The Analysis of Animal Bones
from Archeological Sites

PREHISTORIC ARCHEOLOGY AND ECOLOGY
A Series Edited by Karl W. Butzer and Leslie G. Freeman

The Analysis of Animal Bones from Archeological Sites

Richard G. Klein

and

Kathryn Cruz-Uribe

The University of Chicago Press

Chicago and London

Richard G. Klein is professor in the Department of Anthropology and Biological Science at the University of Chicago. His previous books include *Ice-Age Hunters of the Ukraine*, also published by the University of Chicago Press.
Kathryn Cruz-Uribe was educated at Middlebury College and the University of Chicago. She is currently a research associate in the Department of Anthropology at Brown University.

The University of Chicago Press, Chicago 60637
The University of Chicago Press, Ltd., London
© 1984 by The University of Chicago
All rights reserved. Published 1984
Printed in the United States of America

93 92 91 90 89 88 87 86 85 84   54321

The Library of Congress Cataloging in Publication Data

Klein, Richard G.
    The Analysis of animal bones from archeological sites.

    (Prehistoric archeology and ecology)
    Bibliography: p. 249
    Includes index.
    1. Animal remains (Archaeology)--Analysis--Data
processing. I. Cruz-Uribe, Kathryn. II. Title.
III. Series.
CC79.5.A5K58 1984   930.1'0285   84-247
ISBN 0-226-43957-7
ISBN 0-226-43958-5 (pkb.)

CONTENTS

Series Editors' Foreword ix

Preface xi

PART ONE **The Analysis of Archeological Bone Assemblages** 1

1. The Interpretation of Fossil Faunas 3

Fossil Samples and Populations 3

Controlling Comparisons among Fossil Assemblages 4

Problems in "Controlling" for the Collector 6

Controlled Comparisons vs Taphonomy 8

2. The First Steps in Analysis: Sorting, Identification, Sexing, Aging, and Measurement 11

The Mammalian Skeleton: Terminology 11

Identifiable and Nonidentifiable Bone 17

Identification 21

Sexing and Aging 21

Measurement 22

3. Quantifying Taxonomic Abundance 24

Introduction 24

Indexes of Species Abundance 24

 The Number of Identified Specimens (NISP) 24

 The Minimum Number of Individuals (MNI) 26

 More on NISPs and MNIs 29

 Modified MNIs 32

 Meat Weight Estimates 34

 The Petersen Index 35

Summary and Conclusion 37

4. Sex and Age Profiles of Fossil Species 39

The Utility of Sex and Age Determination 39

Determination of Sex 39

Determination of Age: Epiphyseal Fusion versus Dental Criteria 41

Determining Individual Age from Teeth 44

Ungulate Crown Height and Age 46

Some Problems in Constructing Age Profiles from Crown Heights 52

Interpretation of Age Profiles 55

Comparing Age Profiles 57

Discontinuities in Age Distributions 60

5. Interpreting NISPs, MNIs, Age/Sex Profiles, and
Descriptive Statistics in Faunal Analysis   63
   Skeletal Element Representation   63
       The Transformation from the Death Assemblage to the
       Deposited Assemblage   63
       The Transformation from the Deposited Assemblage to the
       Fossil Assemblage   69
   Species Abundance   75
       Species Abundance and Changes in Environment   76
       Species Abundance and Cultural Change   77
       Species Abundance in Assemblages Created by Carnivores   81
   Age and Sex Profiles   85
       Age/Sex Profiles and Collector Behavior: Example 1   85
       Age/Sex Profiles and Collector Behavior: Example 2   87
       Age/Sex Profiles and Collector Behavior: Example 3   89
       Age/Sex Profiles of a Fossil Species and Its Population
       Dynamics   90
   Mean Individual Size   92
       Mean Individual Size and Climate   94
       Size Variation and Human Predation Pressure   96
   Conclusion   98

PART TWO **BASIC Programs for the Analysis of Animal Bones
from Archeological Sites**   101
   Some Technical Features Common to All the Programs   103
6. Computing the Minimum Number of Individuals in a Fossil Sample:
Programs MNI, BONECODE, DENTCODE, and SKELDIV   107
   *The Assumptions behind MNI: Skeletal Parts Other
   Than Dentitions*   107
   The Assumptions behind MNI: Dentitions   112
   File Names   113
   *Entry of Skeletal Parts Other Than Dentitions: Program
   BONECODE*   114
   Entry of Dentitions: Program DENTCODE   129
   *How MNI Deals with Indeterminacy: Skeletal Parts Other
   Than Dentitions*   141
   How MNI Deals with Indeterminacy: Dentitions   144
   The Entry of Skeletal Part Divisors: Program SKELDIV   146
   A Sample Session with MNI   151
   The Results of an MNI Session   173

7. Computing Age Profiles from Dental Crown Heights: Programs
AGEPROF, DENTDATA, CRNHGT, and SMIRNOV   175
   File Names   175
   Data Entry: Program DENTDATA   175
   *Automatic Entry of Age and Crown Height Parameters:
   Program CRNHGT*   187

Contents

A Sample Session with AGEPROF   194
Results of an AGEPROF Session   205
Comparing Age Profiles: Program SMIRNOV   208

8. Computing Descriptive Statistics from Measurements of Bones
   and Teeth: Programs BONESTAT and BONEDATA   214
   File Names   214
   Entry of Bone Measurements: Program BONEDATA   215
   A Sample Session with BONESTAT   225
   The Results of a BONESTAT Session   239

Appendix. The Principal Variables Used in the Program MNI   243

References   249

Index   261

SERIES EDITORS' FOREWORD

The editors of the Prehistoric Archeology and Ecology Series are pleased to welcome a major study in zooarcheology, *The Analysis of Animal Bones from Archeological Sites*. The authors, Richard Klein and Kathryn Cruz-Uribe, are concerned not only with fossil bone assemblages as biased reflections of past environments, but also with the behavior of the bone collectors. The basic dilemma is how to distinguish the influence of the background context, the impact of postdepositional destruction, and the activity of humans and animal predators.

Although analog studies and laboratory simulations are helpful in this regard, large, well-collected fossil assemblages can provide even more information in their own right. The strategy is based on internal analysis and external comparison, within and between assemblages with definable contexts and associations. Ideally, the sensitive data include the species represented, the abundance of each species, the numbers of different skeletal parts by which it is represented, the age and sex composition of each species sample, and the average size of adults in each species. Klein and Cruz-Uribe discuss in detail how these vital faunal numbers may be obtained, and they present many interesting examples to demonstrate the interpretive potential of the numbers. The examples are based on a combined total of more than twenty years' experience in analyzing and interpreting bone assemblages from more than eighty-five sites in Africa and Europe.

In addition to its clear treatment of the basic theoretical and practical issues confronting faunal analysts, the book makes a unique contribution with a set of computer programs thoughtfully constructed to calculate important faunal numbers with minimum effort and maximum accuracy. Since the programs are written in a dialect of BASIC that is available on nearly all microcomputers, most zooarcheologists should have access to equipment that will run them. The programs have been designed with ease of use in mind, and no prior computer knowledge is required. In fact, the authors' discussion of the programs focuses entirely on the logical or faunal analytic assumptions behind them, not on programming or computers. The program chapters should therefore be interesting even to those who have no intrinsic interest in computers. We believe this book will kindle that interest.

Much of the value of this comprehensive study rests on the corpus of computer-based technology that it provides for scientific faunal analysis. But quantification in and of itself is not the motive, and the authors emphasize as well as demonstrate how their numerical approaches lead to new insights concerning questions of archeological and paleoecological importance. The explicit attention given to the many processes involved in bone accumulation as well as to the issues of assemblage and behavioral interpretation greatly transcends the basic methodology. In this sense the volume is an indispensable guide to the principles of zooarcheology even for those students and professionals who may never punch the keys of a computer. Klein and Cruz-Uribe have carried the subfield a whole generation beyond Ian Cornwall's *Bones for the Archaeologist* (1958). From early indentification manuals we have finally moved to a reasoned assessment of how both taphonomy and behavior can be inferred from bone assemblages.

The Analysis of Animal Bones from Archeological Sites is a unique book that, in our opinion, represents a major advance in bioarcheology. It does so by demonstrating the nature of the variables, by explicating an effective methodology, and finally by showing how scientific rigor can yield a wealth of cultural understanding.

Karl W. Butzer

Leslie G. Freeman

PREFACE

It is now widely recognized that excavated animal bones, like artifacts and ruins, can provide valuable insight into the activities of ancient humans. As a result, a growing number of archeologists are specializing in the study of animal bones. At the same time, specialists in other classes of data must familiarize themselves with the methodology of bone studies in order to critically assess the conclusions of their bone-oriented colleagues. It is with these facts in mind that we have written this book. Our purpose is twofold: to illuminate some of the outstanding issues in bone analysis that must concern all archeologists; and to provide bone specialists with a set of computer programs that we hope will greatly simplify the analytic part of their job. These programs and the discussion that precedes them should also interest those paleontologists who focus on reconstructing past environments or ecologies from animal bones.

In keeping with our twofold purpose, we have divided the book into two basic parts. The first presents concepts and methods that we think are essential for obtaining valid and interesting information from archeological bone assemblages. Our emphasis is on abstracting numbers that characterize the fundamental structure of an assemblage and facilitate comparisons among assemblages. It is from interassemblage comparisons that we believe archeologists are likely to obtain the most reliable, valid, and generally interesting information about the past.

The second part of the book presents a set of BASIC computer programs for calculating those faunal numbers that we think are most useful and important. The programs were designed for the IBM Personal Computer but can be quickly adapted to most other microcomputers. Our emphasis in any case is not microcomputing or even programming, but on the logical assumptions behind the programs we present. There is thus a real sense in which the program chapters constitute more detailed treatments of the methods that are discussed in the first part of the book.

In conceiving the programs, we sought particularly to reduce the time and drudgery involved in analyzing large samples, comprising thousands or even tens of thousands of "identifiable" bones. The tedium and paperwork are so great that some analysts routinely avoid truly large samples. Yet it is precisely such samples (versus a myriad of small ones) that we believe contain most of the information archeologists seek.

Mammals far outnumber other vertebrates in most samples excavated by archeologists. They are also the zoological class with which we have had the most experience. We have therefore prepared the text primarily with mammals in mind, though we are sure that what we have to say here is pertinent to other vertebrates as well. This is particularly true of our review of measures of taxonomic abundance in bone assemblages, and the relevant computer program could readily be modified or expanded to estimate taxonomic abundance for birds, reptiles, amphibians, and even fish.

This book is a direct outcome of our experience in analyzing bone assemblages from numerous sites in Spain and especially in southern Africa. Our research on these assemblages was generously supported by the National Science Foundation. We want to thank the many excavators who made their materials available to us. We also thank K. W. Butzer, J. D. Speth, R. A. Thisted, and an anonymous reviewer for many useful suggestions for improving the text.

PART ONE: THE ANALYSIS OF ARCHEOLOGICAL BONE

ASSEMBLAGES

The study of animal remains from archeological sites is a burgeoning field, commonly known as zooarcheology. The goal of zooarcheology is to reconstruct the environment and behavior of ancient peoples to the extent that animal remains allow. Zooarcheologists are not easy to distinguish from paleontologists whose primary interest is in paleoecology, and some specialists care little whether their samples come from archeological or nonarcheological sites. The overlap between zooarcheology and ecological paleontology is likely to grow, since there is much to be learned by comparing archeological and nonarcheological faunal samples. We illustrate this point with examples. Our broader purpose is to explore some of the methods basic to both fields. Following common informal usage, we will call the shared methodology "faunal analysis."

The pioneers of faunal analysis relied heavily on qualitative data, mainly on the list of taxa represented in a fossil sample. Today nearly all specialists agree that such qualitative data are insufficient. Insofar as it is possible, we must also measure the abundance of each taxon within a faunal sample, count the numbers of different skeletal elements by which each taxon is represented, estimate the proportionate representation of individuals of each sex and of different ages, determine mean individual size and variability in size within each taxon, and so forth. Our purpose in the first part of this book is to show which numbers are especially important in faunal analysis and why.

In chapter 1 we present the interpretive framework that governs our use of numbers in faunal analysis. In essence, we believe that comparisons among fossil samples constitute the most fruitful source of significant information about past environments or the behavior of bone collectors. In chapter 2 we digress briefly from our main theme to define some technical terms that we repeatedly use in later chapters. We also outline the laboratory procedures that provide the raw data for faunal analysis.

In Chapter 3 we survey various measures of taxonomic abundance and conclude that two--the number of identified specimens (NISP) and the minimum number of individuals (MNI)--are jointly necessary and sufficient. In Chapter 4, we review methods for estimating the sex and age composition of a fossil species sample. We focus particularly on age-profile estimation in samples of high-crowned ungulates, which constitute the majority of species in archeological samples in the Americas, Eurasia, and Africa.

Finally, in chapter 5 we present examples from our experience to demonstrate how NISPs, MNIs, sex/age profiles, and other numbers can provide useful and interesting information about the past. Chapter 5 is the pivotal chapter in the book, representing not only the logical conclusion to part 1, but also the bridge to part 2, in which we present a set of computer programs to calculate the numbers whose importance we advocate in part 1.

1: THE INTERPRETATION OF FOSSIL FAUNAS

In the introduction we indicated that we study fossil faunas to reconstruct ancient environments and the behavior of ancient bone collectors. We are especially interested in the information that fossil faunas may contain on the behavior or ecology of ancient people. Unfortunately, in most faunas the effects of the ancient environment are difficult to separate from those of the collector's behavior, and conclusions drawn about the environment may be mistaken for failure to recognize the effects of the collector, and vice versa. In this brief chapter we explore this problem and suggest a means of circumventing it.

Fossil Samples and Populations

A fossil "fauna" is usually just a sample that may be enlarged by further excavation or collection. However, at least implicitly, authors often disagree on what "population" is being sampled. In part, the disagreement stems from the fact that a fossil fauna passes through several stages before it reaches the analyst. As it passes to a new stage, it loses some of the information it previously contained. We have borrowed from Clark and Kietzke (1967), Meadow (1980), and others in proposing five basic stages:

1) The life assemblage (the community of live animals in their "natural" proportions).

2) The death assemblage (the carcasses that are available for collection by people, carnivores, or any other agent of bone accumulation).

3) The deposited assemblage (the carcasses or portions of carcasses that come to rest at a site).

4) The fossil assemblage (the animal parts that survive in a site until excavation or collection).

5) The sample assemblage (the part of the fossil assemblage that is excavated or collected).

If the entire fossil assemblage is carefully excavated, the "sample assemblage" and the "fossil assemblage" will be identical. Excavation of a total fossil assemblage is rare, however. Much more commonly, the characteristics of the fossil assemblage must be estimated from a sample. Clearly, the larger the sample, the better it will be for estimation. Not always so obvious is the importance of careful recovery methods (Payne 1972a, 1975; Clason and Prummel 1977). Without meticulous excavation, sieving, and so forth, the sample may be too "biased" for use in estimating the characteristics of the fossil assemblage.

Inferring the fossil assemblage from the sample assemblage is more a statistical problem than a paleontological or zooarcheological one. Inferring the "deposited assemblage" from the fossil assemblage is quite a different matter. In most instances, if the bones in an assemblage are well preserved and fragmentation is limited, the fossil assemblage probably resembles the "deposited" one quite closely. On the other hand, if bone preservation is poor and fragmentation is extensive, then postdepositional leaching, profile compaction, and other processes may have altered the "deposited assemblage" considerably.

Most fossil assemblages are intermediate in quality of preservation and degree of fragmentation, and the extent to which they resemble the "deposited assemblage" may be indeterminate. This has important implications for studies of bone accumulation under modern conditions. Generally speaking, the assemblages that form under these conditions are "deposited" ones. They are useful for interpreting a fossil assemblage only if there is evidence that the fossil assemblage or some aspect of it has not been altered postdepositionally.

If it is often difficult to infer the "deposited assemblage," in most instances it is all but impossible to infer the "death assemblage" and the "life assemblage." In the case of a hunter-gatherer site, for example, the "life assemblage" is the total community of animals to which the people had access. The "death assemblage" comprises those animals they actually obtained. Assuming that the "fossil assemblage" at the site is a direct reflection of the "deposited assemblage," the "fossil assemblage" will mirror the "death assemblage" only if the hunters brought every species to the site in direct proportion to the frequency with which they killed, scavenged, or otherwise obtained it. Obviously, there is no a priori reason to suppose that ancient hunters regularly did this.

Even if we could somehow reconstruct the "death assemblage" from the fossil assemblage," the "life assemblage" would probably still elude us, since there is no assurance that ancient hunters regularly obtained different species in direct proportion to their live abundance.

Grayson (1979, 1981), Lyman (1982), and others have similarly emphasized the impossibility of inferring the death assemblage or the life assemblage from the fossil assemblage. They suggest that it is an insurmountable obstacle to paleoecological research. We sympathize with their point of view when analysis and interpretation must be confined to a single fossil assemblage. When several comparable assemblages are available, however, we believe that meaningful paleoenviromental and behavioral inferences may be drawn through the process of controlled comparison, without the need to reconstruct the underlying death or life assemblages. We expand on this point in the next section.

Controlling Comparisons among Fossil Assemblages
The statement that every fossil assemblage is preceded by a life assemblage, a death assemblage, and a deposited assemblage is equivalent to saying that the composition of a fossil assemblage is determined by the ancient environment in which it accumulated, the agency that accumulated it, and its postdepositional history. In general, it is not possible to separate the effects of these three factors on a single fossil assemblage. This is another way of saying that it is usually impossible to infer the deposited assemblage, the death assemblage, and the life assemblage from the fossil assemblage.

If several fossil assemblages are available, however, it may be possible to conduct comparisons in which two of the factors that shape assemblages are held constant. Any differences that are observed between the assemblages may then be ascribed to the third factor--postdepositional history, collector, or ancient environment, as the case may be. The two factors that are held constant are "controlled" to isolate the effects of the third.

The principal criteria for determining whether two assemblages share similar postdepositional histories are quality of bone preservation and sedimentologic/geomorphic context. The principal criteria for determining whether they were accumulated by the same agency or in the same environment are context and associations (artifacts, pollens, coprolites, radiometric dates, etc.).

As an example of what is involved, we take the bone assemblages from the two principal layers of the El Juyo Magdalenian Cave Site in northern Spain. The two assemblages differ dramatically in important respects, yet the associated artifacts and pollens indicate they were accumulated by very similar people living in very similar environments. The quality of bone preservation and the sedimentologic context, however, indicate that the bone assemblages have had very different postdepositional histories. Thus, we conclude that the postdepositional factor is responsible for the differences in assemblage composition.

The fossil assemblages from the Middle Stone Age layers of Klasies River Mouth Cave 1 and the Later Stone Age layers of Nelson Bay Cave, situated very near one another in South Africa, also differ strikingly in important respects. In this instance, however, the quality of bone preservation and the sedimentologic/geomorphic context are very similar. In addition, geomorphic/sedimentologic and geochemical observations indicate that the bone assemblages accumulated under very similar environmental conditions. What does vary markedly between the assemblages is the nature of the associated artifacts. In this instance we conclude that the difference between the assemblages reflects a difference in the behavior of their Stone Age accumulators.

Lyman (1982) has suggested that controlled comparisons will always be dubious because the principal controls--pollens, sediments, and so forth--are themselves subject to erroneous interpretation. Certainly the "controls" may be inadequate, but the issue must be addressed in each specific instance, not in the abstract. In chapter 5 we provide details on the controls behind the two examples we have just outlined along with the controls for other comparisons we think have provided interesting and reliable information. Readers can judge for themselves whether the controls seem reasonable. Here we emphasize that the comparative approach requires not only multiple samples, but also a thorough understanding of sample context. Another vital point concerns sample size. This must be large enough so that the role of chance in causing sample differences may be discounted. In the absence of multiple, large, well-controlled samples, faunal analysis will seldom provide truly useful or reliable information about the past.

Problems in "Controlling" for the Collector

The process of controlled comparison we advocate assumes that the agency responsible for a bone accumulation has been satisfactorily inferred. In many cases inferring the bone collector is relatively straightforward; in other cases it is difficult or impossible, and there exist sites where several collectors may have played important roles. Where possible collectors include people and one or more other bone-collecting species, the common problem is to determine how much bone is truly "cultural" (Thomas 1971; Grayson 1979). Among other species known to accumulate bones are owls, carnivores, and, in Africa, the porcupine *Hystrix africaeaustralis* (Brain 1981).

As an example of a straightforward situation, most specialists would agree that people were responsible for the bones of large mammals in a cave where there are also numerous artifacts, fireplaces, or other traces of human activity and where the damage marks on bones may be attributed almost entirely to human action. They would also agree that hyenas probably played the primary role in accumulating bones in an ancient burrow where artifacts are rare or absent, hyena coprolites are abundant, and bone damage may be attributed exclusively to hyena teeth.

These examples show that the principal criteria for inferring the bone collector are sedimentary/geomorphic context, the objects associated with bones, and surficial characters of the bones themselves. Observing surficial characters is clearly a part of the faunal analyst's task, and some analysts have focused specifically on the problem of distinguishing bone damage produced by people from damage produced by carnivores or other creatures. It is now increasingly obvious that simple bone breakage and bone flaking are ambiguous in their implications. Both carnivores and people may break bones spirally, and both may flake bone edges in a way that mimics retouch on stone tools (Binford 1981 or Shipman and Rose 1983, contra Bonnichsen 1979). Additionally, postdepositional trampling or profile compaction may mimic or obscure breakage or flaking caused by either people or carnivores.

A more promising approach is to differentiate the marks made by stone or metal tools on bone surfaces from ones made by carnivore teeth, rodent teeth, or other agents. Some analysts feel that different kinds of marks may be reliably distinguished macroscopically (Bunn 1981, 1982), while others emphasize the need for microscopic examination (Shipman and Rose 1983).

Besides marks from tools or teeth, bones may also show charring or calcining from exposure to fire. When burned bones are abundant in cave deposits or other situations where natural fires are unlikely, they constitute good evidence for an important human role in bone accumulation. In other situations, as in floodplain or lake margin sediments, the implications of burned bones are less clear. For example, burned bones are known from the early Pliocene floodplain deposits of Langebaanweg, South Africa, where they antedate the appearance of people and almost certainly reflect natural veldt fires (Hendey 1982).

Bone surfaces may also exhibit polishing or abrasion resulting from a variety of processes. Bones that have passed through the digestive system of a hyena may take on a distinctive polish, accompanied by surface pitting and a tendency for broken edges to become quite sharp (Sutcliffe 1970). In addition, teeth ingested by hyenas and passed in their scats tend to appear shrunken as a result of gastric acid attack (personal observation).

Surface polishing accompanied by edge rounding may result when weathered bones lie in a body of sand regularly disturbed by trampling (Brain 1981). More commonly, polishing and edge rounding reflect repeated contact between bones and other objects in flowing water. Sedimentological context is perhaps the most important clue to whether water movement has caused rounding and polishing. In such a case, rounding or abrasion on virtually all surfaces implies that a bone was transported some distance from its original resting place. Abrasion that is restricted to only a portion of a bone's surface suggests that the bone itself may have been stationary in a stream bed while other objects brushed by it. Whatever the extent of abrasion on individual bones, its occurrence on many bones usually indicates that flowing water played an important role in the origin and structure of a bone assemblage. This is particularly true if the bones are systematically oriented in a deposit, reflecting current flow (Shipman 1981). An unfortunate side effect of abrasion by any process is its tendency to obliterate prior cut marks or tooth marks, thus masking the contributions of other agencies to the composition of a bone assemblage (Shipman and Rose 1983).

Finally, surficial damage may inform us of the exposure of bones to physical or chemical weathering, either before or after deposition. Such weathering can selectively remove less durable bones, leaving behind an assemblage whose composition closely resembles one created by carnivore chewing (Grigson 1983). Criteria for recognizing and recording predepositional weathering have been suggested by Behrensmeyer (1978). Criteria for recognizing postdepositional affects, primarily chemical leaching, have received less attention, but include the degree of bone friability and obvious corrosion of bone surfaces as a result of acid attack.

Unfortunately, there are many sites throughout the world where context, associations, and the nature of surficial damage, separately or together, suggest that two or more agencies were important in accumulating bones. The problem is particularly acute for many very early "archeological" sites, dating between the late Pliocene, roughly two million years ago, and the end of the Middle Pleistocene, approximately 130,000 years ago. The relevant sites, all in Africa and Eurasia, are mainly "open-air" localities near former lakes or streams. At several of these sites the "mixed" role of people and carnivores in bone accumulation or assemblage composition has now been directly documented by the co-occurrence of stone tools and carnivore coprolites (e.g. at the "Saldanha Man" [Elandsfontein] site in South Africa [Klein 1982b] and the Ambrona Acheulean site in

Spain (Klein and Cruz-Uribe in prep.)] or of stone tool cut marks and carnivore tooth marks [e.g. at Olduvai Gorge and Koobi Fora in East Africa (Bunn 1981, 1982; Potts and Shipman 1981)].

Flowing water is also importantly implicated at some sites [e.g. at Ambrona and its sister site of Torralba (Klein and Cruz-Uribe 1984 and in prep.)], as are the selective destructive effects of postdepositional leaching (e.g. at various Koobi Fora localities described by Bunn 1982 and at Torralba and Ambrona). For the moment, at most very ancient archeological sites, we can only say that several factors contributed to assemblage composition without being able to specify how important each was. Eventually, the relative numbers of chewed, cut, or otherwise damaged bones may prove indicative. For example, in bone assemblages collected by African porcupines, as many as 60-70% of the bones will exhibit very distinctive gnaw marks (Brain 1981). Unfortunately, in most other situations it is not clear how many damaged bones of any kind to expect, even in an assemblage where only one agent was responsible. This is perhaps especially true for bones with cut marks in assemblages created exclusively by people.

In sum, in many complex situations, establishing "controls" particularly for the collector, may be impossible, and maximum, albeit limited, insight into assemblage origin and structure may come mainly from the taphonomic approach discussed in the next section.

Controlled Comparisons versus Taphonomy

Interpretation based on controlled comparisons among fossil assemblages may be compared with a more popular approach often known as "taphonomy." As defined by I. A. Efremov, who coined the word, taphonomy is "the study of the transition (in all its details) of animal remains from the biosphere into the lithosphere, i.e. the study of a process in the upshot of which organisms pass out of the different parts of the biosphere, and being fossilized, become part of the lithosphere" (quoted by Gifford 1981 in a thoughtful overview of taphonomy and archeology.) In the terms we have used here, taphonomy is the study of those factors that cause a fossil assemblage to differ from the deposited, death, and life assemblages that underlie it (Behrensmeyer and Hill 1980; Shipman 1981).

Virtually all taphonomists would agree that a fossil assemblage is generally an imperfect reflection of the underlying life and death assemblages. However, most would probably use the word "biased" in place of "imperfect." The goal of taphonomic research is to strip away the "biases" in the fossil assemblage, so that the death assemblage or the life assemblage may be reconstructed. Most taphonomists pursue this goal by studying the factors that concentrate or destroy bones in modern natural environments or by simulating these factors in laboratories. The assumption is that the factors that affect bones today are essentially the same ones that shaped ancient bone assemblages. The taphonomic approach is thus a logical application of the uniformitarian principle to the interpretation of fossil assemblages.

There is of course a sense in which recent or historical observations underlie all interpretations of fossil assemblages, whether based on controlled comparisons or on explicitly designed taphonomic research. In point of fact, the comparative approach and the taphonomic one are complementary, not opposed. Thus, recent studies of bone collecting by people and carnivores are crucial to the interpretations of fossil bone assemblages we offer in chapter 5. On the other hand, comparisons among the assemblages have revealed aspects of human and carnivore behavior that would never emerge from modern studies.

The principal advantage of modern studies is that causation may be observed; it does not have to be inferred. However, modern studies have numerous limitations. First, the observer may affect the results. This is very clear in the case of an observer whose presence causes bone-collecting carnivores to shift dens or otherwise alter their habits.

Second, in many cases modern studies must be conducted in settings very different from those in which many important fossil assemblages accumulated. This is true, for example, with respect to modern studies of bone collecting by the brown hyena, which is today confined to the most marginal or degraded parts of its former range. More important, it is true with respect to modern studies of bone-collecting human hunter-gatherers, who also tend to live in environments that are marginal by prehistoric standards. In addition, most recently observed hunter-gatherers have been affected to an important extent by contacts with more advanced societies from which they obtain hunting-gathering implements, food and water supplements, and so forth, that are likely to affect their bone-accumulating behavior. Third, modern studies obviously cannot be done on bone-collectors who did not exist historically. Most important in this context are extinct varieties of people whose behavior probably differed in important respects from that of all historically observed people.

A further problem with modern studies of bone accumulation is that they are usually very brief, comprising a year or two at most. More commonly they comprise a few weeks or months. One consequence is that the observed bone sample is usually quite small. Clearly too, the sample may reflect short-term behavioral or environmental aberrations rather than the long-term, "time-averaged" conditions reflected in most fossil samples. It is usually impossible to say precisely how much time is represented in a fossil sample, but decades, centuries, or even millennia are certainly more common than years, months, or weeks.

Finally, by definition, modern samples have no postdepositional history. They are thus "deposited" assemblages whose comparability to any fossil assemblage must be inferred, not assumed. This is especially true for modern samples that are not even "fossil samples in the making"--that is, ones that would probably disappear altogether if left to the forces of nature.

In sum, we stress the comparative approach because we feel that for the moment it is more likely to provide new and significant information about the past, particularly from fossil assemblages accumulated by early people. However, we reiterate our view that the comparative approach and the taphonomic one are complementary. Both are always pertinent, and in any given case the extent to which one or the other is used will be determined by the nature of a fossil assemblage and by what the investigator hopes to learn from it.

2: THE FIRST STEPS IN ANALYSIS: SORTING, IDENTIFICATION,

SEXING, AGING AND MEASUREMENT

Our goal in this chapter is to introduce some technical terms that we use repeatedly in later chapters. Many readers will already be familiar with these terms but may use them in slightly different ways than we do. We hope here to remove any possible ambiguity.

Also in this chapter, we outline the broad steps in sorting and identification that must precede the kind of analysis and interpretation that are our main subject matter. However, we provide no specific instructions on how to identify bones. In large part this is because our focus in this book is on calculating and analyzing numbers from bones that have already been identified. Additionally, we believe that learning to identify bones is mainly a matter of practice under the supervision of an experienced analyst. Written instructions and even illustrations are of limited value in the learning process. However, some useful texts and illustrations do exist. We particularly recommend Cornwall (1974), Gilbert (1980), Olsen (1971), Pales and Garcia (1981), Pales and Lambert (1971), Ryder (1969), and Schmid (1972).

The Mammalian Skeleton: Terminology
As a result of common descent, the skeletons of all mammal species tend to comprise roughly the same variety of skeletal parts arranged in the same anatomical order. Figures 2.1 and 2.2 illustrate the skeletons of an ungulate and a carnivore and give the common names for the large skeletal parts. There is less consensus on the names for small skeletal parts, particularly the carpals and tarsals. The names we use are shown in figures 2.3- 2.6 in relation to the carpals and tarsals of an ungulate and a carnivore.

Figures 2.7, 2.8, and 2.9 illustrate ungulate and carnivore dentitions, giving the names we use for different teeth. Some specialists regard the deciduous teeth as molars rather than premolars, in which case they substitute dm for dP (or dp). Most investigators superscript the number of a tooth to designate the upper jaw (maxilla) and subscript it to designate the lower jaw (mandible). Sometimes a line is drawn above a name to designate "upper" and below it to designate "lower" (often the line is drawn only above or below the number for the tooth). In the event that there is no line and no subscript or superscript, it may be assumed that jaw (upper or lower) could not be established or that it was irrelevant.

Besides names for whole skeletal parts, there are numerous terms for portions of skeletal parts. Ones that we use here and that are especially likely to appear in a faunal analyst's report are epiphysis and diaphysis, proximal and distal, medial and lateral, anterior and posterior, and buccal and lingual.

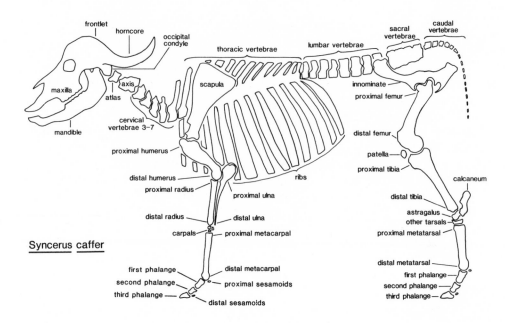

FIGURE 2.1: The principal bones of the skeleton, illustrated for the Cape buffalo (*Syncerus caffer*).

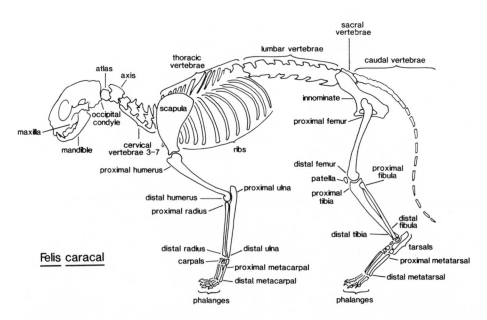

FIGURE 2.2: The principal bones of the skeleton, illustrated for the African lynx or caracal (*Felis caracal*).

12

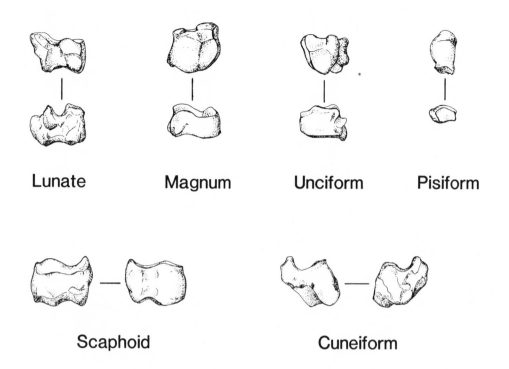

| Lunate | Magnum | Unciform | Pisiform |

Scaphoid   Cuneiform

BOVID CARPALS

FIGURE 2.3: Left carpals of a bovid (the nyala, *Tragelaphus angasi*), showing the names for carpals used in this book.

To accommodate growth, most mammalian skeletal parts possess multiple centers of ossification separated by nonbony tissue, mainly cartilage. The separate centers merge or fuse to form the complete skeletal element only when growth is complete. Most long bones possess three principal centers of ossification--the two ends and the connecting shaft. The ends are commonly known as the epiphyses, while the shaft is often known as the diaphysis. However, many specialists regularly use the term shaft even in technical writing. Epiphyses also occur on vertebrae, where the "shaft" to which they eventually fuse is most often called the centrum or body. On ribs, scapulae, and innominates (pelvises), the main portion of the bone to which epiphyses fuse is often known as the blade.

There are several reasons for recording the state of epiphyseal fusion of a fossil bone. First, it is potentially useful for determining how old the animal was at time of death. Second, it may be used in calculating the minimum number of individuals that provided the bones in a fossil assemblage. Finally, the proportion of fused or unfused pieces within any given element category (e.g. the distal radius) may help explain the relative

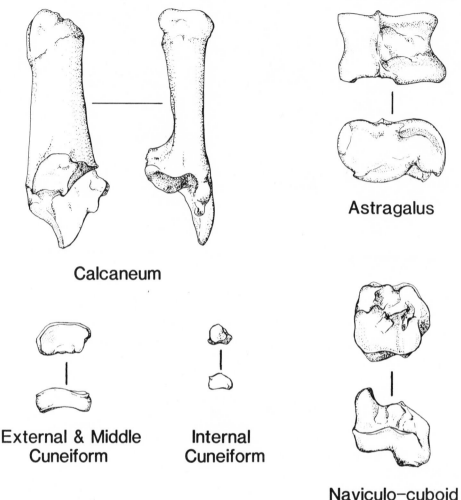

Calcaneum

Astragalus

External & Middle
Cuneiform

Internal
Cuneiform

Naviculo–cuboid

Distal Fibula
(Lateral Malleolus)

BOVID TARSALS

FIGURE 2.4: Left tarsals of a bovid (the nyala, *Tragelaphus angasi*), showing the names for tarsals used in this book.

abundance of the category in an assemblage. This is because there is a relationship between the fusion state of a bone and its durability or likelihood of survival in the face of pre- and postdepositional destructive pressures (Brain 1976).

14

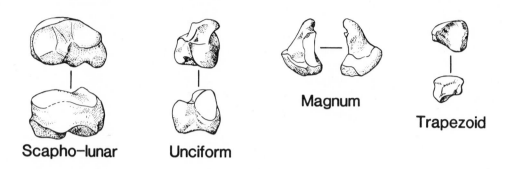

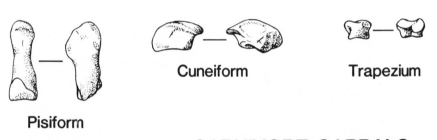

CARNIVORE CARPALS

FIGURE 2.5: Right carpals of a carnivore (the brown hyena, *Hyaena brunnea*), showing the names for carpals used in this book.

Proximal and distal refer to the position of a skeletal element with respect to the head (figs. 2.1 and 2.2). The closer to the head, the more proximal; the farther from the head the more distal. Thus the humerus is more proximal than the radius, and the tibia is more distal than the femur. However, proximal and distal are used mostly for portions of skeletal parts. Thus the proximal humerus is the portion closest to the shoulder, while the distal humerus is the portion closest to the elbow. Similarly, the proximal tibia is the portion closest to the knee; the distal tibia is the portion closest to the ankle.

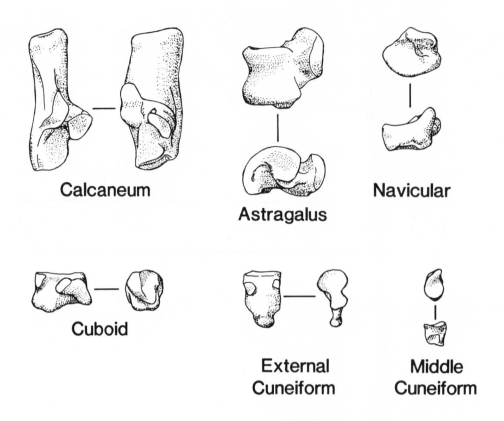

CARNIVORE TARSALS

FIGURE 2.6: Right tarsals of a carnivore (the brown hyena, *Hyaena brunnea*), showing the names for tarsals used in this book.

Medial and lateral refer to position vis-a-vis the midline of the body. Medial means closer to the midline, lateral farther from the midline. Anterior and posterior refer to position in the plane perpendicular to the one defined by medial and lateral. Thus, if medial and lateral can be roughly translated as "inner" and "outer," anterior and posterior can be translated as "fore" and "rear." Unlike proximal and distal, which are used mainly to modify the names of skeletal parts, in faunal analysis, medial/lateral and anterior/posterior are used mainly to define measurements, particularly on epiphyses (fig. 2.10).

Buccal and lingual are used with respect to the jaws and teeth (figs. 2.7-2.9). The buccal side is the one closer to the cheek, the lingual side is the one closer to the tongue. Like medial/lateral and anterior/posterior, in faunal analysis buccal/lingual are used mainly to define the position of measurements. We use anterior and posterior to refer to the dimension

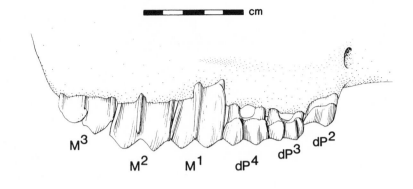

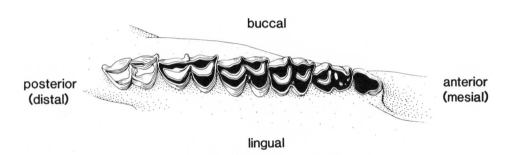

BOVID JUVENILE UPPER DENTITION

(<u>TAUROTRAGUS</u> <u>ORYX</u>, BM-66.850)

FIGURE 2.7: Juvenile upper dentition of a bovid (the eland, *Taurotragus oryx*), showing the dental names used in this book.

perpendicular to the buccal-lingual (or buccolingual) one. Many specialists prefer to call this dimension mesial-distal (or mesiodistal).

Identifiable and Nonidentifiable Bone

Most fossil bone assemblages contain numerous specimens that cannot be assigned to skeletal part and taxon. Such pieces are usually called "nonidentifiable" or "nondiagnostic." Some investigators examine nonidentifiable bones for cut marks, gnaw marks, or other damage, or they study the pattern of fragmentation (see, for example, Brain 1975). However, it is rare that nonidentifiable bones provide any information that is not also available from the identifiable ones. Consequently, the nonidentifiable bones are frequently sorted out at a very early stage in the analysis and ignored thereafter.

The qualities that render a bone nonidentifiable are mainly incompleteness and formlessness, but investigators may disagree on what constitutes formlessness. Thus, few analysts would regard a complete

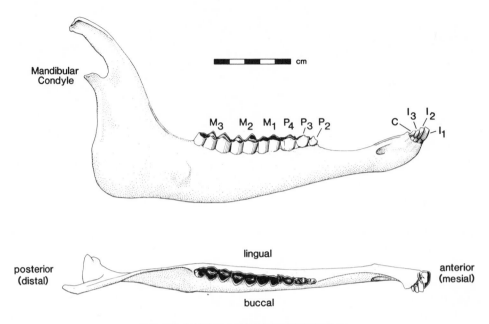

BOVID ADULT LOWER DENTITION

(AEPYCEROS MELAMPUS, SAM–M728)

FIGURE 2.8: Adult lower dentition of a bovid (the impala, *Aepyceros melampus*), showing the dental names used in this book.

epiphysis as nonidentifiable, but they may disagree sharply on a fragmentary one. In many cases this is a matter of experience. Usually an experienced analyst can identify small epiphyseal fragments that a novice must disregard. There is probably more consensus on shaft fragments, particularly small ones to which no epiphysis is attached. Most investigators probably regard such fragments as unidentifiable. We follow this practice ourselves, not only because such fragments are difficult to identify to skeletal part and taxon, but also because it is impossible to incorporate them in the principal index of taxonomic abundance that we use. Similar problems of identification and counting also lead us to assign most small cranial fragments to the "nonidentifiable" category.

There is also disagreement on how to treat vertebrae, ribs, and sesamoids, mainly because they are difficult to identify to species even when they are complete. Some specialists routinely place them in the "nonidentifiable" category. However, even when they are identified only to family, their numbers may elucidate the history of a sample. For example, a very large number of sesamoids may reflect intensive postdepositional destructive pressure, while a high proportion of vertebrae may indicate that a site was a place where animals were killed and dismembered as opposed to one to which parts of previously dismembered animals were introduced.

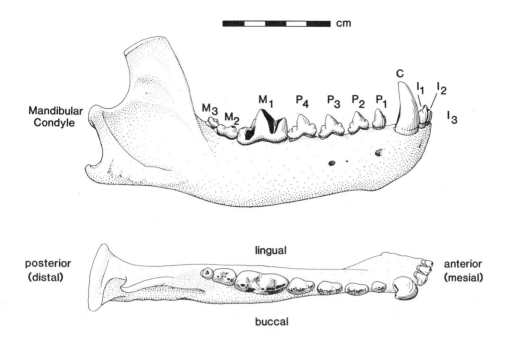

CARNIVORE ADULT LOWER DENTITION

(LYCAON PICTUS, SAM-12245)

FIGURE 2.9: Adult lower dentition of a carnivore (the Cape hunting dog, *Lycaon pictus*), showing the dental names used in this book.

It is probably best, therefore, to treat them as identifiable, even if the identifications must often be crude.

The general point is that there is no simple dichotomy between identifiable and nonidentifiable bone. It is both more realistic and more useful to speak of "levels of identifiability" (Ziegler 1973; Lyman 1979). Thus in many cases it may be possible and useful to identify a bone to genus, family, or order even if it cannot be identified to species. Often in cases like this it is possible to add a size qualifier (e.g. small carnivore or medium-sized bovid).

The precision of identification depends on several factors. Most obvious are the analyst's experience and the degree of fragmentation. Often, however, the most important factor is what the analyst expects or assumes. Thus few analysts would hesitate to assign isolated bovine teeth in a prehistoric North American sample to bison, even though the teeth may be morphologically indistinguishable from the teeth of the European aurochs or the African buffalo. Similarly, otherwise "unidentifiable" ribs, vertebrae. sesamoids, and small long-bone shaft fragments may be readily

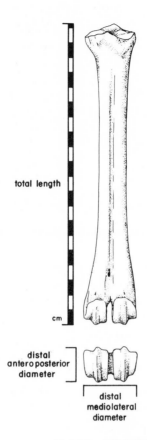

total length

cm

distal
anteroposterior
diameter

distal
mediolateral
diameter

BLACK WILDEBEEST
Right Metatarsal

FIGURE 2.10: Total length and distal mediolateral and anteroposterior diameters of a bovid metatarsal (from the black wildebeest, *Connochaetes gnou*).

assigned to species in a fossil sample where cranial parts suggest there is only one species of the appropriate size and morphology. In short, form is only one criterion used to determine whether a bone is identifiable. *A priori* assumptions about its likely origin are another--often crucial, even if implicit.

Clearly, to avoid potentially misleading comparisons between samples, faunal analysts should make their criteria for identifiability as explicit as possible. It is especially important to note what identifications were based on assumptions about the population from which a fossil sample was drawn.

Identification

All bone identifications are ultimately based on comparisons with the skeletal parts of known taxa. An "identification" is made when the analyst believes there is a satisfactory match between a fossil bone of unknown taxon and a skeletal part whose taxon has been previously established. Most analyses thus depend upon the availability of a "comparative collection," comprising skeletons of those taxa that are likely to be represented in a fossil assemblage. Of course, an experienced analyst can make many identifications from memory, by comparison with mental images of often-seen parts. Gaining sufficient experience to do this is vital if an analyst wants to process large bone samples in a reasonable amount of time.

There are two alternative procedures for processing identifiable bones. The preferred one is to sort bones together that look alike, without necessarily identifying them to taxon. A logical first step is to sort pieces together that clearly represent the same skeletal part, such as the distal humerus. The pieces within each skeletal part can then be sorted more finely on the basis of morphological similarities and differences. Ones that are morphologically indistinguishable will usually derive from a single taxon, whose identity can be established by reference to the comparative collection.

The alternative to sorting before identification is to identify each bone as it is encountered in its container, usually a bag or box with the provenience unit written on it. One advantage of identifying without prior sorting is that individual bones do not have to be labeled with their provenience unit (site, level, square, etc.). Additionally, identification without prior sorting can be done in a very limited space. However, it is generally much more time-consuming than identification after sorting (even considering the time involved in labeling). In addition, the chances of erroneous identification are greatly increased, particularly if the analyst is not very experienced. Lack of space has often forced us to identify with only minimal prior sorting (by square rather than by level or by level rather than by site). However, we do not recommend it.

Whether sorting precedes identification or identification is undertaken directly without sorting, the information that is recorded should be the same. We specify the information we think is essential in chapter 6, where we also suggest forms that facilitate recording and subsequent analysis.

Sexing and Aging

In addition to skeletal part and taxon, for some identifiable bones it is possible to determine the animal's sex and age. If this is possible for many bones of a species, the sex and age composition of the sample may illuminate sample origin or the behavior of the bone accumulator. We discuss this subject in much more detail in chapter 4. Here we note only that "sexing" and "aging" can sometimes be done on qualitative grounds, but more often it is necessary to measure skeletal parts to obtain usable results. "Sexing" and "aging" thus merge into "measurement," the final topic of this chapter.

Measurement

As we have just indicated, identifiable bones may be measured to determine the animal's age or sex. In some cases measurements may also aid taxonomic identification, although they are generally less useful for this than discrete (or qualitative) criteria. Finally, measurements on skeletal parts may be used to infer the live size of an animal or as proxies for live individual size. Live size in turn may be used for many purposes. One of the most interesting is to infer past climates or climatic variation through time. This follows from the correlation between mean adult size and climate in many living species that extend across several climatic zones. We discuss this topic in greater detail in chapter 5.

In most cases it is best to measure bones only after the initial sorting, identification, and recording of skeletal parts has been completed. In addition, it is best to measure only one category of bones (e.g., red deer distal humeri) at a time. This reduces the likelihood of measurement and recording error. Measurements may be made with many different instruments, but, whenever practical, dial-reading calipers are best. In general, they permit maximum precision in the minimum amount of time with the minimum likelihood of misreading.

We ordinarily record and analyze measurements separately from the records of skeletal parts that we use to compute indexes of taxonomic abundance (with the program MNI discussed in chapter 6). We then use the measurements to compute other useful numbers (with the programs AGEPROF and BONESTAT in chaps. 7 and 8). The separate recording systems reflect our belief that the efficient computation of useful numbers should have priority over a comprehensive data storage and retrieval system with limited analytical utility. However, we note that the programs we present in part 2 could process much more comprehensive records containing a wide variety of qualitative and quantitative data. The trade-off would be greatly increased recording and processing time and a greater chance of recording error.

Specialists have often lamented the lack of standardization in measurements, and some have advocated the adoption of a uniform system, such as the very useful one outlined by von den Driesch (1976). Certainly, standardization is desirable whenever it can be achieved, but no system can ever be final--partly because standardized systems usually assume whole bones, while analysts are often forced to measure fragments.

Even more important, a standardized system partly presupposes the uses to which measurements will be put. As problem orientations change or investigators ask new questions, they may have to "invent" new measurements. Clearly, there is no harm in this as long as the measurements reflect the phenomenon (sex, age, size) being investigated and as long as they may be readily replicated by other investigators. High-quality illustrations particularly facilitate replication. The crown height measurements we discuss in chapter 4 meet the requirements we have set, though they are nonstandard and could be replaced by other equally useful measurements if patterns of fragmentation demanded.

Introduction

It is rarely possible to draw interesting and reliable paleoenvironmental and behavioral inferences simply by comparing the taxa two fossil assemblages contain. Generally speaking, we must also have some indication of the relative abundance of the taxa in each assemblage. It is understandable, therefore, that the quantification of taxonomic abundance has been discussed by many authors, especially in zooarcheology (see, for example, Bokonyi 1970; Casteel 1977a,b; Chaplin 1971; Clason 1972; Ducos 1975; Grayson 1973, 1979; Klein 1980a; Lie 1980; Lyman 1982; Payne 1972b; Perkins 1973; Poplin 1976; Smith 1976; Uerpmann 1973; Watson 1979; and Ziegler 1973).

In an especially comprehensive and critical review, Grayson (1979) concluded that it may not be worthwhile to measure taxonomic abundance in most fossil assemblages, because with or without numbers it will still be impossible to infer the underlying death or life assemblage. There may thus be no information in measures of taxonomic abundance that is not available in a presence/absence analysis of the taxonomic list.

We agree that measures of taxonomic abundance have limited utility when only one sample is available, but we think they are critical for comparing two or more samples. Without them, there is no way to argue that the differences or similarities between samples did not arise by chance--that is, that they reflect real differences or similarities in past environments or in the behavior of bone-collecting agents. Comparisons based simply on the presence or absence of taxa are inadequate because without abundance estimates there is no way to show that a species' presence in one sample and its absence in another reflects a "real" (vs. chance) difference. It is from this perspective that we survey various indexes of taxonomic abundance in this chapter.

In most fossil assemblages, the species is the unit whose abundance is estimated. For simplicity's sake in what follows, we have therefore substituted "species" for the more general, but less familiar term "taxon." However, the very same indexes that are used to measure the abundance of a species may be used to measure the abundance of a higher taxon. For example, in the faunas we have studied, many "small bovid" skeletal parts are not readily identifiable to species. We therefore assign them to the category "small bovid" and estimate the abundance of "small bovids" in the same way we estimate the abundance of an individual species.

Indexes of Species Abundance

The Number of Identified Specimens (NISP)

The most obvious and most readily obtainable index of a species abundance is the number of bones or bone fragments that may be assigned to it within a fossil sample. Following Payne (1975) and Grayson (1979), we abbreviate the number of identified bones (specimens) per species as the NISP.

The NISP has two outstanding advantages. First, it may be calculated at the same time the basic bone identifications are done, with no need for any subsequent numerical manipulation. Second, NISP values are additive. Thus, it is easy to update species abundance when excavations at a site are renewed--the new NISP for each species is simply added to the old one. Similarly, if it becomes necessary to lump the contents of two field provenience units, the new NISP is simply the sum of the two original ones.

The NISP also has some serious flaws. To begin with, it ignores the fact that the skeletons of some species have more parts than the skeletons of others. Thus, the NISP may exaggerate the abundance of a monkey species versus an antelope species, since monkeys have clavicles and supplementary metapodials and phalanges that antelopes lack.

The NISP will also overemphasize the importance of a species that tended to reach a site intact versus a species that was usually dismembered before transport. For example, in many instances prehistoric hunters probably butchered a large animal where it fell and brought only selected parts to their home base. In contrast, they probably often imported smaller animals intact. Clearly, the NISPs calculated for a site occupied by such people will exaggerate the importance of small species versus large ones.

Finally and most seriously, the NISP is very sensitive to bone fragmentation. For interassemblage comparisons this might not matter very much, if we could assume that fragmentation affected all species equally. A highly fragmented assemblage would have higher NISPs for all species, but relative species abundance would remain unchanged. However, fragmentation need not affect all species equally.

For example, in many of the fossil samples we have studied, human butchering and/or postdepositional leaching, profile compaction, and so forth, have completely destroyed the maxillary and mandibular bones of large antelopes. The result is an abundance of isolated large antelope teeth. In the same samples, the factors that impacted large antelope jaws operated very differently on small antelope jaws. These often maintain their integrity with the teeth in place. Clearly, for such a sample the NISP will significantly overstate the importance of large antelopes versus small ones. More important, as measured by the NISP, the ratio of small antelopes to large antelopes will be very different from that in an assemblage where large antelope jaws also remain intact.

The disadvantages of the NISP make it unsuitable as the sole index of species abundance. However, it has definite value, particularly when it is considered jointly with the minimum number of individuals from which the identified bones must have come, discussed and abbreviated below as the MNI. For example, if two species differ markedly in their NISP/MNI ratio, it means either that the bones of one are more highly fragmented than the bones of the other, or that one is represented by a much wider range of skeletal elements than the other. The correct alternative may be determined by examining the NISP and MNI values for each skeletal element of each species. Whatever the cause, the contrast in NISP/MNI ratios must itself be explained before the separate NISPs or MNIs are interpreted in paleoenvironmental or behavioral terms.

The Minimum Number of Individuals (MNI)

The minimum number of individuals (MNI) represented in a species sample is simply the number of individuals necessary to account for all the identified bones. White (1953) is generally credited with introducing the MNI to zooarcheology, though it had been used in paleontology for several decades before (Casteel 1977a).

The MNI can never be larger than the NISP and is usually smaller. For example, a species sample comprising two left distal and two right distal humeri would have an NISP of 4 and an MNI of 2. A sample comprising four left distal humeri and no right ones would have an NISP of 4 and an MNI of 4. Of course, most samples include specimens from more than one skeletal part. In such a case, it is necessary to calculate an MNI for each part. The largest such MNI becomes the MNI for the species.

Unlike the NISP, the MNI for one species cannot be larger than the MNI for another simply because the skeleton of the first species has more parts. Further, unlike the NISP, the MNI of a species will be the same whether the bone accumulator commonly introduced whole carcasses to a site or only selected parts, such as the hindquarters. Finally, compared with the NISP, the MNI is relatively insensitive to differences between species or between faunas in the degree of bone fragmentation.

Thus the MNI is strong precisely where the NISP is weak. It is not flawless, however. To begin with, MNI estimates can be tedious to calculate, and there is a strong possibility of calculation error, even in relatively small samples. More seriously, MNI estimates may not be comparable among samples, because there is no consensus on how they should be calculated.

For example, many specialists sort specimens of a paired element such as the distal humerus into lefts and rights. They take the MNI for the element to be the number of lefts or the number of rights, whichever number is larger. Other specialists do not distinguish lefts from rights but simply divide the total number of specimens by two to obtain an MNI. In most cases, it is probably fair to assume that the bone accumulator did not prefer lefts to rights or vice versa. Thus, if the bone sample is very large, the resulting MNIs will probably be very similar whether lefts are separated from rights or the total is simply divided by two. However, in the relatively small samples that zooarcheologists and paleontologists usually work with, the two procedures can produce very different MNIs.

In addition to sorting lefts from rights, some investigators calculate MNIs using a procedure called "matching." Bökönyi (1970) and Chaplin (1971) discuss matching in detail. In essence, it involves the use of size, sex, or age criteria to determine whether two bones could come from the same individual. In theory, matching may be done between different skeletal parts. For example, an investigator could try to determine whether a particular radius could come from the same individual as a humerus or even a femur.

However, most investigators match pieces only within the same element. The question then is whether a particular left piece could come from the same individual as a particular right. Thus, for a particular species, a sample of ten distal humeri might contain six lefts and four rights. Without matching the MNI is 6. However, matching may lead to the conclusion that two of the rights are too small or too young to come from individuals represented among the lefts. The MNI is then 6(L) + 2(R), or 8 total.

Bone size is perhaps the most commonly used matching criterion. It is also the most problematic. This is because differences in bone size among adults are relatively subtle in most species. "Matching" by size therefore requires subjective, even arbitrary decisions on whether a particular left and a particular right actually came from the same individual. It also usually requires fairly complete bones. In many assemblages, however, relatively small fragments abound. Finally, matching by size is impractical in large samples, barring the availability of a computer program such as the one described by Nichol and Creak (1979).

Matching is obviously most satisfactory and most objective when it is based on a discrete trait. Thus, in some species, some skeletal parts differ markedly in form between the sexes. In many bovid species, for example, only male frontal bones bear horns. In these species, the presence or absence of horn-cores may obviously be used to "match" frontals. In most mammal species, it is also possible to use the fusion or nonfusion of epiphyses as a discrete matching criterion. Thus, for a paired element like the distal humerus, a nonfused epiphysis and a fused epiphysis probably come from different individuals, even if one epiphysis is left and the other right.

Like sorting into lefts and rights, matching is more likely to affect MNIs in small samples than in large ones. A more serious problem that is largely independent of sample size concerns the way an investigator treats fragmentary bones. This subject is seldom explicitly addressed, yet it is critical, since fragmentary bones occur in most fossil faunas. In the ones we have studied, fragments constitute the overwhelming majority of identifiable specimens.

There are three basic alternatives: (1) fragments may be totally ignored; (2) they may be treated as if they were complete bones; and (3) they may be recorded as fractions of complete bones. If the third alternative is chosen, the fractions for a skeletal part are summed and added to the number of complete bones. The MNI for the part is the resulting figure, rounded upward to the next whole number. Thus, for a particular species, the left distal humerus category might include three complete specimens and three fragmentary ones, consisting of one-half, one-third, and one-third of a complete distal humerus respectively. The sum for left distal humeri would then be 4.16 (3 + .50 + .33 + .33). The MNI for left distal humeri would be 5.

If fragmentary bones are ignored, MNIs will be artificially depressed. If fragments are treated as whole bones, MNIs will be artificially inflated. In either case, MNI values will become dependent on the degree of fragmentation, which may vary between assemblages or between species within an assemblage. The result will be MNIs that may not be comparable between assemblages or between species.

The estimation of fractions is therefore the preferred alternative. The major objection to it is that it must be subjective to some extent. However, it is probable that the fractions estimated by experienced analysts will be very similar.

A final important problem with MNIs is that they are not additive in the way that NISPs are. Thus, if a species sample contains three left distal humeri, two right distal humeri, two left proximal ulnae, and one right proximal ulna, the MNI is 3 (NISP = 8). If a second sample contains three left distal radii, two right distal radii, two left proximal ulnae, and one right proximal ulna, its MNI is also 3 (NISP = 8). However, if the two samples are now lumped before MNI calculation, the new MNI is 4, not 6 (NISP = 8 + 8 = 16). In most real world cases, lumping samples will similarly reduce MNIs, particularly if the lumped samples are small.

Lumping may occur for a variety of reasons. Perhaps most common is the situation where bones from a renewed excavation must be added to a previous sample. There are also times when an excavator is unsure whether two provenience units (adjacent layers, house floors within a single layer, etc.) really contain mutually exclusive samples. In this case, the bones in one unit may come from the very same animals as the bones in another. It may thus be desirable to compute MNIs for the two units both separately and together.

In sum, the principal problems with the MNI are that: (1) MNIs are tedious to calculate, with a strong possibility of calculation error; (2) MNI estimates may not be comparable among analysts, depending on whether they sort lefts from rights in paired elements, and if so, depending on what criteria they use to determine whether a left-right pair could come from the same animal; (3) MNI estimates may not be comparable among analysts, depending on how they treat fragmentary bones; and (4) MNI values are affected by the size and quality of the field provenience units used to define bone samples.

Clearly, the noncomparability of MNIs owing to differences in the way different analysts compute them would be reduced or eliminated if there were a consensus on whether to sort lefts from rights, what criteria to use in matching, how to treat fragmentary bones, and so on. We suggest that analysts regularly separate rights from lefts, that they employ only discrete criteria such as epiphyseal fusion (or lack of it) in matching, and that they record fragments as specific fractions of whole bones. We have incorporated these suggestions and others in the computer program "MNI" described in chapter 6. In addition to standardizing the criteria behind MNI calculation, the program also significantly reduces the tedium involved in calculation and the likelihood of calculation error.

Finally, the program makes it relatively simple to recompute MNIs when two samples must be lumped. However, it does not address the problem that MNI values are affected by the size and quality of field provenience units. As we see it, the basic issue here is whether the units have been meaningfully defined in terms of sediments, cultural contents, or other relevant criteria. If the units are poorly defined, then MNI comparisons may be unwarranted or misleading. There may also be little point in comparing NISPs or any other numbers.

MNI comparisons should especially be avoided among adjacent provenience units that have been arbitrarily defined, such as squares or spits within a layer. The reason is that the bones in one square or spit may come from the same individuals represented in an adjacent square or spit. It follows that the MNI values in one square or spit may affect those in another. There is an obvious logical, not to mention statistical problem in comparing MNI values that are numerically interdependent.

In sum, the interpretation of MNI values, like the interpretation of other fossil or archeological data, is constrained by the quality and nature of the provenience units from which samples were recovered.

More on NISPs and MNIs

To this point, we have emphasized the strengths of the MNI over the NISP. We have suggested, however, that the NISP and the MNI together may provide information that neither provides alone. In this section, we discuss two additional reasons for considering the NISP and the MNI together. We also argue that they share a basic conceptual weakness. When this is made explicit, it is clear that neither is truly suitable as an index of species abundance, unless one or both is presented for each skeletal part of each species.

First, we consider the mathematical relationship between the NISP and the MNI. It is intuitively obvious that both increase as sample size increases, while the MNI tends to increase more slowly. Casteel (1977b) analyzed paired NISP and MNI values in 610 species samples from around the world. Taking NISP as the independent variable and MNI as the dependent one, he showed that the relationship between them could be broadly modeled by the exponential formula

$$MNI = 0.77(NISP)^{0.52}$$

when NISP was 1,000 or less, and by the linear formula

$$MNI = 5.56 + 0.0225(NISP)$$

when NISP was more than 1,000. Casteel's exponential model for NISP less than 1000 is presented here in figure 3.1.

Casteel's conclusion was that NISP is a good predictor of MNI. However, Casteel did not truly deal with the question of prediction accuracy. (In statistical terms, he did not undertake an analysis of the residuals around his regression lines.) Figure 3.1 shows that, for samples we have studied where NISP is less than 1,000, Casteel's exponential model sometimes predicts MNI quite closely and sometimes does not. (We chose Casteel's exponential model for illustrative purposes only. The same point could be made with respect to the linear model and samples larger than 1,000.)

In some cases, the lack of fit between Casteel's model and our data may be due to chance, but in most instances the reason is basic sample structure. Most important is that our samples vary greatly among themselves in the degree of bone fragmentation. We have already noted that fragmentation will have a greater effect on the NISP than on the MNI. Thus, two samples that are differently fragmented can have identical NISPs and very different MNIs or identical MNIs and very different NISPs. Generally speaking, all other things equal, the greater the fragmentation, the greater the difference between the NISP and the MNI for a species.

Our samples also differ among themselves in the range of skeletal parts that are well represented. Thus, in some of our samples, pre- and/or postdepositional factors have favored an abundance of small hard parts (isolated teeth, carpals, tarsals, and sesamoids). Other parts are rare or absent. In some of our other samples, skeletal-part representation is more even. In particular, various limb bones, vertebrae, and ribs are relatively more common. In the samples with a smaller variety of well-represented parts, the NISP and MNI values are closer than in the samples with a wide range of well-represented parts. This result can be generalized to state that the disparity between the NISP and the MNI will tend to grow as the range of well-represented parts increases.

Thus, the scatter of points around Casteel's line is probably more interesting than the line itself. In sum, NISP and MNI are not so closely related that we can substitute one for the other.

The second aspect of the relationship between NISP and MNI that bears mention is conceptual. If the MNI is the minimum number of individual animals in a species sample, the NISP is the maximum number. The actual number lies between the MNI (the lower limit) and the NISP (the upper limit). At least implicitly, some authors favor the MNI or the NISP because they believe that one measure or the other is closer to the actual number of individuals in a sample.

It is conceivable that in some samples nearly every bone or bone fragment is derived from a different individual (Lie 1980; Perkins 1973; Watson 1979). In this case the NISP will clearly estimate the actual number of individuals better than the MNI will. On the other hand, the MNI will probably estimate the actual number better in samples characterized by extreme fragmentation. However, we see no way to pursue this question rigorously. In virtually all cases, the actual number of individuals in a fossil sample is indeterminate, and there is no sound way to determine its distance from either the MNI or the NISP. This is an aspect of their mathematical independence.

Finally, the NISP and the MNI share a basic conceptual weakness. As

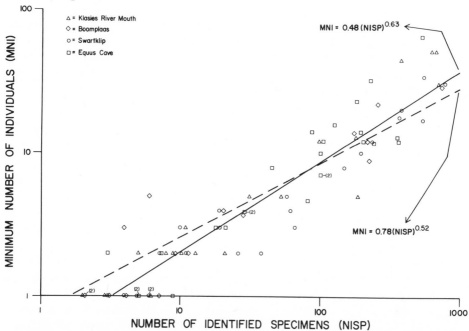

FIGURE 3.1: Paired NISP and MNI values for eighty-four species samples
from the Stone Age archeological sites of Klasies River Mouth Cave 1
and Boomplaas Cave A and the fossil hyena dens of Swartklip and
Equus Cave. All four sites are in South Africa and date from the late
Pleistocene. The samples plotted are all the ones from each site in
which the NISP was between 2 and 1,000. The figure shows that the
MNI tends to rise as the NISP does, which fits intuitive expectations.
However, it also shows that the relation between NISP and MNI is far
from perfect. The solid line is the regression of log(MNI) on log(NISP)
for the plotted samples. The dotted line is a regression of log(MNI) on
log(NISP) for another set of species samples analyzed by Casteel
(1977b). For additional discussion, see the text.

summary measures of species abundance, both ignore the specific skeletal
parts that make up a sample. Thus, two samples may have identical
NISPs or MNIs and still contrast strongly in patterns of skeletal part
representation. The first sample may be dominated by one set of skeletal
parts (e.g. the vertebrae) and the second sample by a different set (e.g. the
limb bones). Or the first sample might contain a wide variety of skeletal
parts all represented to about the same extent, while the second contains
only a few parts represented to the virtual exclusion of others. In either
case, interassemblage differences based on summary MNIs or NISPs alone
are likely to be misinterpreted.

We may illustrate the problem in greater detail with an interassemblage
contrast in skeletal part representation that has been observed
archeologically. Imagine two large fossil assemblages containing exactly
the same species. Imagine further that the relative abundance of the

species in the two assemblages is very similar, whether measured by the NISP or the MNI. If there is contextual evidence that the assemblages share similar postdepositional histories and that they accumulated under similar environmental circumstances, we might well conclude that there was also no difference in behavior between the agents that accumulated them. However, if the principal skeletal parts behind the NISP and the MNI in the first assemblage were vertebrae and the principal parts behind the NISP and the MNI in the second were limb bones, our conclusion would surely be suspect.

The point is of course that bone accumulators do not always deal in whole animals, nor do they necessarily treat all skeletal parts in the same way. Thus, with regard to our hypothetical example, the assemblage rich in vertebrae might reflect human butchering at a kill site from which only the meatier or more useful parts were removed. The assemblage rich in limb bones might reflect human activities at a living site to which only the most useful parts were ordinarily brought.

Clearly, then, it is risky to rely solely on summary NISPs or MNIs in interassemblage comparisons. In virtually all instances, it is far wiser to compare patterns of skeletal part representation between species before proceeding to more general interassemblage comparisons of species abundance. If the patterns for the same species in different assemblages are very different, this fact rather than the summary NISPs or MNIs may be the critical point for interpretation.

In general, MNIs are probably more useful than NISPs for comparing patterns of skeletal part representation between samples. This is especially true if the samples differ in the degree of bone fragmentation and there is evidence that the difference originated postdepositionally. In this case, NISP comparisons will automatically confuse differences that orginated postdepositionally with ones that may be due to differences in ancient environment or collector behavior. More generally, the NISP is more likely than the MNI to exaggerate the abundance of a skeletal part simply because it fragments easily.

In sum, patterns of skeletal part representation must be compared between species samples before species abundance may be meaningfully compared between fossil assemblages. This means that, whatever measure of species abundance is employed, it must be calculated and presented for each skeletal part of each species and not simply for the species as a whole.

Modified MNIs

Some specialists have suggested that modifying MNI calculation may eliminate certain inadequacies. A frequently cited inadequacy is that the MNI exaggerates the importance of "rare" species. The point here is that a species represented by only a few bones may have the same MNI as one represented by many bones. To counteract this problem, Gejvall (1969) and others have suggested that MNIs not be calculated for "small" species samples.

One problem with this suggestion is that there is no truly objective, nonarbitrary way to define "small." A more serious problem is that the suggestion confuses MNIs with the interpretation of MNIs. Analysts who worry that the MNI exaggerates the importance of "rare" species are mainly concerned that the "rare" species will seem more important in an ancient environment or economy than they really were. Thus, in a particular sample, domestic sheep may have an NISP of 200 and an MNI of 3, while red deer have an NISP of 2 and an MNI of 1. If the MNIs are taken at face value, a possible conclusion is that red deer were nearly as common near the site as sheep, or that hunting was nearly as important as herding. If the amount of meat obtainable from the animals is considered, the conclusion might even be that red deer were dietarily more important than sheep.

Certainly, conclusions like these have been repeatedly drawn from MNIs, and we agree that they are not well founded. However, the problem is not in the MNI index; it is in the assumption that the MNIs in a "fossil assemblage" directly reflect those in the "death assemblage" or the "life assemblage" that preceded it. We have already noted that this assumption is not justified. With respect to the site that provided the hypothetical red deer/sheep sample, it might be that red deer were actually much more common than sheep nearby but that the occupants rarely hunted. Or it might be that they often hunted but usually left red deer bones somewhere else. It might even be that red deer did not occur nearby at all, but that their remains were traded in for artifact manufacture.

Narrowing down the alternatives will be possible only when the factors responsible for sample composition are "controlled" through comparison with other relevant samples. MNIs are perfectly adequate for such comparisons, particularly when they are considered together with NISPs and with patterns of skeletal part representation.

Based on an argument that is more complex and less clear than Gejvall's, Perkins (1973) also concluded that there should be a minimum sample size for MNI calculation. He suggested 1,000 bones. Even with such a sample size, he felt that MNI calculation was unjustified unless:

1) The period of time it took for a fossil assemblage to form is known.

2) Preservation is good enough so that the actual number of individuals may be estimated.

3) Essentially the entire fossil assemblage has been recovered.

Since these conditions are almost never met, Perkins suggested replacing standard MNI calculation with the following procedure:

1) For each species, determine which skeletal parts (e.g. the distal humerus, the proximal radius, the proximal femur, etc.) are least affected by cultural or preservational factors. Then count the number of such parts (= A).

2) For each species, sum the number of bones or bone fragments assignable to each of the skeletal parts established in step 1 (the sum = B).

3) Determine the abundance of each species (= f) by dividing the total number of bones or bone fragments established in step 2 by the number of skeletal parts in step 1 (f = B/A). Thus, if the skeletal parts least affected

by pre- or postdepositional destructive pressures were the distal humerus, the proximal radius, and the proximal femur, and a species sample contained thirty distal humeri, fourteen proximal radii, and ten proximal femora, the species abundance would be (30 + 14 + 10)/3 or 18.

Holtzman (1979) has proposed an essentially similar index that he calls the "weighted abundance of elements" or WAE. Paleontologists will also recognize the close similarity of the WAE to "the corrected number of specimens" suggested by Shotwell (1955, 1958).

In Monte Carlo computer simulations, Holtzman found that the WAE was closer to the actual number of individuals than the MNI. However, it clearly has some serious deficiencies. One is that it is useful only for summary measures of species abundance. It cannot be used to measure the abundance of separate skeletal parts. More seriously, there is no objective, nonarbitrary means for deciding what skeletal parts "to weight" or, in Perkins's terms, what skeletal parts "are least affected by cultural or preservational factors." Even if different analysts could somehow agree on the parts for a single sample, their choice would still be sample specific. The WAEs calculated for different samples might therefore not be comparable. In sum, we see little value in the WAE method.

Meat Weight Estimates

Under the heading "meat weight estimates," we consider two methods of measuring species abundance. The first is actually a modification of the MNI method suggested by White (1953) and employed by many archeologists since. In this procedure, the MNI for a species is multiplied by the amount of meat on a carcass. This is supposed to correct for the possibility that the importance of a large species may be underestimated by a small MNI. Thus, if only MNIs are considered, one bison may seem less significant than ten roe deer. But if meat weights are factored in, the bison will clearly "outweigh" the ten deer.

There are many objections to this procedure. One is that it usually assumes that the same meat weight characterizes all members of a species, regardless of sex, age, or season of the year, when this is clearly not the case (Smith 1975; Stewart and Stahl 1977). Thus, one bison might not outweigh ten roe deer, if the bison is very young. Much more important, the meat weight index is flawed by the assumption that each individual in a "fossil assemblage" reflects a complete carcass consumed by the bone collectors. This assumption is clearly not warranted a priori. The one bison in our hypothetical example might be represented by only a few bones to which relatively little meat was attached. Or the bones may have been used for artifact manufacture, in which case nothing from the bison may have been eaten. From a dietary standpoint, it is thus possible that the roe deer were more important after all.

In effect, the meat weight index assumes that the MNIs in a fossil assemblage reflect those in the preceding death assemblage, which they need not. In most cases, calculating meat weights will simply distort basic MNI values without adding any useful or significant information.

The second kind of meat weight index is the *Weigemethode,* literally the "weight method," but better described as the bone weight method. It literally relies on the total weight of the bones assigned to a species. This is multiplied by a factor that is presumed to reflect the ratio between bone weight and meat weight in live animals.

Proponents of the bone weight method have generally assumed that the ratio of bone weight to meat weight is the same for all individuals within a species. However, Casteel (1978) has shown that this does not apply to domestic pigs, in which the percentage of bone weight drops hyperbolically as meat weight increases. The same kind of variation probably characterizes other species, and it is difficult to incorporate this fact into the bone weight method. Casteel shows that ignoring it may produce meat weights that are off by an order of magnitude or more.

Another obvious problem with the bone weight method is that it will exaggerate the importance of a species whose bones retain their identifiability even when they become highly fragmented. It will also exaggerate the importance of a species whose bones are more resistant to leaching or more susceptible to mineralization. Most important, however, it again assumes that "meat weight" is the crucial variable in estimating species abundance. In effect this confuses counting with interpretation.

In sum, we agree with Chaplin (1971), Casteel (1978), and others that the bone weight index is a poor measure of species abundance.

The Petersen Index

We pointed out previously that the NISP and the MNI together bracket the actual number of individual animals in a fossil sample. Together, they constitute an interval estimate of this number rather than a point estimate. Krantz (1968), Lie (1980), and Fieller and Turner (1982) have all suggested that a true point estimate can be obtained for paired elements. Their shared assumption is that for any paired element (e.g. the distal humerus), the numbers of lefts and rights that cannot be assigned to a matched left-right pair provide a good measure of the number of individuals "missing" from a species sample. Fieller and Turner propose an especially ingenious way to use "nonmatchable" rights and lefts, and it is their method we deal with here. Krantz's method is very similar but was presented with less statistical or logical justification. We do not deal further with Lie's method because it has all the flaws of Fieller and Turner's and none of the strong points.

Fieller and Turner perceive an analogy between estimating the number of individuals in a fossil sample and estimating the number in a free-ranging population of wild animals. To census wild animals, biologists commonly employ the "capture-recapture" method, known more formally as the Petersen (or Lincoln) index. This method comprises three steps:

1) A sample of animals is captured, marked, and released.

2) Somewhat later, a second sample is captured, and the proportion of marked individuals is recorded.

3) The proportion of marked animals in the second sample is presumed

to be roughly the same as the proportion of marked animals in the total population. The total population may thus be estimated from the formula (n1 x n2)/P where n1 is the number of individuals in sample 1, n2 is the number in sample 2, and P is the proportion of marked individuals in sample 2.

In applying the Petersen index to fossil samples, Turner and Fieller equate sample 1 (marked individuals) with the number of lefts in a paired element, sample 2 (the recapture sample of marked and unmarked individuals) with the number of rights of a paired element, and P with the number of matched left-right pairs. (n1 x n2)/P (or [nR x nL]/P) is then the number of pairs that must have been present initially. This number is equated in turn with the actual (original) number of individuals in the sample.

Fieller and Turner emphasize that the figure produced by the Petersen index is only an estimate, but one with a known probability distribution. It is therefore possible to calculate a confidence interval for it. This is a highly desirable property not found in the MNI or any other index of species abundance that has been seriously proposed.

We believe Fieller and Turner's application of the Petersen index to fossil samples is thoughtful and intriguing. However, we are not sure that the analogy with the capture-recapture method is truly appropriate. In the case of capture-recapture, the two samples (n1 and n2) on which estimation is based clearly are drawn from the same population. In the fossil situation, the two samples (nL and nR) need not be drawn from the same population. This will happen only if the bone accumulator commonly imported both sides (a left-right pair) of the same carcass or carcass segment to a site. If the collector commonly brought back only one side (sometimes left, sometimes right), the analogy is invalid. In most of the fossil samples we are aware of, there is no a priori reason to suppose that the collector routinely brought back both sides of each carcass or carcass segment.

Furthermore, in the wildlife biology case, establishing P is straightforward. It is simply the proportion of marked individuals in the recapture sample. However, in the fossil case, P is the number of matched pairs, which is itself only an estimate with an unknown probability distribution. Additionally, in the fossil sample, P will usually be depressed by the degree of bone fragmentation. Thus, in a highly fragmented sample the number of individuals estimated by the Petersen index may actually be lower than the MNI.

In an updated discussion of the Petersen Index in fossil studies, Turner (1983) suggests that the method be applied only to paired elements such as pelvises, or mandibles, maxillae, and other cranial bones, whose left and right halves are relatively unlikely to come apart when a carcass is dismembered. These are parts that have the greatest a priori likelihood of entering a fossil assemblage as a matched pair. However, it is difficult to see the value of the method unless it can be applied to all parts equally. What do we conclude, for example, if the "actual number of individuals" estimated from an appropriate part is less than the MNI estimated from an inappropriate one? This raises an even more basic flaw--the method cannot deal at all with vertebrae or other non-paired elements.

In sum, in spite of its statistical allure, we feel that the Petersen index is inferior to the MNI and the NISP as a measure of fossil species abundance.

Summary and Conclusion

Clearly, a good index of species abundance should not attempt to measure something that is not an aspect of the "fossil assemblage." If it simultaneously attempts to measure an aspect of the "deposited assemblage" or the "death assemblage," it is assuming something that in reality should be inferred. This is the principal difficulty with Perkins's modified MNI index, the meat weight methods, or Fieller and Turner's application of the Petersen index. These indexes confound measurement with interpretation. They make unwarranted assumptions about the postdepositional history of a fossil assemblage, the behavior of the bone collector, or the effects of this behavior on a bone assemblage, and they build these assumptions into the measurement method. This is particularly obvious in the case of the meat weight methods which assume that a fossil assemblage is a direct reflection of the bone collector's diet.

We have emphasized that bone accumulators do not necessarily deal in whole animals, while they may distinguish in important ways between the different parts of an animal. Similarly, postdepositional destructive pressures need not affect all skeletal parts equally. This means that patterns of skeletal part representation must be compared between species samples before summary measures of species abundance are compared between assemblages. It follows that a good index of species abundance must measure not only the abundance of each species within a fossil assemblage, but also the abundance of each skeletal part within a species sample. Perkins's modified MNI index, the meat weight methods, and the Petersen index also fail on this criterion--they are essentially designed to measure species abundance alone.

Among the measures of species abundance that we have discussed, the two that do not confuse measurement with interpretation and that may be used to measure both skeletal part and summary species abundance are the NISP and the MNI. For most intersample comparisons, we favor the MNI over the NISP, mainly because it is less sensitive to the effects of bone fragmentation. However, a complete analysis requires that fragmentation itself be described and explained. For this purpose the NISP can be very helpful when it is presented together with the MNI.

One obstacle to the use of MNIs is that they are tedious to calculate, particularly in samples that are large enough for intersample comparisons. Additionally, there is a good chance of calculation error, even in fairly small samples. In chapter 6, we describe a computer program that substantially reduces both the tedium and the likelihood of calculation error in large samples. Input to the program is a list of identifiable bones in a sample and associated data--the skeletal part represented, its provenience unit, side, the fraction present, and so forth. Output is a formatted list of NISPs and MNIs for each skeletal part in the sample, providing the basic information we think is vital for intersample comparisons.

4: SEX AND AGE PROFILES OF FOSSIL SPECIES

The Utility of Sex and Age Determination

In chapter 1 we noted that there are many fossil sites where it is difficult
or impossible to establish the agent of bone accumulation or to separate the
possible contributions of several agents. Fortunately, there are also many
sites where context, associated objects, and bone damage point clearly to
just one agent as the primary bone accumulator. We provide examples of
such sites in chapter 5. At such sites it is obviously reasonable to ask how
the agent of accumulation acquired the bones that are present. For
example, if people were the bone collectors, we want to know whether they
scavenged, hunted, or herded the animals and, if hunting or herding is
implied, what methods they used. Again, site context and associations are
often relevant to the answer, but the sex/age composition of species
samples may be equally or more important. We illustrate this with
examples in chapter 5.

In this chapter we discuss methods for determining and interpreting
fossil sex and age profiles. We note that sex/age profiles may be useful
even at sites where there is uncertainty or confusion about the bone
accumulator. At the very least, the profiles may rule out an accumulator
whose known behavior is inconsistent with them.

Determination of Sex

In many mammal species, some skeletal parts differ in morphology
between the sexes. In equids, for example, the jaws of males usually
contain large canines; the jaws of females usually lack canines or contain
very small "vestigial" ones. Similarly, in bovid and equid species, female
skulls either lack horns or antlers or bear ones different in size or shape
from those of males. In carnivore species, the penis commonly contains a
bone known as the penis bone or baculum. There is no homologous
structure in females. In people, the female pelvis differs significantly in
shape from the male one, because the female pelvis must accommodate the
birth canal. For the same reason, pelvis shape also differs between the
sexes in deer (Taber 1956; Edwards, Marchinton, and Smith 1982),
caprines (Boessneck 1969), and probably many other mammalian species
(Taber 1971).

For a species in which a skeletal part differs in shape between the sexes,
the sex ratio in a fossil sample can be estimated from the ratio of male
parts to female parts or from the proportion of males or females in the total
sample. However, there are many fossil samples in which the parts most
useful for distinguishing the sexes are rare. This can happen because the
bone-accumulating agent did not introduce the parts to a site or selectively
took them away. Additionally, many parts useful for "sexing" are
relatively fragile and therefore subject to selective removal by

postdepositional leaching, profile compaction, and other processes. This pertains particularly to horn-cores and antlers, which are far less durable than many other skeletal parts. Postdepositional destruction is probably responsible for the rarity of horn-cores or antlers in most of the fossil samples we have studied, though other bovid or cervid bones are superabundant.

Postdepositional destructive pressures may also remove the critical parts of one sex more readily than those of the other. Thus, male bovid horn-cores and cervid antlers are generally more durable than female ones (or than the part of the skull to which horn-cores or antlers would attach in females). Similarly, the presence of large canines enhances the durability of male equid jaws versus female ones. Thus, unless bone preservation is excellent, it is probably not safe to assume that the sex ratio in a fossil assemblage closely reflects the ratio in the original deposited assemblage. In most cases, the proportion of males will be higher than it was originally. In the samples we have studied, insofar as the sex ratio for equids, bovids, or cervids can be established from jaws, horn-cores, or antlers, there is a clear tendency for the proportion of males to increase as the quality of bone preservation declines.

As an alternative to differences in bone shape, in some samples it may be possible to use differences in bone size to establish a sex ratio. Male skeletal parts tend to be larger than their female homologues in most mammal species, reflecting larger average male body size (Boessneck and von den Driesch 1978, with references). One clear advantage to this method is that it is applicable to a wide variety of skeletal parts, at least some of which are likely to abound in any large fossil sample. Additionally, for most skeletal parts to which the method is applicable, there is no reason to suppose that postdepositional destructive pressures will selectively remove the bones of either sex.

The method clearly is most promising when applied to a skeletal part that is known to differ in size between the sexes of a species. However, it may be used even when a difference in mean size has not been established from specimens of known sex. The first step is to choose a dimension that is very likely to differ between the sexes. In many species the mediolateral diameter of a limb-bone epiphysis, such as the distal tibia, is a good choice. In species where males bear the extra weight of antlers or horns, a bone of the forelimb is perhaps most appropriate. For example, Altuna (1976) chose the distal metacarpal to analyze the sex ratio in samples of late Pleistocene red deer from northern Spain. Ordinarily, measurements are made only on fused epiphyses, since these do not change size with age. This means there is no danger of confusing size differences due to sex with size differences due to age.

The measurements are subsequently plotted. If the sexes differ in average size for the measurement, if both sexes are well represented in the sample, and if the sample is large enough, the plot will exhibit two distinct modes. The mode comprising smaller bones will be "female"; the mode comprising larger bones will be "male." The sex ratio may be estimated from the ratio between the number of bones in the female mode and the number in the male mode.

There are several obvious problems with the method. One difficulty is that it excludes individuals whose growth is not complete for the bone being measured. In many samples these individuals are very common. There is also a problem introduced by the possible existence of castrates in a domestic species (Chaplin 1971). These may fall squarely between females and uncastrated males in size, blurring the size bimodality.

Most important, however, is the assumption the method makes about size differences between the sexes. In some species, such as otariid seals, adult males and females may not overlap in size at all, and a plot of both sexes will always show two distinct modes. In most species, however, the difference in size is more subtle, and males and females overlap substantially (fig. 4.1). If the sexes do not differ greatly in mean size, bimodality will not emerge even in a large sample comprising subequal numbers of males and females. (It can be shown mathematically that a frequency distribution comprising half males and half females of a species will appear unimodal, even if the male and female means are as much as two standard deviations apart.) In sum, establishing the sex ratio from a bimodal plot will be impossible in many cases. In such cases, the best an analyst can do is to use differences in mean bone size between two samples to suggest a difference between them in the sex ratio (Altuna 1976).

In general, size differences between the sexes may be clearer if more than one measurement is considered at a time. Thus, if a bone is complete, it might be fruitful to measure its total length and the minimum diameter of its shaft in addition to the mediolateral diameter of its distal epiphysis. Two of the measurements may be expressed as a ratio and plotted against the third (Boessneck and von den Driesch 1978; Bedord 1978). Instead of modes the analyst is then seeking two distinct clusters of points in two-dimensional space. However, even with multiple measurements it may be difficult to demonstrate the reality of clusters unless the samples are very large, both sexes are well represented, and the sexes differ strongly in size with respect to the measurements being plotted. A further problem is that many samples, including most of those we have studied, contain very few bones that are complete enough for multiple measurements.

In sum, establishing the sex ratio in a fossil sample is often problematic. However, where the sex ratio is available, it can be very informative. We present some examples from our own experience in chapter 5. We note also that the program BONESTAT discussed in chapter 8 produces histograms that can be used to search for sex-linked bimodality in bone size.

Determination of Age: Epiphyseal Fusion versus Dental Criteria
The skeletal parts most commonly used to determine the age of an animal at time of death are epiphyses and teeth. In virtually all mammalian species, for any given skeletal part (e.g., the humerus), a specimen on which the epiphyses are unfused almost certainly comes from a younger

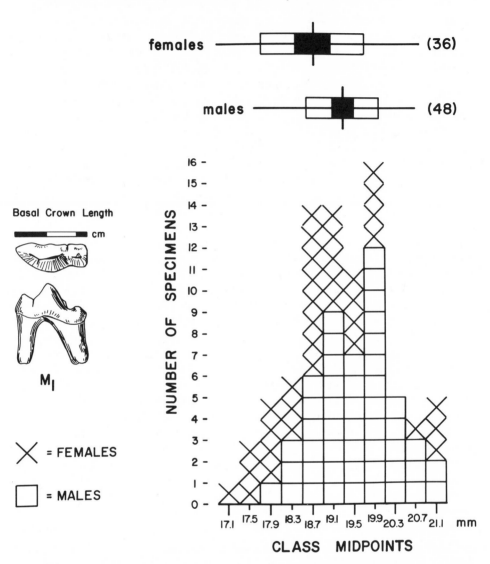

CANIS MESOMELAS (Cape Province)

FIGURE 4.1: Below: Basal crown length in lower M1s of male and female black-backed jackals (*Canis mesomelas*) from the Cape Province, South Africa. Note the clear tendency for male teeth to be larger than female teeth, but also the substantial overlap in size. The result is that the crown length distribution is not clearly bimodal.

Above: The mean (horizontal line), standard deviation (open bar), and 95% confidence limits of the mean (closed bar) for lower M1 length in male and female black-backed jackals from the Cape Province, South Africa.

individual than a specimen on which the epiphyses are fused. For each skeletal part, it is thus possible to form at least two age classes. In fact, it is often possible to form more than two, since many bones have two (or more) epiphyses that fuse at different ages. Thus, in most species the distal epiphysis of the humerus fuses to the shaft before the proximal epiphysis. This obviously permits three age classes (neither epiphysis fused; distal fused and proximal unfused; and both epiphyses fused).

If a fossil sample comes from a population in which the ages of epiphyseal fusion are known, epiphyseal age classes can be translated into chronological ones. Thus, in domestic sheep the distal epiphysis of the humerus tends to fuse to the shaft at about 10 months and the proximal epiphysis at 3-3.5 years (Silver 1969). The humerus age classes are then < 10 months, 10 months to 3-3.5 years, and > 3.5 years. The epiphyses of other skeletal parts generally fuse at somewhat different ages. Hence, by considering different parts concurrently, it may be possible to construct several age classes of individuals before the age at which all epiphyses are fused.

Aging by epiphyseal fusion has sometimes provided interesting results, particularly for samples of domestic stock, where the epiphyseal age classes may be sufficient to reconstruct the strategy of herd management (Chaplin 1971). However, in general the method has serious shortcomings. First, the chronological ages of epiphyseal fusion are not known for most populations of wild mammals. Even the relative sequence of epiphyseal fusion is unknown for many free-ranging populations. Second, in most cases the epiphyseal age classes are probably too coarse to construct an interpretable mortality profile. In particular, the oldest age class (with all epiphyses fused) contains a very wide range of individuals, from prime adults to senile ones. In many cases, separating prime adults from senile ones is vital to understanding the causes of mortality.

Third, unfused epiphyses are generally much less durable than fused ones. Thus, in samples that have been subjected to signficant postdepositional destructive pressure, unfused epiphyses will have been selectively removed, leading to a bias against younger animals. The extent of the bias will vary from case to case but is generally indeterminate. Finally, in many fossil samples, including most of those we have studied, most epiphyses cannot be securely assigned to species. They must be assigned to a broader category such as "large bovid" that probably comprises two or more species. An age profile based on these epiphyses may thus be a misleading blend of two or more different age profiles.

Fortunately, many of the deficiencies of epiphyseal fusion for "aging" may be circumvented by the use of teeth. Unlike epiphyses, teeth monitor age more or less continuously throughout the life of an individual. This means that teeth can be used to define a larger number of more narrowly bounded age classes. In particular, teeth usually permit a clear distinction between prime adults and senile ones; often it is even possible to make distinctions within the prime and senile categories. Also, compared with epiphyses, teeth from individuals of different ages are about equally durable, so that dental age profiles are less likely to be seriously "biased" by selective postdepositional destruction. More generally, the great durability of teeth means that they are often abundant enough to provide an interpretable profile when epiphyses are not. Finally, unlike epiphyses, teeth are almost always identifiable to species, so there is little danger of constructing an age profile that is a meaningless composite of two different age profiles.

Determining Individual Age from Teeth

There are two basic methods for establishing the age of an animal from its teeth. The first method involves counting the growth increments or "annuli" frequently visible in dentine or cementum. The second and more traditional method is based on the evaluation of dental eruption and wear.

The cementum/dentine annulus method is widely used in wildlife biology, where its potential is still being explored. Morris (1972, 1978) and Spinage (1973) provide general reviews. The method is based on two changes that occur in teeth as an animal ages: secondary dentine progressively fills the pulp cavity, while cementum builds up on the roots. In many (probably most) species, the rate of secondary dentine and cementum formation varies from season to season. As a result, neither substance is homogeneous. Instead, both are composed of discrete bands--narrow, dense ones representing periods of slow deposition alternating with broad, less dense ones representing periods of rapid deposition. The bands may be observed by transmitted or reflected light in specially prepared, stained sections. They then appear as alternating light-dark pairs. In many species, there is a close correlation between the number of pairs and the age in years of known-age individuals. Hence, each pair may be regarded as a yearly increment or "annulus," analogous to the growth ring of a tree.

In most mammals, the pulp cavity fills with dentine fairly early in life, so that later dentine increments may be too thin to detect. Routine estimation of advanced ages from secondary dentine increments is possible only in marine mammals. In most terrestrial species, cementum annuli must be used. It is thus only cementum annuli that are likely to interest most faunal analysts.

There are several problems in applying the cementum annulus method. From a theoretical point of view, the principal difficulty is that the causes of annulus formation are not well understood (Grue and Jensen 1979). Seasonal differences in nutrition are commonly thought to be responsible. This is because in many species the broader, less dense band (indicating more rapid deposition) forms during the season of least nutritional stress. However, exactly the same kind of banding appears in zoo animals that never suffer nutritional stress. Additionally, in some species, "secondary" dark bands have been found inside the broad, light ones. In many species, these may form during periods of peak reproductive activity, implying some hormonal control over cementum banding. Secondary bands constitute a potential source of counting error, since what one investigator considers secondary bands another may take as primary.

A potentially more serious source of counting discrepancy derives from the fact that cementum is not equally thick on all parts of all roots. Thus bands that are readily apparent in one part of a cementum pad will not be visible in another. In addition, some cementum may be resorbed during the life of an animal or lost when a tooth is removed from a jaw. In either case, the number of countable bands will be reduced below the "true" number.

From a faunal analytic standpoint, however, the principal shortcoming of the cementum annulus method is not its potential inaccuracy, since this can probably be minimized with care and experience. A greater difficulty is the time, equipment, and expertise in section preparation that the method requires. Even more important, the method is destructive, and most faunal analysts will probably be reluctant to sacrifice a dental sample simply to obtain an age profile.

Furthermore, in wildlife biology it has been shown that the banding pattern is most readily observed when teeth are decalcified before sectioning and staining. Fossil teeth, however, often contain too little organic matter to survive decalcification. The alternative is to section and smooth grind undecalcified specimens (Benn 1974; Bourque, Morris, and Spiess 1978), but this often does not produce a discernible banding pattern (Spiess 1979; personal observation). In sum, it seems unlikely that the cementum annulus method will ever be truly suitable for producing complete age profiles in fossil samples. It may, however, prove useful for establishing the season(s) of the year when bones accumulated at a site. We discuss this possibility below.

In fossil samples, then, the most practical way to estimate individual age from teeth is to evaluate eruption and wear. This can be done subjectively by comparing fossil dentitions with dentitions of known-age individuals in the same species, if the fossil species is still extant, or to dentitions of known-age individuals in closely related species, if the fossil species is extinct. The subjective method works best on a fossil sample derived from a population in which birth and death were seasonally restricted events.

Seasonal mortality may be a result of climate (floods, blizzards) or human activity (seasonally restricted communal drives). In a sample reflecting seasonal birth and death, subjective evaluation of eruption and wear may produce a series of discrete age clusters, with few or no intermediate individuals (for an example, see Voorhies 1969). Usually it is possible to assume that individuals in the youngest age cluster are in their first year of life and that successive age clusters are separated from one another by approximately one year. This means that subjective aging will not require a comparative series of known-age dentitions, which is fortunate, since such series are rare.

An obvious difficulty with the subjective method is that different investigators may produce somewhat different results. A more serious difficulty in applying it to fossil material is that it generally requires complete or nearly complete tooth rows. In many fossil samples, including

45

most of those we have studied, tooth rows are less common than isolated teeth.

For most fossil samples, then, it is desirable to possess an age estimation method that can utilize isolated teeth. The most obvious method is to measure a dental dimension that varies strongly with age. In many species it may be difficult to identify an appropriate dimension, and aging may have to rely on subjective eruption/wear criteria. However, in many carnivores and ungulates there is an obvious relation between crown height and age. So far, little has been done to exploit the relation in carnivores, partly because they are rare in most fossil samples. However, it has been used to estimate age in ungulates, including cervids, bovids, equids, and similar hypsodont species that dominate zooarcheological and many paleontological samples throughout the world. It is on aging from crown height in these species that we focus here.

Ungulate Crown Height and Age

Ungulate crown height can be measured in a variety of ways (see, for example, Ducos 1968 or Davis 1977). The way we measure it is illustrated in figure 4.2. Basically, the measured dimension is the minimum distance between the occlusal surface and the line separating the enamel of the crown from the dentine on the roots, measured on the buccal surface of mandibular teeth and on the lingual surface of maxillary ones. On bilobed or bilophed teeth, we ordinarily measure both lobes or lophs, and on trilobed or trilophed teeth, the two anterior ones. This is because there may be broken teeth that are missing one or another lobe or loph. In constructing an age profile from crown heights, we then use the lobe or loph that is most common in the total sample.

As far as we know, the mathematical relation between advancing age and declining crown height has not been thoroughly established for any ungulate population. However, Spinage (1971, 1972, 1976) has proposed that the relationship between crown height and age is reasonably modeled by the following formula:

$$Y = Y_0[1 - (T/N)^{1/2}]$$

where Y is the height of a tooth, Y_0 is its initial (unworn) crown height, T is the age at height Y, and N is the age at which Y becomes zero.

This model assumes a variable rate of dental wear, such that wear occurs most rapidly when a tooth is freshly erupted (and its occlusal surface is roughest) and most slowly when a tooth is heavily worn (and its surface is smoothest). It further assumes that the maximum possible individual age is the age at which the crowns of permanent teeth are completely worn away. Numerous observations by wildlife biologists support this assumption. In wildlife studies, maximum possible individual age is often known as "potential ecological longevity," a term we will use here. This should not be confused with "average life span" which is usually much

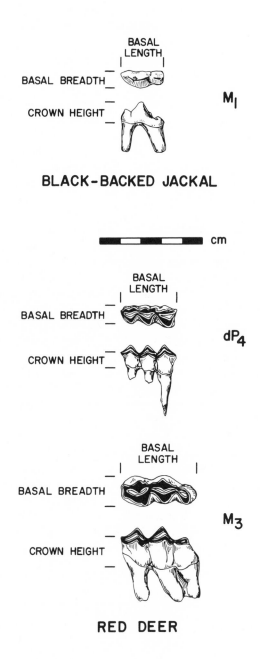

FIGURE 4.2: A red deer lower M3, a red deer lower dP4, and a jackal lower M1, showing the crown height, crown length, and crown breadth measurements made by the authors.

shorter than potential longevity.

Spinage's model may be translated algebraically into the following age estimation formulas:

For a deciduous tooth,

$$AGE = AGEs - 2AGEs(CH/CHo) + AGEs(CH^2/CHo^2)$$

for a permanent tooth:

$$AGE = AGEpel - 2(AGEpel - AGEe)(CH/CHo) +$$
$$(AGEpel - AGEe)(CH^2/CHo^2),$$

where CH is the variable crown height, CHo is initial (unworn) crown height, AGEs is the age at which a deciduous tooth is shed, AGEe is the age at which a permanent tooth erupts, and AGEpel is the maximum possible age of an individual (= age at potential ecological longevity).

Generally speaking, CHo may be estimated from unworn teeth in any fossil sample large enough to warrant age profile construction. Alternatively, it may be based on unworn teeth of the same species in other samples. Given their special importance, we always make certain that the wear state of unworn or very lightly worn teeth is noted on our data recording sheets (see chap. 7). In our experience, there is relatively little variation in unworn crown height within a population, and the mean in a fossil sample will usually provide an adequate estimate, even if it is based on very few specimens. Table 4.1 shows the unworn crown heights of some species that are common in samples we have studied.

For most living ungulate species, estimates of AGEs, AGEe, and AGEpel may be obtained from the wildlife biology literature. For extinct species, or for living ones for which direct estimates have not been published, reasonable approximations can be obtained from publications on close living relatives of similar size. Table 4.2 shows the dental eruption schedules and potential ecological longevity of the same species whose initial unworn crown heights are presented in table 4.1.

Spinage found that his model provided reasonably accurate age estimates for individuals in several species (bovids and equids) whose age was either known or inferred by another method such as cementum annulus counts. In addition, Klein, Allwarden, and Wolf (1983) have shown that the formulas derived from Spinage's model are similar to quadratic regressions of age on crown height in a large sample of known-age Rocky Mountain elk (*Cervus elaphus canadensis*). The elk study showed that crown height is an imperfect estimator of individual age, but that it is almost certainly adequate for the paleobiological purpose of producing an interpretable age profile. This is particularly true when ages are grouped into relatively broad classes, such as the 10% of life span intervals on which we depend. An additional advantage of 10% of life span classes is

TABLE 4.1 Initial Crown Heights (in Tenths of a Millimeter) Used to Calculate Age Profiles for Ungulate Species Common in Late Quaternary Samples from Africa and Europe

	dP4	M3
Eland (*Taurotragus oryx*)	190	448
Greater kudu (*Tragelaphus strepsiceros*)	?131	??
Bushbuck (*T. scriptus*)	65	151
Blue antelope (*Hippotragus leucophaeus*)	168	385
Roan antelope (*H. equinus*)	?191	?420
Lechwe (*Kobus leche*)	162	?370
Southern reedbuck (*Redunca arundinum*)	130	340
Mountain reedbuck (*R. fulvorufula*)	93	270
Vaalribbok (*Pelea capreolus*)	78	240
Cape hartebeest (*Alcelaphus buselaphus*)	210	550
"Giant hartebeest" (*Megalotragus priscus*)	??	?850
Blesbok (*Damaliscus dorcas*)	168	520
Blue wildebeest (*Connochaetes taurinus*)	250	680
Black wildebeest (*C. gnou*)	219	600
Common springbok (*Antidorcas marsupialis*)	140	312
Southern springbok (*A. australis*)	120	285
Bond's springbok (*A. bondi*)	150	416
Gray duiker (*Sylvicapra grimmia*)	74	178
Steenbok (*Raphicerus campestris*)	50	142
Cape grysbok (*R. melanotis*)	47	113
Cape buffalo (*Syncerus caffer*)	218	526
"Giant buffalo" (*Pelorovis antiquus*)	233	715
Aurochs (*Bos primigenius*)	?215	?530

	dP4	M1	M2
Red deer (*Cervus elaphus*)	140	270	296

	dP2	P2	M3
Burchell's zebra (*Equus burchelli*)	270	?600	?750
"Giant Cape horse" (*E. capensis*)	300	??	?900
Wild horse (*E. przewalskii*)	?400	??	?800

Note: The figures are means for unworn first lobe height of mandibular teeth in fossil samples. (See the text and fig. 4.2 for the definition of crown height.)

If possible, the age profile of a fossil species should be calculated using mean unworn crown heights of teeth in the fossil sample. This is because unworn crown height may vary somewhat among populations of a species, following differences in mean individual size. However, if a particular fossil sample lacks measurable unworn crowns, the values below will produce an age profile whose shape should be basically reliable.

TABLE 4.2 Dental Shedding/Eruption Ages and Ages at Potential Ecological Longevity (PEL) Necessary to Calculate Age (Mortality) Profiles from Dental Crown Heights for the Species Listed in Table 4.1

	dP4 shed	M3 erupts	PEL
Eland (*Taurotragus oryx*)	37	24	240
Greater kudu (*Tragelaphus strepsiceros*)	28	21	192
Bushbuck (*T. scriptus*)	26	20	180
Blue antelope (*Hippotragus leucophaeus*)	30	22	216
Roan antelope (*H. equinus*)	30	22	216
Lechwe (*Kobus leche*)	28	18	192
Southern reedbuck (*Redunca arundinum*)	22	16	144
Mountain reedbuck (*R. fulvorufula*)	18	12	120
Vaalribbok (*Pelea capreolus*)	18	12	120
Cape hartebeest (*Alcelaphus buselaphus*)	28	22	216
"Giant hartebeest" (*Megalotragus priscus*)	48	36	288
Blesbok (*Damaliscus dorcas*)	30	22	216
Blue wildebeest (*Connochaetes taurinus*)	30	22	216
Black wildebeest (*C. gnou*)	30	22	216
Common springbok (*Antidorcas marsupialis*)	18	12	108
Southern springbok (*A. australis*)	18	12	108
Bond's springbok (*A. bondi*)	18	12	108
Gray duiker (*Sylvicapra grimmia*)	18	12	108
Steenbok (*Raphicerus campestris*)	12	9.5	72
Cape grysbok (*R. melanotis*)	12	9.5	72
Cape buffalo (*Syncerus caffer*)	48	36	288
"Giant buffalo" (*Pelorovis antiquus*)	60	48	360
Aurochs (*Bos primigenius*)	48	36	288

	dP4 shed	M1 erupts	M2 erupts	PEL
Red deer (*Cervus elaphus*)	26	6	12	192

	dP2 shed	P2 erupts	M3 erupts	PEL
Burchell's zebra (*Equus burchelli*)	36	36	36	264
"Giant Cape horse" (*E. capensis*)	46	46	46	324
Wild horse (*E. przewalskii*)	36	36	36	264

Note: The potential longevity estimates are based mainly on Mentis (1972) and on the assumption that longevity is very similar among closely related species of similar size.

The approximate ages of dental loss and eruption are based on Kerr and Roth (1970) and Attwell and Jeffrey (1980) for eland; on

that they facilitate comparisons among profiles from species with very different potential longevities.

The elk study did highlight one potentially important complication, however. Different permanent teeth do not all approach zero crown height at the same age. For example, in elk and other ungulates M1 approaches zero before M2 and M2 before M3. This reflects the order of eruption (M1 before M2 and M2 before M3), as well as the tendency for later erupting teeth to be higher crowned (M3 higher than M2 and M2 higher than M1). The regressions in the elk study suggest that, in elk, M1 approaches zero at 168 months, M2 at 210 months, and M3 at 215 months. For M1 this is 14% shorter than the potential ecological longevity of elk (= 192 months or 16 years), while for M2 it is 9% and for M3 12% longer. Hence, if a single figure of 192 months is used as potential longevity in calculating age from crown heights of each kind of tooth, ages calculated from M1 will tend to be overestimates, while those calculated from M2 and M3 will tend to be underestimates.

It is tempting to use the elk regressions to "correct" potential ecological longevity, so that each kind of permanent molar has its own figure. Thus, we could use potential longevity minus 14% as the longevity figure (AGEpel) in calculating ages from M1 crown heights. For M2 and M3, the corrected figures would be potential longevity plus 9% and plus 12%. However, we are not convinced that the elk regressions are truly satisfactory for making such corrections. This is particularly true for the regressions of age on M2 and M3 crown height, which are based on relatively few specimens. Additionally, our experimentation suggests that changing age at potential ecological longevity by 10-15% will only rarely alter the shape of an age profile materially, and it is on profile shape that we focus in interpretation. For the moment, then, we continue to use a single age at potential longevity for each tooth.

Simpson (1966) for kudu; on Simpson (1973) for bushbuck; on Robinette and Child (1964) for lechwe; on Irby (1979) for mountain reedbuck; on Mitchell (1965) for Lichtenstein's hartebeest (*Alcelaphus lichtensteini*) (as a proxy for Cape hartebeest); on Attwell (1980) and Attwell and Jeffrey (1980) for blue wildebeest; on von Richter (1971, 1974) for black wildebeest; on Rautenbach (1971) for common springbok; on Wilson and Roth (1967) for gray duiker; on Manson (1974) for grysbok; on Grimsdell (1973) for African buffalo; on Quimby and Gaab (1957), Lowe (1967), and Mitchell (1967) for red deer; and on Klingel (1965) and Smuts (1974) for Burchell's zebra. For the remaining species, the approximate ages of dental loss and eruption are based on those for closely related species of similar size. All ages are in months.

Some Problems in Constructing Age Profiles from Crown Heights

There are both theoretical and practical problems in constructing ungulate age profiles from crown heights. The principal theoretical problem is that the rate of crown attrition may vary significantly among populations of the same species. The principal practical problems are that not all teeth are equally suitable for the crown height method, and that crown height is sometimes difficult or impossible to measure on suitable teeth.

We know of only one case where the rate of crown attrition has been shown to differ significantly among living populations of the same ungulate species. The species is the domestic sheep in New Zealand and Australia, where the rate of incisor wear was found to increase as the amount of ingested soil (grit) increased (Healy 1965; Healy and Ludwig 1965; Ludwig, Healy, and Cutress 1966; Cutress and Healy 1965). In populations that ingested much soil, the incisors commonly wore to nubs at a relatively young age, and many individuals had to be culled in their reproductive prime because they could no longer feed themselves. One economic solution to the problem was simply to cut the stocking rate (number of sheep per hectare), reducing incisor wear and increasing longevity.

We think that the principle observed for these sheep probably applies to most wild ungulates as well. Large differences in dental wear rate probably do not occur among free-ranging populations of a single species, because the wear rate is intimately linked to potential longevity. In most ungulate populations, a dramatic increase in wear rate will lead to the premature death of reproductively active individuals. In the event of a drastic change in forage quality, it will thus be more economic (more adaptive) to reduce population numbers than to increase wear rate. We note that there are few empirical observations relevant to this, but in virtually all ungulate species for which there are data, observed potential longevity is very similar among widespread populations. Circumstantially, this suggests the populations do not differ dramatically in the rate of dental wear.

We note further that the wear rate is a function of potential longevity in the model we use to estimate age from crown height. Thus, for age profile construction, variation in wear rate among populations of one species would not matter, if the potential longevity of each population were known. The problem is, of course, that potential longevity is not known for fossil populations, and we must use a figure derived from observations on living ones. However, it may be shown mathematically that an error of 5-10% in estimated longevity would not materially affect the basic shape of an age profile based on the crown height method. We doubt that potential ecological longevity has ever differed among "natural" populations of one species by more than 10%, except perhaps over a time interval far shorter than that represented by most fossil samples.

The practical problems in constructing age profiles from crown heights may be approached more directly. In any given case, constructing a complete profile requires crown heights for a deciduous tooth and for a permanent tooth that erupts before the deciduous tooth is shed. In most cases, deciduous and permanent incisors and canines are less suitable than cheek teeth, because the rate of incisor and canine wear is clearly more variable among individuals. This is especially true of bovid and cervid incisors and canines (Spinage 1973; personal observation). Additionally, incisors and canines are usually less abundant than cheek teeth in fossil samples, reflecting their relative fragility. Finally, the incisors and canines of closely related species usually resemble each other more than the cheek teeth do. As a result, in many fossil samples, isolated incisors and canines are very difficult to assign to species.

In most cases, then, the most suitable teeth for constructing an age profile are the cheek teeth. In bovids and cervids, the best deciduous tooth is usually dP4, partly because it tends to be the most abundant deciduous tooth in fossil samples, reflecting its robusticity. It is also easy to recognize, even when isolated. In equids, where the deciduous teeth are more similar in durability, the best deciduous tooth is usually dP2 because it is easier to recognize than dP3 and dP4 when the teeth are isolated.

With regard to permanent teeth, in general the ones that replace deciduous precursors are least suitable for age profile construction. One reason is that an individual can have a heavily worn deciduous tooth and its unworn permanent replacement at the same time. If the teeth become isolated, as commonly happens in fossil samples, the same individual could be "aged" twice, biasing the resultant age profile. Additionally, in some species, especially bovids and cervids, the permanent premolars (which replace deciduous cheek teeth) are more variable in wear rate among individuals than the permanent molars (which have no deciduous precursors).

Hence, in most cases the best permanent tooth on which to base an age profile is a permanent molar--M1, M2, or M3. In most species M3 is preferable, because it is readily distinguishable from M1 and M2 when the teeth are isolated, whereas M1 and M2 may be very difficult to distinguish from one another. However, in some species M3 may not be suitable because it erupts only after the deciduous premolars are shed. The choice may thus have to be M1 or M2, and an effort must be made to distinguish isolated M1s from M2s by size or shape. For example, in some cervid and bovid species, the anterior and posterior walls of M1s tend to converge toward the roots, while the anterior and posterior walls of M2's are parallel sided (fig. 4.3). Alternatively, in some species, basal breadth, basal length, or the two together may be used to distinguish isolated M1s from M2s (fig. 4.4).

The second practical problem we address here is that crown height is not always directly measurable on suitable teeth. Crown height, as we define it, clearly cannot be measured on a tooth that lacks roots. In most species, the roots begin to develop long before a tooth is fully erupted, and the measurement of crown height is a problem only for tooth germs. If a germ is deciduous, we record it as "unworn" or "unerupted" and place the owner in the very youngest category in an age profile. (This can be done after the age profile has been calculated or by arbitrarily assigning the highest

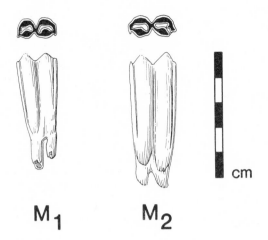

M_1 M_2

Damaliscus dorcas from Nelson Bay Cave

FIGURE 4.3: A lower M1 and M2 of the bontebok (*Damaliscus dorcas*) showing the tendency for the anterior and posterior walls of M1 to converge toward the crown base, while the walls of M2 are more nearly subparallel. A similar difference in shape characterizes M1s and M2s in many bovid and cervid species.

possible crown height to germs during calculation.) If a germ is permanent, we commonly ignore it, since the individual involved will also be represented by whatever deciduous tooth we are measuring.

However, there are some hyperhypsodont species, particularly equids, in which the permanent teeth come into occlusion before the roots are formed. In such species, of course, initial unworn crown height is not directly observable, but must be estimated from the highest crowned, least worn specimens in a sample. We ordinarily assign the estimated initial crown height to all specimens that were obviously in occlusion but had not yet developed roots.

A more common difficulty is measuring teeth that are still mounted in jaws. In relatively lowcrowned species, the base of the crown may be visible above the alveolus even in a freshly erupted tooth. However, in many very high crowned species, the base of the crown emerges from the alveolus only after the tooth has been in wear for some time. (In such species, the tooth continues to erupt at a pace that roughly equals the rate of crown reduction.)

There are two ways to measure the crown height of a tooth whose crown base (enamel/dentine junction) is masked by alveolar bone. One is to cut away the bone as carefully as possible. The other is to X-ray the bone. The X-ray alternative is usually not practical with maxillae. Because of their curvature, they cannot be laid flat on X-ray plates, and the resulting X-ray photographs may distort the crown height dimension. Mandibles,

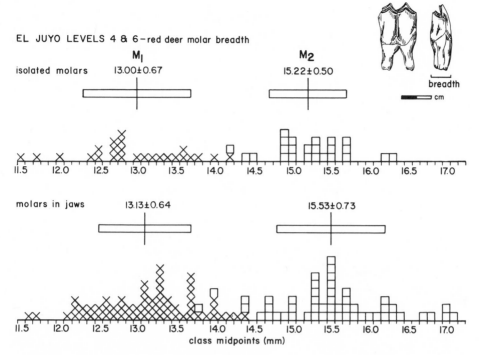

FIGURE 4.4: The basal breadth of red deer lower M1s and M2s from the Magdalenian cave site of El Juyo, Spain. The lower histogram shows breadths for teeth that were still in jaws. Their assignment to M1 or M2 was thus certain. Note that the known M2s tend to be consistently broader than the known M1s. The difference can be used to separate isolated ("unknown") teeth between M1 and M2 with reasonable certainty (upper histogram).

however, are sufficiently flat to avoid such distortion, and we have successfully measured mandibular crown heights from X-ray photos.

We inject one caution, however. In some samples, the age profile provided by mandibular teeth may differ from the one provided by maxillary specimens. This is true, for example, of the age profiles of medium sized antelopes in hyena-accumulated samples we have studied. In these samples, the average maxillary age tends to be significantly younger than the average mandibular age. The reason is probably that the hyenas readily transported antelope mandibles of all ages but had difficulty carrying the skulls of older animals. In any case, it is clear that both mandibular and maxillary age profiles may be necessary in many cases, and the only way to obtain them may be careful, surgical removal of the masking alveolar bone.

Interpretation of Age Profiles

Thanks primarily to studies by Kurtén (1953), Van Valen (1964), and Voorhies (1969) in paleontology and to work by Frison and his colleagues in archeology (Nimmo 1971; Frison 1978a,b; Reher 1978; Wilson 1980), many specialists now appreciate the interpretive possibilities of fossil age profiles. Most frequently, the profiles are interpreted with respect to two theoretically expectable models.

The first model is one in which successively older age classes contain progressively fewer individuals. This is the typical age profile of a living mammal population that is essentially stable in size and structure, a condition to which natural populations tend. This kind of age profile could become fixed in the fossil record if a living population were suddenly wiped out by a catastrophe, such as a flash flood, a volcanic eruption, or an epidemic disease. As a result, it is often known in paleobiology as a "catastrophic" age profile. In the context of a hunter-gatherer archeological site, a catastrophic age profile implies a hunting method such as the communal drive that nets individuals of various ages in proportion to their live abundance.

The second kind of theoretically expectable age profile is one in which prime age (reproductively active) adults are underrepresented relative to their live abundance, while very young and old individuals are overrepresented. Such a profile will contain those population members who die of starvation, accidents, predation, endemic disease, and other routine, attritional mortality factors that affect the very young and the old most heavily. In paleobiology, this kind of profile is commonly referred to as "attritional." In the context of a hunter-gatherer site, an attritional profile could imply scavenging from carcasses dead of "natural" causes. Alternatively, it may imply a hunting method, such as stalking with a thrusting spear, to which the weakest prey--the very young and the old-- are most vulnerable.

In species in which females usually bear one young or fewer per year, corresponding "catastrophic" and "attritional" profiles differ dramatically in shape (fig. 4.5, top). Both profiles have a large number of individuals in the youngest age class, reflecting a high birthrate as well as a high rate of infant mortality. They differ primarily in the representation of adults. A catastrophic profile resembles a flight of stairs descending from left to right (from youngest to oldest). Relative to an attritional profile, it has many prime age adults and few old ones.

The corresponding attritional profile comprises those individuals who die between successive age classes. Since the rate of mortality rises in late adulthood, an attritional mortality profile contains relatively many senile adults versus prime age ones. If the rise in mortality rate is dramatic, the attritional profile will be U-shaped, with a large peak in the youngest age class and a smaller one in a class beyond 40-50% of potential life span. However, if the rise in mortality rate is relatively small, the second peak may be imperceptible, leading to an L-shaped attritional profile with no obvious peaks beyond the one in the youngest age class (Eberhardt 1971; Klein 1982a).

In species in which females commonly bear more than one young per year, the rate of mortality is often high even in young adult age classes.

Corresponding catastrophic and attritional age profiles may then both resemble a flight of stairs descending from left to right (Fig. 4.5, bottom). The rise in mortality that characterizes older age classes may be almost imperceptible, except in samples far larger than faunal analysts are likely to have (Klein 1982a). Fortunately, many species that are common in archeological and paleontological sites are extant mammals in which females are known to bear one young or fewer per year. Alternatively, they are extinct species for which this reproductive rate can be inferred from close living relatives of similar size. This means that for many species it is possible to interpret fossil age profiles with respect to the clearly contrasting theoretical profiles of figure 4.5 (top).

We present some concrete examples of age profile interpretation in chapter 5. Here we note that interpretation of a fossil profile does not depend on identity with either of the two theoretically expectable types. Fossil samples may be deficient or rich in individuals of one or another age class for reasons that have nothing to do with mortality. Thus, very young individuals may be missing because their bones were selectively destroyed pre- or postdepositionally. Alternatively, for large species, older individuals may be underrepresented because the bone collector rarely introduced their bulky skulls to a site. Conversely, in the case of an archeological site, older individuals may be disproportionately abundant because the people valued their bones or teeth for artifact manufacture. The theoretical profiles thus provide only a partial basis for interpretation. Equally important in most cases is a knowledge of site context and associations.

Finally, it is clear that interpretable age profiles cannot be constructed from small samples. However, the minimum sample size for interpretation will depend on the mix of factors shaping an age profile. If only one overriding factor is responsible, then an interpretable profile may result from relatively few individuals; if multiple factors are subequally involved, then many individuals may be necessary. In general, a minimum of twenty-five individuals is probably essential, and larger--even much larger--numbers are highly desirable. This means that constructing an age profile using the quadratic formulae we presented in the previous section can be very tedious, and there is a strong possibility of calculation error. It was mainly to reduce tedium and the possibility of entry error that we wrote the program AGEPROF, described in chapter 7.

Comparing Age Profiles

In many cases, the interpretation of an age profile may depend in part on contrasts with other profiles. In such a case, the first step is commonly to determine the probability that two samples differ simply by chance. The most useful statistical procedure for this purpose is the Kolmogorov-Smirnov test (Siegel 1956; Blalock 1972). This test is not described in many standard statistical texts, and even where a description is available, the use of the test for comparing age profiles may not be obvious. We therefore discuss it briefly here. We note that it also has obvious potential for comparing patterns of skeletal part representation.

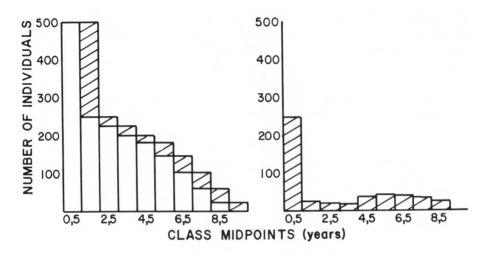

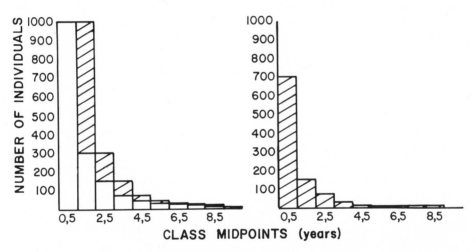

FIGURE 4.5: Top left: The age structure of a hypothetical population of large mammals in which females give birth once a year, total births are 500 per year, and potential individual longevity is 9 years (blank bars), and the number of individuals of each age that must die each year if the population size and age structure are to remain unchanged (hatched bars). Top right: A separate display of the hatched bars, reflecting the age profile of those individuals that die each year in the hypothetical population.

Bottom left: The age structure of a hypothetical population of large mammals in which females give birth twice a year, total births are 1000 per year, and potential individual longevity is 9 years (blank bars), and the number of individuals of each age class that must die each year if

The Kolmogorov-Smirnov test assumes that the categories or classes into which a sample has been subdivided may be arranged in a logical order. In the case of age classes, the obvious order is from younger to older. (In the case of skeletal part categories, the order may be the anatomical order in the skeleton or any other order that makes archeological or paleontological sense.) If two samples are to be compared, they must comprise the same number of classes arranged in the same logical order. Also, for maximum reliability, it is best if each sample comprises at least forty items.

The expression we use for Kolmogorov-Smirnov is

$$\max \text{P.D.}/[(n1 + n2)/(n1 \times n2)]^{1/2} ,$$

where n1 and n2 are the number of items in each of the samples to be compared, and "max P.D." is the greatest difference between the sample distributions expressed in cumulative percentage terms. Imagine, for example, two fossil samples, comprising 121 and 70 aged individuals respectively, divided among ten successive 10% of life span segments as follows:

Age Classes	Sample 1	Sample 2
1	20	44
2	17	2
3	13	3
4	23	0
5	23	2
6	16	9
7	3	5
8	4	5
9	2	0
10	0	0
Total	121	70

the population size and age structure are to remain unchanged (hatched bars). Bottom right: A separate display of the hatched bars, reflecting the age profile of those individuals that die each year in the hypothetical population.

In paleobiology, the patterns on the left, depicted by blank bars, are known as "catastrophic" age (mortality) profiles. The patterns on the right, depicted by hatched bars, are known as "attritional" age (mortality) profiles. Note the readily discernible difference in shape between the corresponding catastrophic and attritional profiles in the population in which females give birth only once a year (top) and the similarity in shape between the corresponding profiles in the population in which females give birth more than once year (bottom).

These profiles may be recast in cumulative terms as follows:

Age Classes	Raw Frequencies		Percentage Frequencies	
	(1)	(2)	(1)	(2)
	121	70	100	100
1	101	27	83	38
2	84	25	69	35
3	71	22	59	31
4	48	22	39	31
5	25	20	20	28
6	9	11	7	15
7	6	6	5	8
8	2	1	2	1
9	0	0	0	0
10	0	0	0	0

The maximum difference between the two cumulative percentage distributions occurs in age class 1. It is 45 (83 - 38), recorded as 0.45 (45%). The Kolmogorov-Smirnov value for determining the likelihood that the two distributions differ by chance alone is then

$$0.45/[(121 + 70)/(121 \times 70)]^{1/2} = 3.09.$$

A Kolmogorov-Smirnov value of 1.22 indicates a difference significant at the .10 level, a value of 1.36 a difference significant at the .05 level, a value of 1.63 a difference significant at the .01 level, and a value of 1.95 a difference significant at the .001 level. As in the case of other statistical tests, a difference significant at the .05 level (or below) is conventionally taken to indicate that two samples do not differ simply by chance. In conventional terms then, the Kolmogorov-Smirnov value calculated in our example could be used to argue that the samples involved reflect different mortality patterns.

Those familiar with the "chi-square test" will recognize a generic similarity to Kolmogorov-Smirnov, but Kolmogorov-Smirnov is more powerful and easier to evaluate in cases where there is a logical order to the categories into which samples are subdivided. In chapter 7, we present a short BASIC program that allows the user to compute Kolmogorov-Smirnov values by simply entering the original (noncumulative) raw frequencies in two age profiles.

Discontinuities in Age Distributions

In many species, virtually all the young are born at the same season each year. The season is usually the one in which conditions are optimal for survival. In addition, in some populations mortality may be largely a seasonal event, as a result of seasonal catastrophes like floods or blizzards or of seasonally restricted human hunts. In such a case, a fossilized sample of the population will exhibit a discontinuous age distribution comprising discrete age clusters with few intermediate individuals. A discontinuous age distribution will also result from seasonally restricted bone accumulation, even if mortality was more or less continuous.

It is sometimes assumed that a discontinuous age distribution can result only from catastrophic mortality, but Hulbert (1982) has shown that it can also result from attritional mortality. Hulbert's example involved a migratory species of fossil horse that was dying attritionally but was present in the area of bone accumulation only seasonally.

We pointed out previously that a discontinuous age distribution created by seasonally restricted birth and death may allow "aging" of fossil dentitions without comparison with modern known-age dentitions. More than this, inferring seasonal birth or seasonal bone accumulation may illuminate the ecology of a species or of the agent that collected its bones. For example, demonstrating seasonally limited bone accumulation at an archeological site is clearly important to reconstructing the total subsistence strategy of its ancient inhabitants. Discontinuous age distributions therefore have an interpretive potential separate from their use in "aging" fossil individuals from their teeth.

If a sample comprises many more or less complete demimandibles or maxillae, then age discontinuities may be obvious from a subjective evaluation of wear and eruption. In addition, Kurtén (1953) pointed out that age discontinuities should be apparent in the crown height distributions of hypsodont ungulates. This is fortunate because it means that seasonality may be detected even if a sample consists mainly of isolated teeth. An appropriate crown height measurement is the same one we suggested for constructing age profiles.

For a species characterized by seasonally restricted birth and death, Kurten reasoned that the crown heights of a permanent tooth (e.g., the M3) should form a series of discrete modes, each separated from adjacent modes by gaps of about the same length. Each mode reflects the mean crown height of a cohort of individuals all born at about the same time. The gaps between modes reflect the period of each year when individuals were wearing their teeth but could not reach the fossil site, either because there was no mortality or because the agent of bone accumulation was absent. The number of modes should be roughly equal to the potential ecological longevity of the species, minus the time between birth and the average age at which the analyzed tooth erupted.

One fruitful application of the method has been to confirm that bison drives at several archeological sites in the western United States were seasonal events (Frison 1978a, with references). However, in general the method has met little success, particularly in zooarcheology. There are several reasons for this.

First, it clearly requires very large samples. This is because there must be a sufficient number of teeth to demonstrate multiple modes. The problem is compounded by the absence of readily applicable statistical methods to confirm multimodality. The reality of the crown height modes must depend mainly on the visual impression they make.

Second, as formulated by Kurten, the method assumes a constant rate of crown height reduction in high crowned ungulates. In fact, the rate probably slows with age, as implied by Spinage's model for estimating age from crown height, discussed previously. This means that older (later) crown height modes will be more closely packed together and may be very difficult to discern except in extremely large samples. One possible way around this problem is to analyze the distribution of ages calculated from crown heights rather than the crown heights themselves. This is why the program AGEPROF, described in chapter 7, produces a list of estimated individual ages, in addition to grouping the ages into successive 10% of life span intervals.

However, the principal problem is that, in most species, like-aged individuals probably vary greatly in crown height. This is clearly true of the known-age Rocky Mountain elk studied by Klein, Allwarden, and Wolf (1983). The crown heights of elk in adjacent age cohorts overlapped extensively even though the mean crown heights of the cohorts differed significantly. Overlap was particularly great among older cohorts. The result was that no multimodal crown height pattern could be discerned even though the elk sample comprised more than 150 individuals whose births and deaths were known to be seasonally restricted.

In general, the crown height method of demonstrating seasonal bone accumulation is most promising when applied to a species that is very high crowned relative to potential individual longevity. In such a species, the individuals in any given age cohort will lose a substantial amount of crown height each year, so that the gaps between mean crown heights in adjacent cohorts will be relatively large. The result should be modes that are easier to discern visually. However, our experience suggests that even for a very high-crowned, short-lived species, truly enormous samples may be necessary to demonstrate convincing multimodality.

It is in this context that the cementum annulus method may perhaps be most useful to faunal analysts. If an annular pattern can be identified in the cementum of a sufficient number of teeth, and if the outer band is consistently the narrow, dense one or the broad, less dense one, it would be reasonable to infer seasonally restricted bone accumulation. Benn (1974) and Kay (1974) demonstrated the principle on white-tailed deer teeth from Woodland sites in Iowa and Missouri. Spiess (1979) extended it to ungulate (mainly reindeer) teeth from an Upper Paleolithic site in southwestern France, while Gordon (1980) is applying it to reindeer from several French Paleolithic sites.

5: INTERPRETING NISPS, MNIS, AGE/SEX PROFILES, AND

DESCRIPTIVE STATISTICS IN FAUNAL ANAYLSIS

In this chapter we show how the NISPs, MNIs, age/sex profiles and descriptive statistics computed by the programs in part 2 can provide meaningful information about the past. We stress numerical comparisons between fossil samples, and we rely heavily on examples from our own experience. However, the issues we address are of broad significance within faunal analysis. They include the interpretation of skeletal part abundance, species abundance, age and sex composition, and mean individual size in fossil samples.

Skeletal Element Representation

Skeletal part abundance in a fossil species sample can be represented by the number of identified specimens (NISP) per part or by the minimum number of individuals (MNI) the specimens come from. The program MNI (chap. 6) provides both numbers for each skeletal part, as illustrated in fig. 6.14. Both are relevant to understanding patterns of skeletal element representation, though we depend more on the MNI for reasons discussed in chapter 3.

In chapter 1 we pointed out that a fossil sample is the product of several stages, beginning with the life assemblage (a live community of animals), the death assemblage (the portion of the live community available to a bone accumulator), the deposited assemblage (the bones actually deposited at a site), and the fossil assemblage (the bones that survive until excavation or collection). By definition, all skeletal parts of a species have identical MNIs in the life and death assemblages, because these comprise whole animals or whole carcasses. Yet in all the fossil samples we are aware of, different skeletal parts of the same species have very different MNIs.

The differences are often too great to be explained by chance (sampling). They must therefore have originated when the death assemblage was transformed into the deposited assemblage, when the deposited assemblage was transformed into the fossil assemblage, or when the fossil assemblage was sampled during excavation. In fact, the MNI discrepancies in most fossil samples are probably due to a complex mix of events that occurred during all three transformations. We focus here on the first two transformations, since their effects on a particular sample cannot be established experimentally. Rather, they must be inferred using NISPs, MNIs, and information on sample context and associations.

The Transformation from the Death Assemblage to the Deposited Assemblage

The transformation from the death assemblage to the deposited assemblage is primarily a reflection of collector behavior. Since most analysts study skeletal part abundance to reconstruct this behavior, it is natural that they have focused primarily on this transformation. It is also the transformation that is most readily observed under modern, natural conditions or in laboratory simulations.

There are two ways in which a collector may cause the MNIs for different skeletal parts of a species to diverge from parity. First, it may selectively destroy certain parts in dismembering or consuming a carcass. Second, it may carry the most portable or desirable parts to another locality, leaving less portable or less desirable parts at the carcass site.

Brain (1981, with references) has illustrated how human butchering and consumption practices may favor the survival of some skeletal parts over others. He studied goat bones found in and around Hottentot villages along the Kuiseb River in the Namib Desert. The causes of bone destruction were directly observable. They included killing, butchering and skinning, cooking, marrow extraction, and finally chewing both by people and by domestic dogs. Brain found a clear correlation between bone hardness and the likelihood that a bone would survive these destructive pressures. Thus, with regard to a given goat limb bone, the epiphysis that was denser and fused earlier was invariably more common than the epiphysis that was less dense and fused later. He also found that small, compact bones such as the astragalus had a better chance of survival than broad, thin ones like the scapula blade.

Brain's elegant study demonstrates that MNI discrepancies among skeletal parts of a fossil species are to be expected, if only because different parts differ in durability. Brain's study pertains only to the transformation from the death assemblage to the deposited assemblage, but durability factors are surely important in the transformation from the deposited assemblage to the fossil assemblage as well. We return to this point below.

Several authors have stressed transportation as a factor that can alter skeletal part numbers between the death assemblage and the deposited assemblage. Perkins and Daly (1968) pointed out that transportation would be particularly important in the case of a large animal whose carcass was far from the home base of a human hunter-gatherer group. The hunters would butcher the carcass where it lay and take home only the choicest or most useful parts. In the case of a small animal or one whose carcass was obtained near home, the hunters would bring back a wider variety of parts, perhaps even the whole animal. Perkins and Daly used these considerations to explain a striking difference between wild sheep and wild cattle at the "Neolithic" hunter-gatherer site of Suberde in Turkey. The sheep were well represented by a much wider variety of skeletal parts than the cattle were. Perkins and Daly coined the term "schlepp effect" to describe the portability factors that probably explain the difference.

The schlepp effect has been observed in many archeological faunal samples, including most of those we have studied. As an example, we present data for bovids of two very different sizes from the Upper Pleistocene and early Holocene layers of Boomplaas Cave A, South Africa. The bovid bones were introduced to Boomplaas primarily, if not entirely, by its Stone Age inhabitants. Based on MNIs, figure 5.1 shows that the smaller bovids are well represented by a wider range of skeletal parts than the larger bovids are. Kolomogorov-Smirnov results presented in the caption of figure 5.1 show that there is only a small probability that the difference in skeletal part representation is due to chance.

To some extent, the difference may reflect a durability bias in favor of small bovid bones and an excavation-recovery bias against them, especially against the very smallest ones. However, given the magnitude and nature of the difference, we think the schlepp effect is the principal cause. The Boomplaas people probably brought back only selected parts of larger bovids but introduced smaller bovids intact. The MNI differences within the smaller bovid category largely follow the pattern predictable from differences in bone durability, as described by Brain. Hence, these differences probably arose mainly from selective pre- and postdepositional destruction after introduction to the site.

Binford (1978, 1981) has focused on the qualities of a bone that determine whether hunters will transport it from a carcass site to another locality. He argues that the utility of a bone depends on the meat, marrow, and bone grease that can be obtained from it. By quantifying the amount of each substance on different skeletal parts, he arrives at a "general utility index" (GUI) for each part. Binford also notes that butchering practices may cause some "low-utility" parts to be transported as "riders" attached to "high-utility" parts. Taking this into account, he arrives at a "modified general utility index" (MGUI) for each part.

The MGUI is directly useful only for interpreting skeletal part numbers in assemblages that have not suffered much attrition during and after deposition. Speth (1983) has used the MGUI to analyze such an assemblage from the Garnsey Site, a fifteenth century bison kill site in New Mexico. As at many kill sites throughout the world, low utility bones such as skulls, atlases, and axes were disproportionately well represented at Garnsey. The implication is that high-utility bones were selectively removed for processing of meat, marrow, or grease elsewhere. Interestingly, Speth found a difference between the sexes in the extent to which high-utility bones had been removed. Among the high utility bones, male ones had been taken away more commonly than female ones. The reason is probably that males were in better condition than females during the season of the year (spring) when the kill occurred. In other words, within the general high-utility category at Garnsey, male bones were of higher utility than female bones.

One important methodological implication of Speth's work is that the sex ratio for a skeletal part in the deposited assemblage may differ greatly from the ratio in the death assemblage if the part differs in utility between the sexes. In species such as bison, where one sex tends to be in better condition than the other depending upon the season, the sex ratio really should be calculated for each skeletal part if it is to be meaningfully interpreted. Unfortunately, there are few archeological faunal samples in which it is possible to calculate a sex ratio for more than one or two skeletal parts.

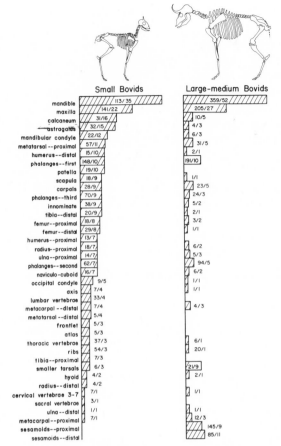

	Small Bovids	Large-medium Bovids
mandible	113/35	359/52
maxilla	141/22	205/27
calcaneum	31/16	10/5
astragalus	32/15	4/3
mandibular condyle	22/12	6/3
metatarsal--proximal	57/11	31/5
humerus--distal	15/10	2/1
phalanges--first	148/10	191/10
patella	19/10	
scapula	18/9	1/1
carpals	28/9	23/5
phalanges--third	70/9	24/3
innominate	38/9	5/2
tibia--distal	20/9	2/1
femur--proximal	18/8	3/2
femur--distal	29/8	1/1
humerus--proximal	13/7	
radius--proximal	18/7	6/2
ulna--proximal	14/7	5/3
phalanges--second	62/7	94/5
naviculo-cuboid	16/7	6/2
occipital condyle	9/5	1/1
axis	7/4	1/1
lumbar vertebrae	33/4	
metacarpal--distal	7/4	4/3
metatarsal--distal	5/4	
frontlet	5/3	
atlas	5/3	
thoracic vertebrae	37/3	6/1
ribs	54/3	20/1
tibia--proximal	7/3	
smaller tarsals	6/3	21/9
hyoid	4/2	2/1
radius--distal	4/2	
cervical vertebrae 3-7	7/1	1/1
sacral vertebrae	3/1	
ulna--distal	1/1	1/1
metacarpal--proximal	7/1	12/3
sesamoids--proximal		145/9
sesamoids--distal		85/11

BOOMPLAAS

FIGURE 5.1: The minimum number of individuals (MNI) per skeletal part of small bovids and large-medium bovids in the fossil sample from the Upper Pleistocene and Holocene layers of Boomplaas Cave A. For the purposes of MNI calculation, the bones in each size category were treated as if they came from a single species in a single layer. In the context of the Boomplaas sample, small bovids include steenbok/grysbok (*Raphicerus* spp.) and klipspringer (*Oreotragus oreotragus*). Large medium bovids comprise wildebeest (*Connochaetes* spp.), hartebeest (*Alcelaphus buselaphus*), blesbok (*Damaliscus dorcas*), blue antelope (*Hippotragus leucophaeus*), and kudu (*Tragelaphus strepsiceros*). Background information on the Boomplaas site may be found in H. J. Deacon (1979). The skeletal parts have been ordered according to their abundance in the small bovids (where a tie occurred, the more proximal element was placed first).

The figure shows that there is a sharp difference in skeletal part representation between the two bovid size classes (Kolmogorov-Smirnov $Z = 2.61$, $p < .001$). In general, skeletal part representation in the large medium bovids is skewed toward a smaller range of skeletal parts. This probably means that many parts of large medium bovids were left with the carcass, and only selected parts were commonly returned to the

Transportation factors may also affect skeletal part numbers in assemblages formed by flowing water (Voorhies 1969; Behrensmeyer 1975; Hanson 1980). We have suggested that water transport accounts for the paucity of relatively small bones and the abundance of large flat ones in the faunal sample from the Acheulean (mid-Pleistocene) site of Torralba, central Spain (Klein and Cruz-Uribe 1984). At Torralba, as at other sites where flowing water has played a prominent role in bone accumulation, many of the bones are obviously abraded (rounded).

Transportation also affects skeletal part numbers in assemblages deposited by carnivores. We illustrate this from our analysis of two large early Upper Pleistocene samples collected by hyenas at Swartklip 1 and Equus Cave, both in the Cape Province, South Africa. At both sites, hyena coprolites abound, while artifacts and porcupine-gnawed bones are rare or absent. It is this above all that establishes hyenas as the principal bone collectors versus the other two prime candidates--people and porcupines.

Using MNIs, table 5.1 shows that, at both Swartklip and Equus Cave, small ungulates are proportionately better represented by cranial bones, while large ungulates are proportionately better represented by postcranial bones. In other words, in both samples the cranial/postcranial ratio tends to decrease with ungulate size.

We have not observed the same tendency in samples that were accumulated by people, as indicated by the abundance of artifacts, hearths, and so forth, and the rarity or absence of carnivore coprolites and porcupine-gnawed bones. Table 5.1 shows, for example, that the cranial/postcranial ratio tends to increase with ungulate size in the samples from the Upper Pleistocene archeological sites of Boomplaas Cave A and Klasies River Mouth Cave 1, also in the Cape Province, South Africa. We specifically chose these samples because they are broadly comparable in size to the hyena samples and also because they allow us to control for the effects of bone preservation. Preservation is similar between Klasies 1 and Swartklip and much better than at Boomplaas and Equus Cave, between which it is also similar. Yet, in respect to the gross cranial/postcranial ratio, Klasies is clearly like Boomplaas, and Swartklip is just as clearly like Equus Cave.

---

site. In contrast, small bovid carcasses were probably often returned intact. Pre- and postdepositional destructive pressures probably account for most of the discrepancies in skeletal part abundance within the small bovid category, and also for some of the discrepancies within the large medium category.

The same kind of contrast between small and large ungulates in skeletal part representation has been observed at many sites. The general reasons are probably the same in all cases, though the precise patterns of skeletal part representation differ from site to site, reflecting complex differences in pre- and postdepositional histories.

TABLE 5.1 Minimum Number of Bovid and Equid Individuals Represented by Cranial Parts and by Postcranial Parts in the Fossil Hyena Lairs at Swartklip 1 and Equus Cave (layers 1b-2b) and in the Stone Age Sites of Klasies River Mouth Cave 1 (Upper Pleistocene levels) and Boomplaas Cave A (Upper Pleistocene and Holocene levels)

	Hyena Lairs		Stone Age Sites	
	Swartklip 1	Equus Cave	Klasies 1	Boomplaas
Small bovids	*1.5* (27:18)	*5.81* (64:11)	*0.51* (26:51)	*2.19* (35:16)
Small-medium bovids	*1.8* (18:10)	*5.56* (606:109)	*0.29* (15:51)	*3.25* (39:12)
Large-medium bovids	*0.59* (26:44)	*2.26* (183:81)	*0.94* (32:34)	*4.78* (52:11)
Zebra/quagga	*1.00* (1:1)	*1.55* (62:40)	*1.00* (1:1)	*4.00* (12:3)
Large bovids	*0.60* (6:10)	*0.77* (10:13)	*1.10* (50:46)	*6.50* (13:2)
Very large bovids	*1.00* (1:1)	----	*3.00* (30:10)	---- (3:0)

Note: Each MNI was calculated as if the skeletal parts involved came from a single species in a single layer. The ungulate categories are listed in order of increasing size from top to bottom. The italicized figures are the quotients obtained by dividing the postcranial MNIs into the cranial ones. The MNIs (cranial:postcranial) are presented in parentheses.

The table shows the clear tendency for the cranial:postcranial ratio to decrease with ungulate size in the hyena lairs and to increase with size in the Stone Age sites. This almost certainly reflects a difference in bone collecting behavior between hyenas and people, as discussed in the text. For any given size category, the ratios tend to be higher in the Equus Cave and Boomplaas samples because they are much more highly fragmented. As a result there are fewer identifiable postcranial bones relative to teeth.

There are no published observations on living hyenas that could explain the tendency for the cranial/postcranial ratio to decrease with ungulate size in fossil hyena samples. However, the reason is probably that hyenas tend to destroy small bones completely, while they have difficulty transporting bulky bones like large ungulate skulls from a carcass site. In support of this, we note that large ungulate postcranial bones in the fossil hyena samples come almost entirely from adults, whose limb bones are most durable, while large ungulate cranial bones come overwhelmingly from very young animals, whose skulls are most portable. We have not observed the same phenomenon in undoubted archeological samples.

The reason the ungulate cranial/postcranial ratio behaves differently in archeological samples is probably because people destroy fewer small bones completely, and, unlike hyenas, they can cooperate to carry bulky items from a carcass site. The fact that large ungulate cranial bones in hyena lairs may come from younger animals than the postcranial bones has important methodological implications. Vrba (1975, 1976, 1980), for example, used the percentage of juvenile antelopes in bone samples from South African australopithecine sites to determine whether the bone collector was a primary predator or a scavenger. She suggested that a high proportion of juveniles, comparable with that in a living antelope population, implied primary predation. Whatever the merits of this idea, Vrba used only cranial material (teeth) to determine the proportion of juveniles in her fossil assemblages. Our data indicate that the proportion might be very different if postcranial material were also taken into account. More generally, our data suggest that the percentage of juveniles in an assemblage may say more about the collector's ability to transport or destroy bones than about its role as a scavenger or a primary predator.

There are additional contrasts between fossil samples accumulated by hyenas and those accumulated by people. For example, at Swartklip, there are a very large number of nearly complete long bone shafts lacking epiphyses, while at Klasies 1 there are hardly any. The reason is almost certainly that hyenas often chew off the epiphyses, while people tend to enter a long bone through the shaft. This contrast cannot be demonstrated between Equus Cave and Boomplaas because postdepositional processes at these sites broke both shafts and epiphyses into small fragments. This is an example of how information contained in a deposited assemblage may be lost in the transformation to the fossil assemblage.

The Transformation from the Deposited Assemblage to the Fossil Assemblage
We know of no studies that have focused in detail on the transformation from the deposited assemblage to the fossil assemblage. In fact, specialists have commonly assumed that this transformation is relatively unimportant. For example, it has sometimes been assumed that bone fragmentation can be attributed entirely to collector behavior. Thus, Brain (1981 and elsewhere) has suggested that a high degree of bone fragmentation indicates human as opposed to carnivore activity, based on the assumption that human food preparation is generally more destructive.

However, in the eighty-five African and European samples we have studied, the degree of fragmentation clearly varies independently of the accumulator. For example, compared with most African Pleistocene assemblages, the one from Klasies River Mouth Cave 1 is hardly fragmented at all. It contains numerous complete epiphyses and many complete or nearly complete tooth rows. In contrast, the assemblage from Boomplaas is more typical. Fragmentation is extensive. Most epiphyses are incomplete, and tooth rows are rare. Yet in both cases the principal bone accumulators were certainly people.

The assemblage from Swartklip resembles the one from Klasies in the low degree of fragmentation, while the Equus Cave assemblage is highly fragmented like that from Boomplaas. Yet the principal accumulators at Swartklip and Equus Cave were probably hyenas. These examples and others we could cite show clearly that bone fragmentation is not simply a function of the collector. In fact, in the samples we have studied, the only qualities that correlate closely with a high degree of fragmentation are the extent to which a sample has been leached and the extent to which it has been compacted in the ground. We conclude that that these postdepositional factors are a major cause of bone fragmentation.

In sum, based on our experience, the transformation from the deposited assemblage to the fossil assemblage cannot be ignored. In many cases, it was probably as eventful as the transformation from the death assemblage to the deposited assemblage.

One reason that postdepositional factors have attracted so little explicit attention is that they are difficult or impossible to recreate or to observe directly. It is here that the comparative approach we advocated in chapter 1 becomes especially relevant. We illustrate this with an example from El Juyo Cave in northern Spain (Klein, Allwarden, and Wolf 1983; Freeman, Klein, and Gonzalez Echegaray 1983; Barandiaran et al. 1984).

El Juyo contains three meters of deposits with artifacts, animal bones, and "features," all assigned to the north Spanish "Lower Magdalenian Culture." So far the excavations have been confined mainly to levels 4 and 6 at the top of the sequence. (The layers overlying level 4 are largely sterile and are substantially younger than the Magdalenian occupation. Level 5 is a mostly sterile layer between 4 and 6.) Charcoal from level 4 has been dated to $13,920 \pm 240$ B.P. (I-10736). Level 6 is bracketed between this date and one of $14,440 \pm 180$ B.P. (I-10738) on charcoal from underlying level 7.

The faunal samples from levels 4 and 6 are identical in species composition. Red deer bones dominate heavily, followed by bones of roe deer, horse, bison or aurochs, and ibex. Carnivores are represented as traces. The age profiles calculated from the abundant red deer teeth are "catastrophic" in both levels. The implication is that the occupants of levels 4 and 6 acquired red deer in much the same way. They probably drove whole herds over cliffs or into corrals, deep snow, or other traps where individuals were equally vulnerable regardless of age.

The faunal samples obviously differ in one important respect, however--the bones in level 4 are much more heavily fragmented than those in level 6. This is clearly reflected in in the overall red deer NISP/MNI ratios. Level 4 has provided more red deer bones than level 6 (1,662 vs. 1,462), but fewer than half the minimum number of individuals (17 vs. 38).

There is no reason to suppose that the difference in fragmentation is due to a difference in human behavior. The artifacts associated with bones in both layers are virtually identical, while associated pollens imply the same external environment (Boyer-Klein 1982). Certainly there is no evidence for the kind of environmental deterioration that might have induced people to seek more nourishment from bones.

What does differ between the two levels is sedimentary context, largely reflecting a change in drainage within the cave. Thus, level 4 is mainly a 1-2 cm band within a thick stalagmitic boss, while level 6 is mainly a 20-30 cm layer of clay below the boss. Clearly, the bones in level 4, resting on a hard substrate, would have been far more subject to trampling, kicking, and other postdepositional destructive pressures than those in level 6. This is almost certainly what accounts for the greater fragmentation in level 4.

Given that postdepositional factors probably explain the difference in fragmentation between the two levels, it is instructive to compare their patterns of skeletal part abundance, as shown by MNIs in figure 5.2. As in most fossil samples, the most common elements in both cases are dentitions, reflecting their great durability. We note, however, that the dentitions in level 4 are almost all isolated teeth, while those in level 6 are mainly demimandibles and maxillae. This can be inferred from the mandibular and maxillary NISP/MNI ratios, which are much higher in level 4 than in level 6.

In addition, the levels contrast sharply in the abundance of various postcranial parts, and the difference is highly "significant" as shown by the Kolmogorov-Smirnov results in the caption to figure 5.2. Relative to level 6, level 4 is particularly rich in carpals, tarsals, and sesamoids, all small, hard, compact bones that are particularly likely to survive mechanical crunching against a hard stalagmitic substrate. Level 4 is also rich in phalanges. These too are relatively hard, compact bones. Equally important, compared with many other bones, they tend to retain their identifiability, even when they are highly fragmented.

In sum, the difference in skeletal part representation between levels 4 and 6 is precisely what would be expected if the level 4 bones had been subjected to much more severe post-depositional destructive pressure. On the model of level 4, we suggest that any archeological assemblage that is comparably rich in small, hard, compact bones has probably suffered greatly from postdepositional destruction.

This is particularly true if most of the teeth in the assemblage are isolated and if identifiable fragments of mandibular or maxillary bone are very rare, as in level 4. We think it is highly unlikely that people could remove the mandibular and maxillary bone so thoroughly without damaging the teeth. It is far more likely that the removal occurred in the ground, after the relatively thin alveolar bone had been significantly weakened by the loss of collagen and by partial decalcification. Human activity may have hastened the process, since many of the mandibles in level 6 show considerable butchering damage. Particularly common is the removal of the inferior margin of the mandible to expose the marrow cavity. Noe-Nygaard (1977) has illustrated several red deer mandibles from northern European Mesolithic sites, "butchered" in this way.

Most of the southern African samples we have studied are even more highly fragmented than the one from El Juyo level 4. At the southern African sites, examining the bones and their context indicates that the

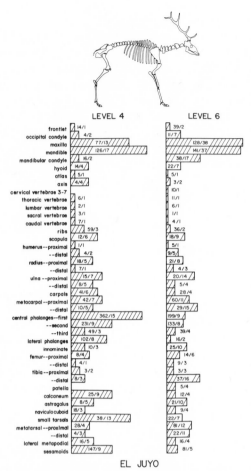

FIGURE 5.2: Skeletal parts of red deer (*Cervus elaphus*) from levels 4 and 6 of El Juyo Cave (1978-79 excavations). In this case, the skeletal parts have been ordered anatomically from most proximal to most distal. "-/-" is the number of bones or bone fragments (NISP)/the minimum number of individuals (MNI) represented. The bars are proportional to the MNI's. Whether judged by the NISPs or the MNIs, the patterns of skeletal part representation differ strongly between the two levels (Kolmogorov-Smirnov value for the difference between the levels in MNI's = 1.58, p < .05). The reason for the difference is probably a difference in postdepositional history, as discussed in the text.

principal cause of extreme fragmentation was postdepositional leaching, coupled with very slow sedimentation. Like the El Juyo level 4 sample, the southern African samples are usually dominated by isolated teeth, and they lack identifiable pieces of mandibular and maxillary bone.

Figure 5.3 shows that there is a basic resemblance between the pattern of skeletal part representation in the red deer sample from El Juyo 4 and in the highly fragmented sample of red deer-sized bovids from Boomplaas

Cave. This was the expected result, since the collectors in both cases were Stone Age people, while intense postdepositional pressure was the principal cause of fragmentation. However, figure 5.3 also shows that there is a difference between El Juyo 4 and Boomplaas on the one hand and the highly fragmented sample of red deer-sized bovids from Equus Cave on the other. Carpals, tarsals, and sesamoids are proportionately much rarer at Equus Cave. These bones are also proportionately much rarer at Swartklip than at Klasies River Mouth, at both of which postdepositional destruction and fragmentation were much more restricted. We think that carpals, tarsals, and sesamoids are rarer at Equus Cave and Swartklip because the hyena collectors frequently swallowed them whole. Even in the unlikely event that carpals and other small bones retained their form in the hyena's digestive system, they would often have been deposited in scats away from the site.

There are several general conclusions to be drawn from the El Juyo example. First, we cannot assume that the pattern of skeletal part representation in a fossil sample simply reflects the behavior of the bone collector. Binford (1981), for example, assumes that the only factors affecting skeletal part numbers in a fossil assemblage are predepositional transportation and destruction by the collector. To establish the effects of transportation, he "corrects" for destruction by multiplying skeletal part numbers in a fossil assemblage by a factor reflecting differential bone durability. The "pristine" numbers that result are the original numbers in the assemblage before it was "ravaged" by a predepositional destructive agent (e.g., a carnivore).

This procedure is seductive, but the same differential durability factors that promote bone survival in the face of predepositional destructive pressures also promote it in the face of postdepositional ones. Hence, there is no way to know whether the "corrected" numbers that Binford obtains closely resemble the original ("pristine") numbers (in the transported assemblage) or not. More generally, unless the effects of pre- and postdepositional destructive pressures can somehow be separated, we see little point in pursuing a method like Binford's. There is the further problem of determining whether Binford's multiplier or any other adequately reflects differential bone durability in the face of a variable and often complex mix of pre- and postdepositional destructive pressures.

Considered with the samples from Klasies River Mouth, Boomplaas, Equus Cave, and Swartklip, the El Juyo case shows further that MNI and NISP comparisons between samples should be controlled for quality of preservation and degree of fragmentation. Samples that are very differently preserved or fragmented may differ in structure for this reason alone, and not because of a difference in ancient environment or in collector behavior. Yet most faunal reports, including ones we have published, treat the degree of fragmentation and the quality of preservation very casually, if at all. At the very least, reports should provide some indication of how common isolated teeth are compared with tooth rows and how common broken epiphyses are compared with whole ones. More generally, we

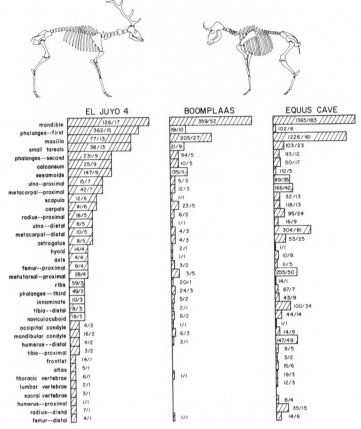

FIGURE 5.3: Skeletal part representation in red deer from El Juyo Cave level 4, in red-deer-sized (large medium) bovids from Boomplaas Cave A (Upper Pleistocene and Holocene levels), and in red deer-sized bovids from Equus Cave (layers 1b-2b). The bars are proportional to the MNIs. The skeletal parts have been ordered according to their abundance in the El Juyo sample.

All three patterns differ from one another in the strictly statistical sense (Kolmogorov-Smirnov Z for the MNIs > 1.36, p < .05), reflecting differences in bone collector and in postdepositional history. The El Juyo and Boomplaas samples were collected by Stone Age people, while the Equus Cave sample was collected by hyenas. Postdepositional leaching and compaction have strongly affected all three samples, particularly the ones from Equus Cave and Boomplaas. In the Boomplaas sample, even teeth have begun to decompose.

Given the high degree of postdepositional destruction, it is understandable that teeth predominate in all three samples. Teeth are especially abundant in the Boomplaas and Equus Cave samples, which suffered the most. After teeth, the most abundant bones in the El Juyo and Boomplaas samples are carpals, tarsals, sesamoids, first phalanges, and second phalanges. This is understandable since, after teeth,

emphasize the utility of the MNI/NISP index as a succinct and reasonably objective measure of fragmentation, particularly when it is presented for each skeletal part.

Finally, it is clear from the El Juyo case that a knowledge of the context of a fossil sample is vital to understanding its structure. A faunal analyst should always request pertinent information from the excavator and should avoid samples where the information is vague or otherwise inadequate. Better yet, the faunal analyst should visit the site and, if possible, participate in the excavations.

Species Abundance

In general, the initial effect of postdepositional destructive pressure will be to raise NISPs and depress MNIs. Later, NISPs will fall as well, and in the extreme case all bone will be leached from a site. Thus, postdepositional destructive factors may greatly alter absolute species abundance, whether measured by the NISP or the MNI. In general, they probably affect relative abundance much less. However, we cannot assume that relative abundance will be unaltered, and it is probably unwise to compare relative species abundance between samples with very different postdepositional histories. This is particularly true if the analyst is searching for differences in relative abundance that reflect differences in ancient environment or collector behavior.

Like the interpretation of skeletal part abundance, the interpretation of species abundance depends heavily on a knowledge of site context. Particularly important are associated cultural debris, coprolites, or other items that inform mainly on the collector, and pollens, sediments, or geochemical/geophysical analyses that inform mainly on the ancient environment. If associated items indicate that two faunal samples were collected by the same agent, then the most likely reason for any difference in relative species abundance is a difference in ancient environment. This is especially so if associated pollens, sediments, or geochemical data point to a difference in environment. The reverse is true as well. If associated objects suggest different collectors, while sediments, pollen, and so on, imply a similar paleoenvironment, collector behavior probably explains any difference in relative species abundance.

Establishing adequate controls on the environment and the collector is the essence of the comparative approach that we outlined in chapter 1. It is not possible to judge controls in the abstract; they must be evaluated for

---

carpals, tarsals, and sesamoids would resist postdepositional destructive pressure best, while first and second phalanges tend to remain identifiable even when highly fragmented. Yet carpals, tarsals, sesamoids, and phalanges are relatively much less common in the Equus Cave sample. This probably reflects their predepositional destruction by hyenas, as discussed in the text.

each case. We present four major cases here where we think the controls are very good. The cases illustrate differences in species abundance that are probably due to differences in environment, to differences in behavior between different kinds of Stone Age people, and to differences in behavior between Stone Age people and hyenas.

Species Abundance and Changes in Environment
We are mainly interested in faunal samples from the Quaternary period, because of their special potential to illuminate the evolution of human behavior. We think that most long-term changes in relative species abundance that are apparent from Quaternary samples probably reflect changes in environment. We outline a European case in which shifts in abundance have been documented by a mixture of NISPs and MNIs and an African case where they have been shown mainly by MNIs. The NISPs, MNIs, or both have been published previously in sources we cite.

Bordes and Prat (1965) and Delpeche (1975) have shown that the later Pleistocene faunal history of southwestern France was characterized by three distinct reindeer peaks separated by periods during which horse, bison/aurochs, or red deer dominated separately or together. The first reindeer peak occurred during the late Acheulean, the second during the early Mousterian, and the third during the late Upper Paleolithic (Solutrean/Magdalenian). Thus, there is no obvious correlation with "culture." There is, however, a clear correlation with cold, dry climate, as reflected in both sediments and pollens. The implication is that the reindeer peaks reflect changes in climate rather than changes in human behavior.

Klein (1980a, with references) has shown a comparable pattern of faunal change at the extreme southwestern tip of Africa. This region has a Mediterranean climate and a very distinctive vegetation commonly known as "Cape Macchia" and locally as fynbos. Fynbos communities typically include many shrubs with small, hard leaves that are capable of withstanding summer drought. Other plants vary in abundance from community to community, but grasses are generally rare. Accordingly, the historical large mammal fauna of the fynbos region was dominated by grysbok, steenbok, bushbuck, bushpig, Cape buffalo, and other species that are at home in shrubby or bushy settings. Typical African grassland species such as zebra, wildebeest, and springbok were rare or absent. Yet there are many late Middle and Upper Pleistocene faunal samples in which such grassland species dominate completely.

Some of the Pleistocene samples were collected by Middle Stone Age people, some by Later Stone Age people, and some by carnivores. For some of the samples, independent paleoenvironmental evidence is lacking. However, there are several others with associated sedimentological and less commonly paleobotanical data. In each case where grassland species dominate, the associated data suggest a much cooler, generally drier climate than the historical (or Holocene) one. In contrast, where late Pleistocene samples similar in species composition to the historical one are known, sedimentological evidence, geochemical evidence, or both point to a relatively warm, moist climate similar to the historical one. In sum, as in the French case, the implication is that climate rather than collector behavior was the cause of the observed species shifts.

We stress that the French case and the southern African case share important major features. In both instances, changes in species abundance occur independent of changes in "culture." Even more striking, in both cases the changes are long term, spanning many millennia, and they are cyclical. The cycles in turn correspond to climatic cycles that have been documented locally and that can be correlated with global cycles revealed in the deep-sea record. In situations like this, it is surely reasonable to implicate climate rather than human behavior as the cause of changes in species abundance.

Species Abundance and Cultural Change
Climatic change rather than culture was probably responsible for most long-term shifts in species abundance that are visible in the Pleistocene archeological record. However, some shifts must reflect the evolution of culture, which surely involved changes in the way people dealt with other animals. One reason such culturally caused shifts have remained elusive is the difficulty of separating them from shifts caused by environmental change. Additionally, large, well-controlled, appropriately analyzed archeological samples are necessary to document the shifts. These are rare, even from later Pleistocene sites. One region where they exist is southern Africa, where a contrast between Middle Stone Age and Later Stone Age faunal samples strongly suggests an advance in human ability to obtain animals.

The Middle Stone Age (MSA) of southern Africa has recently been summarized by Volman (1984) and the Later Stone Age (LSA) by Deacon (1984). MSA people succeeded Early Stone Age (Acheulean) people in southern Africa at least 130,000 years ago, if not before. They were in turn replaced by LSA people 40,000-30,000 years ago, the exact time perhaps depending on the place. LSA people still survived in parts of the subcontinent at the time of European contact, only a few hundred years ago. So far, very few early LSA sites have been found, and our picture of the LSA is based overwhelmingly on sites occupied after 20,000 B.P. For simplicity's sake here, however, we have assumed the information from these sites pertains to the entire LSA. Even if this should turn out to be incorrect, it would not materially affect our faunal discussion.

The contrasting MSA and LSA faunal samples we discuss come from the same fynbos ("macchia") region discussed in the previous section. This area contains numerous LSA sites that were occupied during the Holocene or Present Interglacial, spanning the past 12,000-10,000 years. Dating of the sites is secure, thanks to the radiocarbon method. The Holocene site that has provided the largest faunal sample is the coastal cave at Nelson Bay (Klein 1972; Deacon 1978). The region also contains a handful of MSA sites with deposits dating to warm phases within the Last Interglacial, mainly between 130,000 and 95,000 years ago. By far the most important of these MSA sites is the coastal cave known as Klasies River Mouth 1 (Singer and Wymer 1982).

The Last Interglacial deposits at Klasies 1 are beyond the range of radiocarbon, but their age has been well established on geomorphic grounds (Butzer 1978a). The MSA sequence at Klasies 1 dates mainly from the earlier, warmer part of the Last Interglacial, between 130,000 and 95,000 B.P. However, it extends into the relatively cool part after 95,000 B.P. and perhaps into the early Last Glacial proper after about 70,000 B.P. Climatic fluctuations at Klasies have been reconstructed from sand granulometry and the oxygen-isotope composition of intertidal shells brought to the site by its Middle Stone Age inhabitants. The sand granulometry informs on the position of the coast, which was very near its present position during warm phases and many kilometers seaward during cool ones. The oxygenisotope analyses inform on offshore water temperatures. As expected, warm temperatures indicated by isotope composition correlate well with high sea levels implied by granulometry. The proximity of the sea in "warm" intervals is also implied by numerous intertidal mollusk shells, seal bones, and penguin bones introduced to Klasies 1 by its MSA inhabitants.

Unlike faunal samples from "glacial" sites in the region, the samples from warm "interglacial" levels at Klasies 1 are poor in typical African grassland species (Klein 1976). Instead, they contain numerous bones of grysbok, bushbuck, Cape buffalo, and other species that were common in the region historically and that dominate local Holocene fossil samples. However, unlike the Holocene samples and the historical fauna, the Klasies interglacial samples are remarkably poor in bushpig and very rich in eland. The spectacular abundance of eland is readily apparent from the number of individuals in the buffalo and eland age profiles at Klasies versus the numbers in the age profiles from the Holocene levels of nearby Nelson Bay Cave. Figure 5.4 shows that eland are more than twice as common as buffalo in the Klasies sample, but only a third as common as buffalo in the Nelson Bay sample. The ratio of buffalo to eland at Nelson Bay closely reflects the historical ratio in the area.

We emphasize that the available sedimentological and geochemical evidence, as well as other aspects of the faunal samples, indicate that the Klasies layers antedating 95,000 B.P. accumulated under conditions very similar to the Holocene conditions at Nelson Bay. Certainly there is no evidence for the kind of dramatic environmental difference that would lead eland to far outnumber not only buffalo, but all other mammal species at Klasies. The rarity of eland at Nelson Bay in fact reflects the historical situation not only in the Klasies/Nelson Bay region, but also almost everywhere else that eland occurred. Historically, they were extremely widespread in Africa, but nowhere were they particularly common.

The abundance of eland at Klasies thus almost certainly reflects the behavior of its MSA occupants, not the abundance of eland in the environment. The MSA layers that postdate 95,000 B.P. further support this conclusion. The sediments indicate a cooler climate, and zebra and alcelaphine antelopes are more abundant relative to grysbok and bushbuck, implying a change in vegetation. Yet eland retains its number one position in the faunal sample.

The faunal difference between Klasies and Nelson Bay is associated with a striking difference between their artifact assemblages. Thus, like other LSA sites, Nelson Bay is rich in standardized bone artifacts ("awls," "points," "hide burnishers," etc.) and in art objects or items of personal adornment ("beads," "pendants," engraved bones, etc.). At Klasies and other MSA sites where preservation is appropriate, formal bone tools and art objects are rare or absent. Where they do occur, their rarity makes it easy to imagine natural or accidental displacement from overlying LSA layers.

There are also contrasts in the stone artifacts. Particularly striking is the high proportion of "microlithic" artifacts at Nelson Bay and other LSA sites. Both ethnographic observations and occasional archeological finds indicate that these were commonly mounted on wooden or bone handles or shafts to serve as scrapers, arrowheads, and such. In form, some of the microliths, and also some of the formal bone artifacts, are indistinguishable from pieces used historically to arm arrows. It thus seems likely that the Nelson Bay people, like all LSA people from at least 20,000 B.P. on, possessed the bow and arrow. There is no artifactual evidence for its presence in the MSA.

We think that the kind of technological advance implied by the bow and arrow explains the abundance of eland at Klasies relative to species like buffalo and bushpig that were probably more abundant on the ground. Compared with buffalo and bushpig, eland are far more likely to flee from hunters than to counterattack. In addition, eland are far more amenable to driving, which probably explains the "catastrophic" shape of the eland age profile, as discussed below. In short, compared with bushpig, buffalo, and other relatively dangerous or elusive species, eland would be especially vulnerable to hunters armed only with thrusting spears or other weapons that required a close approach. Only with the invention of weapons like the bow and arrow could hunters regularly acquire other species more in proportion to their live abundance.

In sum, it seems likely that the new items in Later Stone Age artifact assemblages at least partly reflect technological innovations that allowed Later Stone Age people to kill dangerous or elusive species more often. Thus, eland are more abundant at Klasies than at LSA sites not because MSA people killed eland more, but because they killed other more dangerous or elusive species less. We will return to this point when we discuss the age profiles from Klasies and Nelson Bay.

There is other evidence that MSA people were behaviorially less advanced than LSA people. First, coastal MSA sites like Klasies contain numerous shells of intertidal mollusks and bones of seals and penguins, indicating exploitation of the adjacent coast. Notably rare in these sites, however, are bones of flying seabirds and especially of fish. In coastal LSA sites like Nelson Bay, bones of flying seabirds and of fish are

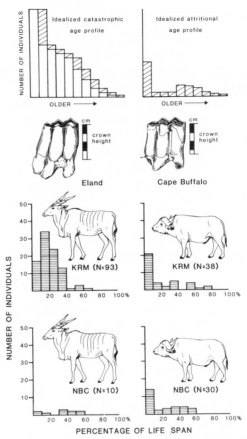

FIGURE 5.4: Top left: The numbers of individuals in successive age classes in an idealized, schematic catastrophic age (mortality) profile (blank bars), and the number of individuals who die between successive age classes (hatched bars). Top right: an idealized, schematic attritional age (mortality) profile, comprising a separate display of the hatched bars in the profile immediately to the left. Although the basic shapes of catastrophic and attritional profiles will be the same for all ungulate populations that are approximately stable in size and age structure, the precise shapes will vary from population to population, depending upon species biology and upon the mortality factors that affect the population.

Center: Lower third molars (M3s) of eland (*Taurotragus oryx*) and Cape buffalo (*Syncerus caffer*) showing the crown height dimension the authors measure.

Bottom: Mortality profiles based on the crown heights of eland and Cape buffalo teeth from the Middle Stone Age layers of Klasies River Mouth Cave 1 (KRM) and Nelson Bay Cave (NBC). It is probable that postdepositional leaching, profile compaction, and other destructive factors have selectively destroyed teeth of very young eland and buffalo at both sites. Keeping this in mind, the eland profile from Klasies is clearly catastrophic, while the buffalo profiles from both sites are

superabundant. The implication is that only LSA people possessed a well-developed fishing and fowling technology. LSA artifact assemblages in fact contain "net sinkers," "fish gorges," and other items that are readily interpretable as fishing or fowling gear. No such pieces are known in MSA assemblages.

Additionally, it is pertinent that tortoises and limpets are larger on average in MSA sites than in LSA sites occupied under broadly similar conditions. Both tortoises and limpets grow continuously, and larger average individual size in the MSA implies less predation pressure, probably because MSA population density was relatively low, reflecting a lower level of technological development. We briefly discuss some of the relevant tortoise and limpet measurements under "Mean Individual Size" below.

It is possible that the cultural advance represented by the Later Stone Age was linked to the appearance of anatomically modern people in Africa, much as the cultural advance represented by the Upper Paleolithic was linked to the appearance of anatomically modern people in Europe. However, we must reserve judgment on this pending the discovery of many more welldocumented and reasonably complete MSA and early LSA human fossils. More research will also be necessary to determine whether the behavioral advances of the LSA arose suddenly or relatively gradually between perhaps 40,000 and 20,000 B.P. Faunal analysis will surely play an important role in this research. Faunal analysis may also one day help to document other, probably more subtle behavioral advances that occurred during earlier phases of human evolution. The limitations are not methodological. Mostly what is lacking are sufficiently large, well-excavated faunal samples from well-controlled contexts.

Species Abundance in Assemblages Created by Carnivores
Little research has been done on species abundance in carnivore bone accumulations, particularly regarding possible contrasts with human accumulations. However, we have analyzed eight fossil or subfossil samples from southern Africa that were collected by hyenas. Hyenas are implicated by abundant coprolites and by the absence or rarity of stone artifacts or gnawed bones that would indicate a major role for people or porcupines.

Our hyena samples date from the Late Pleistocene and Holocene. During this interval, there were two hyena species in southern Africa--the

---

attritional. The eland profile from Nelson Bay contains too few individuals for assignment to profile type. (Kolmogorov-Smirnov Z for the difference between the Klasies eland and Klasies buffalo profiles is 1.90 [p < .01]; for the difference between the Klasies eland and Nelson Bay buffalo profiles 1.36 [p = .05]; and for the difference between the Klasies buffalo and Nelson Bay buffalo profiles 0.54 [p > .10].)

brown hyena (*Hyaena brunnea*) and the spotted hyena (*Crocuta crocuta*). Both species collect bones in dens (Sutcliffe 1970; Kruuk 1972; Bearder 1977; Mills 1973, 1978a,b; Mills and Mills 1977; M. Owens and Owens 1978, 1979; D. Owens and Owens 1979; Henschel, Tilson, and von Blottnitz 1979; Bunn 1982), but the brown hyena does so on a larger scale. This is because brown hyena females actively provision their young, while spotted hyena females do not.

The sheer quantity of bones in the sites providing our fossil assemblages suggests that the brown hyena was the collector in each instance. The sites are also all in areas where the brown hyena was historically far more numerous than the spotted hyena. Further, the samples are all dominated by ungulates in the springbok-reedbuck size range more commonly eaten by the brown hyena than by ungulates in the wildebeest-zebra size range more commonly eaten by the spotted hyena. Finally, in all the assemblages, the brown hyena itself is far more common than the spotted hyena, while brown hyena individuals come from all age groups, including very young cubs. The spotted hyena is represented almost exclusively by full-grown (usually old) adults. The brown hyena age distribution suggests natural deaths in long-occupied dens. It is unlikely that the relatively fragile bones of very young brown hyenas would have survived in such numbers if the individuals had been eaten. In contrast, the bones of spotted hyena adults could easily have come from scavenged carcasses.

In sum, we think that brown hyenas accumulated our samples, but we recognize that the evidence remains circumstantial. It is unfortunate that coprolites of the two species are not readily distinguished.

Whichever hyena was responsible, all the bone assemblages differ from contemporaneous archeological ones in a series of features. We discussed some of these under "Skeletal Part Representation." Table 5.2 lists all the distinctions we have recognized. Here we focus on a very clear contrast in relative species abundance.

In all the archeological samples we have studied, carnivores are relatively rare, particularly those jackal-size and larger. Carnivores usually compose less than 10% of the total of carnivores plus ungulates and never more than 13%, whether measured by the NISP or the MNI. In contrast, in the hyena assemblages carnivores always constitute at least 20% of the total. Table 5.3 presents absolute figures for some archeological and hyena assemblages that are clearly large enough to demonstrate a statistically significant difference in carnivore representation.

The relative rarity of carnivore remains in the archeological samples probably reflects a long-term mutual avoidance between people and carnivores. Carnivores are similarly rare in Stone Age sites throughout the world, save in sites where skeletal part representation implies trapping for furs (for example, some Ukrainian Upper Paleolithic sites mentioned in Klein 1973). The abundance of carnivores in the fossil hyena assemblages may reflect active hyena predation or confrontations around carcasses. It is notable in this regard that the most abundant carnivore in the hyena samples is the black-backed jackal (*Canis mesomelas*), which has often been

TABLE 5.2 Differences the Authors Have Observed between Bone Assemblages from Fossil Hyena Dens and from Stone Age Archeological Sites in Southern Africa

Feature	Hyena Dens	Archeological Sites
Cranial/post-cranial ratio	Ratio tends to decrease with ungulate size (smaller ungulates better represented by cranial bones; large ungulates better represented by post-cranial bones). In addition, large ungulate post-cranial bones tend to come from adults, while large ungulate cranial bones derive from juveniles.	Ratio tends either to be independent of ungulate body size or to increase with body size.
Long bone representation	Long bone shafts tend to be complete but missing epiphyses.	Long bone shafts tend to be broken, while epiphyses are still present.
Skeletal part representation	Small, hard bones (carpals, tarsals, sesamoids) always rare.	Small, hard bones always present; will be superabundant if the assemblage is very fragmented.
Carnivore/ungulate ratio	Carnivores at least 20% of total carnivore + ungulate MNI.	Carnivores often less than 10% of the carnivore + ungulate MNI; never more than 13%.
Age profiles	Tend to be attritional.	May be catastrophic or attritional, depending on species, technology, and hunting method.

Note: For further discussion, see text.

TABLE 5.3 Carnivores as a Percentage of Carnivores Plus Ungulates in Fossil Hyena Dens and Stone Age Archeological Sites in Southern Africa

	Middle (MSA) and Later Stone Age (LSA) Archeological Sites				
	Klasies 1 (MSA)	Die Kelders (MSA)	Nelson Bay (LSA)	Boom-plaas (MSA & LSA)	Border Cave (MSA & LSA)
Carnivores	38	28	46	50	13
Carnivores and ungulates	426	266	589	419	132
Percentage of carnivores	9%	11%	8%	12%	10%

	Fossil Hyena Dens				
	Equus Cave	Swartklip	Sea Harvest	Hoedjies Punt	Elandsfontein "Bone Circle"
Carnivores	448	44	48	13	17
Carnivores and ungulates	1479	185	115	42	57
Percentage of carnivores	30%	24%	42%	36%	30%

Note: The abundance estimates for both carnivores and ungulates are MNIs. At all sites, the principal ungulates are bovids, followed by equids and suids. Hyracoids have been excluded, though they are ungulates in a strict technical sense. Note that carnivores are relatively much less abundant in the archeological sites, probably reflecting a mutual avoidance relationship with people.

observed at carcasses with hyenas. Further, our subjective evaluation of dental eruption and wear indicates that the fossil jackals were mainly very young adults. Such individuals would not have been foraging long on their own and would have had relatively little experience with hyenas.

Unfortunately, there are few pertinent observations on recent hyenas. The rather solitary, secretive brown hyena is particularly difficult to observe, and the presence of the observer may affect the behavior of both species. This is especially true of behavior (including bone collecting) at the den. Additionally, no hyena dens have been located that contain bone samples whose size approaches the largest of our fossil samples (from Swartklip and Equus Cave). With respect to the brown hyena at least, we suspect that marginal environmental conditions or human disturbance forces them to change dens too often to accumulate large assemblages.

There is an interesting contrast, however, between small bone assemblages collected by Mills and Mills (1977) from brown hyena and spotted hyena dens in the Kalahari Desert. Carnivores, especially jackals, are well represented in the brown hyena samples, but not in the spotted hyena samples. This supports our hypothesis that brown hyenas collected the fossil samples, but it also indicates that an abundance of carnivores need not characterize all assemblages created by carnivores versus ones created by people.

The extent of carnivore representation and other aspects of bone assemblages created by carnivores clearly deserve further study. This is especially true, given the possibility that one or more carnivores were primarily responsible for accumulating bones in the Transvaal australopithecine sites (Brain 1981). The focus may always have to be on fossil samples where carnivores are implicated by context or associations, since samples accumulated by living carnivores are difficult to locate and tend to be very small.

Age and Sex Profiles

In this section, we show how fossil age/sex profiles may be used to infer the behavior of both a bone collector and the species whose bones it collected.

Age/Sex Profiles and Collector Behavior: Example 1

Bone preservation is poor to moderate in most of the samples we have studied. This means that postdepositional destructive pressures may have seriously biased age profiles and sex ratios. The bias in age profiles will be against very young animals, whose bones are less durable than those of adults. The bias in sex ratios will generally be against females, since in most species the best parts for sexing are more durable in males. This is especially true of bovid and cervid species in which the most readily "sexable" part of the skull is the frontlet--the part that bears horns or antlers. In general, male frontlets are far more durable, particularly in species where only males have horns or antlers. Unfortunately, bovids or cervids dominate many fossil samples, including all those we have studied.

We have one sample, however, in which bone preservation is excellent and postdepositional pressures have probably not seriously affected age and sex composition. This sample comes from the Later Stone Age levels at Die Kelders Cave 1, Cape Province, South Africa. The context of the sample and its cultural associations have been described in detail by Schweitzer (1974, 1979). Radiocarbon dates bracket it firmly between 2000 and 1500 B.P.

In addition to indigenous animals, the Die Kelders sample contains domestic sheep, which were introduced to southern Africa only about 2000 B.P. Before this date, people in the Die Kelders area, as elsewhere in southern Africa, subsisted entirely by hunting and gathering. It would be interesting to know if the people who occupied the site between 2000 and 1500 B.P. were still hunter-gatherers who stole sheep from their neighbors or were sheepherders themselves. It is in this context that the age/sex composition of the fossil flock is pertinent.

The available sheep sample comprises a minimum (MNI) of twenty-three individuals, as determined from the jaws. Only male sheep bear horns, and in theory a sex ratio could be established on this basis. Unfortunately, the Later Stone Age inhabitants of Die Kelders smashed the sheep skulls, perhaps to obtain the brains, and only six "sexable" frontlets survived. Interestingly, all six came from young to very young males. Smashing of the skull could explain the total absence of female frontlets, but not of frontlets from adult males, which should have survived best of all. We conclude that the seventeen "missing" individuals were overwhelmingly females or additional juvenile males.

Sheep jaws at Die Kelders are complete enough to allow age estimation by comparison with dentitions from animals of known age. The resultant age profile contains seven individuals between 0 and 6 months, eleven between 6 and 18 months, two between 18 months and 48 months, and three older than 48 months. These last three were probably much older than 48 months, judging by the very advanced wear on their teeth.

Like the braincases, sheep limb bones suffered from human butchering or food preparation, but enough are present to provide some check on the dental age profile. Using the ages of epiphyseal fusion for domestic sheep reported by Silver (1969:285-86), the Die Kelders epiphyses imply two individuals between 0 and 10 months, six between 10 and 18 months, one between 18 and 36 months, and six between 36 months and then potential life span in sheep (about 10 years). Within the limitations imposed by the method and materials, the epiphyseal age profile resembles the dental profile quite closely. Particularly notable in both cases is the large bulge in the age class between 6-10 months and 18 months.

In interpreting the data, we stress the abundance of individuals between 6-10 months and 18 months. These are far more numerous than they would be in a live flock. At the same time prime adults are far rarer. It is difficult to see thieves producing such a pattern. Presumably, they would concentrate on adults whose meat yield would better justify the effort and risk of stealing. On the other hand, the Die Kelders pattern might well reflect rational culling of 10-18-month-olds, whose future weight gain would be small relative to their feeding requirements (Payne 1973). It would be particularly rational to cull 10-18- month-old males, since few would be necessary for reproduction and their developing sexual appetites could complicate flock management. Regular, selective culling of young males would of course explain the otherwise puzzling absence of adult males in the Die Kelders sample.

In sum, the age/sex pattern suggests that the occupants of Die Kelders were probably herders rather than thieves. A firmer statement may become possible when sheep age/sex profiles become available from other local sites, particularly sites where context or associations (e.g., the ruins of a kraal) indicate herder occupation.

Age/Sex Profiles and Collector Behavior: Example 2
Our second example concerns the age profiles of eland and Cape buffalo from Klasies River Mouth Cave 1 and Nelson Bay Cave, mentioned previously under "Species Abundance." We present no corresponding eland or buffalo sex ratios, because they could not be calculated at either site. Frontlets of both species are very rare at both sites, owing to a combination of pre- and postdepositional factors. Measurements on postcranial bones could not be used instead because the most suitable bones at both sites tend to be incomplete (fragmented). In this state not only are they unmeasurable, but they often cannot be reliably identified to species. It is particularly difficult to distinguish fragmentary eland postcranial bones from those of Cape buffalo, since the species are very similar in size and skeletal morphology.

The eland and buffalo age profiles were computed from crown heights using the program AGEPROF (chap. 7), which automatically assigns individuals to 10% of life span intervals. This facilitates comparison of profiles between species with different potential life spans (20 years in eland and 24 in buffalo). The profiles are presented graphically in figure 5.4, where they can be compared to the two idealized types discussed in chapter 4. Individuals in the first 10% of life span are probably underrepresented in all four profiles because their teeth are relatively fragile. Taking this into account, the eland profile from Klasies is essentially "catastrophic," while the buffalo profiles from both sites are "attritional." The eland profile from Nelson Bay contains too few individuals for adequate characterization. It has been included precisely to show the contrast between Klasies and Nelson Bay in the abundance of eland, as discussed above under "Species Abundance."

Kolmogorov-Smirnov results in the legend to figure 5.4 show that the difference between the two buffalo profiles on the one hand and the eland profile on the other is highly "significant" from a statistical point of view. It is thus highly unlikely to reflect simple chance. We stress also that it cannot reflect a difference in portability between the species, since they are essentially identical in size. Nor does it reflect a difference in the skeletal parts used to calculate the age profiles, since the mandible was used in both cases. The most likely explanation for the difference is a contrast in the way the people hunted the species. Such a contrast could be expected from important differences in behavior between the species.

Cape buffalo are irascible and aggressive. They live in herds that tend to charge potential predators, including people and lions. Lions in fact hunt them with great care and are normally unable to obtain prime-age adults (Sinclair 1977). Mainly, they take very young animals (in the first 10% of potential lifespan) and old ones (beyond 40% of life span). Very young buffalo are more vulnerable because of their size and physical weakness. Newborn individuals are particularly vulnerable because they are usually born away from the herd and must be led to it over several hours. Old buffalo are more vulnerable because of physical weakness and exclusion from herds (in the case of males).

Like buffalo killed by recently observed lions, the buffalo samples from Klasies and Nelson Bay contain far smaller numbers of prime adults (between 10% and 40% of life span) than occur in live herds and disproportionately many very young and old individuals. We add that at both sites the young include many newborn individuals whose special vulnerability we mentioned above. Their original number was probably even larger, since their teeth would be particularly susceptible to removal by postdepositional destructive pressures.

The shape of the archeological profiles clearly suggests that the Stone Age hunters were constrained by the same factors of buffalo behavior that constrain lions. In fact, it could even be argued that the people did not hunt buffalo at all but scavenged carcasses found in the veldt. This is because the archeological profiles resemble not only those created by lion predation, but the more general profile that reflects mortality from various predators, endemic disease, accidents, starvation, and other "attritional" factors. Like lion predation, these other factors affect mainly the very young and the old. However, to scavenge so many very young buffalo, the Klasies and Nelson Bay people would have had to find their carcasses before hyenas, lions, and other scavengers whose special senses are better suited to the purpose. Recent observations indicate that once these other scavengers locate the carcass of a young buffalo they consume it quickly and completely. There would thus be nothing left for people to scavenge.

The abundance of very young individuals in the Klasies and Nelson Bay profiles therefore implies active hunting, or perhaps a mixture of active hunting of young animals and scavenging of adults (Klein 1982a). The similarity of the age profiles between the two sites may seem to contradict our earlier argument that the Nelson Bay people were more proficient hunters, in large part because they possessed the bow and arrow while the Klasies people did not. However, our argument is that the bow and arrow would have allowed the Nelson Bay people to kill more buffalo overall, not that it would have significantly increased the vulnerability of prime-age adults compared with very young and old individuals. Before the introduction of rifles, it is unlikely that people ever obtained prime adult buffalo in direct proportion to their live abundance.

Like buffalo, eland live in herds, but unlike buffalo they are remarkably docile. They tend to flee from predators, and many observers have commented on how easy they are to drive. It is probably this feature that allowed the Klasies people to obtain so many prime adult eland relative to very young and old individuals. At minimal risk to themselves, the Klasies hunters could have driven eland herds over cliffs (there are suitable ones near Klasies) or into traps where differences in the animals' size or age would have no meaning.

The attritional mortality pattern of the Klasies and Nelson Bay buffalo is the one that probably characterizes most longstanding predator-prey relationships. This is because the reproductive potential of most species is so great that large losses among the very young can be sustained indefinitely. In fact, such losses must occur if a species is not to outstrip its food supply. Similarly, most species can readily afford the loss of old (postreproductive) adults. However, no species can long sustain a predation pattern that results in "catastrophic" mortality, that is, one in which reproductively active adults are taken in proportion to their live abundance. The immediate result will be a reduction in population numbers. The end result will be extinction. This makes the eland mortality profile at Klasies especially intriguing. The eland obviously survived, and there is no evidence that its numbers declined during the many millennia it was hunted near Klasies.

The reason is probably that the eland was a relatively rare species near Klasies, as it was historically. We noted under "Species Abundance" that eland were historically very widespread in Africa, but they were nowhere very common. In addition, eland herds tend to wander widely, and it was probably difficult for the Klasies people to locate one in a position suitable for driving. As a consequence, they probably obtained very few eland relative to the total number available. In other words, in spite of their ability to obtain prime-age adults in those eland herds they did obtain, the Klasies people were probably not very good at hunting eland. This makes it particularly interesting that eland are the most abundant ungulate in the site. The Klasies people must have been even poorer at hunting other species that are less common in the site but were more abundant on the ground.

The eland and buffalo profiles from Nelson Bay and Klasies can be supplemented with profiles for other species at both sites and with profiles for eland, buffalo, and other species at yet other Middle and Later Stone Age sites, particularly Die Kelders Cave 1, Byneskranskop Cave 1, and Elands Bay Cave (Klein 1978, 1981, and unpublished). Overall, the profiles suggest that, in both Middle and Later Stone Age sites, species that were amenable to driving or snaring tend to exhibit catastrophic profiles, while species that were probably hunted individually with hand-held weapons tend to exhibit attritional ones.

Age/Sex Profiles and Collector Behavior: Example 3
We also have age profiles of various ungulates from the "hyena" sites discussed in the previous example. The profiles tend to be attritional,

indicating that hyenas obtain relatively few prime-age adults in most species. Finally, we have age profiles from the mid-Pleistocene water hole site of Elandsfontein and the early Pliocene river channel/floodplain site at Langebaanweg (Klein 1982b). Some of the Elandsfontein profiles are catastrophic and some are attritional, but we are hesitant to interpret them because they are based largely on material whose context was not (sometimes could not be) recorded. At the same time, it is clear that the Elandsfontein site in fact incorporates many different occurrences--hyena lairs, porcupine lairs, carnivore kills or natural deaths near ancient water holes, and perhaps some hominid kills or campsites. Perhaps the principal lesson to be learned from Elandsfontein is that, like any other aspect of faunal analysis, the interpretation of age profiles depends on a sound knowledge of sample context and associations.

Context is well-established for the Langebaanweg samples, which come from two distinct sedimentary situations--ancient river channels and the fringing floodplain (Hendey 1981, 1982). Flowing water concentrated the bones in the channel deposits, whereas bones in the floodplain sediments are dispersed and probably lie very near the places where the animals died. Some floodplain skeletons were apparently dismembered by carnivores, but there are no bone concentrations indicating lairs. Age profiles for ungulates in the channel deposits are catastrophic, suggesting death by drowning during flash floods. Age profiles in the floodplain sediments are attritional, suggesting death from predation, endemic disease, accidents, and other everyday mortality factors.

Interestingly, the attritional profiles of large ungulates at Langebaanweg contain far fewer very young individuals than the buffalo profiles from Klasies and Nelson Bay. This cannot reflect greater selective postdepositional destruction of very young bones at Langebaanweg, since bone preservation at the site is far better than at either Klasies or Nelson Bay. More likely, it reflects complete consumption of many very young carcasses by the numerous hyenas and other probable scavengers that prowled the area in early Pliocene times.

In essence, the animals represented in the Langebaanweg attritional profiles are the ones that would have been available to human scavengers (if people had been present at Langebaanweg, which they were not). We predict that such attritional profiles, far poorer in very young animals than the buffalo profiles from Klasies and Nelson Bay, will eventually be found to characterize hominid sites of late Pliocene or early Pleistocene age. The problem will be to locate late Pliocene/earlier Pleistocene sites where context and associations clearly implicate people as the primary bone accumulators. So far, such sites have proved remarkably elusive.

Age/Sex Profiles of a Fossil Species and Its Population Dynamics
In the previous three examples we reconstructed the behavior of a bone collector from the age/sex profiles of species it collected. Here we focus on reconstructing the behavior of collected species. As examples, we use two small (10-14 kg), solitary, highly territorial antelopes--the Cape grysbok

(*Raphicerus melanotis*) and its close relative the steenbok (*R. campestris*).

The Cape grysbok is endemic to the same "macchia" or fynbos zone at the southwestern tip of Africa that we have discussed before. The steenbok is more widely distributed, occurring with minor discontinuities throughout southern Africa and also in parts of Tanzania and Kenya. The steenbok tends to occupy somewhat more open countryside, but both species require substantial patches of bush or shrub, where they seek food and protection from predators. Because of their secretive nature, both species are difficult to observe or census systematically. As a consequence, some aspects of their biology are poorly established.

One significant fact that remains unknown is the sex ratio in free-ranging populations. In both species only the males bear horns, but these are relatively small, and the sexes are otherwise difficult to distinguish externally, especially from a distance or in bush. This perhaps explains why different observers have reported widely divergent sex ratios for populations living in circumstances where no difference would be expected (Mentis 1972). The reported differences are especially striking, since a uniform ratio near 1:1 would be expected from the territorial spacing and behavior of the species (Jarman 1974).

Given the difficulty of observing live, free-ranging grysbok and steenbok, we propose that a large archeological sample might provide a reasonable estimate of the common sex ratio. Certainly there is nothing in the behavior of either species to indicate that one sex would be more vulnerable to Stone Age hunting than the other. Nor is there any reason to suppose Stone Age hunters would prefer one sex over the other. Of course, it is vital that the sample be one in which the sex ratio has probably not been seriously affected by pre- and postdepositional destructive pressures.

The large grysbok sample from the Later Stone Age levels of Die Kelders 1 meets these criteria. As we noted earlier, bone preservation in this sample is excellent, suggesting little postdepositional destruction. Also, the Die Kelders people did not fragment grysbok skulls to any great extent. In particular, nearly complete grysbok frontlets are abundant (MNI = 91). The ratio of male to female frontlets is 41:50, which is not significantly different from 1:1 (the binomial probability of a difference is approximately .25). We conclude that the Die Kelders evidence supports theoretical expectations of a sex ratio close to parity. The Die Kelders ratio is at least as pertinent in this regard as ratios derived from observations on recent populations, and it has the advantage of being based on material spanning several centuries. It is thus far less likely to reflect temporary aberrations.

A second aspect of grysbok/steenbok biology that remains uncertain from modern observations is the reproductive rate. In both species, the gestation period (approximately 5.5 months) would easily permit females to average more than one birth per year. However, it is difficult to determine whether such a reproductive rate is usual. This reflects the difficulty of recognizing individual females and their young, combined with the tendency of females to give birth at any time of year (there is no distinct seasonal peak or peaks). Once again, recent observations are clearly inadequate, and observations on fossil samples can provide important circumstantial evidence. Here we focus on age profiles.

We have age profiles of Cape grysbok and steenbok from a wide variety of sites, including both archeological and hyena sites (fig. 5.5). In all cases, the profiles exhibit the downstaircase shape that is usually interpreted as "catastrophic." However, we think it is unlikely that grysbok/steenbok mortality could be catastrophic in such a wide range of sites, including "hyena" localities where other species exhibit attritional profiles. It is far more likely that some of our profiles are attritional. This could be so, however, only if grysbok and steenbok are species in which females commonly average more than one young per year. We recall (from chap. 4) that in such species attritional profiles will be very similar to catastrophic ones, because population stability in such species requires heavy mortality even in young adults.

The grysbok/steenbok example underlines the need to consider context or associations in interpreting age profiles. To emphasize this further, we cite the age profile of the large extinct suid *Nyanzachoerus* sp(p). in the floodplain deposits of the early Pliocene site of Langebaanweg discussed above. The *Nyanzachoerus* profile also shows the down-staircase form that reflects catastrophic mortality in most large mammals (Klein 1982b). However, from the sedimentary context catastrophic mortality seems unlikely, and all other species in the same context exhibit attritional profiles. The other species are ones whose living relatives are characterized by a birthrate of one young or fewer per female per year. In contrast, the extant relatives of *Nyanzachoerus* usually have multiple young (litters). With this fact in mind, the *Nyanzachoerus* profile could in fact be attritional rather than catastrophic. Given its sedimentary context and associations, we suggest that it is attritional and provides evidence that, like living suid females, *Nyanzachoerus* commonly bore multiple young.

Together, the grysbok and *Nyanzachoerus* examples show that fossil samples may be used to infer population structure or aspects of reproductive biology that are difficult or impossible to infer from living populations. We add that, even in the case of extant species, fossil samples may sometimes be preferable to living ones, because they are often larger, they are "time averaged," and they may be less affected by observer or environmental "biases." Perhaps this aspect of faunal analysis will become more important in coming decades as truly free-ranging populations of large mammals become ever smaller and rarer.

Mean Individual Size

We are primarily interested in mean individual size in fossil species as an index of Quaternary climate. However, climate is not the only factor affecting individual size. For example, Davis (1981) and many previous authors have noted that domestication commonly leads to size reduction ("dwarfing") in mammal species. We present no examples to illustrate this because we have not analyzed samples from areas where domestication took place. The domestic species that occur in some of our samples were all

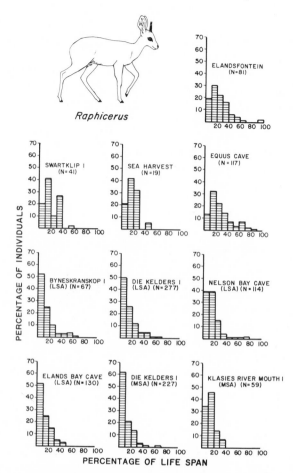

FIGURE 5.5: Age (mortality) profiles of grysbok/steenbok (*Raphicerus* spp.) from the mid-Pleistocene "water hole" site of Elandsfontein, the late Pleistocene fossil hyena lairs at Swartklip, Sea Harvest, and Equus Cave, the Middle Stone Age layers of Die Kelders Cave 1 and Klasies River Mouth Cave 1, and the Later Stone Age levels of Byneskranskop Cave 1, Nelson Bay Cave, Elands Bay Cave, and Die Kelders Cave 1. Very young individuals are probably underrepresented in several of the profiles because of the relative fragility of their jaws and teeth. Keeping this fact in mind, the profiles all display a general tendency for successively older age classes to contain progressively fewer individuals. Since some (most?) of the profiles are probably attritional, while others may be catastrophic, the implication is that grysbok/steenbok females commonly bear more than one young per year, as discussed in the text.

introduced from other areas, and they are readily distinguishable from local wild species on morphological grounds. In any case, in the absence of morphological or contextual evidence for domestication, size reduction is an inadequate criterion because there are various other factors that may produce it.

In this section, we present an example from our own experience in which size variation is linked to climate. The species involved is the black-backed jackal of southern and eastern Africa. In addition, we present two examples of size variation in nonmammals, one involving the angulate tortoise (*Chersina angulata*) of southern Africa and the other the common limpet (*Patella vulgata*) of Cantabrian Spain. Size variation in these species perhaps reflects a change in predation pressure rather than a change in climate. However, our principal purpose in these examples is to show that the methods and computer programs presented in this book may be extended to lower vertebrates and invertebrates in fossil samples.

Mean Individual Size and Climate
Mean individual size is known to vary with climate in numerous mammalian species, particularly carnivores and micromammals (small rodents and insectivores). For instance, Guilday (1971) used correlations between climate and mean size in several North American micromammals to infer late Pleistocene climate from fossil samples excavated at Appalachian caves. Similarly, Kurtén (1959, 1965) has demonstrated a relation between late Quaternary climatic change and mean size in several Near Eastern and European carnivore species.

Kurten noted that in general size variation can be ascribed to two main causes--Bergmann's rule and "population density factors." Bergmann's rule (formulated by C. Bergmann in the previous century) states that, if all other things are equal, individuals of a species will be larger in colder climates. This is because as an animal grows its volume, which produces heat, increases more rapidly than its skin area, which dissipates it.

Bergmann's rule characterizes many species for which size and climatic data are available, but there are also many exceptions. The reason is that "other things" are not always equal. Probably most important is the fact that individuals must be able to find sufficient food to maintain a larger body. It is in this context that "population density factors" are relevant. In particular, increased body size will be selected against if it reduces the number of individuals the environment can support below the level necessary for successful reproduction. Through its effect on food supply, a change in climate--even greater cold--might thus actually induce a reduction in mean individual body size.

Attempts to identify species that obey Bergmann's rule have been limited mainly to the Northern Hemisphere, where there are many species that range through several climatic zones, and where dramatic Quaternary climatic change has long been established. Africa and other regions straddling the equator have been largely ignored, in part because they exhibit less climatic variability through time and space. It is also pertinent that they have provided fewer large Quaternary fossil samples.

Climatic change was probably less dramatic in equatorial areas narrowly defined, but there is evidence for significant climatic change, including temperature variation, in southern Africa (Butzer 1978b). With this in mind, Avery (1982) analyzed mean individual size in fossil samples of micromammals from late Quaternary sites in the same fynbos zone we have discussed before. She found a clear correlation between mean individual size in several species and climatic change, as inferred from other evidence.

Encouraged by Avery's results, we have analyzed mean individual size in several species of carnivores and small herbivores that are well represented in middle and late Quaternary samples from the same fynbos region. Our study involves both modern specimens and fossil ones. In general, we have found that mean size in the carnivores increases with decreasing temperature, as known in modern environments or as inferred from sedimentary evidence in fossil contexts. The situation is far more complex in the small herbivores, where size appears to increase with precipitation in browsers and to decrease with precipitation in grazers. This probably reflects the increase in browse relative to grass during moister episodes in the fynbos zone.

To illustrate the nature of our data, figure 5.6 summarizes measurements of lower first molar (M1) length in recent and fossil black-backed jackals. The underlying statistics were obtained from the program BONESTAT, with data formatted by the program DENTDATA, as described in chapters 7 and 8 below. We measured a tooth (rather than a postcranial bone) because we cannot readily distinguish the postcranial bones of black-backed jackals from those of other jackal species that might occur in our samples. We did not want to confuse a change in mean individual size with one due to a change in jackal species. A further reason for focusing on teeth was that jackal dentitions are far more numerous than limb bones in the museum comparative collections we studied. Teeth, particularly the relatively robust lower M1, also dominate our fossil samples.

Figure 5.6 shows first that modern black-backed jackals do conform to the expectations of Bergmann's rule. The largest modern jackals occur farthest from the equator, in the Cape Province of South Africa, at the southern tip of the continent. The smallest ones occur in equatorial East Africa, at the northern limit of the black-backed jackal's range. Jackals from a geographically intermediate area, the Transvaal Province of South Africa, are intermediate in average size. The differences in mean individual size between the three samples are "statistically significant" at the .05 level or below, as indicated by lack of overlap between the respective 95% confidence limits for the means (see chap. 8).

Our fossil data further support a link between larger jackal size and colder climate. Jackals clearly tend to be larger in those samples where sediments or other aspects of the fauna indicate very cool conditions during bone accumulation. For instance, the largest jackals we have encountered occur in the Swartklip fossil hyena den, where the sediments indicate very cool climate (Butzer unpublished data) and the fossil fauna is totally dominated by grazing species that did not occur in the region historically (Klein 1975).

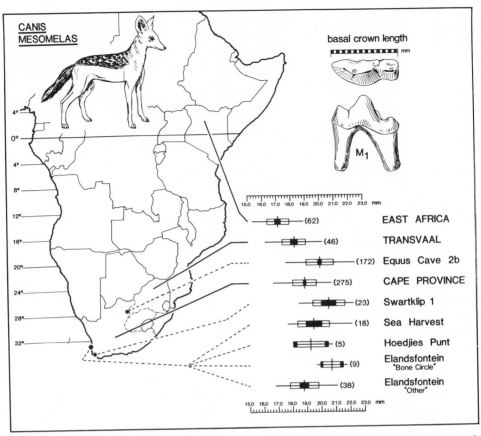

FIGURE 5.6: The anteroposterior diameter ("basal crown length") of black-backed jackal lower M1s in modern and fossil samples. The names of the modern samples are in upper case; the names of the fossil samples are in upper and lower case. For each sample, the mean is indicated by a vertical line, the observed range by a horizontal line, the standard deviation by a solid bar, and the 95% confidence limits of the mean by an open bar. The number of specimens in each sample is shown in parentheses. The figure shows that black-backed jackals tend to be larger in cooler climates.

Ultimately, it should be possible to use size variation in fossil jackals and other species to construct a detailed curve of climate change in the fynbos zone. This is especially fortunate because local sites rarely preserve paleobotanical remains. The size change data thus provide a welcome independent supplement and check on schemes of climatic change derived mainly from geomorphic/sedimentological studies.

Size Variation and Human Predation Pressure
Here we deal briefly with mean individual size in tortoises and mollusks, in which growth occurs more or less continuously throughout life. Mean

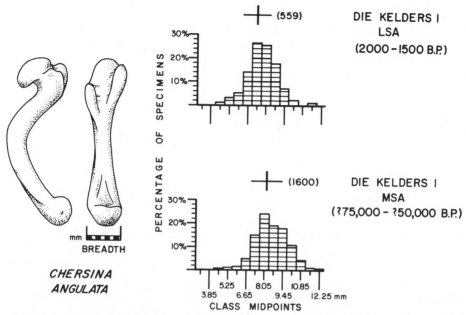

FIGURE 5.7: Angulate tortoise distal humerus "breadth" in the Middle Stone and Later Stone Age layers of Die Kelders Cave 1, Cape Province, South Africa. The vertical line above each histogram is the arithmetic mean; the horizontal line is the standard deviation. The Middle Stone Age humeri clearly tend to be larger (broader) than the Later Stone Age humeri (Kolmogorov-Smirnov Z = 5.78, p < .001). The implication is that Middle Stone Age people preyed less intensively on tortoises, probably because Middle Stone Age people were less numerous than Later Stone Age people.

individual size established from a tortoise bone or mollusk shell is therefore the mean for the population as a whole, not simply for adults. Adults in a strictly physiological sense in fact include individuals of very different sizes, depending on their ages. In archeological contexts, a reduction in mean individual size in such species might imply a slowing of the growth rate as a result of environmental change or an increase in human predation pressure.

Increased predation pressure reflecting greater human population density has been proposed to explain a reduction in limpet size between the Middle Stone Age and Later Stone Age in South Africa (Klein 1979) and also within the 20,000-10,000 B.P. span of the Solutrean and Magdalenian in northern Spain (Straus *et al.* 1981; Clark and Straus 1983; Bailey 1983). We have also recently proposed that low predation pressure reflecting low human population density explains the relatively large size of the tortoises in the Middle Stone Age layers of Die Kelders Cave 1 (Klein and Cruz-Uribe 1983b).

The limpet cases are more equivocal, because it is possible that size reduction reflects a change in offshore water temperatures, in turn caused by a change in offshore currents or upwelling. We think warmer waters are particularly likely to explain size reduction in the Spanish case. Climatic or environmental change is a less likely explanation for the difference in tortoise size, however, since the sediments enclosing the very large Middle Stone Age tortoises imply much cooler, wetter conditions than those incorporating smaller Later Stone Age tortoises. Cool, wet climate would probably inhibit, not promote, rapid growth in tortoises.

Figures 5.7 and 5.8 illustrate some of the data on which the limpet and tortoise size changes are based. In both cases the averages and histograms were computed with the program BONESTAT, with data formatted by BONEDATA, as described in chapter 8 below. The measurement providing the data for tortoises was the maximum mediolateral diameter of the distal humerus, as illustrated in figure 5.7. We also measured the anteroposterior diameter, and where possible total humerus length, exactly as we would do in mammals.

The measurement providing the data for the limpets was the maximum shell "length," as illustrated in figure 5.8. We also measured the maximum "breadth" (= the greatest dimension perpendicular to the "length") and the "height" (defined as the distance between the apex of the shell and its basal plane). (For entry via the program BONEDATA, we treated limpet length as the mediolateral diameter, breadth as the anteroposterior diameter, and height as total [bone] length. We of course responded N when asked "Is Side Known (Y/N).")

Conclusion

In conclusion, we address three potential flaws in the examples we have presented to illustrate the importance of various numbers in faunal analysis. First, the examples are far from exhaustive, reflecting our experience more than the total range of faunal studies. Second, and more important, they are artificial, since they proceed as if species abundance, age/sex composition, and mean individual size can be treated separately from one another. In fact, these aspects are interrelated, and, as some of the examples do show, there are times when the interpretation of one aspect (e.g., mean individual size) very much depends on the nature of another (e.g., species abundance).

Finally, like our general approach, some of our examples may strike some investigators as over inductive. Thus, in many cases, it is clear that we produced the numbers first and interpreted them afterward, with no a priori expectations or predictions. We think this reflects the state of the field in which there have been too few prior observations to make reasonable predictions. We note further that our a posteriori interpretations do involve prior information (e.g., known aspects of species behavior) and a concern for plausibility and consistency. Perhaps most important, they now constitute predictions for what we and others could expect to find in future samples. We hope that the methods and programs we present in this book will facilitate the search.

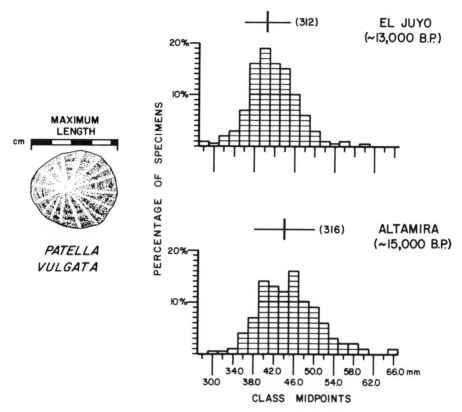

FIGURE 5.8: Common limpet shell length in the Lower Magdalenian layers of Altamira and El Juyo caves, northern Spain. The vertical line above each histogram is the arithmetic mean; the horizontal line is the standard deviation. The Altamira limpets clearly tend to be larger (longer) than the El Juyo ones (Kolmogorov-Smirnov Z = 3.49, p < .001). This may indicate a change in offshore water temperatures between the Altamira and El Juyo occupations. Alternatively, it may reflect more intensive limpet exploitation by the El Juyo people.

PART TWO: BASIC **PROGRAMS FOR THE ANALYSIS OF ANIMAL**

BONES FROM ARCHEOLOGICAL SITES

In this part of the book, we present a set of BASIC programs to compute the numbers whose faunal analytic utility we demonstrated in Part 1. The programs evolved over a period of eighteen months, during which they saved us considerable analysis time and effort. They also reduced the likelihood of erroneous results, which could now come only from erroneous data, not from calculation errors. Finally, the programs forced us to think carefully about calculation assumptions we had taken for granted before. This was particularly significant in the case of the program that produces MNIs. We believe that the description of this program (in chap. 6) is the most detailed and explicit treatment of MNI calculation in print. The description should therefore be of general interest to faunal analysts, whether or not they choose to use the program.

We wrote the programs in BASIC mainly because it is the one language that is implemented on virtually all microcomputers. As these become increasingly cheaper and more widely available, few faunal analysts will be excluded from using the programs for lack of computer facilities. We also chose BASIC because we were impressed by the ease with which recent versions handle data files and process alphanumeric or "string" variables. From a faunal analyst's point of view, this enhanced ability to manipulate strings is especially important, since it completely obviates the need to assign arbitrary numeric codes to the names of species, skeletal parts, and other variables.

The principal disadvantage of BASIC is that it permits the programmer to write "unstructured" programs that are difficult to read and modify. This is in sharp contrast to Pascal which encourages legibility in program construction. Pascal is particularly better than BASIC for long, relatively complex programs like the one that calculates MNIs. However, the Microsoft Corporation dialect of BASIC supplied with the IBM Personal Computer and most other late model microcomputers includes several Pascal-like features, and we have made extensive use of these. As a consequence, we believe that even a relatively inexperienced BASIC programmer will find it easy to read and modify our programs.

Many commercially available microcomputer programs are based on complex algorithms or on assumptions that the ordinary user cannot hope to understand. The user furnishes input and the program furnishes output; what occurs in between is largely a mystery, except to the programmer. We stress that this is not true of the programs in this book. For each program, we have detailed the logical assumptions behind it, so that the user should have no difficulty in understanding how input is transformed into output.

All the programs are interactive in the sense that they ask the user to supply information as it is needed. We have tried to make the requests ("prompts") for information as clear and as unambiguous as possible, and we have also incorporated "traps" for the kinds of incorrect responses that are most likely to occur. Each program will reject such a response, instruct the user of the mistake, and reprompt for correct information. In those situations where an appropriate response is an abbreviation (for a bone name, epiphyseal fusion state, etc.) that the user may have forgotten, we have made it possible to obtain a complete list of abbreviations and other instructions by entering "HELP" in response to a program prompt. Finally, for each program, we have provided complete sample sessions and sample output. We have also provided complete tables of the program prompts and appropriate responses.

The name of each program reflects the task it performs. Thus the program MNI (chap. 6) calculates the minimum number of individuals ("MNI") and the number of bones or bone fragments ("NISP") for each skeletal part of a species. The programs BONECODE and DENTCODE create the data "files" that MNI processes. BONECODE prompts the user for background information on each identifiable bone; DENTCODE does the same for each dentition. In each case, the proper responses to the prompts are mnemonic abbreviations for provenience units, skeletal parts, portions of a skeletal part, side of a skeletal part, and so forth.

The program AGEPROF (chap. 7) constructs age profiles for high-crowned ungulates, using a quadratic relationship between age and crown height. It is a far simpler program than MNI, since it relies mainly on a single mathematical formula rather than on a complex series of assumptions about whether two bones are likely to come from the same animal. We previously published a simpler version of AGEPROF that assumed a user would enter crown heights either from the keyboard or from a computer "file" that contained only crown heights and no other dental measurements or associated provenience information (Klein and Cruz-Uribe 1983a). The version of AGEPROF in this book assumes that crown heights will be entered from files that contain other dental measurements and associated provenience data. The supporting program DENTDATA prompts the user for the information and measurements to create such "files."

In many cases, the user will want to compare the age profiles of two species. It is particularly important to ask what the likelihood is that the profiles differ strictly by chance. In general, the simplest and most powerful statistical "test" for this purpose is the Kolmogorov-Smirnov test. Since this test is rarely incorporated in standard statistical packages, we have included a program for it here, called SMIRNOV (chap. 7). The program SMIRNOV can also be profitably used to compare patterns of skeletal part representation between species samples.

Finally, we present the program BONESTAT (chap. 8), which produces descriptive statistics and histograms from measurements on bones and teeth. It differs from standard statistical programs in that it will accept data in a format that we think most faunal analysts will find especially convenient. For teeth, this format is created by the data entry program DENTDATA, which also formats data for AGEPROF. For skeletal parts other than teeth, the format is created by the program BONEDATA.

Among the programs we present, MNI is clearly the most complicated and the most unusual. It differs sharply from previously published bone-counting programs such as those described by Bonnichsen and Sanger (1977), Gifford and Crader (1977), Meadow (1978), McArdle (1975-77), Redding, Pires-Ferreira, and Zeder (1975-77), Redding, Zeder, and McArdle (1978), and Uerpmann (1978). These earlier programs were designed primarily as cataloging systems. They accept far more information on each bone than MNI, but their function is mainly to store and retrieve the information, not to manipulate it. In addition, these programs process only data that has been numerically coded in advance. This not only complicates data entry, but enhances the possibility of entry error. These programs clearly had utility in the 1970s, but a user interested in their cataloging and sorting functions would probably obtain greater satisfaction today from one of the powerful data-base management systems available on mini- and microcomputers.

The data "files" created by BONECODE, DENTCODE, DENTDATA, and BONEDATA also constitute electronic catalogs. They could be sorted very much like the files created by the earlier programs, and they are more suitable for visual scanning, since they are made up of mnemonic abbreviations rather than arbitrary numerical codes. To enhance their potential as electronic catalogs, we have made it possible for BONECODE, DENTCODE, DENTDATA, and BONEDATA to record an individual identification (catalog) number for each bone or dentition. These catalog numbers (and any other information in the files) can then be manipulated using one of the commercially available data-base management programs (such as Ashton-Tate's dBASE II) that can read files in BASIC format.

We stress, however, that the primary purpose of our data files is to allow the programs MNI, AGEPROF, and BONESTAT to transform basic bone identifications and measurements into summary or composite numbers. The numbers involved are ones that we feel are especially useful for reconstructing ancient environments and the behavior of bone accumulators. Catalog numbers are not relevant in this context, and their entry may take considerable time, particularly for large faunal samples. Yet it is for processing large samples that the programs are most helpful, and it is large samples that are most likely to provide meaningful information about the past. Consequently, each of our data entry programs allows the user the option of not entering catalog numbers, and it is this option we routinely choose ourselves. In fact, many of the samples we have studied are so large that simply assigning each bone an individual catalog number would have exhausted our research time.

Some Technical Features Common to All the Programs
We have already indicated that the programs MNI, AGEPROF, and BONESTAT obtain their data from "files" specially created and stored on

the computer system. Some further comments on files are essential to facilitate use of the programs.

Technically, a "file" is any collection of text or data stored on a computer under a single name. From the computer's point of view, each of our programs is a file, though a special ("executable") one. However, in this book, we use the term file to refer mainly to a list of skeletal parts, a series of measurements, or some other data set to be processed by a program.

Commonly, computer systems allow or encourage two-part file names comprising a basic "description" separated by a period from an "extension". The file naming conventions employed by the IBM Personal Computer Disk Operating System are reasonably typical. On the IBM system, the description may consist of one to eight characters, the extension of one to three. If the extension is omitted, the period may be left out as well. The characters may be letters, numbers, or a mixture of the two. Most systems also permit special characters, like the dash (-) or exclamation point (!) in file names, but the precise ones that are permissible vary from system to system. In general, the user has considerable discretion in choosing the one-to-eight character description. Choice of the one-to-three character extension is more limited, depending on system or program requirements. For example, the IBM Personal Computer system assumes that a BASIC program will have the extension "BAS". The full names of the programs MNI, AGEPROF, and BONESTAT are then MNI.BAS, AGEPROF.BAS, and BONESTAT.BAS. In the following chapters, we suggest conventions for naming the data files these programs process.

Although we have designed the data entry programs BONECODE, DENTCODE, DENTDATA, and BONEDATA to reduce the risk of erroneous entries, mistakes will still occur. As described below, all four programs permit a user to prevent an erroneous entry from being written to a file if the error is spotted early enough. However, once an error is in a file, it may be altered or deleted only by a text editor such as MicroPro Corporation's WordStar (in nondocument mode) or Edlin (a line editor provided with the disk operating system on the IBM Personal Computer).

As written in IBM Personal Computer BASIC, all four data entry programs place new records at the end of an existing file, that is, they do not overwrite existing records when a file is reopened for the addition of more data. Additionally, all four programs accept lower-case, upper-case, or mixed-case input. However, they force all input into upper case before recording or processing it. This ensures that data recorded in a "file" matches the expectations of the data processing programs, all of which also automatically convert user input to upper case.

Strictly speaking, a computer can execute only a program in machine language, not one written in a higher-level language like BASIC. On many computers, including the IBM Personal Computer, there are two ways around this problem. Most common for BASIC is the use of an "interpreter." This is a program resident in the computer that causes a sequence of preexisting machine-language programs to run in response to each BASIC instruction. The effect is to "translate" each BASIC instruction into machine language as the instruction is encountered.

The alternative, which is the rule on large computers and usually possible on small ones, is the use of a "compiler" that translates an entire program into machine language before it is run. In general, an interpreter is superior for "debugging" a program, while a compiler is superior for executing the finished product. This is because the compiled version of a program will often run far faster than the interpreted one. The difference in speed is immaterial for data entry programs (like BONECODE, DENTCODE, DENTDATA, and BONEDATA), but it is very important for programs (like MNI, AGEPROF, SMIRNOV, and BONESTAT) that manipulate or transform data. A BASIC compiler is almost essential for serious, sustained use of our data manipulation programs.

An Inconvenience Common to All the Programs

As we developed and applied the programs presented here, we realized that they share one important, inconvenient feature. To process a single sample (e.g. all the bones from one site) with each program, the user must create multiple data files. For example, in the case of the program that computes MNIs, the user must create separate files for the bones of each species rather than a single file containing all the bones in the sample. Then, in order to obtain NISPs and MNIs for the entire sample, the user must run the program MNI repeatedly, at least once for each species. This is not a serious problem for samples that contain relatively few species, but it can become tedious for those that contain many. Clearly, even greater savings in human time and effort would be achieved by a program that did not demand multiple files and that would calculate NISPs and MNIs for an entire sample in one run.

We have now in fact written such a program and the data entry programs that support it. An added advantage of the data entry programs is that they allow records to be edited (altered or deleted) internally, without the need for a separate text editor. We have not presented the enhanced programs here for two reasons. First, they are very complex and we want to test and refine them much further to ensure that they work correctly and efficiently.

Second, in order to describe their use fully, we would have to discuss some of the programming behind them, particularly the way in which they create and manage files. One result would be a longer book. Another and particularly undesirable result would be a book that was partly a programming manual rather than one about faunal analysis, which is our major interest. It is the logical or faunal analytic assumptions behind the programs on which we wish to focus here, and these are the same for both the simpler programs and their enhanced replacements. Furthermore, a person who understands the use of the programs we present here will have no difficulty in making immediate use of the new ones, and we will happily supply listings of the new programs to anyone who asks. Although the new MNI program cannot process the files created by the data entry programs in this book, the new data entry programs can automatically convert the old files into ones the new MNI program can process.

In conclusion, we note that it is often more difficult to describe the use of a computer program than to use it. This is clearly the case with our programs. We have found that students with little or no computer experience can use the programs effectively within minutes of their first attempt. Persons who have access to an IBM Personal Computer or compatible machine can easily verify this. Simply send us a blank single- or double-sided five-and-one-quarter inch diskette with a stamped, self-addressed return mailing container. We will return the diskette with the programs (original and enhanced) ready for immediate use.

6: COMPUTING THE MINIMUM NUMBER OF INDIVIDUALS IN A FOSSIL SAMPLE: PROGRAMS **MNI**, **BONECODE**, **DENTCODE**, AND **SKELDIV**

In chapter 4, we explained our preference for the minimum number of individuals (MNI) as an index of taxonomic abundance, particularly when it is presented with the number of identified specimens (NISP). In this chapter, we discuss the assumptions behind the BASIC computer program "MNI" that calculates MNIs and NISPs, given certain pertinent information on each bone and dentition in a fossil species sample. We also discuss three companion programs--"BONECODE" and "DENTCODE," which format the information MNI requires, and "SKELDIV," which creates a file containing various parameters needed to calculate MNIs. Finally, we illustrate the use of "MNI" in a sample session.

The Assumptions behind MNI: Skeletal Parts Other Than Dentitions

There are many ways to calculate MNIs. However, it is clear that some degree of standardization is desirable so that the MNIs calculated by different investigators will be at least broadly comparable. We have a preferred calculation method that we believe most analysts will find acceptable, and we have imposed this method on the program MNI, though the user has some flexibility in applying it. So, for example, we ordinarily separate paired skeletal elements between lefts and rights and take the MNI for a paired element to be the larger number, left or right. However, a user of the program who chooses to ignore the left/right distinction may simply record the side for all paired elements as "indeterminate." The program will then calculate the MNI for each paired element as the total number of (whole) elements divided by two.

Similarly, for a skeletal element with epiphyses (e.g. the proximal humerus), we ordinarily record the fusion state (fused or unfused). We take the MNI for the skeletal part to be the MNI for the fused specimens plus the MNI for the unfused ones. Sometimes it is impossible to determine whether an epiphysis was fused or not. In this instance we record fusion as indeterminate. The way MNI treats such indeterminacy is discussed below. If a user records fusion as indeterminate for all epiphyses, MNI will calculate the MNI for a skeletal part essentially as if fusion had not been recorded at all.

Furthermore, the user may tell the program MNI to calculate MNIs as if the left/right distinction, fused/unfused distinction, or both were immaterial, even if left/right and fused/unfused have been recorded in data files. Among other things, this permits the user to determine the effects of specifying side or state of fusion on MNI calculations.

In the fossil samples we have studied, the majority of identifiable bones are only fragments of once-whole specimens. We commonly ignore fragments that are identifiable to some degree but that cannot be used in MNI calculation. These include long bone shaft fragments, most cranial fragments, vertebral spines, and the blades (mostly blade fragments) of the scapula and pelvis. For the skull, we regularly record only the teeth, the mandibular and occipital condyles, and the frontlet (the part of the skull that bears antlers or horns in cervids or bovids). For vertebrae (excepting the atlas and axis), we record only centra (or centra fragments). For the scapula we record only the glenoid and for the innominate only the acetabulum.

We pointed out in chapter 4 that even when fragments are suitable for MNI calculations, recording them remains a problem. One possibility is to treat fragments as if they were complete. The result will be artificially inflated MNIs. Another possibility is to ignore fragments altogether. This will produce artificially depressed counts. A more serious difficulty with either alternative is that fragmentation does not necessarily affect all skeletal elements to the same extent. Thus the degree of MNI inflation or depression will vary from skeletal part to skeletal part, complicating the interpretation of skeletal part numbers.

Our solution to this dilemma is to record the fraction by which an identifiable bone is represented (e.g. one-third [0.33] or one half [0.5] of the right proximal metacarpal [fig. 6.1]). We use common and intuitively obvious fractions (e.g. 0.25, 0.33, 0.5, 0.67) and do not attempt great precision. Our fraction estimates are admittedly subjective, but other experienced analysts would probably replicate them closely. The program MNI expects fraction estimates, which it totals for each element. In calculating the MNI for an element, the program always rounds the total to the next whole number. For example, a total of 5.4 for the left distal humerus will result in an MNI of 6, as will 5.25 or 5.95. A total of 6.1 will result in an MNI of 7.

In most cases, we find it difficult or impossible to estimate the portion of a long bone shaft represented by a shaft fragment. Consequently, we do not ordinarily enter shaft fragments into MNI calculations (except incidentally when they are attached to fused epiphyses). However, we have encountered fossil samples where many nearly complete shafts are represented and where their ratio to epiphyses could be an interesting datum. The program MNI thus allows the entry of shaft fragments without epiphyses. There are two possible fusion states --shafts to which epiphyses have not yet fused and shafts that do not allow an assessment of epiphyseal fusion. In calculating the MNI represented by a particular bone, MNI first calculates the MNIs for unfused shafts and for unfused epiphyses. The "unfused" MNI is taken as the larger of the two separate MNIs and this is added to the MNI of epiphyses fused to shafts to obtain a final MNI for the skeletal part. It should be noted that while shaft fragments without epiphyses may be entered and are included in the bone counts, they do not enter into the MNI calculations.

We believe that the effort put into identifying the precise skeletal origin

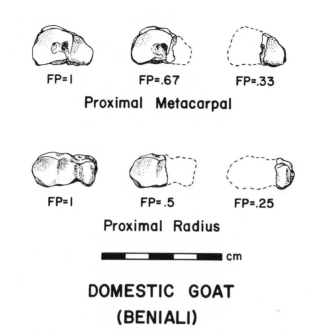

FP=1   FP=.67   FP=.33

Proximal Metacarpal

FP=1   FP=.5   FP=.25

Proximal Radius

cm

DOMESTIC GOAT
(BENIALI)

FIGURE 6.1: Complete and fragmentary proximal metacarpals and proximal radii of domestic goat (*Capra hircus*) to show the fraction estimates the authors would make. These are the fractions (FP = proximal fraction) that would be entered into the program BONECODE.

of some bones is often not justified by the results. We are satisfied to assign such bones to a relatively broad category. We then divide the total for the category by an appropriate figure to obtain the MNI. The categories involved are vertebrae, ribs, metapodials, phalanges, and (phalangeal) sesamoids. Table 6.1 shows the pertinent divisors for some taxa that are common in samples we have studied.

Regarding vertebrae, we usually ignore caudals because they are very difficult to assign to taxon. For each species, we record the atlas and axis separately, but we assign cervicals 3- 7, thoracics, and lumbars to broad categories by those names. We then divide the total number of vertebrae in a category by a number appropriate to the category and species (e.g. by five in the case of cervicals for all species). The sacral vertebrae could be treated in the same way, but they present a problem since they are usually fused into a single "sacrum." In most cases, we record the sacrum only when the first sacral vertebra is present since taxonomic assignment is difficult or impossible otherwise. Hence our divisor for the sacral category is usually one.

Regarding the ribs, we ordinarily do not record "side," though this is technically feasible. We divide the total for ribs by a divisor appropriate to the taxon.

For most species, we distinguish phalanges only as first, second, or third

TABLE 6.1 The Approximate Number of Vertebrae, Ribs, Phalanges, Metapodials, and Sesamoids per Individual in Some Mammalian Familes That Are Common in Quaternary Fossil Samples. The numbers are broadly suitable for calculating MNIs from the bones of species within the listed families.

| Family | Vertebrae | | | | Ribs |
	Cervicals 3 to 7	Thoracic	Lumbar	Sacral	
Leporidae	5	12	7	4	24
Cercopithecidae	5	13	6	3	26
Canidae	5	13	7	3	26
Mustelidae	5	15	6	3	30
Viverridae	5	14	6	3	28
Hyaenidae	5	15	5	3	30
Felidae	5	13	7	3	26
Procaviidae	5	21	7	6	42
Elephantidae	5	19	4	4	38
Equidae	5	18	6	5	36
Suidae	5	14	6	5	28
Bovidae	5	14	6	5	28
Cervidae	5	13	6	5	26

| | Metapodials per Side | | Phalanges per Side per Individual | | | Sesamoids (phalangeal) | |
	Meta-carpals	Meta-tarsals	1st	2nd	3rd	Prox-imal	Distal
Leporidae	5	5	8	10	10	?	?
Cercopithecidae	5	5	8	10	10	?	?
Canidae	4*	4*	8	10	10	?	?
Mustelidae	5	5	8	10	10	?	?
Viverridae	4*	4*	8	10	10	?	?
Hyaenidae	4	4*	8	10	10	?	?
Felidae	5	4*	8	10	10	?	?
Procaviidae	4	3	7	7	7	?	?
Elephantidae	5	5	6	10	10	?	?
Equidae	1*	1*	2	2	2	8	4
Suidae	4	4	8	8	8	32	8
Bovidae	1	1	4	4	4	16	8
Cervidae	1*	1*	4*	4*	4*	16	4

Source: Partly after Grasse (1955, 1967).
Note: *principal

and, where practical, as left or right. We then divide the totals by appropriate figures to obtain the MNIs. (For example, by four to obtain the MNI for the left first phalange of a bovid species. Left in this instance refers to side on the foot, not to side on the body). Regarding sesamoids, we generally make only one distinction--between proximal and distal. The MNI for either kind is then obtained by dividing the total for that kind by the total number in a single animal (e.g. by four in the case of the distal sesamoid in equids).

The metapodials are a complex case, since the way we treat them depends very much on the species. For most ungulates we distinguish between metacarpals and metatarsals and between lefts and rights within each category. In the case of bovids, which possess only one metapodial per foot, the result is that the MNI for metatarsals or metacarpals is the number of lefts or the number of rights, whichever is larger. (In the case of the distal end, of course, fusion is also taken into account). In other species (suids, carnivores, primates, etc). with multiple metapodials per extremity, the metacarpal or metatarsal category must be divided by an appropriate figure (e.g. by four in the case of suid left metacarpals).

In many species, the lateral metapodials are much different from the central ones in form and size. When this is the case (as in equids), we distinguish them as a separate category "lateral metapodials," which must have its own divisor to obtain an MNI (e.g. eight in the case of equid lateral metapodials, ignoring side).

There are also species for which it may be uneconomic or even impossible to distinguish between metacarpals and metatarsals. In particular, in most species, when the proximal end is missing, a distal metacarpal may be very difficult to distinguish from a distal metatarsal. In such a case, we call the problematic bone simply a "metapodial." In calculating MNIs, we assume that half of such bones are metacarpals and half are metatarsals. This is what the program MNI does as well.

Some analysts may object to this procedure, and other solutions are possible. One would be to calculate an MNI for the indeterminate metapodials as if they were a skeletal part completely distinct from definite metacarpals and metatarsals. Another would be to divide the indeterminate metapodials between metacarpals and metatarsals in the same ratio in which definite metacarpals and metatarsals occur. Alternatively, where indeterminate metapodials are very common, a composite metapodial MNI could be computed, incorporating all metapodials whether identified as metacarpals, metatarsals, or indeterminate metapodials.

The program MNI requires a user to enter divisors for the various categories of vertebrae, ribs, metapodials, phalanges, and sesamoids, depending upon the species. In most zoological families the divisors are the same for all species, or such differences as exist among species are too small to affect MNI calculations materially. The program MNI is therefore equipped to obtain average values for a family from a background file found on the same computer system as the program. This file can be created by the companion program SKELDIV (skeletal divisors) described below. The existence of an appropriate background file obviates the need to enter skeletal part divisors in response to a prompt series during each MNI run.

Table 6.2 lists the skeletal parts that MNI deals with, as it is now written. With minimal rewriting the program could easily deal with finer categories within the vertebrae, ribs, metapodials, phalanges, and sesamoids. Alternatively, the user could be given the option of deciding whether to use finer or broader categories or some combination of the two. This would require more substantial program revision.

The Assumptions behind MNI: Dentitions

In the fossil samples we have studied, teeth tend to occur as isolated specimens, separated from mandibles and maxillae. However, partial and even complete mandibles and maxillae do occur. Sometimes they contain only empty sockets or a combination of empty sockets and teeth in place. The various ways teeth and jaws occur forces us to calculate MNIs on a tooth by tooth basis.

In addition to tooth type (e.g. I2, M3, or dP4), we ordinarily record jaw (upper or lower) and side (left or right). It is usually easy to determine side, but determining jaw may be problematic, especially for incisors and canines. There are various ways such indeterminacy may be handled in MNI calculations. The way the program MNI does this is discussed below. If jaw, side, or both are consistently recorded as indeterminate, MNI essentially ignores one or both categories in calculating MNIs.

In addition to jaw and side, we also note whether a tooth is in place or isolated or whether only an empty socket is present. We then calculate three preliminary MNIs for each tooth (e.g. the lower left M3)--one on empty sockets, another on isolated specimens, and a third on teeth in sockets. We then add the number of specimens in sockets to the number that are isolated or to the number of empty sockets, whichever is larger. We regard the sum as the final MNI for the tooth. The program MNI follows the same procedure.

We regard the MNI for the mandible as the largest of the MNIs for individual mandibular teeth, and the MNI for the maxilla as the largest of the MNIs for maxillary teeth. It is technically possible for an individual to possess both a deciduous tooth and its permanent replacement at the same time, but this is rare, except for clearly unerupted permanent tooth crowns and for even rarer near-shed deciduous tooth caps. We record these but do not enter them into MNI calculations. This permits us to compute an MNI for a particular dental position (e.g. that occupied first by dP4 and then by P4). This is the sum of the MNI for the deciduous tooth in that position plus the MNI for the permanent tooth there. MNI uses such composite deciduous and permanent sums to calculate the final MNIs for the mandible and maxilla.

In some species, it may be very difficult to distinguish adjacent teeth from one another. In such instances, we record a tooth simply as a left lower incisor, an upper right molar, and so forth. MNI permits the entry of

TABLE 6.2 The Skeletal Parts (Other Than Teeth) That May Be Entered into the Program MNI, with the Abbreviations That the Program Expects

Skeletal Part	Abbreviation	Skeletal Part	Abbreviation
Frontlet	FR	Trapezium	TM
Occiptal condyle	OC	Metacarpal	MC
Mandibular condyle	MD	First phalange	1P
Hyoid	HY	Second phalange	2P
Atlas	AT	Third phalange	3P
Axis	AX	Innominate	IN
Cervical vertebrae 3 to 7	CE	Femur	FE
Thoracic vertebrae	TH	Patella	PA
Lumbar vertebrae	LU	Tibia	TI
Sacral vertebrae	SA	Fibula	FI
Rib	RI	Astragalus	AS
Clavicle	CL	Calcaneum	CA
Scapula	SC	Cuboid	CD
Humerus	HU	Navicular	NA
Radius	RA	External Cuneiform	C1
Ulna	UL	Internal Cuneiform	C2
Cuneiform (carpal)	CU	Middle Cuneiform	C3
Unciform	UN	Metatarsal	MT
Lunate	LN	Proximal sesamoid	PS
Magnum	MA	Distal sesamoid	DS
Scaphoid	SD	Metapodial	MP
Pisiform	PI	Lateral metapodial	LM
Trapezoid	TD		

such loosely defined dental (even the type "cheek tooth"). The way it deals with this kind of indeterminacy in calculating MNIs is discussed in the section on indeterminacy below.

File Names

We have developed a convention for naming data files that are to be processed by MNI. It assumes that a single file will contain skeletal parts from only one site and one species. The first two to four letters of the file name denote the site (e.g. KRM for Klasies River Mouth), and the next two to four letters denote the species. Ordinarily, we select the first letter of the genus name and the first letter of the species name (e.g. PC for *Procavia capensis*), but if such a combination of letters could represent more than one species, we add letters to make the designation unique (e.g., PRCA for *Procavia capensis* in a site that also contains *Pelea capreolus*).

MNI treats teeth and jaws very differently from other skeletal elements.

As a consequence, two kinds of files are required. For ones that contain all skeletal parts except teeth (that is, bones in the narrow sense), we use the file extension ".BON". For files that contain only teeth (dentitions), we use the extension ".DEN". Examples of complete file names then are KRMPC.BON for Klasies River Mouth *Procavia capensis* skeletal parts and KRMPC.DEN for Klasies River Mouth *Procavia capensis* teeth.

It is not necessary to follow our file-naming conventions precisely, but as now written MNI requires that a file name end in "BON" if the user has previously indicated that the file to be processed contains bones other than teeth. Similarly, it requires that a file name end in "DEN" if the user has indicated that the file to be processed contains only teeth.

Entry of Skeletal Parts other than Dentitions: Program BONECODE
MNI assumes there will be ten items of information on each skeletal part. Additionally, the ten items must occur in the following order:

   1) Provenience unit within a site.
   2) Skeletal part name.
   3) Side (left, right, or indeterminate).
   4) Bone portion (proximal, distal, or complete).
   5) State of fusion of the proximal end.
   6) Fraction of the proximal end represented.
   7) State of fusion of the distal end.
   8) Fraction of the distal end represented.
   9) Qualitative condition of bone (Burned, carnivore-Chewed, rodent-Gnawed, Rolled, Weathered, and/or Cut).
   10) Catalog Number of a bone.

To ensure that all ten items are recorded in the necessary order, we have written the program BONECODE that prompts the user for them. BONECODE includes "error traps" to reduce possible entry error, and it automatically enters an item of information when this has been predetermined by a previous entry. For example, if the user has indicated that only the proximal end of a bone is present, BONECODE does not prompt for information on the distal end. Instead, it automatically records distal state of fusion as not relevant ("N") and distal fraction as zero.

Figure 6.2 lists BONECODE and figure 6.3 shows a sample session. Figure 6.4 shows the file created by the session. Table 6.3 summarizes the BONECODE prompts, with possible responses and their effects.

BONECODE asks first for the name of the file into which the skeletal data will be placed. We suggested a naming procedure in the last section. The only vital point is that the name end in the letters "BON". If the user enters a file name without an extension, BONECODE will automatically add the extension ".BON".

BONECODE next asks "Do you want to enter a comment on each bone (Y/N)". This option enables the user to include qualitative information about each bone, such as whether it is burned, cut, or carnivore-chewed. If the answer is Y, in the subsequent session BONECODE will prompt for this information on each bone. Otherwise it will automatically record it as

FIGURE 6.2: Listing of the program BONECODE for entering skeletal parts into a computer file.

```
1000 REM IBM Personal Computer BASIC (R. G. Klein, 23 January 1984)
1010 CLS
1020 DEFINT A-Z
1030 KEY OFF
1040 DIM SKPT$(46,2),FUST$(5,2),CMMT$(6,2)
1050 '
1060 REM Lookup table for skeletal parts and abbreviations
1070 FOR I=1 TO 46:FOR J=1 TO 2:READ SKPT$(I,J):NEXT:NEXT
1080 DATA HU,humerus,RA,radius,UL,ulna,MC,metacarpal,FE,femur,TI,tibia
1090 DATA FI,fibula,MT,metatarsal,CA,calcaneum,CL,clavicle,SC,scapula
1100 DATA 1P,first phalange,2P,second phalange,3P,third phalange
1110 DATA MP,metapodial,LM,lateral metapodial,RI,rib,AX,axis,CE,cervicals 3-7
1120 DATA TH,thoracics,LU,lumbars,SA,sacral,CU,cuneiform,UN,unciform,LN,lunate
1130 DATA MA,magnum,SD,scaphoid,PI,pisiform,TD,trapezoid,TM,trapezium
1140 DATA PA,patella,AS,astragalus,NA,navicular,CD,cuboid,C1,lateral cuneiform
1150 DATA C2,medial cuneiform,C3,middle cuneiform,HY,hyoid
1160 DATA MD,mandibular condyle,IN,innominate,FR,frontlet,OC,occipital condyle
1170 DATA PS,proximal sesamoid,DS,distal sesamoid,AT,atlas,??,indeterminate
1180 '
1190 REM Lookup table for fusion states and abbreviations
1200 FOR I=1 TO 5:FOR J=1 TO 2:READ FUST$(I,J):NEXT:NEXT
1210 DATA EF,epiphysis fused,EU,epiphysis unfused
1220 DATA EI,epiphyseal fusion indeterminate,SU,shaft unfused
1230 DATA SI,shaft indeterminate
1240 '
1250 REM Lookup table for comments and abbreviations
1260 FOR I=1 TO 6:FOR J=1 TO 2:READ CMMT$(I,J):NEXT:NEXT
1270 DATA B,Burned,C,(carnivore-)Chewed,G,(rodent-)Gnawed,R,Rolled
1280 DATA W,Weathered,X,Cut
1290 '
1300 REM Function keys
1310 KEY 1,"CHANGE"+CHR$(13):KEY 2,"QUIT"+CHR$(13):KEY 3,"HELP"+CHR$(13)
1320 KEY 4,"MULT"+CHR$(13)
1330 '
1340 PRINT "BONECODE. Creates bone files for MNI. To see abbreviations for"
1350 PRINT "bones, bone conditions, or fusion states, type 'HELP' in response"
1360 PRINT "to requests for 'Skeletal element', 'Fusion state', or 'Comment.'"
1370 PRINT
1380 '
1390 CONTINUE=-1 'File name entry
1400 WHILE CONTINUE
1410   INPUT "File Name for bones ".BON"";ANS$:GOSUB 3840:FLNM$=ANS$
1420   IF INSTR(FLNM$,":")=0 AND LEN(FLNM$)<=12 AND RIGHT$(FLNM$,4)=".BON"
         THEN CONTINUE=0
1430   IF INSTR(FLNM$,":")=2 AND LEN(FLNM$)<=14 AND RIGHT$(FLNM$,4)=".BON"
         THEN CONTINUE=0
1440   IF INSTR(FLNM$,":")=2 AND INSTR(FLNM$,".")=0 AND LEN(FLNM$)<=10
         THEN FLNM$=FLNM$+".BON":CONTINUE=0
1450   IF INSTR(FLNM$,":")=0 AND INSTR(FLNM$,".")=0 AND LEN(FLNM$)<=8
         THEN FLNM$=FLNM$+".BON":CONTINUE=0
1460   IF CONTINUE THEN BEEP:PRINT "Illegal File Name!"
1470 WEND
1480 CLOSE:OPEN FLNM$ FOR APPEND AS #1
1490 '
1500 CTYN$=""
1510 WHILE CTYN$<>"Y" AND CTYN$<>"N"
1520   INPUT "Do you want to enter a comment on each bone (Y/N)";ANS$:
         GOSUB 3840:CTYN$=ANS$
1530   IF CTYN$<>"Y" AND CTYN$<>"N" THEN BEEP
```

```
1540 WEND
1550 '
1560 CNYN$=""
1570 WHILE CNYN$<>"Y" AND CNYN$<>"N"
1580   INPUT "Do you want to enter a catalog number for each bone (Y/N)";ANS$:
          GOSUB 3840:CNYN$=ANS$
1590   IF CNYN$<>"Y" AND CNYN$<>"N" THEN BEEP
1600 WEND
1610 '
1620 REM Provenience unit entry
1630 LV$="":CHANGE=0
1640 WHILE LV$=""
1650 INPUT "Provenience Unit";ANS$:GOSUB 3840:LV$=ANS$
1660   IF LV$="QUIT" THEN CLOSE:CLS:END
1670   IF LV$="CHANGE" THEN CHANGE=-1
1680   IF LV$="" THEN BEEP:PRINT "Must enter a provenience unit!"
1690 WEND
1700 IF CHANGE THEN 1500 'ask about comment and cat no again
1710 '
1720 REM Skeletal element entry
1730 NSK=1 'number of times to write bone to file
1740 SK=0:QUIT=0:CHANGE=0
1750 WHILE SK=0
1760   INPUT "Skeletal element";ANS$:GOSUB 3840:SK$=ANS$
1770   IF SK$="QUIT" THEN QUIT=-1:SK=-1
1780   IF SK$="CHANGE" THEN CHANGE=-1:SK=-1
1790   FOR I=1 TO 46
1800     IF SK=-1 THEN I=46
1810     IF SK$=SKPT$(I,1) THEN SK=I:I=46
1820   NEXT
1830   IF SK$="MULT" THEN GOSUB 3910
1840   IF SK$="HELP" THEN GOSUB 3540
1850   IF SK=0 AND SK$<>"MULT" AND SK$<>"HELP" THEN BEEP:
          PRINT "Illegal skeletal part!"
1860 WEND
1870 IF QUIT THEN CLOSE:CLS:END
1880 IF CHANGE THEN 1630 'new level
1890 '
1900 REM Side entry
1910 CONTINUE=-1
1920 IF SK>=17 AND SK<=22 THEN LR$="N":CONTINUE=0  'non-paired prox/dist bones
1930 IF SK>=43 THEN LR$="N":CONTINUE=0  'non-paired non-prox/dist bones
1940 CHANGE=0:QUIT=0
1950 WHILE CONTINUE
1960   IF SK$="IN" OR SK$="FR" OR SK$="OC" THEN
          PRINT "Left, Right, Indeterminate, or Both (L/R/B/I)"; ELSE
          PRINT "Left, Right, or Indeterminate (L/R/I)";
1970   INPUT ANS$:GOSUB 3840:LR$=ANS$
1980   IF LR$="QUIT" THEN QUIT=-1:CONTINUE=0
1990   IF LR$="CHANGE" THEN CHANGE=-1:CONTINUE=0
2000   IF LR$="L" OR LR$="R" OR LR$="I" THEN CONTINUE=0
2010   IF SK$="IN" AND LR$="B" THEN CONTINUE=0
2020   IF SK$="FR" AND LR$="B" THEN CONTINUE=0
2030   IF SK$="OC" AND LR$="B" THEN CONTINUE=0
2040   IF CONTINUE THEN BEEP:PRINT "Must be CHANGE, QUIT, L, R, I, (OR B)!"
2050 WEND
2060 IF CHANGE THEN 1630 'new level
2070 IF QUIT THEN CLOSE:CLS:END
2080 '
```

```
2090 REM Proximal/distal entry
2100 CONTINUE=-1
2110 IF SK$="SC" THEN PD$="P":CONTINUE=0
2120 IF SK>=23 THEN PD$="N":CONTINUE=0 'non-prox/dist bones
2130 CHANGE=0:QUIT=0
2140 WHILE CONTINUE
2150   INPUT "Proximal, Distal, or Complete (P/D/C)";ANS$:GOSUB 3840:PD$=ANS$
2160   IF PD$="P" OR PD$="D" OR PD$="C" THEN CONTINUE=0
2170   IF PD$="CHANGE" THEN CHANGE=-1:CONTINUE=0
2180   IF PD$="QUIT" THEN QUIT=-1:CONTINUE=0
2190   IF CONTINUE THEN BEEP:PRINT "Must be CHANGE, QUIT, P, D, or C!"
2200 WEND
2210 IF CHANGE THEN 1630 'new level
2220 IF QUIT THEN CLOSE:CLS:END
2230 '
2240 CONTINUE=-1:UNNECESSARY=0 'Proximal fusion entry
2250 IF SK>=23 AND SK$<>"FR" THEN PES$="N":CONTINUE=0 'non-prox/dist bones
2260 IF PD$="D" THEN PES$="N":CONTINUE=0
2270 IF SK$="MP" OR SK$="MC" OR SK$="MT" OR SK$="LM" OR SK$="3P"
        THEN UNNECESSARY=-1
2280 IF PD$="P" AND UNNECESSARY THEN PES$="EF":CONTINUE=0
2290 IF PD$="C" AND UNNECESSARY THEN PES$="EF":CONTINUE=0
2300 IF CONTINUE THEN ES=1:GOSUB 2990:PES$=ES$
2310 IF CHANGE THEN 1630 'new level
2320 IF QUIT THEN CLOSE:CLS:END
2330 '
2340 CONTINUE=-1 'proximal fraction entry
2350 IF PD$="D" OR SK$="??" THEN FP!=0:CONTINUE=0
2360 WHILE CONTINUE
2370   IF SK<=22 THEN INPUT "Fraction-proximal";ANS$:GOSUB 3840:
        GOSUB 3220:FP!=VAL(ANS$) 'prox/dist bones
2380   IF SK>=23 AND LR$="B" THEN INPUT "Fraction-left";ANS$:GOSUB 3840:
        GOSUB 3220:FP!=VAL(ANS$) 'paired,non-prox/dist
2390   IF SK>=23 AND LR$<>"B" THEN INPUT "Fraction";ANS$:GOSUB 3840:
        GOSUB 3220:FP!=VAL(ANS$) 'non-paired non-prox/dist
2400 WEND
2410 IF CHANGE THEN 1630 'new level
2420 IF QUIT THEN CLOSE:CLS:END
2430 '
2440 REM Distal fusion entry
2450 CONTINUE=-1:UNNECESSARY=0
2460 IF SK$="1P" OR SK$="2P" OR SK$="3P" OR SK$="CA" OR SK$="RI"
        THEN UNNECESSARY=-1
2470 IF PD$="D" AND UNNECESSARY THEN DES$="EF":CONTINUE=0
2480 IF PD$="C" AND UNNECESSARY THEN DES$="EF":CONTINUE=0
2490 IF PD$="P" THEN DES$="N":CONTINUE=0
2500 IF SK>=23 THEN DES$="N":CONTINUE=0 'non prox/dist bones
2510 IF CONTINUE THEN ES=2:GOSUB 2990:DES$=ES$
2520 IF CHANGE THEN 1630 'new level
2530 IF QUIT THEN CLOSE:CLS:END
2540 '
2550 REM Distal fraction entry
2560 CONTINUE=-1
2570 IF PD$="P" OR SK$="??" THEN FD!=0:CONTINUE=0
2580 IF SK>=23 AND LR$<>"B" THEN FD!=0:CONTINUE=0 'non-paired,non prox/dist
2590 WHILE CONTINUE
2600   IF SK<=22 THEN INPUT "Fraction-distal";ANS$ 'prox/dist bones
2610   IF SK>=23 AND LR$="B" THEN INPUT "Fraction-right";ANS$
        'paired,non-prox/dist
```

```
2620   GOSUB 3840:GOSUB 3220:FD!=VAL(ANS$)
2630 WEND
2640 IF CHANGE THEN 1630 'new level
2650 IF QUIT THEN CLOSE:CLS:END
2660 '
2670 REM Comment entry
2680 CORRECTLET=0
2690 IF CTYN$="N" THEN CT$="N":CORRECTLET=-1
2700 WHILE CORRECTLET=0
2710   UNUSUAL=0
2720   INPUT "Comment (Car Ret or B,C,G,R,X, and/or W)";ANS$:
          GOSUB 3840:CT$=ANS$
2730   IF CT$="" THEN CT$="N":UNUSUAL=-1:CORRECTLET=-1
2740   IF CT$="CHANGE" THEN CHANGE=-1:UNUSUAL=-1:CORRECTLET=-1
2750   IF CT$="QUIT" THEN QUIT=-1:UNUSUAL=-1:CORRECTLET=-1
2760   IF CT$="HELP" THEN UNUSUAL=-1:GOSUB 3540
2770   IF NOT UNUSUAL THEN GOSUB 3300 'check for proper letters
2780   IF CORRECTLET=0 AND NOT UNUSUAL THEN BEEP:PRINT "Illegal comment!"
2790 WEND
2800 IF CHANGE THEN 1630 'new level
2810 IF QUIT THEN CLOSE:CLS:END
2820 '
2830 REM Catalog number entry
2840 CN$=""
2850 IF CNYN$="N" THEN CN$="#"
2860 WHILE CN$=""
2870   INPUT "Catalog Number";CN$
2880   IF LEN(CN$)=0 THEN CN$="#"
2890   IF CN$="CHANGE" OR CN$="change" THEN CHANGE=-1
2900   IF CN$="QUIT" OR CN$="quit" THEN QUIT=-1
2910 WEND
2920 IF CHANGE THEN 1630
2930 IF QUIT THEN CLOSE:CLS:END
2940 '
2950 GOSUB 3440 'write to file
2960 SK$="":LR$="":PD$="":PES$="":FP$="":DES$="":FD$="":CT$="":CN$=""
2970 GOTO 1730 'start again from skeletal part
2980 '
2990 REM Fusion state entry
3000   CHANGE=0:QUIT=0
3010   WHILE CONTINUE
3020     UNUSUAL=0
3030     IF SK$="FR" THEN PRINT "Male, Female or Indeterminate (M/F/I)";
3040     IF ES=1 AND SK$<>"FR" THEN
            PRINT "State of fusion-proximal (EF/EU/EI/SU/SI)";
3050     IF ES=2 THEN PRINT "State of fusion-distal (EF/EU/EI/SU/SI)";
3060     INPUT ANS$:GOSUB 3840:ES$=ANS$
3070     FOR I=1 TO 5
3080       IF SK$<>"FR" AND ES$=FUST$(I,1) THEN CONTINUE=0
3090     NEXT
3100     IF SK$="FR" AND ES$="M" THEN CONTINUE=0
3110     IF SK$="FR" AND ES$="F" THEN CONTINUE=0
3120     IF SK$="FR" AND ES$="I" THEN CONTINUE=0
3130     IF ES$="CHANGE" THEN CHANGE=-1:CONTINUE=0
3140     IF ES$="HELP" THEN UNUSUAL=-1:GOSUB 3540
3150     IF ES$="QUIT" THEN QUIT=-1:CONTINUE=0
3160     IF ES$="EU" AND PD$="C" THEN UNUSUAL=-1:CONTINUE=-1:BEEP:
            PRINT "Cannot be complete bone with unfused epiphysis!"
3170     IF ES$="EI" AND PD$="C" THEN UNUSUAL=-1:CONTINUE=-1:BEEP:
```

```
          PRINT "Cannot be complete bone with indeterminate epiphysis!"
3180    IF CONTINUE AND NOT UNUSUAL THEN BEEP:PRINT "Illegal entry!"
3190  WEND
3200 RETURN
3210 '
3220 REM Fraction entry
3230    CHANGE=0:QUIT=0
3240    IF ANS$="CHANGE" THEN CHANGE=-1:CONTINUE=0
3250    IF ANS$="QUIT" THEN QUIT=-1:CONTINUE=0
3260    IF VAL(ANS$)>0 AND VAL(ANS$)<=1 THEN CONTINUE=0
3270    IF CONTINUE AND CHANGE=0 AND QUIT=0 THEN BEEP:
          PRINT "Must be CHANGE, QUIT, or >0 and <=1!"
3280 RETURN
3290 '
3300 REM Check for correct letters in comment
3310    CORRECTLET=-1
3320    FOR I=1 TO LEN(CT$)
3330       L$(I)=MID$(CT$,I,1)
3340       IF L$(I)<>"B" AND L$(I)<>"C" AND L$(I)<>"G" AND L$(I)<>"R" AND
          L$(I)<>"X" AND L$(I)<>"W" THEN CORRECTLET=0
3350    NEXT I
3360    IF CORRECTLET=0 THEN RETURN
3370 '
3380 REM Check for duplicate letter in comment
3390    FOR F=1 TO LEN(CT$):FOR S=F+1 TO LEN(CT$)
3400       IF L$(F)=L$(S) THEN CORRECTLET=0
3410    NEXT S:NEXT F
3420 RETURN
3430 '
3440 REM Write to file
3450    FOR I=1 TO NSK
3460       PRINT#1,LV$","SK$","LR$","PD$","PES$","FP!","DES$","FD!","CT$","CN$
3470    NEXT
3480    CLS
3490    LOCATE 25,1:PRINT "Last Entry:";
3500    PRINT LV$","SK$","LR$","PD$","PES$","FP!","DES$","FD!","CT$","CN$;
3510    LOCATE 1,1
3520 RETURN
3530 '
3540 REM HELP
3550    CLS
3560    LOCATE 1,1:COLOR 0,7:PRINT "SKELETAL PART ABBREVIATIONS" SPC(5)
3570    FOR I=1 TO 21:FOR J=1 TO 2
3580       LOCATE I+1,1:COLOR 7,0:PRINT SKPT$(I,1) TAB(6) SKPT$(I,J)
3590       LOCATE I+1,39:COLOR 7,0:PRINT SKPT$(I+21,1) TAB(45) SKPT$(I+21,J)
3600    NEXT:PRINT:NEXT
3610    LOCATE 25,1:PRINT "Press <ENTER> to continue ...";
3620    ZZ$=INKEY$:WHILE ZZ$="":ZZ$=INKEY$:WEND
3630    CLS
3640    LOCATE 1,1:COLOR 0,7:PRINT "More skeletal part abbreviations"SPC(5)
3650    FOR I=22 TO 23:FOR J=1 TO 2
3660       LOCATE I-20,1:COLOR 7,0:PRINT SKPT$(I+21,1) SPC(3) SKPT$(I+21,J)
3670       LOCATE I-20,39:COLOR 7,0:PRINT SKPT$(I+23,1) SPC(3) SKPT$(I+23,J)
3680    NEXT:PRINT:NEXT
3690    LOCATE 5,1:COLOR 0,7:PRINT "FUSION STATE ABBREVIATIONS" SPC(5)
3700    LOCATE 6,1
3710    FOR I=1 TO 5:FOR J=1 TO 2
3720       COLOR 7,0:PRINT FUST$ (I,J),
3730    NEXT:PRINT:NEXT
```

```
3740   LOCATE 12,1:COLOR 0,7:PRINT "BONE STATE ABBREVIATIONS" SPC(3)
3750   LOCATE 13,1
3760   FOR I=1 TO 6:FOR J=1 TO 2
3770     COLOR 7,0:PRINT CMMT$ (I,J),
3780   NEXT:PRINT:NEXT
3790   LOCATE 25,1:PRINT "Press enter to return to program operation...";
3800   ZZ$=INKEY$:WHILE ZZ$="":ZZ$=INKEY$:WEND
3810   CLS
3820 RETURN
3830 '
3840 REM Capitalization
3850   FOR N=1 TO LEN(ANS$)
3860     LTR$=MID$(ANS$,N,1)
3870     IF "a"<=LTR$ AND LTR$<="z" THEN MID$(ANS$,N,1)=CHR$(ASC(LTR$)-32)
3880   NEXT
3890 RETURN
3900 '
3910 REM Write bone to file multiple times
3920   NSK=0
3930   WHILE NSK<1
3940     INPUT "How many times to write same bone to file";NSK
3950     IF NSK<1 THEN BEEP:PRINT "Must be >1!"
3960   WEND
3970 RETURN
```

not relevant (N) for each bone.

BONECODE next asks "Do you want to enter a catalog number for each bone (Y/N)". If the answer is Y, BONECODE will prompt for a catalog (or serial) number for each bone in the subsequent session. Otherwise it will automatically record the catalog number as "#". The answer must be Y or N, or BONECODE will repeat the question. For reasons discussed in the introduction to Part II, we routinely answer N.

BONECODE next prompts for "Provenience Unit". We suggest easily entered, mnemonic abbreviations for field units (e.g. 14 for level 14 or BOL3 for Brown Orange Loam 3). If the response to "Provenience Unit" is "CHANGE", BONECODE asks again if the user wants (first) to enter a comment for each bone and (second) a catalog number. Thus a user who has separated bones between ones with comments or catalog numbers and ones without can economically enter them all in the same session.

If the user types "QUIT" in response to "Provenience Unit," BONECODE closes the file and terminates the session. QUIT has the same effect in response to all succeeding prompts.

The next prompt is for "Skeletal element." The proper response is a two-letter abbreviation, ordinarily comprising the first two letters of a skeletal element name. Table 6.2 lists the abbreviations the program expects. If the user is not entering individual catalog numbers and has grouped multiple occurrences of identical bones from the same provenience unit, the proper response to "Skeletal element" is "MULT". BONECODE will then ask "How many times to write same bone to file", followed by a renewed request for "Skeletal element". It will then automatically record the same bone and associated information in the file as many times as the user specified. For example, if the user has ten identical left distal fused humeri, replying "10" to "How many times to write same bone to file" will cause BONECODE to write ten separate but identical humeri to file.

If the response to "Skeletal element" is "HELP", BONECODE will list the abbreviations for skeletal parts on the screen. If the response is "CHANGE", BONECODE will reinitiate the prompt sequence from "Provenience Unit". CHANGE has the same effect in response to all succeeding prompts. If the response to "Skeletal element" is anything other than one of the bone abbreviations in table 6.2, MULT, HELP, CHANGE, or QUIT, the program prints an error message and requests "Skeletal element" again.

What happens next depends on what skeletal part has been entered. If the part is a humerus, radius, ulna, metacarpal, femur, tibia, fibula, metatarsal, calcaneum, clavicle, scapula, first phalange, second phalange, third phalange, metapodial or lateral metapodial, the program prompts for side--"Left, Right, or Indeterminate (L/R/I)." The response must be L, R, I, QUIT, or CHANGE. Otherwise BONECODE prints an error message and reprompts for side.

For all the above-listed bones but the scapula, BONECODE next requests bone portion--"Proximal, Distal, or Complete (P/D/C)." For the scapula, it assumes that only the glenoid fossa is being entered and thus automatically records "P" for the portion of bone present. With regard to the other skeletal parts, if the response to the bone portion prompt is anything but P, D, C, CHANGE, or QUIT, BONECODE prints an error message and reprompts for bone portion.

If the response to bone portion was P or C, BONECODE then seeks information on state of proximal epiphyseal fusion. If the skeletal part is a proximal or complete metacarpal, metatarsal, metapodial, or third phalange, BONECODE automatically enters fused ("EF") for proximal state of fusion. If the skeletal part is a proximal or complete humerus, radius, ulna, femur, tibia, fibula, calcaneum, clavicle, first phalange, or second phalange, BONECODE asks the user for "State of fusion-proximal." There are five possible responses: (1) EF (epiphysis, fused to shaft); (2) EU (epiphysis, unfused to shaft); (3) EI (epiphysis, fusion indeterminate); (4) SU (shaft, unfused to epiphysis); and (5) SI (shaft, fusion indeterminate). A response of HELP causes the codes for fusion state to be listed on the screen. Any response but EF, EU, EI, SU, SI, CHANGE, HELP, or QUIT causes BONECODE to print an error message and to reprompt for "State of fusion-proximal."

FIGURE 6.3: A BONECODE sample session, involving bones of the grysbok (*Raphicerus melanotis*) from Klasies River Mouth, South Africa.

BONECODE -- Creates bone files for MNI. To see abbreviations for bones, bone conditions, or fusion states, type 'HELP' in response to requests for 'Skeletal element', "Fustion state' or 'Comment.'

File Name for Bones [.BON] ? KRMRM.BON
Do you want to enter a comment on each bone ? Y
Do you want to enter a catalog number for each bone (Y/N) ? N
Provenience Unit ? 17B
Skeletal element ? FR
Left, Right, Indeterminate, or Both (L/R/B/I) ? R
Male, Female, or Indeterminate ? M
Fraction ? 1
COMMENT (Car Ret or B,C,G,R,X, and/or W) ? B

Skeletal element ? OC
Left, Right, Indeterminate, or Both (L/R/B/I) ? B
Fraction-left ? .75
Fraction-right ? 1
COMMENT (Car Ret or B,C,G,R,X, and/or W) ? BC

Skeletal element ? TH
Proximal, Distal, or Complete (P/D/C) ? C
State of fusion-proximal (EF/EU/EI/SU/SI) ? EF
Fraction-proximal ? .5
State of fusion-distal (EF/EU/EI/SU/SI) ? EF
Fraction-distal ? .5
COMMENT (Car Ret or B,C,G,R,X, and/or W) ? GRW

Skeletal element ? CHANGE
Provenience Unit ? 18
Skeletal element ? HU
Left, Right, or Indeterminate (L/R/I) ? R
Proximal, Distal, or Complete (P/D/C) ? D
State of fusion-distal (EF/EU/EI/SU/SI) ? EU
Fraction-distal ? .67
COMMENT (Car Ret or B,C,G,R,X, and/or W) ?

Skeletal element ? LN
Left, Right, or Indeterminate (L/R/I) ? L
Fraction ? .5
COMMENT (Car Ret or B,C,G,R,X, and/or W) ?

Skeletal element ? 1P
Left, Right, or Indeterminate (L/R/I) ? R

Proximal, Distal, or Complete (P/D/C) ? C
State of fusion-proximal (EF/EU/EI/SU/SI) ? SU
Fraction-proximal ? 1
Fraction-distal ? 1
COMMENT (Car Ret or B,C,G,R,X, and/or W) ? C

Skeletal element ? MC
Left, Right, or Indeterminate (L/R/I) ? I
Proximal, Distal, or Complete (P/D/C) ? P
Fraction-proximal ? .2
COMMENT (Car Ret or B,C,G,R,X, and/or W) ?

Skeletal element ? QUIT

BONECODE next asks for "Fraction-proximal." The fraction should be entered as a decimal (e.g. .33 or .5). The response must be CHANGE, QUIT, or a number between 0 and 1. Any other response leads to an error message and a renewed request for "Fraction-proximal."

Once "Fraction-proximal" has been successfully entered, BONECODE seeks information on distal state of fusion and distal fraction. If the response to bone portion was P, BONECODE automatically enters N (not relevant) for distal state of fusion and 0 for distal fraction. Otherwise, it asks the user for "State of fusion-distal." Acceptable responses are EF, EU, EI, SU, SI, CHANGE, QUIT, or HELP, exactly as for "State of fusion-proximal." Any other response evokes an error message and a renewed request. Appropriate responses to "Fraction-distal" are CHANGE, QUIT, or a decimal fraction, just as for "Fractionproximal."

If the response to "Proximal, Distal, or Complete (P/D/C)" was D, BONECODE automatically records proximal state of fusion as N (not relevant) and proximal fraction as 0. It prompts the user only for "State of fusion-distal" and "Fraction-distal." If the skeletal element is a phalange, calcaneum or rib, it automatically records distal state of fusion as EF and prompts only for "Fraction-distal."

> 17B,FR,R,N,M,1,N,0,B,#
> 17B,OC,B,N,N,.75,N,1,BC,#
> 17B,TH,N,C,EF,.5,EF,.5,GRW,#
> 18,HU,R,D,N,0,EU,.67,N,#
> 18,LN,L,N,N,.5,N,0,N,#
> 18,1P,R,C,SU,1,EF,1,C,#
> 18,MC,I,P,EF,.2,N,0,N,#

FIGURE 6.4: The file created by the BONECODE sample session in figure 6.3.

TABLE 6.3 BONECODE Prompts with Accepted Responses and Their Effects

Prompts	Responses and Effects
1) File Name for for bones ".BON"	Name must have the extension ".BON". If no extension is entered, ".BON" will be added automatically.
2) Do you want to enter a comment on each bone (Y/N)	Y -- causes program to prompt for information on state of each bone. N -- causes program to record state of each bone as N (not relevant).
3) Do you want to enter a catalog number for each bone (Y/N)	Y -- causes program to prompt for a catalog catalog number for each bone. N -- causes program to record the catalog number for each bone as "#".
4) Provenience Unit	Any combination of letters and numbers (easily entered, mnemonic abbreviations of field units are recommended.) CHANGE -- causes program to begin again from prompts 2 and 3. QUIT -- closes file and terminates session.
5) Skeletal Element	A 2-character abbreviation for a bone name, as listed in table 6.2. MULT -- if the same bone is to be recorded in the file multiple times. Leads to prompt 6. HELP -- causes bone name abbreviations to be listed on the screen. CHANGE -- causes the prompt sequence to begin again from "Provenience Unit". QUIT -- closes file and terminates session.
6) (If response to 5 was MULT) How many times to write same bone to file.	An integer indicating the number of times a a particular bone is to be automatically recorded in the file.
7a) Left, Right, or Indeterminate	L, R, B, or I -- causes side to be recorded, leading to next prompt. CHANGE -- causes the prompt sequence to begin again from "Provenience Unit."

7b) Left, Right, Both, or Indeterminate	QUIT -- closes file and terminates session.
8) Proximal, Distal, or Complete	P, D, or C -- causes bone portion to be recorded, leading to next prompt. CHANGE -- causes the prompt sequence to begin again from "Provenience Unit". QUIT -- closes file and terminates session.
9) Male Female, or Indeterminate	M, F, or I -- causes sex to be recorded, leading to next prompt. CHANGE -- causes prompt sequence to begin again from "Provenience Unit". QUIT -- closes file and terminates session.
10a) Fraction 10b) Fraction-left 10c) Fraction-right 10d) Fraction-proximal 10e) Fraction-distal	CHANGE -- causes prompt sequence to begin again from "Provenience Unit". QUIT -- closes file and terminates session. Decimal fraction between 0 and 1 (including 1).
11a) Fusion state-proximal 11b) Fusion state-distal	EF (= epiphysis fused), EU (= epiphysis unfused), EI (= epiphysis, fusion state indeterminate), SU (= shaft unfused), SI (= shaft, fusion state indeterminate) CHANGE -- causes prompt sequence to begin again from "Provenience Unit". QUIT -- closes file and terminates session. HELP -- causes codes for fusion states to be listed on the screen.
12) COMMENT (Car Ret or Combination of B, C,G,R,W, and/ or X).	Carriage Return for "No Comment". B (for Burned), C (for carnivore-Chewed), G (for rodent-Gnawed), R (for Rolled), W (for Weathered), and/or X (for Cut). CHANGE -- causes prompt sequence to begin again from "Provenience Unit". HELP -- causes codes for bone states to be listed on screen. QUIT -- closes file and terminates session.
13) Catalog Number	Carriage Return for no number. CHANGE -- causes prompt series to begin again

from "Provenience Unit."
QUIT -- closes file and terminates session.
Any combination of letters and numbers
representing a catalog (serial) number.

Note: Each response must be followed by a carriage return.

After "Fraction-distal" has been successfully entered, BONECODE asks "COMMENT (Car Ret or combination of B,C,G,R,W and/or X)". (If the user indicated at the start that no comments were to be entered, BONECODE will skip this request). Acceptable answers are QUIT, HELP, CHANGE, a carriage return (for "no comment"), or some combination of the letters B (for Burned), C (for carnivore-Chewed), G (for rodent-Gnawed), R (for Rolled), W (for Weathered), and X (for artifactually Cut). HELP causes the meanings of the letters to be printed on the screen. As in the case of previous prompts, a response of CHANGE causes the prompt sequence to begin again from "Provenience Unit". The letters B, C, G, R, W, and/or X can be entered in any order but must not be separated by a space or any other character. BONECODE will print an error message and reprompt for COMMENT if the entry includes any letters besides B, C, G, R, W, or X or includes one of these letters twice.

The purpose of including the comment variable is to allow MNI to calculate NISPs and MNIs for bones that possess the specified characteristics (Burned, or Burned and Cut, or Burned, Cut and Gnawed, etc). With minimal rewriting, BONECODE and MNI could be made to accept and process other qualitative information on bone condition or modifiers to the present information (e.g. lightly rolled or heavily weathered). For the moment, BONECODE allows entry only of those qualitative characteristics we routinely record.

Once the comment variable has been entered, BONECODE asks "Catalog Number." (BONECODE will skip this request if the user indicated previously that no catalog numbers were to be entered). Acceptable answers are QUIT, CHANGE, a carriage return (for no number), or a catalog number, comprising any combination of letters and numbers. As in previous cases, CHANGE reinitiates the prompt series from "Provenience Unit."

BONECODE writes information to a file only after the Catalog Number has been successfully entered. This is the reason for allowing a return to "Provenience Unit" by responding CHANGE to any prompt--the result is that an erroneous response to a previous prompt can be erased before it is permanently recorded.

Once the Catalog Number has been sucessfully entered, BONECODE requests information on the next skeletal element. A response of CHANGE causes the program to prompt for (a new) "Provenience Unit." Otherwise the provenience unit that was recorded with the previous skeletal element will be recorded with the new one. Grouping skeletal elements by provenience unit before running BONECODE thus saves data entry time and reduces the possibility of entering erroneous provenience units.

If the user responds to "Skeletal element" with the two-letter abbreviation for rib, axis, cervical vertebra, thoracic vertebra, lumbar vertebra, or sacrum, BONECODE automatically records side as N (not relevant). The prompt series then begins with "Proximal, Distal, or Complete (P/D/C)" and proceeds as in the case of the humerus, radius, and so forth.

If the user responds to "Skeletal element" with the two-letter abbreviation for mandibular condyle, hyoid, cuneiform (carpal), unciform, lunate, magnum, scaphoid, pisiform, trapezoid, trapezium, patella, astragalus, navicular, cuboid, external cuneiform, internal cuneiform, or middle cuneiform, BONECODE automatically records portion of bone, state of proximal fusion, and state of distal fusion as N (not relevant). It prompts first for side--"Left, Right, or Indeterminate (L/R/I)." If the answer is anything but L, R, I, CHANGE, or QUIT, it prints an error message and repeats the prompt. If the answer is L, R, or I, it then requests "Fraction." An answer of CHANGE causes the prompt sequence to start again from "Provenience Unit." A number less than 0 or greater than 1 leads to an error message and a renewed request for "Fraction." (To meet the formatting requirements of MNI, an answer between 0 and 1 is recorded in the file space for "Fraction-proximal." "Fraction-distal" is automatically recorded as 0.)

If the user responds to "Skeletal element" with the two-letter abbreviation for occipital condyle or innominate, BONECODE again automatically records portion of bone, state of proximal fusion, and state of distal fusion as N (not relevant). The next prompt is for side--"Left, Right, Both, or Indeterminate (L/R/B/I)." If the answer to this request is L, R, or I, BONECODE asks for "Fraction", exactly as in the case of mandibular condyle, hyoid, and so forth. However, if the answer is B, it first requests "Fraction-left", followed by "Fraction-right". (In the file, "Fraction-left" is recorded in the space for "Fraction-proximal" and "Fraction-right" in the space for "Fraction-distal.") In the case of the innominate, fraction refers to the fraction of the total acetabulum present, whether on the ilium, ischium, pubis, or some combination of these.

A response of CHANGE to either fraction request restarts the prompt sequence with "Provenience Unit". The only other acceptable responses are QUIT and a decimal fraction between 0 and 1 (including 1). Once the fractions have been successfully entered, BONECODE asks first for "COMMENT (Car Ret or Combination of B,C,G,R,W and/or X)" and then for "Catalog Number." It then writes the accumulated information to the file.

If the user responds to "Skeletal element" with the two-letter abbreviation for frontlet, the prompt series also begins with "Left, Right, Both, or Indeterminate (L/R/B/I)." However, the next prompt is for "Male, Female, or Indeterminate" (recorded in the space for proximal fusion state; distal fusion state is recorded as N). The subsequent prompts are the same as for innominate, occipital, and so forth.

We anticipate that most users will record frontlet only for species that have horns or antlers. "Fraction" is to be understood as fraction of the pedicel, that is, as the fraction of a horn or antler at its junction with the frontal or, in the case of a female lacking horns or antlers, as the fraction of the frontal that would bear horns or antlers in a male.

If the user responds to "Skeletal element" with the two-letter abbreviation for proximal sesamoid, distal sesamoid, or atlas, BONECODE prompts only for fraction. All other information is automatically recorded to meet the requirements of MNI.

In some species, two skeletal parts regarded as separate by BONECODE and MNI are fused as one bone. A prominent example is the navicular and the cuboid, normally fused together as the "naviculo-cuboid" in bovids and cervids. For the purposes of MNI calculation, such a bone should be recorded under one skeletal part or the other. We use navicular (abbreviation NA) to record bovid and cervid naviculocuboids.

Another special case is the ulna, which fuses to the radius in some species. In this case, the user may opt to record a fused radius and ulna as two separate bones. However, this procedure will inflate the total NISP. One solution is to hand-tabulate the number of "double-counted" bones and subtract them from the final counts. Another alternative is to record ulnae separately from radii only if they are indeed separate bones. Otherwise a fused radioulna could be recorded as a radius, accompanied by a written note that the fused ulna was also present. We generally use the second alternative, since in samples we have analyzed fused radioulnae are extremely rare.

Ulnae present a further problem. The actual proximal end is frequently not preserved, while the articular surface (which is technically a part of the shaft) is more frequently found. In keeping with our treatment of other long bones, we record an ulna fragment as "proximal" only if it retains part of the actual epiphysis. Shaft fragments with the articular surface present may then be recorded as proximal shaft of indeterminate fusion (coded "SI").

In some species, some skeletal parts have atrophied, leaving behind vestiges that are commonly assigned special names. An example is the distal fibula in bovids and cervids, frequently called the "lateral malleolus." For the purposes of BONECODE and MNI, such bones should be assigned their original (more general) anatomical names.

With two exceptions, MNI (via BONECODE and DENTCODE discussed below) does not allow the user to enter skeletal parts that were originally joined by bone. The two exceptions are for the skull, where the occipital condyle, frontlet, and maxilla are all allowed, and the mandible, where both teeth and condyle may be entered. If the user enters both the frontlet and occipital condyle for a skull on which they are joined, or the teeth and condyle for a mandible that has both, MNI calculations will not be affected, but MNI will increase the total number of bones entered by two rather than by one.

In faunal samples where complete or semicomplete skulls or mandibles are common, we therefore recommend that the user hand-tabulate them (for later subtraction). Alternatively, in most cases, the user may choose to enter only dentitions into MNI, and hand tabulate frontlets and condyles. We do not regard this as a serious flaw in the present version of MNI, because the samples we have studied are nearly devoid of complete or semicomplete skulls. Such samples are almost certainly the rule, particularly in archeological contexts.

We feel that the maxilla, frontlet, and occipital condyle are adequate to represent the skull in highly fragmented samples. If MNI were to be regularly applied to samples in which complete skulls or large, identifiable cranial fragments were common, BONECODE (and MNI) should probably be rewritten to treat the skull basically as DENTCODE (and MNI) now treat the jaws. In essence, this means that a successor to BONECODE would take an abbreviation for the skull (e.g. SK or CR) and then prompt for the number of skull parts present. This would be followed by a request for the list of parts (e.g. TE for temporal, PL for parietal, and OC for occipital), one "part" at a time.

Samples with mandibles containing both teeth and condyles are much more common than ones containing complete or nearly complete skulls. However, in such samples we feel that the mandibular condyle may be ignored altogether with no serious loss of interpretable results.

We have found that data entry via BONECODE is greatly facilitated by the use of a coding form like the one illustrated in figure 6.5. An experienced osteologist will have no difficulty in remembering which items of information must be coded on the form and which ones are automatically coded by BONECODE. The form also includes a space for "notes" that are not directly relevant to BONECODE or MNI.

In its present form, BONECODE does not allow entry of measurements and other data that might be very important to some users. For the moment, we see no advantage to placing measurements in a BONECODE file. We usually record measurements separately for processing by other programs (see below). Similarly, we use the "notes" section on forms like the one in figure 6.5 to record qualitative variables that MNI does not at present take into account. We then manipulate this information by hand or by programs other than MNI.

Entry of Dentitions: Program DENTCODE
MNI expects eight items of information on each tooth or dentition, formatted in the following order:
1) Provenience unit.
2) Upper or lower dentition.
3) Opposite side of dentition attached or not.
4) Side entered (left or right).
5) Number of teeth (or sockets) in dentition.
6) A list of the teeth (or sockets) present.

Site **KLASIES RIVER MOUTH**   Date **4/25/82**   BONES

Species **RAPHICERUS MELANITIS**

LV$	SK$	LR$	PD$	PES$	FP	DES$	FD	CT$	CN$	NOTES
12	FR	B		F	1		1	X		
"	CC	L			.5					
"	MD	R			1					
"	AT				.5					
"	AX		C	SU	1	SU	1	B		
"	CE		D			EV	1			
"	LV		C	EF	.75	EF	1			
"	RI		P	EF	1			X		
"	SC	R		EF	1					
13	HU	L	C	EF	.5	EF	1			
"	UL	R	P	EF	.75					
"	UN	R			.5					
"	MA	R			1			B		
"	PI	I			.5					
"	MC	R	D			EF	1			
"	1P	L	C	SU	1		.5			
"	1P	I	D				.5			
"	2P	R	D				1			
"	3P	I	P		.33					
"	IN	R			1			X		
"	FE	I	D			EF	.2			
"	TI	L	C	SU	1	EF	.5			
"	FI	L	D			EF	1			
"	AS	I			.1					
"	CA	R	P	SU	1					
"	NA	L			.33					
16	MT	R	C		.75	EF	1	XC		
"	PS				1					
"	MP	I	D			EF	.5	WBX		
"	LN	L			1					
"	MA	I			.2					

Department of Anthropology, University of Chicago
1126 East 59th St., Chicago, IL 60637 USA   BONES OF **R. MELANITIS**

FIGURE 6.5: A coding form for bones to be entered into a file by the program BONECODE. The columns are labelled with the names for the variable in the program. LV$ stands for level or provenience unit within a site, SK$ for skeletal element, LR$ for side (left, right, or indeterminate), PD$ for part of a bone (proximal, distal, or complete),

7) Qualitative condition of dentition (Burned, carnivore-Chewed, rodent-Gnawed, Rolled, Weathered, or Cut).

8) Catalog Number of dentition.

In contrast to the way it treats bones, regarding teeth MNI does not work with fractions. The reason is partly the relative rarity of fragmentary teeth (compared with fragmentary bones) in most fossil samples. Additionally, it is usually possible to determine the kind of tooth and the species only from relatively large dental fragments. For the purposes of MNI computations, therefore, our procedure is to ignore all dental fragments that comprise less than half of an original tooth. We treat fragments that comprise more than half of the original tooth as if they were whole teeth, assuming of course that we can determine the species from which they derive.

To ensure that all the necessary dental information is entered in the proper order, we have constructed the entry program DENTCODE. Like BONECODE, DENTCODE contains "error traps" to reduce the risk of entry error, and it automatically enters an item of information that has been determined by a previous entry.

Figure 6.6 lists DENTCODE, and figure 6.7 shows a sample session. Figure 6.8 shows the file created by the session. Table 6.4 summarizes DENTCODE prompts, acceptable responses, and their effects.

DENTCODE asks first for the name of the file into which the dentitions will be placed. The only file name extension it accepts is ".DEN". If a name is entered without an extention, DENTCODE will add .DEN automatically.

DENTCODE next asks "Do you want to enter a comment on each dentition (Y/N)," meaning information on condition (burned, chewed, rolled, etc.). If the answer is Y, DENTCODE will prompt for this information on each dentition. Otherwise it will automatically record it as not relevant (N).

DENTCODE asks next "Do you want to enter a catalog number for each dentition (Y/N)." If the answer is Y, DENTCODE will prompt for the catalog number of each dentition in the subsequent session. If the answer is N, it will automatically record the catalog number as "#". For reasons discussed in the introduction to Part 2, we routinely answer N.

DENTCODE next prompts for "Provenience Unit." This should be an easily entered, mnemonic abbreviation for a provenience unit recognized in the field. If the response to "Provenience Unit" is "HELP", DENTCODE

PES$ for state of proximal fusion, FP for proximal fraction, DES$ for state of distal fusion, FD for distal fraction, CT$ for comment, and CN$ for catalog number. Note that provenience unit (or level) need be recorded only when the provenience unit changes. The catalog number (CN$) column is totally blank because bones in the example assemblage were not assigned individual catalog numbers.

FIGURE 6.6: Listing of the program DENTCODE for entering dentitions into a computer file.

```
1000 REM IBM Personal Computer BASIC (R. G. Klein, 21 January 1984)
1010 CLS
1020 KEY OFF
1030 DEFINT A-Z
1040 DIM TOOTH$(24,2),CMMT$(6,2),L$(6),TH$(11)
1050 '
1060 REM Lookup table for teeth and abbreviations
1070 FOR I=1 TO 24:FOR J=1 TO 2:READ TOOTH$(I,J):NEXT:NEXT
1080 DATA DI,deciduous incisor,DI1,deciduous incisor 1,DI2,deciduous incisor 2
1090 DATA DI3,deciduous incisor 3,DC,deciduous canine,I,incisor,I1,incisor 1
1100 DATA I2,incisor 2,I3,incisor 3,C,canine,DP,deciduous premolar
1110 DATA DP1,deciduous premolar 1,DP2,deciduous premolar 2
1120 DATA DP3,deciduous premolar 3,DP4,deciduous premolar 4
1130 DATA P,premolar,P1,premolar 1,P2,premolar 2,P3,premolar 3,P4,premolar 4
1140 DATA M,molar,M1,molar 1,M2,molar 2,M3,molar 3
1150 '
1160 REM Lookup table for comments and abbreviations
1170 FOR I=1 TO 6:FOR J=1 TO 2:READ CMMT$(I,J):NEXT:NEXT
1180 DATA B,burnt,C,(carnivore-)Chewed,G,(rodent-)Gnawed,R,rolled
1190 DATA W,weathered,X,cut
1200 '
1210 REM Function keys
1220 KEY 1,"CHANGE"+CHR$(13):KEY 2,"QUIT"+CHR$(13):KEY 3,"HELP"+CHR$(13)
1230 KEY 4,"MULT"+CHR$(13)
1240 '
1250 PRINT "DENTCODE. Creates dental files for MNI.  To see tooth and bone"
1260 PRINT "bone state abbreviations type <HELP> in response to 'Upper/Lower'"
1270 PRINT "Type 'S' before a tooth (e.g. SM3) to indicate an empty socket,"
1280 PRINT "'S/' (e.g. S/M3) to indicate a tooth in a socket."
1290 PRINT
1300 '
1310 CONTINUE=-1
1320 WHILE CONTINUE
1330   INPUT "File name for teeth ".DEN"";ANS$:GOSUB 3120:FLNM$=ANS$
1340   IF INSTR(FLNM$,":")=0 AND LEN(FLNM$)<=12 AND RIGHT$(FLNM$,4)=".DEN"
         THEN CONTINUE=0
1350   IF INSTR(FLNM$,":")=2 AND LEN(FLNM$)<=14 AND RIGHT$(FLNM$,4)=".DEN"
         THEN CONTINUE=0
1360   IF INSTR(FLNM$,":")=2 AND INSTR(FLNM$,".")=0 AND LEN(FLNM$)<=10
         HEN FLNM$=FLNM$+".DEN":CONTINUE=0
1370   IF INSTR(FLNM$,":")=0 AND INSTR(FLNM$,".")=0 AND LEN(FLNM$)<=8
         THEN FLNM$=FLNM$+".DEN":CONTINUE=0
1380   IF CONTINUE=-1 THEN BEEP:PRINT "Illegal File Name!"
1390 WEND
1400 '
1410 CLOSE:OPEN FLNM$ FOR APPEND AS #1
1420 CTYN$=""
1430 WHILE CTYN$<>"Y" AND CTYN$<>"N"
1440   INPUT "Do you want to enter a comment on each dentition (Y/N)";ANS $:
         GOSUB 3120:CTYN$=ANS$
1450   IF CTYN$<>"Y" AND CTYN$<>"N" THEN BEEP
1460 WEND
1470 '
1480 CNYN$=""
1490 WHILE CNYN$<>"Y" AND CNYN$<>"N"
1500   INPUT "Do you want to enter a catalog number for each dentition";
         ANS$:GOSUB 3120:CNYN$=ANS$
1510   IF CNYN$<>"Y" AND CNYN$<>"N" THEN BEEP
1520 WEND
```

```
1530 '
1540 REM Provenience Unit Entry
1550 LV$="":CHANGE=0
1560 WHILE LV$="" OR LV$="HELP"
1570    INPUT "Provenience Unit";ANS$:GOSUB 3120:LV$=ANS$
1580    IF LV$="CHANGE" THEN CHANGE=-1
1590    IF LV$="HELP" THEN GOSUB 2950
1600    IF LV$="QUIT" THEN CLOSE:CLS:END
1610    IF LV$="" THEN BEEP
1620 WEND
1630 IF CHANGE THEN 1420
1640 '
1650 REM Upper/lower entry
1660 NDE=1 'number of times to write dentition to file
1670 CONTINUE=-1:QUIT=0:CHANGE=0
1680 WHILE CONTINUE
1690    INPUT "Upper, Lower, or Indeterminate (U/L/I)";ANS$:
           GOSUB 3120:UL$=ANS$
1700    IF UL$="QUIT" THEN QUIT=-1:CONTINUE=0
1710    IF UL$="CHANGE" THEN CHANGE=-1:CONTINUE=0
1720    IF UL$="U" OR UL$="L" OR UL$="I" THEN CONTINUE=0
1730    IF UL$="MULT" THEN GOSUB 2620
1740    IF UL$="HELP" THEN GOSUB 2950
1750    IF CONTINUE AND UL$<>"MULT" AND UL$<>"HELP" THEN BEEP:
           PRINT "Must be U, L, I, CHANGE, QUIT, HELP, or MULT!"
1760 WEND
1770 IF QUIT THEN CLOSE:CLS:END
1780 IF CHANGE GOTO 1550    'new level
1790 '
1800 REM Side entry
1810 CONTINUE=-1:CHANGE=0:QUIT=0
1820 WHILE CONTINUE
1830    INPUT "Left, Right, Both, or Indeterminate (L/R/B/I)";ANS$:
           GOSUB 3120:LRB$=ANS$
1840    IF LRB$="QUIT" THEN QUIT=-1:CONTINUE=0
1850    IF LRB$="HELP" THEN GOSUB 2950
1860    IF LRB$="CHANGE" THEN CHANGE=-1:CONTINUE=0
1870    IF LRB$="L" OR LRB$="R" OR LRB$="I" OR LRB$="B" THEN CONTINUE=0
1880    IF CONTINUE AND LRB$<>"HELP" THEN:BEEP:
           PRINT "Must be L, R, B, I, CHANGE, or QUIT!"
1890 WEND
1900 IF CHANGE THEN GOTO 1550 'new level
1910 IF QUIT THEN CLOSE:CLS:END
1920 '
1930 REM Entry of teeth
1940 WHILE LRB$="B"
1950    LR$="L":PRINT "How many teeth on left side (1-11)";
1960       GOSUB 2710:IF WRONG THEN 1950
1970       GOSUB 2780
1980       IF CHANGE THEN 1950
1990       GOSUB 2200:GOSUB 2440 'comment and cat no
2000       GOSUB 2490 'write to file
2010    LR$="R":LOCATE 1,1:PRINT "How many teeth on right side (1-11)";
2020       GOSUB 2710:IF WRONG THEN CLS:GOTO 2010
2030       GOSUB 2780
2040       IF CHANGE THEN CLS:GOTO 2010
2050       GOSUB 2490 'write to file
2060    LRB$="N"
2070 WEND
```

```
2080 '
2090 WHILE LRB$="L" OR LRB$="R" OR LRB$="I"
2100   LR$=LRB$:PRINT "How many teeth in series (1-11)";
2110     GOSUB 2710:IF WRONG THEN 2100 ELSE GOSUB 2780
                'number of teeth and teeth
2120     IF CHANGE THEN 2100
2130     GOSUB 2200:GOSUB 2440 'comment and cat no
2140     GOSUB 2490 'write to file
2150     LRB$="N"
2160 WEND
2170 '
2180 LOCATE 1,1:GOTO 1650 'start again from UL$
2190 '
2200 REM Comment entry
2210 CORRECTLET=0
2220 IF CTYN$="N" THEN CT$="N":CORRECTLET=-1
2230 WHILE CORRECTLET=0
2240   INPUT "Comment (<CR> or combination of B,C,G,R,W,X)";CT$
2250   IF LEN(CT$)=0 THEN CT$="N":CORRECTLET=-1
2260   IF CORRECTLET=0 THEN ANS$=CT$:GOSUB 3120:CT$=ANS$:GOSUB 2300
            'capitalize and check for proper letters
2270   IF CORRECTLET=0 THEN BEEP:PRINT "Illegal comment!"
2280 WEND
2290 '
2300 REM Check for correct letters in comment
2310 CORRECTLET=-1
2320 FOR I=1 TO LEN(CT$)
2330   L$(I)=MID$(CT$,I,1)
2340   IF L$(I)<>"B" AND L$(I)<>"C" AND L$(I)<>"G" AND L$(I)<>"R" AND
            L$(I)<>"X" AND L$(I)<>"W" THEN CORRECTLET=0
2350 NEXT I
2360 IF CORRECTLET=0 THEN RETURN
2370 '
2380 REM Check for duplicate letter in comment
2390 FOR F=1 TO LEN(CT$):FOR S=F+1 TO LEN(CT$)
2400   IF L$(F)=L$(S) THEN CORRECTLET=0
2410 NEXT S:NEXT F
2420 RETURN
2430 '
2440 REM Catalog number entry
2450 IF CNYN$="N" THEN CN$="#" ELSE INPUT "Catalog Number";CN$
2460 IF CN$="" THEN CN$="#"
2470 RETURN
2480 '
2490 REM Write to file
2500 FOR N=1 TO NDE
2510   PRINT#1, LV$,"UL$","LRB$","LR$","NT","CT$","CN$
2520   FOR J=1 TO NT:PRINT#1,TH$(J):NEXT
2530 NEXT N
2540 CLS:GOSUB 2570 'write last entry
2550 RETURN
2560 '
2570 REM Last entry
2580 LOCATE 25,1:PRINT "Last Entry:";
2590 LOCATE 25,14:PRINT LV$,"UL$","LRB$","LR$","NT "teeth,"CT$","CN$
2600 RETURN
2610 '
2620 REM Write dentition to file multiple times
2630 NDE=0
```

```
2640 WHILE NDE<1
2650 INPUT "How many times to write same dentition to file";NDE$
2660   NDE=VAL(NDE$)
2670   IF NDE<1 THEN BEEP:PRINT "Must be > 1."
2680 WEND
2690 RETURN
2700 '
2710 REM Number of teeth
2720 WRONG=0
2730 INPUT NT$
2740 NT=VAL(NT$)
2750 IF NT<1 OR NT>11 THEN WRONG=-1:BEEP:
        PRINT "Nobody has that many teeth in a series!"
2760 RETURN
2770 '
2780 REM Teeth
2790 FOR J=1 TO NT
2800   CONTINUE=-1:CHANGE=0
2810   WHILE CONTINUE
2820     INPUT "Tooth";ANS$:GOSUB 3120:TH$(J)=ANS$
2830     FOR I=1 TO 24
2840       IF TH$(J)=TOOTH$(I,1) THEN CONTINUE=0:I=24
2850       IF TH$(J)="S"+TOOTH$(I,1) THEN CONTINUE=0:I=24
2860       IF TH$(J)="S/"+TOOTH$(I,1) THEN CONTINUE=0:I=24
2870       IF TH$(J)="CHANGE" THEN CHANGE=-1:CONTINUE=0:I=24:J=NT
2880     NEXT I
2890     IF CONTINUE THEN BEEP:PRINT "Invalid tooth name!"
2900   WEND
2910 NEXT J
2920 RETURN
2930 '
2940 '
2950 REM HELP
2960   CLS
2970   LOCATE 1,1:COLOR 0,7:PRINT "TOOTH ABBREVIATIONS" SPC(5)
2980   FOR I=1 TO 12:FOR J=1 TO 2
2990     LOCATE I+1,1:COLOR 7,0:PRINT TOOTH$(I,1) TAB(6) TOOTH$(I,J)
3000     LOCATE I+1,39:COLOR 7,0:PRINT TOOTH$(I+12,1) TAB(45) TOOTH$(I+12,J)
3010   NEXT:PRINT:NEXT
3020   COLOR 0,7:PRINT "BONE STATE ABBREVIATIONS" SPC(3)
3030   PRINT
3040   FOR I=1 TO 6:FOR J=1 TO 2
3050     COLOR 7,0:PRINT CMMT$ (I,J),
3060   NEXT:PRINT:NEXT
3070   LOCATE 25,1:PRINT "Press enter to return to program operation...";
3080   YY$=INKEY$:WHILE YY$="":YY$=INKEY$:WEND
3090 CLS
3100 RETURN
3110 '
3120 REM Capitalization
3130 FOR LTR=1 TO LEN(ANS$)
3140   LTR$=MID$(ANS$,LTR,1)
3150   IF "a"<=LTR$ AND LTR$<="z" THEN MID$(ANS$,LTR,1)=CHR$(ASC(LTR$)-32)
3160 NEXT
3170 RETURN
```

FIGURE 6.7: A DENTCODE sample session, involving dentitions of the grysbok (*Raphicerus melanotis*) from Klasies River Mouth, South Africa.

DENTCODE -- Creates dental files for MNI. To see tooth names and bone state abbreviations type HELP in response to 'Upper/Lower' request. Type 'S' before a tooth (e.g. SM3) to indicate an empty socket, 'S/' (e.g. S/M3) to indicate a tooth in a socket.

File name for teeth [.DEN] ? KRMRM.DEN
Do you want to enter a comment on each dentition (Y/N) ? N
Do you want to enter a catalog number for each dentition ? Y
Provenience Unit ? 15B
Upper, Lower, or Indeterminate (U/L/I) ? U
Left, Right, Both, or Indeterminate (L/R/B/I) ? R
How many teeth in series (1-11) ? 1
Tooth ? M1
COMMENT (<CR> or combination of B,C,G,R,W,X) ?

Upper, Lower, or Indeterminate (U/L/I) ? U
Left, Right, Indeterminate, or Both (L/R/B/I) ? L
How many teeth in series (1-11) ? 2
Tooth ? S/M2
Tooth ? S/M3
COMMENT (<CR> or combination of B,C,G,R,W,X) ? X

Upper, Lower, or Indeterminate (U/L/I) ? L
Left, Right, Indeterminate, or Both (L/R/B/I) ? R
How many teeth in series (1-11) ? 3
Tooth ? SP2
Tooth ? SP3
Tooth ? S/P4
COMMENT (<CR> or combination of B,C,G,R,W,X) ? G

Upper, Lower, or Indeterminate (U/L/I) ? L
Left, Right, Indeterminate, or Both (L/R/B/I) ? R
How many teeth in series (1-11) ? 2
Tooth ? SP2
Tooth ? SP3
COMMENT (<CR> or combination of B,C,G,R,W,X) ? RB

Upper, Lower, or Indeterminate (U/L/I) ? CHANGE
Provenience Unit ? 16A
Upper, Lower, or Indeterminate (U/L/I) ? L
Left, Right, Indeterminate, or Both (L/R/B/I) ? I
How many teeth in series (1-11) ? 1
Tooth ? I
COMMENT (<CR> or combination of B,C,G,R,W,X) ?

Upper, Lower, or Indeterminate (U/L/I) ? L
Left, Right, Indeterminate, or Both (L/R/B/I) ? B
How many teeth on left side (1-11) ? 4
Tooth ? SI1
Tooth ? SI2
Tooth ? SI3
Tooth ? SC
COMMENT (<CR> or combination of B,C,G,R,W,X) ? X

How many teeth on right side (1-11) ? 4
Tooth ? SI1
Tooth ? SI2
Tooth ? SI3
Tooth ? S/C

Upper, Lower, or Indeterminate (U/L/I) ? U
Left, Right, Indeterminate, or Both (L/R/B/I) ? L
How many teeth in series (1-11) ? 1
Tooth ? P2
COMMENT (<CR> or combination of B,C,G,R,W,X) ?

Upper, Lower, or Indeterminate (U/L/I) ? QUIT

---

will print a list of acceptable tooth names and bone-state abbreviations to the screen. HELP has the same effect in response to the prompts for "Upper, Lower, or Indeterminate" and "Left, Right, Both, or Indeterminate."

If the response to "Provenience Unit" is "CHANGE", DENTCODE reinitiates the prompt series with "Do you want to enter a comment on each dentition (Y/N)." This facilitates the entry of dentitions that have been previously separated between ones with comments or catalog numbers and ones without.

If the response to "Provenience Unit" is "QUIT", DENTCODE closes the file and terminates the session. QUIT similarly terminates the session in response to the prompts for "Upper, Lower, or Indeterminate" and "Left, Right, Both, or Indeterminate."

Once provenience unit has been entered, DENTCODE asks "Upper, Lower, or Indeterminate (U/L/I)." If the user is not entering separate catalog numbers for each dentition and has grouped multiple occurrenes of the same dentition from the same provenience unit, the proper response to "Upper, Lower, or Indeterminate" is "MULT". DENTCODE will then ask "How many times to write same dentition to file", followed by a renewed request for "Upper, Lower, or Indeterminate." It will then automatically record the same dentition and associated information in the file as many times as the user has specified.

```
15B,U,R,R,1,N,#
M1
15B,U,L,L,2,X,#
S/M2
S/M3
15B,L,R,R,3,G,#
SP2
SP3
S/P4
15B,L,R,R,2,RB,#
SP2
SP3
16A,L,I,I,1,N,#
I
16A,L,B,L,4,X,#
SI1
SI2
SI3
SC
16A,L,B,R,4,X,#
SI1
SI2
SI3
S/C
16A,U,L,L,1,N,#
P2
```

FIGURE 6.8: The file created by the DENTCODE session in figure 6.7.

If the response to "Upper, Lower, or Indeterminate" is "CHANGE", DENTCODE will reinitiate the prompt series from "Provenience Unit". CHANGE has the same effect in response to the prompt for "Left, Right, Both, or Indeterminate." This feature is designed to expedite the entry of dentitions that have been previously grouped by provenience unit. However, it also allows an incorrectly entered provenience unit or jaw type (upper or lower) to be altered before it is written to file.

If the response to "Upper, Lower, or Indeterminate" is anything but U, L, I, MULT, HELP, CHANGE, or QUIT, DENTCODE will repeat the prompt.

Once the information on Upper or Lower has been entered, DENTCODE asks "Left, Right, Both, or Indeterminate (L/R/B/I)". If the response is not L, R, B, I, HELP, CHANGE, or QUIT, DENTCODE asks again. If the user responds B (for Both), DENTCODE then asks "How many teeth on the left side (1-11)." If the number entered is not between 1 and 11, DENTCODE will request the number again.

Once the number of teeth has been successfully entered, DENTCODE requests a list of the teeth, repeating the prompt "Tooth" as many times as

TABLE 6.4 DENTCODE Prompts, with Accepted Responses and Their
Effects

Prompts	Responses and Effects
1) File name for teeth ".DEN"	Extension must be .DEN. If no extension is entered, .DEN will be added automatically.
2) Do you want to enter a comment on each dentition (Y/N)	Y -- causes program to prompt for information on the state of each dentition. N -- causes program to record the state of each dentition as N (not relevant).
3) Do you want to enter a catalog number for each dentition (Y/N)	Y -- causes program to request a catalog number for each dentition. N -- causes program to record the catalog number of each dentition as "#".
4) Provenience Unit	Any combination of letters and numbers (easily entered, mnemonic abbreviations of field units are recommended.) HELP -- causes abbreviations for teeth and bone states to be listed on the screen. CHANGE -- causes program to begin again with prompts 2 and 3. QUIT -- closes file and terminates session.
5) Upper, Lower, or Indeterminate	U, L, or I -- causes jaw type to be recorded, leading to prompt for "Left, Right, Both, or Indeterminate". MULT -- if same dentition is to be written to file more than once. Leads to prompt 6. HELP -- causes abbreviations for teeth and bone states to be listed on the screen. CHANGE -- causes prompt series to begin again from "Provenience Unit". QUIT -- closes file and terminates session.
6) [If response to 5 was "MULT" How many times to write same dentition to file.	An integer indicating the number of times a particular dentition is to be automatically recorded in the file.
7) Left, Right, Both, or	B -- causes program to expect further entries for both left and right sides; next prompt

Indeterminate	will be "How many teeth on left side".
	L, R, or I -- causes side to be recorded, leading to the prompt "How many teeth in series".
	HELP -- causes abbreviations for teeth and bone states to be listed on the screen.
	CHANGE -- causes prompt series to begin again from "Provenience Unit".
	QUIT -- closes file and terminates session.

8a) How many teeth on left side	The proper number between 1 and 11 -- causes request for teeth comprising a dentition, one "Tooth" at a time.
8b) How many teeth on right side	
8c) How many teeth in series	

---

9) Tooth	CHANGE -- causes prompt series to begin again from prompt 8.
	DI, DI1, DI2, DI3, DC, DP, DP1, DP2, DP3, DP4, I, I1, I2, I3, C, P, P1, P2, P3, P4, M, M1, M2, or M3, freestanding (for isolated teeth), preceded by S/ (for teeth in sockets), or by S (for sockets without teeth).

---

10) COMMENT (Car Ret or B,C,G, R,W,and/or X)	Carriage Return for "No Comment".
	B (for Burned), C (for carnivore-Chewed), G (for rodent-Gnawed), R (for Rolled), W (for Weathered), and/or X (for Cut).

---

11) Catalog Number	Carriage Return for no number.
	A Catalog Number, comprising any combination of letters and numbers.

Note: Each response must be followed by a carriage return.

there are teeth to be entered. A response of "CHANGE" to any request for "Tooth" will cause DENTCODE to reprompt for number of teeth, and none of the teeth entered before CHANGE will be recorded. CHANGE has the same effect in response to "Tooth" following "How many teeth on the right side (1-11)" and "How many teeth in series (1-11)." This is designed to allow easy correction of an erroneous entry for number of teeth.

The tooth names DENTCODE accepts are shown in table 6.4. If a tooth is still in its socket, its name should be prefixed by an "S/" (e.g. S/P2 or S/M3). If only the socket for the tooth is present, the name should be preceded by an "S" (e.g. SP2 or SM3). If the entry is not CHANGE or one of the tooth names in Table 6.4 (freestanding or preceded by S/ or S), DENTCODE prints an error message and requests "Tooth" again.

When the last tooth in the series has been entered, DENTCODE asks "How many teeth on the right side (1-11)." Again, the number entered must be between 1 and 11 or DENTCODE will reprompt. Once the number has been entered, DENTCODE prompts for the list of teeth (on the right side).

If the user initially responds L, R, or I (for Left, Right or Indeterminate) to the prompt "Left, Right, Both, or Indeterminate," DENTCODE asks simply "How many teeth in series (1-11)." Again, it only accepts a number between 1 and 11. It then asks for the list of teeth.

When the last tooth in the series has been entered (the last tooth on the right side in the case of a dentition with both left and right sides), DENTCODE requests "COMMENT (Car Ret or Combination of B,C,G,R,W and/or X)." (If the user indicated previously that no comments were to be entered, DENTCODE will skip this request.) Acceptable answers are a carriage return (for no comment), or some combination of the letters B (for Burned), C (for carnivore-Chewed), G (for rodent-Gnawed), R (for Rolled), W (for Weathered), and X (for artifactually Cut), exactly as in the case of BONECODE.

If the user previously indicated a desire to enter catalog numbers, the final prompt will be for "Catalog Number." Acceptable responses are an appropriate combination of letters and numbers or a carriage return (for no number).

When the last piece of information on a dentition has been successfully entered, DENTCODE seeks information on the next dentition, beginning with the request for "Upper, Lower, or Indeterminate (U/L/I)." As indicated previously, a response of CHANGE will cause the prompt series to begin with "Provenience Unit." Otherwise the provenience unit recorded with the previous dentition will be recorded with the new one. This feature has been incorporated on the assumption that the user will often group dentitions by provenience unit before coding, so that entry time is saved if the program can automatically record provenience unit.

As in the case of BONECODE, we have found that data entry via DENTCODE is facilitated by the use of a coding form, such as the one illustrated in figure 6.9. Like the form for BONECODE in figure 6.5, the one for DENTCODE in figure 6.9 provides space for "notes" that are not relevant to MNI. It does not provide space for measurements which we record and process separately (see chaps. 7 and 8).

How MNI Deals with Indeterminacy: Skeletal Parts Other Than Dentitions

In previous sections, we noted that a user of MNI may record the side of a bone, its fusion state, and the sex of a frontlet as indeterminate. He or she may also enter the skeletal element "metapodial" (MP) when it is either not possible or not useful to distinguish between metacarpals and metatarsals.

Site **KLASIES RIVER MOUTH**   Date **4/25/82**   DENTITIONS

Species **RAPHICERUS MELANOTIS**

LV$	UL$	LRB$	LR$	NT	TH$	TH$	TH$	TH$	TH$	TH$	CT$	CN$	NOTES
14	L	R		5	S/P3	S/P4	S/M1	S/M2	S/M3				
"	L	L		4	S/P4	S/M1	S/M2	S/M3					
"	L	R		1	I								
"	L	R		3	SP2	SP3	SP4						
"	L	I		1	I								
"	U	R		5	SP2	SP3	S/P4	S/M1	S/M2		B		
"	U	R		2	S/M2	S/M3							
"	U	L		3	SP2	SP3	SP4						
15	U	R		1	P								
"	U	L		2	S/P2	S/P3							
"	U	L		3	S/M1	S/M2	S/M3						
"	L	R		5	S/P3	S/P4	S/M1	S/M2	S/M3		X		
"	L	L		3	SP2	SP3	SP4						
"	L	R		1	M								
17B	L	B	(L)	4	SI1	SI2	SI3	SC					
			(R)	6	SI1	SI2	SI3	SC	S/P2	S/P3			
"	L	L		1	M3								
"	L	R		1	M3								

Department of Anthropology, University of Chicago,
1126 East 59th Street, Chicago, IL 60637 USA

DENTITIONS OF **R. MELANOTIS**

FIGURE 6.9: A coding form for dentitions to be entered into a file by the program DENTCODE. The columns are labeled with the names of the variables in the program. LV$ stands for level or provenience unit within a site, UL$ for jaw (upper, lower, or indeterminate), LRB$ for side (left, right, both, or indeterminate), LR$ for side to enter (left or

In this section, we explain explicitly how MNI deals with these cases of indeterminacy.

In each case, there are two possible determinate categories --left or right, fused or unfused, male or female, and metacarpal or metatarsal. In each case, MNI assumes that an indeterminate piece has an equal chance of belonging to one category or the other. Regarding side, for any given skeletal part (e.g. the distal humerus), it sums the fractions for the indeterminate pieces. It then adds half this sum to the sum of the fractions for left pieces and half to the sum of the fractions for right pieces. Whichever new sum is larger (left or right) is taken as the MNI for the skeletal part, rounded upward to the nearest whole number.

Regarding fusion, MNI alternately assigns each indeterminate piece to the fused or unfused category. The first indeterminate piece it encounters is placed in the fused category, the second in the unfused, the third in the fused, the fourth in the unfused, and so forth. This is done without regard for the skeletal part that a piece represents.

MNI uses a broadly similar procedure for frontlets of indeterminate sex and for metapodials. The first indeterminate frontlet is processed as "Male," the second as "Female," the third as "Male," and so forth. The first (indeterminate) metapodial is assigned to the category "metacarpal," the second to the category "metatarsal," the third to "metacarpal," and so forth.

Most users will probably find the treatment of indeterminate side satisfactory. In the overwhelming majority of faunal samples, it is certainly reasonable to suppose that half of the indeterminate pieces are lefts and half are rights. The principal alternative in MNI calculation is to ignore pieces whose side is indeterminate. In highly fragmented bone assemblages, such pieces may be very numerous because of the difficulty of "siding" small fragments. In such assemblages, ignoring pieces with indeterminate side would thus artificially depress MNI counts, perhaps differently for different skeletal parts.

The way MNI treats pieces with indeterminate fusion, frontlets of indeterminate sex, and indeterminate metapodials is more problematic. One difficulty is that the resultant MNIs will be affected by the order in which bones occur in a file. However, the effect will almost certainly be negligible, unless the user has somehow deliberately arranged the file to

---

right), NT for number of teeth (or sockets) in jaw, TH$ for the name of each tooth, CT$ for comment, and CN$ for catalog number. Note that side to enter (LR$) should be left blank except for jaws with both sides present. For such jaws, the left side should be recorded first, then the right. Note also that provenience unit (or level) need be recorded only when the provenience unit changes. The catalog number (CN$) column is totally blank because dentitions in the example assemblage were not assigned individual catalog numbers.

create an effect.

A more serious difficulty is that in most cases there is no *a priori* reason to suppose that the indeterminate pieces will be half fused and half unfused, half male and half female, or half metacarpals and half metatarsals. In this instance, a more appropriate procedure might be to allocate the indeterminate pieces according to the ratio in the determinate ones. Thus, for example, if the ratio of definite male to definite female frontlets were 4:1, MNI could assign 80% of the indeterminate frontlets to the male category and 20% to the female category before undertaking a final MNI calculation.

We have not built such an alternative into the MNI program, partly because it would add substantially to the length and complexity of the program and partly because it would not materially affect the results in the vast majority of faunal samples with which we are familiar. In these samples, fusion state is readily determined on nearly all identifiable bones, excluding only long bone shaft fragments. However, we ordinarily do not enter shaft fragments into MNI calculations, because of the difficulty of estimating the fraction of a whole bone they represent. Additionally, in most samples with which we are familar, it is often difficult to ascertain the species represented by a shaft fragment.

Basically the same situation pertains for frontlets--the overwhelming majority are immediately determinate to sex. Regarding metapodials, a consistent problem arises only with respect to distal fragments, which can be difficult to sort between metacarpals and metatarsals. Where there are many indeterminate distal fragments, we use only the proximal ends to estimate the metacarpal/metatarsal ratio.

In these circumstances, some analysts may feel that MNI should not work at all with pieces of indeterminate fusion, frontlets of indeterminate sex, or metapodials that may be either metacarpals or metatarsals. In most cases, treating these may increase MNI numbers slightly, but it will not increase the information content of the numbers. It is after all the information in the numbers, not the numbers themselves, that is important. Others may feel that we should change the present procedure for handling indeterminacy or that we should offer alternatives. We would be glad for specialist feedback on this issue.

How MNI Deals with Indeterminacy: Dentitions

In most cases, it is easy to determine the side (left or right) of a dentition, even if it consists of only a single tooth. MNI, however, allows a user to specify side as indeterminate. Dentitions or teeth whose side is specified this way are treated in basically the same way as bones that lack a definite side specification. For any given tooth (e.g. lower M3), half of the indeterminate specimens are added to the right category and half to the left. The MNI for the tooth is then taken to be the larger number, whether left or right.

MNI also allows a user to specify jaw (upper or lower) as indeterminate. It assigns the first indeterminate specimen it encounters to the category "lower," the second to the category "upper," the third to the category "lower," and so forth.

Finally, MNI permits a user to specify "kind of tooth" rather generally, as simply a deciduous incisor (dI), incisor (I), deciduous premolar (dP), premolar (P), or molar (M). In many species, neighboring teeth (e.g. I2 and I3 or P3 and P4 or M1 and M2) are very difficult to distinguish when they are isolated. It is therefore this option for indeterminacy that most users will invoke most often. It is certainly the only option that we regularly use.

To deal with this kind of indeterminacy in MNI calculations, for each broad dental category MNI asks how many dental types are indeterminate (indistinguishable). It will next ask for a list of these types. For example, the user may be calculating MNIs for a species whose isolated I3s are readily distinguished, but whose isolated I1s and I2s are difficult to separate. In such a case, "2" is the correct response to the program request for "Number of Indistinguishable I's per individual." MNI then asks for a list of the two indistinguishable incisor types. I1 and I2 are the proper responses. MNI will now allocate indeterminate incisors (ones designated "I") alternately between I1 and I2-- that is, the first indeterminate incisor encountered will be assigned to I1, the second to I2, the third to I1, the fourth to I2, and so forth.

If the user can distinguish isolated I1s, but not I2s from I3s, the appropriate response to "Number of indistinguishable I's" is still 2. This time, however, I2 and I3 should be entered as the two indistinguishable types. The assignment sequence will then be I2, I3, I2, I3, I2, I3, and so forth.

If the user cannot readily distinguish I1s from I2s from I3s, the appropriate response to "Number of indistinguishable I's" is "3". The list of indistinguishable teeth will then include all three incisor types. Order of entry is immaterial. If they are entered · in the order I1, I2, I3, the assignment sequence will be I1, I2, I3, I1, I2, I3, I1, I2, I3, and so forth.

Since there are species in which it is difficult to distinguish the canine from the incisors, it is possible to respond "4" to "Number of indistinguishable I's." Assuming the indistinguishable tooth types are entered as I1, I2, I3, and C, the assignment sequence will be I1, I2, I3, C, I1, I2, I3, C, I1, I2, I3, C, and so forth.

MNI follows exactly the same procedure for the deciduous incisors, deciduous premolars, and permanent molars. For all except the molars, it accepts up to four indistinguishable tooth types. Regarding the molars, it accepts up to seven. This is because there are many species (hyraxes, lagomorphs, many rodents, and others) whose isolated molars are difficult to distinguish not only from one another, but also from isolated premolars. If all such indeterminate teeth are entered (via DENTCODE) as molars (M), MNI can then allocate them between both premolars and molars. Thus, if the user responds "5" to "Number of indistinguishable M's per individual," the subsequent list of indeterminate (indistinguishable) tooth types might include P3, P4, M1, M2, and M3. The assignment sequence for indeterminate molars (specimens simply labelled M in a dental file) will then be P3, P4, M1, M2, M3, P3, P4, M1, M2, M3, and so forth.

It is possible to have both indeterminate and determinate teeth in the same file. Thus, if there are some specimens that have been labeled I1, I2, and I3 and others that have been labeled only I, MNI will reallocate only the ones labeled I.

The Entry of Skeletal Part Divisors: Program SKELDIV

To compute the MNI for a species in a fossil sample, the program MNI must know the numbers of different kinds of vertebrae, metapodials, phalanges, and sesamoids that occur in each individual of the species. These may be entered from the keyboard in each MNI session. Alternatively, they may be retrieved from a file created specifically for the purpose by the program SKELDIV, discussed in this section.

Figure 6.10 lists SKELDIV, and figure 6.11 shows a sample session. Figure 6.12 shows the file created by the session. Table 6.5 lists the SKELDIV prompts, acceptable responses, and their effects.

Within most mammalian families, the numbers of different kinds of vertebrae, metapodials, phalanges, and sesamoids per individual are the same among species, or the differences are too small to affect MNI calculations materially. SKELDIV thus records appropriate figures by family rather than by species.

SKELDIV first requests "File Name," meaning the name of the file in which the skeletal part divisors will be stored. Any name acceptable to the user's system will do. We suggest the name SKELDIV.DAT.

Once the file name has been entered, the program checks to see if a file by that name already exists. If not, it informs the user "New File." If the file does exist, the program lists the families for which skeletal part divisors have already been entered. This is to prevent the user from entering the same family twice. Once a family and divisors have been entered, the divisors may be amended only with an external editor (such as WordStar in non-document mode). Alternatively, the editor may be used to eliminate the entire record for a family. The record may then be replaced in a subsequent SKELDIV session.

SKELDIV's first request after "File Name" is for "Family (in Latin)." Appropriate responses are QUIT, which will cause SKELDIV to close the file and terminate the session, or a family name ending in "idae." Any other response will cause SKELDIV to request family name again.

Once family name has been successfully entered, SKELDIV asks serially for the "Number of thoracic vertebrae per individual (10-25)," the "Number of lumbar vertebrae per individual (3-10)," the "Number of sacral vertebrae per individual (1-7)," the "Number of ribs per individual (20-50)," the "Number of metacarpals per side per individual (1-5)," the "Number of metatarsals per side per individual (1-5)," the "Number of lateral metapodials per side per individual (0-4)," the "Number of first phalanges per side per individual (1-10)," the "Number of second phalanges per side per individual (1-10)," the "Number of third phalanges per side per individual (1-10)," the "Number of proximal sesamoids per individual

FIGURE 6.10: Listing of the program SKELDIV for creating a file containing zoological families and the average numbers of different kinds of vertebrae, metapodials, phalanges, and sesamoids per individual in each family.

```
1000 REM IBM Personal Computer BASIC (R. G. Klein, 23 January 1984)
1010 DEFINT A-Z
1020 ON ERROR GOTO 2040
1030 PRINT "SKELDIV -- creates a file containing family names (in Latin) and"
1040 PRINT "the numbers of different kinds of vertebrae, metapodials,"
1050 PRINT "phalanges, and sesamoids per individual.  To exit, type 'QUIT'"
1060 PRINT "in response to 'Family'."
1070 PRINT
1080 INPUT "File name";FILE$
1090 OPEN FILE$ FOR INPUT AS #1
1100 PRINT "These familes are already on file:"
1110 WHILE NOT EOF(1)
1120   INPUT#1,FM$,NTH,NLU,NSA,NRI,NMC,NMT,NLM,NP1,NP2,NP3,NPS,NDS
1130   PRINT FM$
1140 WEND
1150 CLOSE#1:OPEN FILE$ FOR APPEND AS #1
1160 ENTER=-1
1170 WHILE ENTER
1180   FM$=""
1190   WHILE RIGHT$(FM$,4)<>"IDAE" AND FM$<>"QUIT"
1200     INPUT "Family (in Latin)";ANS$:GOSUB 1970:FM$=ANS$
1210     IF RIGHT$(FM$,4)<>"IDAE" AND FM$<>"QUIT" THEN BEEP
1220   WEND
1230   IF FM$="QUIT" THEN CLOSE:CLS:END
1260     NTH=0
1270     WHILE NTH<10 OR NTH>25
1280       INPUT "Number of thoracic vertebrae per individual (10-25)";NTH
1290       IF NTH<10 OR NTH>25 THEN BEEP
1300     WEND
1310     NLU=0
1320     WHILE NLU<3 OR NLU>10
1330       INPUT "Number of lumbar vertebrae per individual (3-10)";NLU
1340       IF NLU<3 OR NLU>10 THEN BEEP
1350     WEND
1360     NSA=0
1370     WHILE NSA<1 OR NSA>7
1380       INPUT "Number of sacral vertebrae per individual (1-7)";NSA
1390       IF NSA<1 OR NSA>7 THEN BEEP
1400     WEND
1410     NRI=0
1420     WHILE NRI<20 OR NRI>50
1430       INPUT "Number of ribs per individual (20-50)";NRI
1440       IF NRI<20 OR NRI>50 THEN BEEP
1450     WEND
1460     NMC=0
1470     WHILE NMC<1 OR NMC>5
1480       INPUT "Number of metacarpals per side per individual (1-5)";NMC
1490       IF NMC<1 OR NMC>5 THEN BEEP
1500     WEND
1510     NMT=0
1520     WHILE NMT<1 OR NMT>5
1530       INPUT "Number of metatarsals per side per individual (1-5)";NMT
1540       IF NMT<1 OR NMT>5 THEN BEEP
1550     WEND
1560     NLM=5
1570     WHILE NLM>4
1580       INPUT "Number of lateral metapodials per side per individual (0-4)";
             NLM
1585       IF NLM = 0 THEN NLM = -1
```

```
1590        IF NLM>4 THEN BEEP
1600     WEND
1610     NP1=0
1620     WHILE NP1<1 OR NP1>10
1630        INPUT "Number of first phalanges per side per individual (1-10)";NP1
1640        IF NP1<1 OR NP1>10 THEN BEEP
1650     WEND
1660     NP2=0
1670     WHILE NP2<1 OR NP2>10
1680        INPUT "Number of second phalanges per side per individual (1-10)";
              NP2
1690        IF NP2<1 OR NP2>10 THEN BEEP
1700     WEND
1710     NP3=0
1720     WHILE NP3<1 OR NP3>10
1730        INPUT "Number of third phalanges per side per individual (1-10)";NP3
1740        IF NP3<1 OR NP3>10 THEN BEEP
1750     WEND
1760     NPS=0
1770     WHILE NPS<8 OR NPS>32
1780        INPUT "Number of proximal sesamoids per individual (8-32)";NPS
1790        IF NPS<8 OR NPS>32 THEN BEEP
1800     WEND
1810     NDS=0
1820     WHILE NDS<4 OR NDS>20
1830        INPUT "Number of distal sesamoids per individual (4-20)";NDS
1840        IF NDS<4 OR NDS>20 THEN BEEP
1850     WEND
1860 '
1870     YN$=""
1880     WHILE YN$<>"Y" AND YN$<>"N"
1890        INPUT "Are all entries satisfactory (Y/N)";ANS$:GOSUB 1970:YN$=ANS$
1900        IF YN$<>"Y" AND YN$<>"N" THEN BEEP
1910     WEND
1920     IF YN$="Y" THEN PRINT#1,FM$,"NTH","NLU","NSA","NRI","NMC","NMT",
              "NLM","NP1","NP2","NP3","NPS","NDS
1930 PRINT
1950 WEND
1960 '
1970 REM Capitalization
1980   FOR N=1 TO LEN(ANS$)
1990     LTR$=MID$(ANS$,N,1)
2000     IF "a"<=LTR$ AND LTR$<="z" THEN MID$(ANS$,N,1)=CHR$(ASC(LTR$)-32)
2010   NEXT
2020 RETURN
2030 '
2040 REM Error trap for new file
2050   IF ERR=53 THEN BEEP:PRINT "New file.":RESUME 1150
```

SKELDIV -- creates a file containing family names (in Latin) and
the numbers of different kinds of vertebrae, metapodials,
phalanges, and sesamoids per individual. To exit, type 'QUIT'
in response to 'Family (in Latin)'.

File Name ? SKELDIV.DAT
These families are already on file:
BOVIDAE
Family (in Latin) ? EQUIDAE
Number of thoracic vertebrae per individual (10-25) ? 18
Number of lumbar vertebrae per individual (3-10) ? 6
Number of sacral vertebrae per individual (1-7) ? 1
Number of ribs per individual (20-50) ? 36
Number of metacarpals per side per individual (1-5) ? 1
Number of metatarsals per side per individual (1-5) ? 1
Number of lateral metapodials per side per individual (0-4) ? 4
Number of first phalanges per side per individual (1-10) ? 2
Number of second phalanges per side per individual (1-10) ? 2
Number of third phalanges per side per individual (1-10) ? 2
Number of proximal sesamoids per individual (8-32) ? 8
Number of distal sesamoids per individual (4-20) ? 4
Are all entries satisfactory ? Y

Family (in Latin) ? QUIT

FIGURE 6.11: A SKELDIV sample session.

BOVIDAE,14,6,1,28,1,1,-1,4,4,4,16,8
EQUIDAE,18,6,1,36,1,1,4,2,2,2,8,4

FIGURE 6.12: The file created by the SKELDIV session in figure
6.11. Note the "-1" entry in the record for Bovidae. The
actual entry was "0", but SKELDIV converted this to -1 to
prevent division by 0 in an MNI run.

(8-32)," and the "Number of distal sesamoids per individual (4-20)."
Suitable responses for some of the families that are important in samples
we have studied are presented in table 6.1.

For thoracic vertebrae, SKELDIV will accept only a number between 10
and 25, for lumbars between 3 and 10, for sacrals between 1 and 7, for ribs
between 20 and 50, for metacarpals and metatarsals between 1 and 5, for
lateral metapodials 4 or less, for first, second, and third phalanges a
number between 1 and 10, for proximal sesamoids between 8 and 32, and
for distal sesamoids between 4 and 20.

When the number of distal sesamoids has been entered, SKELDIV asks
"Are all entries satisfactory (Y/N)." If the answer is Y, SKELDIV writes

TABLE 6.5 SKELDIV Prompts and Acceptable Responses

Prompt	Responses
1) File Name	Name of the file in which skeletal part divisors are to be placed. SKELDIV.DAT recommended.
2) Family (in Latin)	The name of the zoological family whose skeletal part divisors are to be entered. Must end in "idae". QUIT -- closes file and terminates session.

3) Number per individual of:

thoracic vertebrae	A number between 10 and 25, depending on the family.
lumbar vertebrae	A number between 3 and 10, depending on the family.
sacral vertebrae	A number between 1 and 7, depending on the family.
ribs	A number between 20 and 50, depending on the family.
metacarpals per side	A number between 1 and 5, depending on the family.
metatarsals per side	A number between 1 and 5, depending on the family.
lateral metapodials per side	A number between 0 and 4, depending on the family.
first phalanges per side	A number between 1 and 10, depending on the family.
second phalanges per side	A number between 1 and 10, depending on the family.
third phalanges per side	A number between 1 and 10, depending on the family.
proximal sesamoids	A number between 8 and 32, depending on the family.
distal sesamoids	A number between 4 and 20, depending on the family.

Prompt	Responses
4) Are all entries satisfactory (Y/N)	Y -- causes entries to be written to file, leading to prompt for (next) "Family (in Latin)". N -- leads immediately to prompt for same (or next) "Family (in Latin)", without writing previous entries to file.

Note: Each response must be followed by a carriage return.

the entire record to file. If the answer is N, it reprompts for family name, and none of the previous entries will be written to file unless reentered in the new prompt series.

A Sample Session with MNI

Figure 6.13 lists MNI. In this section, we present a sample session with MNI. Figure 6.14 is a "photo" of the session with the output. Table 6.6 lists the MNI prompts, acceptable responses, and their effects.

MNI asks first for "Site Name" and then for "Species". The responses are used solely for labeling the printout. They may be virtually any combination of letters and numbers, including embedded blanks. We recommend restricting site and species names to no more than fifty characters each to improve legibility in program output.

MNI next requests "Skeletal part divisors from File or Keyboard (F/K)." These are the numbers of different kinds of vertebrae, metapodials, phalanges, and sesamoids per individual in the species whose MNI is to be computed. If the response is F, MNI then asks "Family (in Latin)." Only a name ending in "idae" will be accepted. Once the family has been entered, MNI requests "Name of file with skeletal part divisors." If the file cannot be located in the system, MNI will print "No such file" and ask again "Skeletal part divisors from File or Keyboard (F/K)."

If the file is located but contains no record for the specified family, MNI will inform the user that the skeletal part divisors must be entered from the keyboard, followed by the prompts for "Number of thoracic vertebrae per individual," "Number of lumbar vertebrae per individual," and so on, exactly as listed in the previous section on the program SKELDIV. If the file does contain a record for the specified family, MNI will print the record to the screen for visual checking by the user.

If the answer to "Skeletal part divisors from File or Keyboard (F/K)" was K, MNI asks immediately for "Number of thoracic vertebrae per individual," followed by "Number of lumbar vertebrae per individual," "Number of sacral vertebrae per individual," "Number of ribs per individual," and so forth. The appropriate response in each case is a number specific to the species whose skeletal parts are to be processed. For each category, MNI accepts only numbers within the limits specified in the preceding section on the program SKELDIV (see also tables 6.5 and 6.6).

Once the skeletal part divisors have been entered, whether from file or keyboard, MNI asks "Ignore or Recognize Left/Right Distinction (I/R)" and "Ignore or Recognize Fused/Unfused Distinction (I/R)." If the answer to either question is R, MNI will take side (left or right), fusion state, or both into account in calculating MNIs, assuming side and fusion state have been specifically recorded in data files. If the answer to either question is I, MNI will treat side, fusion state, or both as indeterminate, regardless of how they appear in data files.

MNI next asks "Number of indistinguishable dI's per individual (0-4)." If the response is a number larger than four, it asks again. If the response is a number between one and four, it requests a list of the indistinguishable

FIGURE 6.13: Listing of the program MNI for calculating NISPs and MNIs from files created by BONECODE and DENTCODE. The variables the program employs are listed in the appendix.

```
1000 REM IBM Personal Computer BASIC (R. G. Klein, 25 January 1984)
1010 CLS
1020 DEFINT A-Z
1030 ON ERROR GOTO 6990
1040 DIM PU$(30),TP(22),TD(22),L!(22,10),R!(22,10),I!(22,10),TL(22,10)
1050 DIM TR(22,10),T(22,10),TPFE(22),TDFE(22),TPUE(22),TDUE(22),TPU(22)
1060 DIM TDU(22),MNIP(22),MNID(22),LMAX(19,3),RMAX(19,3),IMAX(19,3)
1070 DIM LMAND(19,3),RMAND(19,3),IMAND(19,3),RMX!(19),LMX!(19)
1080 DIM RMN!(19),LMN!(19),MAX(27),MAND(27),LB!(48),RB!(48),IB!(48),TLB(48)
1090 DIM TRB(48),TB(50),MNI(50),LMNT!(19),LMNS!(19),RMNT!(19),RMNS!(19)
1100 DIM LMXT!(19),LMXS!(19),RMXT!(19),RMXS!(19),LS!(2),RS!(2),IS!(2),TLS(2)
1110 DIM TRS(2),TS(2),T$(7),TH$(7),DI$(4),I$(4),DP$(4),P$(4),M$(7),CR$(6)
1120 DIM CCR$(6),SKPT$(46),TOOTH$(24),FUST$(5),PPU$(10)
1130 '
1140 REM Bone Lookup Table
1150 FOR Q=1 TO 46:READ SKPT$(Q):NEXT
1160 DATA HU,RA,UL,MC,FE,TI,FI,MT,CA,CL,SC,1P,2P,3P,MP,LM,RI,AX,CE,TH,LU,SA,CU
1170 DATA UN,LN,MA,SD,PI,TD,TM,PA,AS,NA,CD,C1,C2,C3,HY,MD,IN,FR,OC,PS,DS,AT,??
1180 '
1190 REM Tooth Lookup Table
1200 FOR Q=1 TO 24:READ TOOTH$(Q):NEXT
1210 DATA DI1,I1,DI2,I2,DI3,I3,DC,C,DP1,P1,DP2,P2,DP3,P3,DP4,P4,M1,M2,M3
1220 DATA DI,I,DP,P,M
1230 '
1240 PRINT "MNI -- Computes NISPs and MNIs from bones and teeth stored"
1250 PRINT "in files.  Files for bones must end in 'BON'; files for teeth"
1260 PRINT "must end in 'DEN'."
1270 PRINT
1280 '
1290 INPUT "Site Name";S$
1300 INPUT "Species";SP$
1310 '
1320 FK$=""
1330 WHILE FK$<>"F" AND FK$<>"K"
1340   INPUT "Skeletal part divisors from File or Keyboard (F/K)";ANS$:
         GOSUB 6920:FK$=ANS$
1350   IF FK$<>"F" AND FK$<>"K" THEN BEEP
1360 WEND
1370 IF FK$="F" THEN GOSUB 7050 ELSE GOSUB 7370
1380 '
1390 IR$=""
1400 WHILE IR$<>"I" AND IR$<>"R"
1410   INPUT "Ignore or Recognize Left/Right Distinction (I/R)";ANS$:
         GOSUB 6920:IR$=ANS$
1420   IF IR$<>"I" AND IR$<>"R" THEN BEEP
1430 WEND
1440 '
1450 RI$=""
1460 WHILE RI$<>"I" AND RI$<>"R"
1470   INPUT "Ignore or Recognize Fused/Unfused Distinction (I/R)";ANS$:
         GOSUB 6920:RI$=ANS$
1480   IF RI$<>"I" AND RI$<>"R" THEN BEEP
1490 WEND
1500 PRINT
1510 '
1520 REM Indeterminate teeth
1530 NDI=5
1540 WHILE NDI>4
1550   INPUT "Number of indistinguishable dI's per individual (0-4)";NDI
```

```
1560   IF NDI>4 THEN BEEP
1570 WEND
1580 IF NDI>=2 THEN NT=NDI:TOOTH$="dI (dI1,dI2,dI3,dC)":T=4:T$(1)="DI1":
         T$(2)="DI2":T$(3)="DI3":T$(4)="DC":GOSUB 8020:FOR I=1 TO NDI:
         DI$(I)=TH$(I):NEXT
1590 NI=5
1600 WHILE NI>4
1610   INPUT "Number of indistinguishable I's per individual (0-4)";NI
1620   IF NI>4 THEN BEEP
1630 WEND
1640 IF NI>=2 THEN NT=NI:TOOTH$="I (I1,I2,I3,C)":T=4:T$(1)="I1":T$(2)="I2":
         T$(3)="I3":T$(4)="C":GOSUB 8020:FOR I=1 TO NI:I$(I)=TH$(I):NEXT
1650 NDP=5
1660 WHILE NDP>4
1670   INPUT "Number of indistinguishable dP's per individual (0-4)";NDP
1680   IF NDP>4 THEN BEEP
1690 WEND
1700 IF NDP>=2 THEN NT=NDP:TOOTH$="dP (dP1,dP2,dP3,dP4)":T=4:T$(1)="DP1":
         T$(2)="DP2":T$(3)="DP3":T$(4)="DP4":GOSUB 8020:FOR I=1 TO NDP:
         DP$(I)=TH$(I):NEXT
1710 NP=5
1720 WHILE NP>4
1730   INPUT "Number of indistinguishable P's per individual (0-4)";NP
1740   IF NP>4 THEN BEEP
1750 WEND
1760 IF NP>=2 THEN NT=NP:TOOTH$="P (P1,P2,P3,P4)":T=4:T$(1)="P1":T$(2)="P2":
         T$(3)="P3":T$(4)="P4":GOSUB 8020:FOR I=1 TO NP:P$(I)=TH$(I):NEXT
1770 NM=8
1780 WHILE NM>7
1790   INPUT "Number of indistinguishable M's per individual (0-7)";NM
1800   IF NM>7 THEN BEEP
1810 WEND
1820 IF NM>=2 THEN NT=NM:TOOTH$="M (P1,P2,P3,P4,M1,M2,M3)":T=7:T$(1)="P1":
         T$(2)="P2":T$(3)="P3":T$(4)="P4":T$(5)="M1":T$(6)="M2":T$(7)="M3":
         GOSUB 8020:FOR I=1 TO NM:M$(I)=TH$(I):NEXT
1830 '
1840 PRINT
1850 NCR=0
1860 WHILE NCR<1 OR NCR>6
1870   INPUT "How many bone states to include (ALL or 1-6)";ANS$:
           GOSUB 6920:NCR$=ANS$
1880   NCR=VAL(NCR$)
1890   IF NCR$<>"ALL" AND NCR>0 AND NCR<=6 THEN GOSUB 2880 'enter bone state(s)
1900   IF NCR$="ALL" THEN NCR=1:CR$(1)="ALL"
1910   IF NCR<1 OR NCR>6 THEN BEEP
1920 WEND
1930 '
1940 NPU=0
1950 WHILE NPU<1 OR NPU>30
1960   CONTINUE=-1
1970   INPUT "Number of provenience units to enter (ALL or 1-30)";ANS$:
           GOSUB 6920:NPU$=ANS$
1980   NPU=VAL(NPU$)
1990   IF NPU$="ALL" THEN NPU=1:PU$(1)="ALL":CONTINUE=0
2000   WHILE CONTINUE
2010     IF NPU<1 OR NPU>30 THEN BEEP ELSE GOSUB 8150 'enter individual units
2020     CONTINUE=0
2030   WEND
2040 WEND
```

```
2050 '
2060 ENTER=-1
2070 WHILE ENTER
2080   CLS
2090   BT$=""
2100   WHILE BT$<>"B" AND BT$<>"T" AND BT$<>"QUIT"
2110     INPUT "Enter Bones or Teeth (B, T, or QUIT)";ANS$:GOSUB 6920:BT$=ANS$
2120     IF BT$<>"B" AND BT$<>"T" AND BT$<>"QUIT" THEN BEEP
2130   WEND
2140   IF BT$="B" THEN GOSUB 2280 'read bone file and sum fractions
2150   IF BT$="T" THEN GOSUB 2560 'read dental file and calculate MNI's for
           individual teeth
2160   IF BT$="QUIT" THEN ENTER=0
2170 WEND
2180 IF NOT ENTER THEN CLS:LOCATE 25,1:PRINT "Now calculating MNI's. Hang on!";:
         GOSUB 4580 'calculate MNI's
2190 '
2200 YN$=""
2210 WHILE YN$<>"Y" AND YN$<>"N"
2220   INPUT "Want to run program again (Y/N)";ANS$:GOSUB 6920:YN$=ANS$
2230   IF YN$<>"Y" AND YN$<>"N" THEN BEEP
2240 WEND
2250 IF YN$="Y" THEN RUN 1000
2260 IF YN$="N" THEN CLOSE:CLS:END
2270 '
2280 REM Open bone file
2290 BONEFILE$=""
2300 WHILE RIGHT$(BONEFILE$,3)<>"BON"
2310   INPUT "Name of file with bones ".BON"";ANS$:GOSUB 6920:BONEFILE$=ANS$:
           FILE$=BONEFILE$
2320   IF RIGHT$(BONEFILE$,3)<>"BON" THEN BEEP
2330 WEND
2340 CLOSE#1:OPEN BONEFILE$ FOR INPUT AS #1
2350 REC=0
2360 WHILE NOT EOF(1)
2370   INPUT #1,LV$,SK$,LR$,PD$,PES$,FP!,DES$,FD!,CT$,CN$
2380   REC=REC+1
2390   IF LEFT$(LV$,1)="#" THEN LV$=MID$(LV$,2)
2400   LR$=LEFT$(LR$,1):PD$=LEFT$(PD$,1)
2410   IF IR$="I" THEN LR$="I"
2420   IF RI$="I" AND LEFT$(PES$,1)="E" THEN PES$="EF"
2430   IF RI$="I" AND PES$="SU" THEN PES$="SI"
2440   IF RI$="I" AND LEFT$(DES$,1)="E" THEN DES$="EF"
2450   IF RI$="I" AND DES$="SU" THEN DES$="SI"
2460   REM Select out good records
2470   GOODREC=-1
2480   IF CR$(1)<>"ALL" THEN GOSUB 2990: 'check bone state
2490   IF GOODREC A..D PU$(1)<>"ALL" THEN GOSUB 3050
           'check provenience unit
2500   IF GOODREC THEN GOSUB 3120: 'count bones & sum fractions
2510   LOCATE 25,1:PRINT "Now looking at bone"REC"for "LEFT$(SP$,21) SPC(9);:
           LOCATE 25,70:IF GOODREC THEN PRINT "True ";ELSE PRINT "False";
2520 WEND
2530 PRINT
2540 RETURN
2550 '
2560 REM Open dental file
2570   DENTFILE$=""
2580   WHILE RIGHT$(DENTFILE$,3)<>"DEN"
```

```
2590      INPUT "Name of file with dentitions ".DEN"";ANS$:GOSUB 6920:
             DENTFILE$=ANS$:FILE$=DENTFILE$
2600      IF RIGHT$(DENTFILE$,3)<>"DEN" THEN BEEP
2610   WEND
2620   REC=0
2630   CLOSE#1:OPEN DENTFILE$ FOR INPUT AS #1
2640   WHILE NOT EOF(1)
2650      INPUT #1,LV$,UL$,LRB$,LR$,NT,CT$,CN$
2660      REC=REC+1
2670      IF LEFT$(LV$,1)="#" THEN LV$=MID$(LV$,2)
2680      UL$=LEFT$(UL$,1):LRB$=LEFT$(LRB$,1):LR$=LEFT$(LR$,1)
2690      WHILE LRB$="B"
2700         B=B+1
2710         IF B=1 THEN LR$="L" ELSE LR$="R"
2720         IF B=2 THEN B=0
2730         LRB$="N"
2740      WEND
2750      IF IR$="I" THEN LR$="I"
2760 REM Select out good records
2770      GOODREC=-1
2780      IF CR$(1)<>"ALL" THEN GOSUB 2990: 'check bone state
2790      IF GOODREC AND PU$(1)<>"ALL" THEN GOSUB 3050
             'check provenience unit
2800      IF NOT GOODREC THEN FOR J=1 TO NT:INPUT#1,TH$:NEXT
2810      IF GOODREC THEN GOSUB 3840 'count dentitions
2820      LOCATE 25,1:PRINT "Now looking at dentition"REC"for "LEFT$(SP$,21)
             SPC(9);:LOCATE 25,70:IF GOODREC THEN PRINT "True ";
             ELSE PRINT "False";
2830   WEND
2840 PRINT
2850 RETURN
2860 '
2870 '
2880 REM Enter bone state(s)
2890 FOR Q=1 TO NCR
2900   CR$=""
2910   WHILE CR$<>"B" AND CR$<>"C" AND CR$<>"G" AND CR$<>"R" AND
          CR$<>"W" AND CR$<>"X"
2920      INPUT "State (B,C,G,R,W,or X)";ANS$:GOSUB 6920:CR$=ANS$
2930      IF CR$<>"B" AND CR$<>"C" AND CR$<>"G" AND CR$<>"R" AND
             CR$<>"W" AND CR$<>"X" THEN BEEP:PRINT "Bad letter!"
2940   WEND
2950   CR$(Q)=CR$
2960 NEXT Q
2970 RETURN
2980 '
2990 REM Check bone state
3000 FOR Q=1 TO NCR
3010   IF INSTR(1,CT$,CR$(Q))=0 THEN GOODREC=0
3020 NEXT
3030 RETURN
3040 '
3050 REM Check provenience unit
3060 GOODREC=0
3070 FOR Q=1 TO NPU
3080   IF LV$=PU$(Q) THEN GOODREC=-1
3090 NEXT
3100 RETURN
3110 '
```

```
3120 REM Count number of bones entered
3130   SK=SK+1
3140 REM Assign number codes to skeletal parts
3150   WHILE SK$="MP"
3160     MP=MP+1
3170     IF MP=1 THEN SK$="MC" ELSE SK$="MT"
3180     IF MP=2 THEN MP=0
3190   WEND
3200   FOR J=1 TO 46
3210     IF SK$=SKPT$(J) THEN Q=J:J=46
3220   NEXT
3230 REM Numbers for bones
3240   TB(Q)=TB(Q)+1
3250 REM Sum fractions for proximal/distal bones
3260   IF PD$="P" OR PD$="C" THEN TP(Q)=TP(Q)+1:GOSUB 3500
                'assign proximal fusion state numbers & sum fractions
3270   IF PD$="P" THEN RETURN
3280   IF PD$="D" OR PD$="C" THEN TD(Q)=TD(Q)+1:GOSUB 3670:RETURN
                'assign distal fusion state numbers & sum fractions
3290 REM Sum fractions for non-proximal/distal bones
3300   IF LR$="L" THEN LB!(Q)=LB!(Q)+FP!
3310   IF LR$="R" THEN RB!(Q)=RB!(Q)+FP!
3320   IF LR$="I" OR LR$="N" THEN IB!(Q)=IB!(Q)+FP!
3330   IF LR$="B" THEN LB!(Q)=LB!(Q)+FP!:RB!(Q)=RB!(Q)+FD!
3340   IF SK$ <> "FR" THEN RETURN
3350 REM Sum of sex for frontlets
3360   PES$=LEFT$(PES$,1)
3370   WHILE PES$="I"
3380     SEX=SEX+1
3390     IF SEX=1 THEN PES$="M" ELSE PES$="F"
3400     IF SEX=2 THEN SEX=0
3410   WEND
3420   IF PES$="M" THEN N=1
3430   IF PES$="F" THEN N=2
3440   IF LR$="L" THEN LS!(N)=LS!(N)+FP!
3450   IF LR$="R" THEN RS!(N)=RS!(N)+FP!
3460   IF LR$="I" OR LR$="N" THEN IS!(N)=IS!(N)+FP!
3470   IF LR$="B" THEN LS!(N)=LS!(N)+FP!:RS!(N)=RS!(N)+FD!
3480 RETURN
3490 '
3500 REM Assign proximal fusion state numbers
3510   WHILE PES$="EI"
3520     PEI=PEI+1
3530     IF PEI=1 THEN PES$="EF" ELSE PES$="EU"
3540     IF PEI=2 THEN PEI=0
3550   WEND
3560   IF PES$="EF" THEN N=1
3570   IF PES$="EU" THEN N=2
3580   IF PES$="EI" THEN N=3
3590   IF PES$="SU" THEN N=4
3600   IF PES$="SI" THEN N=5
3610 REM Sum fractions by side
3620   IF LR$="L" THEN L!(Q,N)=L!(Q,N)+FP!
3630   IF LR$="R" THEN R!(Q,N)=R!(Q,N)+FP!
3640   IF LR$="I" OR LR$="N" THEN I!(Q,N)=I!(Q,N)+FP!
3650 RETURN
3660 '
3670 REM Assign distal fusion state numbers & sum fractions
3680   WHILE DES$="EI"
```

```
3690        DEI=DEI+1
3700     IF DEI=1 THEN DES$="EF" ELSE DES$="EU"
3710     IF DEI=2 THEN DEI=0
3720   WEND
3730   IF DES$="EF" THEN N=6
3740   IF DES$="EU" THEN N=7
3750   IF DES$="EI" THEN N=8
3760   IF DES$="SU" THEN N=9
3770   IF DES$="SI" THEN N=10
3780 REM Sum fractions by side
3790   IF LR$="L" THEN L!(Q,N)=L!(Q,N)+FD!
3800   IF LR$="R" THEN R!(Q,N)=R!(Q,N)+FD!
3810    IF LR$="I" OR LR$="N" THEN I!(Q,N)=I!(Q,N)+FD!
3820 RETURN
3830 '
3840 REM Count number of dentitions entered
3850   WHILE UL$="I"
3860      UL=UL+1
3870      IF UL=1 THEN UL$="U" ELSE UL$="L"
3880      IF UL=2 THEN UL=0
3890   WEND
3900   IF UL$="U" AND LRB$<>"B" THEN UT=UT+1
3910   IF UL$="U" AND LRB$="B" THEN BUT=BUT+1
3920   IF UL$="L" AND LRB$<>"B" THEN LT=LT+1
3930   IF UL$="L" AND LRB$="B" THEN BLT=BLT+1
3940 REM Enter teeth
3950   FOR J=1 TO NT
3960      INPUT#1,TH$
3970 REM Allocate indeterminate teeth
3980   WHILE TH$="DI"
3990      IDI=IDI+1:XDI=NDI-IDI
4000      IF XDI=3 THEN TH$=DI$(4)
4010      IF XDI=2 THEN TH$=DI$(3)
4020      IF XDI=1 THEN TH$=DI$(2)
4030      IF XDI=0 THEN TH$=DI$(1):IDI=0
4040      IF DI$(1)="" THEN TH$="":BADTOOTH$="DI":GOSUB 8240 'error message
4050   WEND
4060   WHILE TH$="I"
4070      II=II+1:XI=NI-II
4080      IF XI=3 THEN TH$=I$(4)
4090      IF XI=2 THEN TH$=I$(3)
4100      IF XI=1 THEN TH$=I$(2)
4110      IF XI=0 THEN TH$=I$(1):II=0
4120      IF I$(1)="" THEN TH$="":BADTOOTH$="I":GOSUB 8240
4130   WEND
4140   WHILE TH$="DP"
4150      IDP=IDP+1:XDP=NDP-IDP
4160      IF XDP=3 THEN TH$=DP$(4)
4170      IF XDP=2 THEN TH$=DP$(3)
4180      IF XDP=1 THEN TH$=DP$(2)
4190      IF XDP=0 THEN TH$=DP$(1):IDP=0
4200      IF DP$(1)="" THEN TH$="":BADTOOTH$="dP":GOSUB 8240
4210   WEND
4220   WHILE TH$="P"
4230      IP=IP+1:XP=NP-IP
4240      IF XP=3 THEN TH$=P$(4)
4250      IF XP=2 THEN TH$=P$(3)
4260      IF XP=3 THEN TH$=P$(2)
4270      IF XP=0 THEN TH$=P$(1):IP = 0
```

```
4280      IF P$(1)="" THEN TH$="":BADTOOTH$="P":GOSUB 8240
4290   WEND
4300   WHILE TH$="M"
4310      IM=IM+1:XM=NM-IM
4320      IF XM=6 THEN TH$=M$(7)
4330      IF XM=5 THEN TH$=M$(6)
4340      IF XM=4 THEN TH$=M$(5)
4350      IF XM=3 THEN TH$=M$(4)
4360      IF XM=2 THEN TH$=M$(3)
4370      IF XM=1 THEN TH$=M$(2)
4380      IF XM=0 THEN TH$=M$(1):IM=0
4390      IF M$(1)="" THEN TH$="":BADTOOTH$="M":GOSUB 8240
4400   WEND
4410   IF TH$="" THEN RETURN
4420 REM Assign number codes to teeth
4430   FOR K=1 TO 19
4440      IF TH$=TOOTH$(K) THEN Q=K:N=1:K=19
4450      IF TH$="S/"+TOOTH$(K) THEN Q=K:N=2:K=19
4460      IF TH$="S"+TOOTH$(K) THEN Q=K:N=3:K=19
4470   NEXT
4480 REM MNI's for individual teeth
4490   IF LR$="L" AND UL$="L" THEN LMAND(Q,N)=LMAND(Q,N)+1
4500   IF LR$="R" AND UL$="L" THEN RMAND(Q,N)=RMAND(Q,N)+1
4510   IF LR$="I" AND UL$="L" THEN IMAND(Q,N)=IMAND(Q,N)+1
4520   IF LR$="L" AND UL$="U" THEN LMAX(Q,N)=LMAX(Q,N)+1
4530   IF LR$="R" AND UL$="U" THEN RMAX(Q,N)=RMAX(Q,N)+1
4540   IF LR$="I" AND UL$="U" THEN IMAX(Q,N)=IMAX(Q,N)+1
4550   NEXT J
4560 RETURN
4570 '
4580 REM Sums for limbbone epiphyses and shafts
4590   FOR Q=1 TO 17
4600      FOR N=1 TO 10
4610         TL(Q,N)=INT(L!(Q,N)+(I!(Q,N)/2)+.9899999)
4620         TR(Q,N)=INT(R!(Q,N)+(I!(Q,N)/2)+.9899999)
4630         IF TL(Q,N)>TR(Q,N) THEN T(Q,N)=TL(Q,N) ELSE T(Q,N)=TR(Q,N)
4640      NEXT N
4650   NEXT Q
4660 REM Sums for vertebral epiphyses and bodies
4670   FOR Q=18 TO 22
4680      FOR N=1 TO 10
4690         T(Q,N)=INT(I!(Q,N)+.9899999)
4700      NEXT N
4710   NEXT Q
4720 REM Sums for fused and unfused epiphyses
4730   FOR Q=1 TO 22
4740      TPFE(Q)=T(Q,1)
4750      TDFE(Q)=T(Q,6)
4760      TPUE(Q)=T(Q,2)
4770      TDUE(Q)=T(Q,7)
4780      IF TPUE(Q)>T(Q,4) THEN TPU(Q)=TPUE(Q) ELSE TPU(Q)=T(Q,4)
4790      IF TDUE(Q)>T(Q,9) THEN TDU(Q)=TDUE(Q) ELSE TDU(Q)=T(Q,9)
4800   NEXT Q
4810 REM MNI's for limbbones and scapula
4820   FOR Q=1 TO 11
4830      MNIP(Q)=TPFE(Q)+TPU(Q)
4840      MNID(Q)=TDFE(Q)+TDU(Q)
4850   NEXT Q
4860 REM MNI's for metapodials
```

```
4870    MNIP(4)=INT((MNIP(4)/NMC)+.9899999)
4880    MNID(4)=INT((TDFE(4)/NMC)+.9899999)+INT((TDU(4)/NMC)+.9899999)
4890    MNIP(8)=INT((MNIP(8)/NMT)+.9899999)
4900    MNID(8)=INT((TDFE(8)/NMT)+.9899999)+INT((TDU(8)/NMT)+.9899999)
4910    MNIP(16)=INT((MNIP(16)/NLM)+.9899999)
4920    MNID(16)=INT((TDFE(16)/NLM)+.9899999)+INT((TDU(16)/NLM)+.9899999)
4930 REM MNI'S for phalanges
4940    MNIP(12)=INT((TPFE(12)/NP1)+.9899999)+INT((TPU(12)/NP1)+.9899999)
4950    MNID(12)=INT((TDFE(12)/NP1)+.9899999)
4960    MNIP(13)=INT((TPFE(13)/NP2)+.9899999)+INT((TPU(13)/NP2)+.9899999)
4970    MNID(13)=INT((TDFE(13)/NP2)+.9899999)
4980    MNIP(14)=INT((TPFE(14)/NP3)+.9899999)+INT((TPU(14)/NP3)+.9899999)
4990    MNID(14)=INT((TDFE(14)/NP3)+.9899999)
5000 REM MNI's for ribs and vertebrae
5010    MNIP(17)=INT((TPFE(17)/NRI)+.9899999)+INT((TPU(17)/NRI)+.9899999) 'ribs
5020    MNID(17)=INT((TDFE(17)/NRI)+.9899999)+INT((TDU(17)/NRI)+.9899999)
5030    MNIP(18)=INT(TPFE(18)+.9899999)+INT(TPU(18)+.9899999) 'axis
5040    MNID(18)=INT(TDFE(18)+.9899999)+INT(TDU(18)+.9899999)
5050    MNIP(19)=INT((TPFE(19)/5)+.9899999)+INT((TPU(19)/5)+.9899999) 'cervicals
5060    MNID(19)=INT((TDFE(19)/5)+.9899999)+INT((TDU(19)/5)+.9899999)
5070    MNIP(20)=INT((TPFE(20)/NTH)+.9899999)+INT((TPU(20)/NTH)+.9899999)
            'thoracics
5080    MNID(20)=INT((TDFE(20)/NTH)+.9899999)+INT((TDU(20)/NTH)+.9899999)
5090    MNIP(21)=INT((TPFE(21)/NLU)+.9899999)+INT((TPU(21)/NLU)+.9899999)
            'lumbars
5100    MNID(21)=INT((TDFE(21)/NLU)+.9899999)+INT((TDU(21)/NLU)+.9899999)
5110    MNIP(22)=INT((TPFE(22)/NSA)+.9899999)+INT((TPU(22)/NSA)+.9899999)
            'sacral
5120    MNID(22)=INT((TDFE(22)/NSA)+.9899999)+INT((TDU(22)/NSA)+.9899999)
5130 REM Summary MNI's for limbbones, phalanges, and vertebrae
5140    FOR Q=1 TO 22
5150      IF MNIP(Q)>MNID(Q) THEN MNI(Q)=MNIP(Q) ELSE MNI(Q)=MNID(Q)
5160    NEXT Q
5170    MNI(45)=INT(IB!(45)+.9899999) 'atlas
5180 REM MNI's for remaining bones
5190    FOR Q=23 TO 44
5200      TLB(Q)=INT(LB!(Q)+(IB!(Q)/2)+.9899999)
5210      TRB(Q)=INT(RB!(Q)+(IB!(Q)/2)+.9899999)
5220      IF TLB(Q)>TRB(Q) THEN MNI(Q)=TLB(Q) ELSE MNI(Q)=TRB(Q)
5230    NEXT Q
5240 REM MNI for frontlet
5250    FOR N=1 TO 2
5260      TLS(N)=INT(LS!(N)+(IS!(N)/2)+.9899999)
5270      TRS(N)=INT(RS!(N)+(IS!(N)/2)+.9899999)
5280      IF TLS(N)>TRS(N) THEN TS(N)=TLS(N) ELSE TS(N)=TRS(N)
5290    NEXT N
5300    MNI(41)=TS(1)+TS(2)
5310 REM MNI's for sesamoids
5320    MNI(43)=INT((IB!(43)/NPS)+.9899999) 'proximal sesamoids
5330    MNI(44)=INT((IB!(44)/NDS)+.9899999) 'distal sesamoids
5340 REM Numbers and MNI's for carpals
5350    TB(47)=TB(23)+TB(24)+TB(25)+TB(26)+TB(27)+TB(28)+TB(29)+TB(30)
5360    MNI(47)=MNI(23)
5370    FOR Q=24 TO 30
5380      IF MNI(Q)>=MNI(47) THEN MNI(47)=MNI(Q)
5390    NEXT Q
5400 REM Numbers and MNI's for cuneiform tarsals
5410    TB(48)=TB(35)+TB(36)+TB(37)
5420    MNI(48)=MNI(35)
```

```
5430    FOR Q=36 TO 37
5440       IF MNI(Q)> =MNI(48) THEN MNI(48)=MNI(Q)
5450    NEXT Q
5460 REM MNI's for teeth
5470    FOR Q=1 TO 19
5480       LMNT!(Q)=LMAND(Q,1)+LMAND(Q,2)+(IMAND(Q,1)/2)+(IMAND(Q,2)/2)
5490       LMNS!(Q)=LMAND(Q,2)+LMAND(Q,3)+(IMAND(Q,2)/2)+(IMAND(Q,3)/2)
5500       RMNT!(Q)=RMAND(Q,1)+RMAND(Q,2)+(IMAND(Q,1)/2)+(IMAND(Q,2)/2)
5510       RMNS!(Q)=RMAND(Q,2)+RMAND(Q,3)+(IMAND(Q,2)/2)+(IMAND(Q,3)/2)
5520       LMXT!(Q)=LMAX(Q,1)+LMAX(Q,2)+(IMAX(Q,1)/2)+(IMAX(Q,2)/2)
5530       LMXS!(Q)=LMAX(Q,2)+LMAX(Q,3)+(IMAX(Q,2)/2)+(IMAX(Q,3)/2)
5540       RMXT!(Q)=RMAX(Q,1)+RMAX(Q,2)+(IMAX(Q,1)/2)+(IMAX(Q,2)/2)
5550       RMXS!(Q)=RMAX(Q,2)+RMAX(Q,3)+(IMAX(Q,2)/2)+(IMAX(Q,3)/2)
5560       IF LMNT!(Q)>LMNS!(Q) THEN LMN!(Q)=LMNT!(Q) ELSE LMN!(Q)=LMNS!(Q)
5570       IF RMNT!(Q)>RMNS!(Q) THEN RMN!(Q)=RMNT!(Q) ELSE RMN!(Q)=RMNS!(Q)
5580       IF LMXT!(Q)>LMXS!(Q) THEN LMX!(Q)=LMXT!(Q) ELSE LMX!(Q)=LMXS!(Q)
5590       IF RMXT!(Q)>RMXS!(Q) THEN RMX!(Q)=RMXT!(Q) ELSE RMX!(Q)=RMXS!(Q)
5600       LMN!(Q)=INT(LMN!(Q)+.9899999):RMN!(Q)=INT(RMN!(Q)+.9899999)
5610       LMX!(Q)=INT(LMX!(Q)+.9899999):RMX!(Q)=INT(RMX!(Q)+.9899999)
5620       IF RMX!(Q)> =LMX!(Q) THEN MAX(Q)=RMX!(Q) ELSE MAX(Q)=LMX!(Q)
5630       IF RMN!(Q)> =LMN!(Q) THEN MAND(Q)=RMN!(Q) ELSE MAND(Q)=LMN!(Q)
5640    NEXT Q
5650       MAX(20)=MAX(1)+MAX(2):MAND(20)=MAND(1)+MAND(2)
5660       MAX(21)=MAX(3)+MAX(4):MAND(21)=MAND(3)+MAND(4)
5670       MAX(22)=MAX(5)+MAX(6):MAND(22)=MAND(5)+MAND(6)
5680       MAX(23)=MAX(7)+MAX(8):MAND(23)=MAND(7)+MAND(8)
5690       MAX(24)=MAX(9)+MAX(10):MAND(24)=MAND(9)+MAND(10)
5700       MAX(25)=MAX(11)+MAX(12):MAND(25)=MAND(11)+MAND(12)
5710       MAX(26)=MAX(13)+MAX(14):MAND(26)=MAND(13)+MAND(14)
5720       MAX(27)=MAX(15)+MAX(16):MAND(27)=MAND(15)+MAND(16)
5730    FOR Q=17 TO 27
5740       IF MAX(Q)> =MNI(49) THEN MNI(49)=MAX(Q)
5750       IF MAND(Q)> =MNI(50) THEN MNI(50)=MAND(Q)
5760    NEXT Q
5770 REM Calculate final MNI
5780    FOR Q=1 TO 50
5790       IF MNI(Q)>MNI THEN MNI=MNI(Q)
5800    NEXT Q
5810    FOR Q=1 TO 48
5820       IF MNI(Q)>MNIB THEN MNIB=MNI(Q)
5830    NEXT Q
5840    IF MNI(49)>MNI(50) THEN MNIT=MNI(49) ELSE MNIT=MNI(50)
5850 REM Total number of bones and teeth
5860    TB(49)=INT(UT+(BUT/2)+.9899999)  'total upper dentitions
5870    TB(50)=INT(LT+(BLT/2)+.9899999)  'total lower dentitions
5880    TT=TB(49)+TB(50)     'total dentitions
5890    NISP=SK+TT           'total all bones
5900 REM Print results
5910    CLS
5920    N$=SPACE$(9)
5930    FOR Q=1 TO NCR
5940       IF CR$(Q)="B" THEN CCR$(Q)="Burnt"
5950       IF CR$(Q)="C" THEN CCR$(Q)="Chewed"
5960       IF CR$(Q)="G" THEN CCR$(Q)="Gnawed"
5970       IF CR$(Q)="R" THEN CCR$(Q)="Rolled"
5980       IF CR$(Q)="W" THEN CCR$(Q)="Weathered"
5990       IF CR$(Q)="X" THEN CCR$(Q)="Cut"
6000       F CR$(Q)="ALL" THEN CCR$(Q)="All"
6010    NEXT Q
```

160

```
6020 CLOSE:SOFTCOPY=-1:HC$=""
6030 WHILE SOFTCOPY
6040   IF HC$="" THEN OPEN "SCRN:" FOR OUTPUT AS #1
6050   IF HC$="Y" THEN SOFTCOPY=0:CLOSE#1:OPEN "LPT1:" FOR OUTPUT AS #1
6060   PRINT#1,N$ "              ";DATE$;" ";TIME$
6070   PRINT#1,
6080   PRINT#1,N$  S$
6090   PRINT#1,N$ SP$
6100   PRINT#1,N$  "From provenience units:"
6110   I=1:PPU$(I)=""
6120   FOR Q=1 TO NPU
6130     PPU$(I)=PPU$(I)+PU$(Q)+" "
6140     IF LEN(PPU$(I))>=40 THEN I=I+1:PPU$(I)=""
6150   NEXT Q
6160   FOR Q=1 TO I
6170     IF PPU$(Q)<>"" THEN PRINT#1,N$ PPU$(Q)
6180   NEXT
6190   PRINT#1,N$ "Bone States: ";
6200   CCR$=""
6210   FOR Q=1 TO NCR
6220     CCR$=CCR$+CCR$(Q)+" "
6230   NEXT Q
6240   PRINT#1,TAB(24) CCR$
6250   IF IR$="I" THEN IR$="Ignored" ELSE IR$="Recognized"
6260   IF RI$="I" THEN RI$="Ignored" ELSE RI$="Recognized"
6270   PRINT#1,N$ "Left/Right Distinction: "; IR$
6280   PRINT#1,N$ "Fused/Unfused Distinction: "; RI$
6290   PRINT#1,
6300   PRINT#1,N$ "SKELETAL ELEMENT" TAB(35)"NO. OF BONES" TAB(50)"MNI"
6310   PRINT#1,N$ "Frontlet" TAB(35) TB(41) TAB(50) MNI(41)
6320   PRINT#1,N$ "Occipital condyle" TAB(35) TB(42) TAB(50) MNI(42)
6330   PRINT#1,N$ "Maxilla" TAB(35) TB(49) TAB(50) MNI(49)
6340   PRINT#1,N$ "Mandible" TAB(35) TB(50) TAB(50) MNI(50)
6350   PRINT#1,N$ "Mandibular condyle" TAB(35) TB(39) TAB(50) MNI(39)
6360   PRINT#1,N$ "Hyoid" TAB(35) TB(38) TAB(50) MNI(38)
6370   PRINT#1,N$ "Atlas" TAB(35) TB(45) TAB(50) MNI(45)
6380   PRINT#1,N$ "Axis" TAB(35) TB(18) TAB(50) MNI(18)
6390   PRINT#1,N$ "Cervical vertebrae 3-7" TAB(35) TB(19) TAB(50) MNI(19)
6400   PRINT#1,N$ "Thoracic vertebrae" TAB(35) TB(20) TAB(50) MNI(20)
6410   PRINT#1,N$ "Lumbar vertebrae" TAB(35) TB(21) TAB(50) MNI(21)
6420   PRINT#1,N$ "Sacral vertebrae" TAB(35) TB(22) TAB(50) MNI(22)
6430   PRINT#1,N$ "Ribs" TAB(35) TB(17) TAB(50) MNI(17)
6440   PRINT#1,N$ "Scapula (glenoid)" TAB(35) TB(11) TAB(50) MNI(11)
6450 IF HC$="" THEN PRINT "Press any key to continue ...";:YY$=INKEY$:
     WHILE YY$="":YY$=INKEY$:WEND:PRINT#1,
6460   PRINT#1,N$ "Clavicle--proximal" TAB(35) TP(10) TAB(50) MNIP(10)
6470   PRINT#1,N$ "Clavicle--distal" TAB(35) TD(10) TAB(50) MNID(10)
6480   PRINT#1,N$ "Humerus--proximal" TAB(35) TP(1) TAB(50) MNIP(1)
6490   PRINT#1,N$ "Humerus--distal" TAB(35) TD(1) TAB(50) MNID(1)
6500   PRINT#1,N$ "Radius--proximal" TAB(35) TP(2) TAB(50) MNIP(2)
6510   PRINT#1,N$ "Radius--distal" TAB(35) TD(2) TAB(50) MNID(2)
6520   PRINT#1,N$ "Ulna--proximal" TAB(35) TP(3) TAB(50) MNIP(3)
6530   PRINT#1,N$ "Ulna--distal" TAB(35) TD(3) TAB(50) MNID(3)
6540   PRINT#1,N$ "Carpals" TAB(35) TB(47) TAB(50) MNI(47)
6550   PRINT#1,N$ "Metacarpal--proximal" TAB(35) TP(4) TAB(50) MNIP(4)
6560   PRINT#1,N$ "Metacarpal--distal" TAB(35) TD(4) TAB(50) MNID(4)
6570   PRINT#1,N$ "Phalanges--first" TAB(35) TB(12) TAB(50) MNI(12)
6580   PRINT#1,N$ "Phalanges--second" TAB(35) TB(13) TAB(50) MNI(13)
6590   PRINT#1,N$ "Phalanges--third" TAB(35) TB(14) TAB(50) MNI(14)
```

```
6600    PRINT#1,N$ "Innominate (acetabulum)" TAB(35) TB(40) TAB(50) MNI(40)
6610    PRINT#1,N$ "Femur--proximal" TAB(35) TP(5) TAB(50) MNIP(5)
6620    PRINT#1,N$ "Femur--distal" TAB(35) TD(5) TAB(50) MNID(5)
6630    PRINT#1,N$ "Patella" TAB(35) TB(31) TAB(50) MNI(31)
6640    PRINT#1,N$ "Tibia--proximal" TAB(35) TP(6) TAB(50) MNIP(6)
6650    PRINT#1,N$ "Tibia--distal" TAB(35) TD(6) TAB(50) MNID(6)
6660    PRINT#1,N$ "Fibula--proximal" TAB(35) TP(7) TAB(50) MNIP(7)
6670    PRINT#1,N$ "Fibula--distal" TAB(35) TD(7) TAB(50) MNID(7)
6680 IF HC$="" THEN PRINT "Press any key to continue ...";:YY$=INKEY$:
        WHILE YY$="":YY$=INKEY$:WEND:PRINT#1,
6690    PRINT#1,N$ "Metatarsal--proximal" TAB(35) TP(8) TAB(50) MNIP(8)
6700    PRINT#1,N$ "Metatarsal--distal" TAB(35) TD(8) TAB(50) MNID(8)
6710    PRINT#1,N$ "Calcaneum" TAB(35) TB(9) TAB(50) MNI(9)
6720    PRINT#1,N$ "Astragalus" TAB(35) TB(32) TAB(50) MNI(32)
6730    PRINT#1,N$ "Navicular" TAB(35) TB(33) TAB(50) MNI(33)
6740    PRINT#1,N$ "Cuboid" TAB(35) TB(34) TAB(50) MNI(34)
6750    PRINT#1,N$ "Cuneiforms (tarsals)" TAB(35) TB(48) TAB(50) MNI(48)
6760    PRINT#1,N$ "Lateral metapodials" TAB(35) TB(16) TAB(50) MNI(16)
6770    PRINT#1,N$ "Proximal sesamoids" TAB(35) TB(43) TAB(50) MNI(43)
6780    PRINT#1,N$ "Distal sesamoids" TAB(35) TB(44) TAB(50) MNI(44)
6790    PRINT#1,N$ "----------------------------------------------"
6800    PRINT#1,N$ "TOTALS FOR BONES = " TAB(35) SK TAB(50) MNIB
6810    PRINT#1,N$ "TOTAL FOR DENTITIONS = " TAB(35) TT TAB(50) MNIT
6820    PRINT#1,
6830    PRINT#1,N$ "GRAND TOTALS = " TAB(35) NISP TAB(50) MNI
6840 '
6850    WHILE HC$<>"Y" AND HC$<>"N"
6860      INPUT "Want hard copy (Y/N)";ANS$:GOSUB 6920:HC$=ANS$
6870      IF HC$<>"Y" AND HC$<>"N" THEN BEEP
6880    WEND
6890    IF HC$="N" THEN SOFTCOPY=0
6900 WEND
6910 '
6920 REM Capitalization
6930    FOR N=1 TO LEN(ANS$)
6940      LTR$=MID$(ANS$,N,1)
6950      IF "a"<=LTR$ AND LTR$<="z" THEN MID$(ANS$,N,1)=CHR$(ASC(LTR$)-32)
6960    NEXT
6970 RETURN
6980 '
6990 REM Error traps
7000 IF ERR=53 AND FILE$=BONEFILE$ THEN BEEP:PRINT "No such file":RESUME 2290
7010 IF ERR=53 AND FILE$=DENTFILE$ THEN BEEP:PRINT "No such file":RESUME 2570
7020 IF ERR=53 AND FILE$=DIVFILE$ THEN BEEP:PRINT "No such file":RESUME 1320
7030 IF ERR=27 THEN BEEP:PRINT "Turn on the Printer! Press any key to continue":
        YY$=INKEY$:WHILE YY$="":YY$=INKEY$:WEND:RESUME 6050
7040 '
7050 REM Divisors from file
7060 FAM$=""
7070 WHILE RIGHT$(FAM$,4)<>"IDAE"
7080    INPUT "Family (in Latin)";ANS$:GOSUB 6920:FAM$=ANS$
7090    IF RIGHT$(FAM$,4)<>"IDAE" THEN BEEP
7100 WEND
7110 INPUT "Name of file with skeletal part divisors";DIVFILE$:FILE$=DIVFILE$
7120 OPEN DIVFILE$ FOR INPUT AS #1
7130 WHILE NOT EOF(1) AND FM$<>FAM$
7140    INPUT #1,FM$,NTH,NLU,NSA,NRI,NMC,NMT,NLM,NP1,NP2,NP3,NPS,NDS
7150    IF FM$=FAM$ THEN GOSUB 7210
7160 WEND
```

```
7170 IF FM$<>FAM$ THEN BEEP:PRINT "Named family not on file.":
      PRINT "Divisors must be entered from the keyboard."
7180 RETURN
7190 '
7200 REM Print divisor results from file
7210   PRINT:PRINT FM$
7220   PRINT "Number of thoracic vertebrae per individual is"NTH
7230   PRINT "Number of lumbar vertebrae per individual is"NLU
7240   PRINT "Number of sacral vertebrae per individual is"NSA
7250   PRINT "Number of ribs per individual is"NRI
7260   PRINT "Number of metacarpals per side per individual is"NMC
7270   PRINT "Number of metatarsals per side per individual is"NMT
7280   PRINT "Number of lateral metapodials per side is"NLM
7290   PRINT "Number of first phalanges per side per individual is"NP1
7300   PRINT "Number of second phalanges per side per individual is"NP2
7310   PRINT "Number of third phalanges per side per individual is"NP3
7320   PRINT "Number of proximal sesamoids per individual is"NPS
7330   PRINT "Number of distal sesamoids per individual is"NDS
7340   PRINT:PRINT
7350 RETURN
7360 '
7370 REM Divisors from Keyboard
7380 NTH=0
7390 WHILE NTH<10 OR NTH>25
7400   INPUT "Number of thoracic vertebrae per individual (10-25)";NTH
7410   IF NTH<10 OR NTH>25 THEN BEEP
7420 WEND
7430 NLU=0
7440 WHILE NLU<3 OR NLU>10
7450   INPUT "Number of lumbar vertebrae per individual (3-10)";NLU
7460   IF NLU<3 OR NLU>10 THEN BEEP
7470 WEND
7480 NSA=0
7490 WHILE NSA<1 OR NSA>7
7500   INPUT "Number of sacral vertebrae per individual (1-7)";NSA
7510   IF NSA<1 OR NSA>7 THEN BEEP
7520 WEND
7530 NRI=0
7540 WHILE NRI<20 OR NRI>50
7550   INPUT "Number of ribs per individual (20-50)";NRI
7560   IF NRI<20 OR NRI>50 THEN BEEP
7570 WEND
7580 NMC=0
7590 WHILE NMC<1 OR NMC>5
7600   INPUT "Number of metacarpals per side per individual (1-5)";NMC
7610   IF NMC<1 OR NMC>5 THEN BEEP
7620 WEND
7630 NMT=0
7640 WHILE NMT<1 OR NMT>5
7650   INPUT "Number of metatarsals per side per individual (1-5)";NMT
7660   IF NMT<1 OR NMT>5 THEN BEEP
7670 WEND
7680 NLM=5
7690 WHILE NLM>4
7700   INPUT "Number of lateral metapodials per side per individual (0-4)";NLM
7710   IF NLM>4 THEN BEEP
7720   IF NLM=0 THEN NLM=-1
7730 WEND
7740 NP1=0
```

```
7750 WHILE NP1<1 OR NP1>10
7760  INPUT "Number of first phalanges per side per individual (1-10)";NP1
7770  IF NP1<1 OR NP1>10 THEN BEEP
7780 WEND
7790 NP2=0
7800 WHILE NP2<1 OR NP2>10
7810  INPUT "Number of second phalanges per side per individual (1-10)";NP2
7820  IF NP2<1 OR NP2>10 THEN BEEP
7830 WEND
7840 NP3=0
7850 WHILE NP3<1 OR NP3>10
7860  INPUT "Number of third phalanges per side per individual (1-10)";NP3
7870  IF NP3<1 OR NP3>10 THEN BEEP
7880 WEND
7890 NPS=0
7900 WHILE NPS<8 OR NPS>32
7910  INPUT "Number of proximal sesamoids per individual (8-32)";NPS
7920  IF NPS<8 OR NPS>32 THEN BEEP
7930 WEND
7940 NDS=0
7950 WHILE NDS<4 OR NDS>20
7960  INPUT "Number of distal sesamoids per individual (4-20)";NDS
7970  IF NDS<4 OR NDS>20 THEN BEEP
7980 WEND
7990 PRINT:PRINT
8000 RETURN
8010 '
8020 REM Individual indeterminate teeth
8030 FOR I=1 TO NT
8040  CONTINUE=-1
8050  WHILE CONTINUE
8060   PRINT "Indeterminate "TOOTH$ I;:INPUT ANS$:GOSUB 6920:TH$(I)=ANS$
8070   FOR Q=1 TO T
8080    IF TH$(I)=T$(Q) THEN CONTINUE=0:Q=T
8090   NEXT Q
8100   IF CONTINUE THEN BEEP
8110  WEND
8120 NEXT I
8130 RETURN
8140 '
8150 REM Individual provenience units
8160  CHANGE=0
8170  FOR Q=1 TO NPU
8180   INPUT "Provenience unit";ANS$:GOSUB 6920:PU$(Q)=ANS$
8190   IF PU$(Q)="CHANGE" THEN CHANGE=-1:Q=NPU
8200  NEXT
8210  IF CHANGE THEN NPU=0
8220 RETURN
8230 '
8240 REM Error message when indeterminate teeth are in a file and cannot be
8250 REM allocated.
8260 BEEP:CLS
8270 PRINT"There is an indeterminate "BADTOOTH$" in the file, but you did not"
8280 PRINT"specify this in advance. It will be counted in the NISP, but not"
8290 PRINT "in the MNI. Press any key to continue..."
8300 YY$=INKEY$:WHILE YY$="":YY$=INKEY$:WEND
8310 RETURN
```

deciduous incisor (dI) types, one at a time, with the prompt "Indeterminate dI (dI1/dI2/dI3/dC)." If the answer is not dI1, dI2, dI3, or dC, it repeats the prompt.

When the list of indistinguishable deciduous incisors has been entered, MNI asks "Number of indistinguishable I's per individual (0-4)," followed by a request for a list of the indistinguishable I (incisor) types. In sequence, the next requests are for "Number of indistinguishable dP's per individual (0-4)," a list of the indistinguishable dP (deciduous premolar) types, "Number of indistinguishable P's per individual (0-4)," a list of the indistinguishable P (premolar) types, "Number of indistinguishable M's per individual (0-7)," and a list of indistinguishable M (molar) types. The number entered may not exceed four for Is, dPs, and Ps. It may not exceed seven for Ms.

The list of indeterminate (indistinguishable) incisor categories may include only I1, I2, I3, and C; the list of indeterminate deciduous premolars only dP1, dP2, dP3, and dP4; the list of indeterminate Ps only P1, P2, P3, and P4; and the list of indeterminate M's only P1, P2, P3, P4, M1, M2, and M3. If the user does not wish to designate any tooth types within a category as indeterminate, the best response to a request for the "number" in that category is a simple carriage return.

After the list of indeterminate Ms has been entered, MNI asks "How many bone states to include (ALL or 1-6)." This is to determine whether the user wants NISPs and MNIs for bones and dentitions in just one state or a combination of states (e.g. Burned, Burned and Cut, or Cut, Rolled, and Chewed). If the answer to number of states is ALL, MNI will calculate NISPs and MNIs for all bones and dentitions, regardless of state. If the answer is a number between 1 and 6, MNI will then repeat the prompt "State (B,C,G,R,W, or X)" that many times. The only acceptable response to each State request is a single letter indicating a state the user is interested in (B for Burned, C for carnivore-Chewed, G for rodent-Gnawed, R for Rolled, W for Weathered, and X for Cut).

For example, if a user wanted MNI to work only with bones that were burned and cut, the proper answer to the number of states to include would be "2". The proper answers to the two subsequent state requests would be B and X or X and B. (The order of entry is immaterial). It is important to stress that by specifying burned and cut, the user is instructing MNI to work with bones that are both burned and cut, not bones that are (only) burned plus ones that are (only) cut plus bones that are both burned and cut.

MNI next asks "Number of provenience units to enter (ALL or 1-30)." If the user wants MNI to perform calculations on all bones and dentitions regardless of provenience unit, the proper answer is ALL. Otherwise the answer must be a number between 1 and 30. This is the number of provenience units that the user wishes MNI to treat as a single provenience unit for the sake of NISP and MNI calculations. We have arbitrarily limited the number to thirty. However, there is no fundamental programmatic reason why the number could not be increased if the user

FIGURE 6.14: An MNI sample session with output, involving bones of domestic goat from the Medieval site of Beniali, eastern Spain (excavations reported in Butzer, n.d).

MNI -- Computes NISPs and MNIs from bones and teeth stored in files. Files for bones must end in 'BON'; files for teeth must end in 'DEN'.

Site Name ? BENIALI
Species ? Capra hircus
Skeletal part divisors from File or Keyboard (F/K) ? F
Family (in Latin) ? Bovidae
Name of file with skeletal part divisors ? SKELDIV.DAT

BOVIDAE
Number of thoracic vertebrae per individual is 14
Number of lumbar vertebrae per individual is 6
Number of sacral vertebrae per individual is 1
Number of ribs per individual is 28
Number of metacarpals per side per individual is 1
Number of metatarsals per side per individual is 1
Number of lateral metapodials per side per individual is -1
Number of first phalanges per side per individual is 4
Number of second phalanges per side per individual is 4
Number of third phalanges per side per individual is 4
Number of proximal sesamoids per side per individual is 16
Number of distal sesamoids per side per individual is 8

Ignore or Recognize Left/Right Distinction (I/R) ? R
Ignore or Recognize Fused/Unfused Distinction (I/R) ? R

Number of indistinguishable dI's per individual ? 4
Indeterminate dI (dI1/dI2/dI3/dC) 1 ? dI1
Indeterminate dI (dI1/dI2/dI3/dC) 2 ? dI2
Indeterminate dI (dI1/dI2/dI3/dC) 3 ? dI3
Indeterminate dI (dI1/dI2/dI3/dC) 4 ? dC
Number of indistinguishable I's per individual ? 4
Indeterminate I (I1/I2/I3/C) 1 ? I1
Indeterminate I (I1/I2/I3/C) 2 ? I2
Indeterminate I (I1/I2/I3/C) 3 ? I3
Indeterminate I (I1/I2/I3/C) 4 ? C
Number of indistinguishable dP's per individual ? 0
Number of indistinguishable P's per individual ? 2
Indeterminate P (P1/P2/P3/P4) 1 ? P3
Indeterminate P (P1/P2/P3/P4) 2 ? P4
Number of indistinguishable M's per individual ? 2
Indeterminate M (P1/P2/P3/P4/M1/M2/M3) 1 ? M1

Indeterminate M (P1/P2/P3/P4/M1/M2/M3) 2 ? M2

How many bone states to include (ALL or 1-6) ? 2
Bone State (B,C,G,R,W, or X) ? B
Bone State (B,C,G,R,W, or X) ? C
Number of provenience units to enter (ALL or 1-30) ? ALL
Enter Bones or Teeth (B, T, or QUIT) ? B
Name of file with bones [.BON] ? BENCH.BON
Enter Bones or Teeth (B, T, or QUIT) ? T
Name of file with dentitions [.DEN] ? BENCH.DEN
Enter Bones or Teeth (B/T or QUIT) ? QUIT

03-23-83 20:27:00

BENIALI
Capra hircus
From provenience units:
ALL
Bone States: Burnt Chewed
Left/Right Distinction: Recognized
Fused/Unfused Distinction: Recognized

SKELETAL ELEMENT	NO. OF BONES	MNI
Frontlet	4	1
Occipital condyle	5	3
Maxilla	338	54
Mandible	347	60
Mandibular condyle	37	24
Hyoid	23	9
Atlas	18	5
Axis	21	11
Cervical vertebrae 3-7	50	7
Thoracic vertebrae	75	5
Lumbar vertebrae	50	6
Sacral vertebrae	6	1
Ribs	116	5
Scapula (glenoid)	27	11

Press any key to continue ...

Clavicle--proximal	0	0
Clavicle--distal	0	0
Humerus--proximal	8	3
Humerus--distal	54	26
Radius--proximal	67	29
Radius--distal	26	12
Ulna--proximal	9	5

Ulna--distal	2	1
Carpals	20	6
Metacarpal--proximal	133	47
Metacarpal--distal	57	21
Phalanges--first	196	21
Phalanges--second	6	1
Phalanges--third	2	1
Innominate (acetabulum)	66	13
Femur--proximal	171	6
Femur--distal	15	5
Patella	13	6
Tibia--proximal	13	8
Tibia--distal	40	19
Fibula--proximal	0	0
Fibula--distal	0	0

Press any key to continue ...

Metatarsal--proximal	124	45
Metatarsal--distal	63	30
Calcaneum	42	14
Astragalus	37	18
Navicular	21	11
Cuboid	0	0
Cuneiforms (tarsals)	1	1
Lateral metapodials	0	0
Proximal sesamoids	0	0
Distal sesamoids	0	0

TOTALS FOR BONES =	1457	47
TOTAL FOR DENTITIONS =	685	60
GRAND TOTALS =	2142	60

Want hard copy (Y/N) ? N
Want to run program again (Y/N) ? N

---

wished. The only practical limitation is memory space in the user's computer.

When the number of provenience units has been accepted, MNI asks the user to list them, one at a time, in response to the prompt "Provenience Unit." Entries should correspond exactly to ones that MNI will encounter in the files it is going to process. In its calculations, MNI will treat the bones from all provenience units listed as if they all came from a single unit, that is, as if bones in any one unit could derive from the same individual animals as bones found in any other unit. Among other things, this feature allows the user to determine the effect on MNIs of lumping different provenience units.

TABLE 6.6: MNI Program Prompts and Acceptable Responses

Prompt	Responses
1) Site Name	Site name, including embedded blanks, if desired.
2) Species	Species name, Latin or vernacular, including embedded blanks, if desired
3) Skeletal part divisors from File or Keyboard (F/K)	F -- leads to prompts 4 and 5, by which program obtains skeletal part divisors from a file. K -- Leads to prompt series 6, by which program obtains skeletal part divisors from the keyboard.
4) (If response to 3 was F) Family (in Latin)	The name of the appropriate zoological family, ending in "idae".
5) (If response to 3 was F) Name of file with skeletal part divisors	The name of the file containing divisors for family specified in prompt 4.
6) (If response to 3 was K) Number per individual of:	
thoracic vertebrae	A number between 10 and 25, depending on the species.
lumbar vertebrae	A number between 3 and 10, depending on the species.
sacral vertebrae	A number between 1 and 7, depending on the species.
ribs	A number between 20 and 50, depending on the species.
metacarpals per side	A number between 1 and 5, depending on the species.
metatarsals per side	A number between 1 and 5, depending on the species.
lateral meta-podials per side	A number between 0 and 4, depending on the species.
first phalanges per side	A number between 1 and 10, depending on the species.

second phalanges per side	A number between 1 and 10, depending on the species.
third phalanges per side	A number between 1 and 10, depending on the species.
proximal sesamoids	A number between 8 and 32, depending on the species.
distal sesamoids	A number between 4 and 20, depending on the species.

---

7) Ignore or Recognize Left/Right Distinction (I/R)	I -- causes program to treat the side of all bones as "Indeterminate", even if Left or Right is recorded in data files. R -- causes program to use Left/Right specification in calculating MNIs.

---

8) Ignore or Recognize Fused/Unfused Distinction (I/R)	I -- causes program to treat the fusion state of all bones as "Indeterminate", even if fused and unfused are specified in data files. R -- causes program to use Fused/Unfused specification in calculating MNIs

---

9) Number per individual of indistinguishable:

dI's	A number between 0 and 4, depending on the species.
I's	A number between 0 and 4, depending on the species.
dP's	A number between 0 and 4, depending on the species.
P's	A number between 0 and 4, depending on the species.
M's	A number between 0 and 7, depending on the species.

NB: a simple carriage return is equivalent to 0 followed by a carriage return. Entry of any number between 0 and 4 (or between 0 and 7 for M's) causes the program to request a list of indistinguishable teeth within a particular category.

---

10) Indeterminate:

dI (dI1/dI2/dI3/dC)	dI1, dI2, dI3, or dC
I (I1/I2/I3/C)	I1, I2, I3, or C
dP (dP1/dP2/dP3/dP4)	dP1, dP2, dP3, or dP4
P (P1/P2/P3/P4)	P1, P2, P3, or P4
M (P1/P2/P3/P4/M1/M2/M3)	P1, P2, P3, P4, M1, M2, or M3

---

11) How many bone states to include	ALL -- if MNI is to process all bones and dentitions regardless of bone state (burned, cut, etc).
	A number between 1 and 6 indicating the number of bone states that MNI is to use in determining which bones or dentitions to process. Leads to prompt 12.
12) State (B,C,G R, W, or X)	B (for Burned), C (for carnivore-Chewed), G (for rodent-Gnawed), R (for Rolled), W (for Weathered), or X (for Cut).
13) Number of provenience units to enter	ALL -- if MNI is to process all bones in a file regardless of provenience unit.
	A number between 1 and 30.
14) Provenience unit	Any combination of letters and numbers -- combinations must match combinations used to designate provenience units in data files.
	CHANGE -- causes prompt sequence to begin again from "Number of provenience units to enter".
15) Enter Bones or teeth (B, T, or QUIT)	B -- if data file to be processed contains bones.
	T -- if data file to be processed contains teeth.
	QUIT -- if no more data files are to be entered; causes results to be displayed on screen.
16) Name of file with:	
bones	A combination of letters and numbers designating a file containing bones. Must end in BON.
dentitions	A combination of letters and numbers designating a file containing teeth. Must end in DEN.
17) Want hard copy (Y/N)	Y -- forces results to printer, followed by prompt 18.
	N -- leads immediately to prompt 18.
18) Run program again (Y/N)	Y -- starts program from scratch, with prompt for "Site".
	N -- terminates session.

Note: Each response must be followed by a carriage return.

A response of CHANGE to "Provenience Unit" causes MNI to reprompt from "Number of provenience units to enter." The previous number and any previously entered provenience units will be erased. Hence, CHANGE is the appropriate response if the user wants to "correct" a misentered number or provenience unit.

Once the last provenience unit has been entered, MNI asks "Enter Bones or Teeth (B, T, or QUIT)". Either B or T may be chosen. It is also possible to answer QUIT. This causes MNI to calculate NISPs and MNIs and to display the results on the screen. QUIT is an appropriate response only at a later stage in the program, when the user has entered all the desired data (files). Any response but B, T, or QUIT causes MNI to print an error message and reprompt "Enter Bones or Teeth (B, T, or QUIT)."

If the response to the bones or teeth request is B, MNI next asks "Name of file with bones [.BON]." MNI will repeat the request if the answer does not end in BON or if it cannot locate the named file in the system.

Processing begins as soon as the file name has been successfully entered. When processing is finished, MNI asks again "Enter Bones or Teeth (B, T, or QUIT)." The possible responses to this request are the same as they were the first time, as described above. QUIT terminates data entry and causes the results to be displayed on the screen. In most cases, if the initial response to "Enter Bones or Teeth (B, T, or QUIT)" was B, the second response will be T. Similarly, if the initial response was T, the second response will be B. This is because, having already processed the bones of a species, the user will now want to process the teeth. Or having processed the teeth, he or she will now want to process the bones.

However, there are situations in which a user will want to enter two or more bone files and two or more tooth files. One such situation is where it was necessary to create multiple files for a single species because of the sheer number of its bones or teeth. (Most microcomputer systems restrict file length in one way or another). Alternatively, there will probably be situations in which the user wants to calculate MNIs from files that were originally assigned to different species.

In the faunal samples we have studied, for example, there are commonly several bovid species of similar size whose postcranial bones are very difficult to distinguish, particularly when they are fragmented. Therefore we often assign bovid postcranial bones only to size category (small, small-medium, large-medium, large, and very large), while we assign teeth and jaws to species. We calculate MNIs for the species on teeth and jaws alone, but we calculate MNIs for the size categories on both teeth and postcranial bones. To obtain the MNIs for a size category, we must therefore enter at least one file for bones and several for teeth.

If the response to "Enter Bones or Teeth (B, T, or QUIT)" is T, MNI asks "Name of file with teeth [.DEN]." If the named file does not end in DEN or if it cannot be found in the system, MNI repeats the question.

When the file name has been successfully entered, processing begins again. When processing is finished, MNI asks yet again "Enter bones or teeth (B, T, or QUIT)." If the answer is B or T, the subsequent prompt will be for a file name, as described above. If the answer is QUIT, summary NISPs and MNIs are displayed on the screen, followed by the request "Want Hard Copy (Y/N)." If the response is Y, the results will be sent to an attached printer. Whatever the response, the next request is "Want to run program again (Y/N)." Only Y or N will be accepted. Y causes a completely fresh session, with all earlier entries and results erased. N leads to program termination.

The Results of an MNI Session

The results of an MNI session are shown in figure 6.14. For each kind of skeletal part, MNI provides the total number of identifiable pieces and the minimum number of individuals (MNI) from which the pieces must have come. It also provides the total number of bones, the MNI for bones, the total number of dentitions, and the MNI for dentitions in a sample.

The "Total for Bones" and the "Total for Dentitions" are the total numbers of pieces processed. The "Total for Dentitions" should always equal the "No. of Bones" for the maxilla plus the "No. of Bones" for the mandible. The "Total for Bones" may be smaller than the cumulative sum of the "No. of Bones" for each listed skeletal element, however. This is because the list includes the "No. of Bones" for both the proximal and distal ends of the limb bones. In some cases the proximal and distal ends may have been joined in a single specimen, counted then as "1" (not 2) in calculating the "Total for Bones."

In printing results, MNI collapses several skeletal part categories it considered separately during processing. Thus, for the maxilla and mandible, MNI initially computes an MNI for each maxillary and mandibular tooth category. However, in printing the results, it selects the largest maxillary and the largest mandibular MNIs as the MNIs for the maxilla and the mandible respectively. For both the maxilla and the mandible, however, the "No. of bones" includes all maxillary and mandibular dentitions, not just those in the categories responsible for the largest MNIs.

Similarly, for the carpals and cuneiform tarsals, MNI initially computes an MNI for each carpal and tarsal type. It then selects the largest of the carpal MNIs and the largest of the tarsal ones as the MNIs for carpals and tarsals (cuneiforms) respectively. Again, however, the total "No. of bones" for carpals and cuneiform tarsals includes all specimens, not just those responsible for the highest MNI.

For the axis, cervical vertebrae 3 to 7, thoracic, lumbar, and sacral vertebrae, calcaneum, first, second, and third phalanges, and lateral metapodials, MNI initially calculates separate MNIs for the proximal and distal portions. It then selects the larger MNI, proximal or distal, as the MNI for the category.

The purpose of collapsing categories is to provide reasonably compact results in a form that we have found useful for subsequent interpretation. However, it would certainly be possible for MNI to print bone counts and MNIs for the full set of skeletal parts it processes. It could also print some of the intermediate results used to calculate final MNIs.

For example, in calculating dental MNIs, MNI determines the MNI for each deciduous tooth and for its permanent replacement. It sums these two MNIs to obtain a final MNI for a dental position. Similarly, in calculating MNIs for a skeletal part with an epiphysis (e.g. the distal humerus), MNI first determines the MNI for pieces with fused epiphyses and for pieces with unfused ones. It sums these to obtain the final MNI.

It is important to point out that for skeletal parts that lack epiphyses (especially the carpals and most tarsals), MNI does not use any comparable "age" criteria to calculate final MNIs. It is thus possible that the final MNIs for jaws and for elements with epiphyses will be biased (upward) in relation to those for elements without epiphyses. This is likely to be a serious problem only in small samples to which it would not be worth applying MNI. MNI itself may be used to test this proposition with regard to fusion state, simply by processing the same sample twice. The first time, the user should instruct MNI to recognize the fused/unfused distinction in data files. The second time, the program should be told to ignore it.

Some analysts may feel it would be better if MNI printed out separate MNIs for deciduous and permanent dentitions and for fused and unfused elements, perhaps combining (summing) them in a separate printout. This would obviously lead to a much less compact result, but it might also provide some indication of the age distribution in a species sample. We would be happy to hear from potential users on this issue.

7: THE COMPUTATION OF AGE PROFILES FROM DENTAL CROWN

HEIGHTS: PROGRAMS **AGEPROF, DENTDATA, CRNHGT,** AND

SMIRNOV

In chapter 4, we argued that reliable age profiles can be calculated from ungulate dental crown heights using a quadratic model proposed by C. A. Spinage. However, calculating age profiles with this model can be very tedious, and there is a strong likelihood of calculation error. This is particularly true when many crown heights are involved, yet large samples are the ones most likely to produce interpretable results. It is to reduce drudgery and the likelihood of calculation error that we have written the program AGEPROF.

File Names

We have developed a convention for naming files that are to be processed by AGEPROF. It assumes that a single file will contain crown height measurements and associated data for only one species from one site. The first 2 to 3 letters of the file name denote the site (e.g. KRM for Klasies River Mouth) and the next 2 to 3 letters denote the species. Ordinarily we select the first letter of the genus name and the first letter of the species name (e.g. TS for *Tragelaphus scriptus*), but if such a combination of letters could represent more than one species, we add letters to make the designation unique (e.g. TSC for *Tragelaphus scriptus* in a site that also contains *Tragelaphus strepsiceros* .)

The final two letters before the period in the file name are LO for "lower" or UP for "upper," denoting the jaw of the tooth whose crown height measurements are in the file. The kind of tooth (e.g. dP4 or M3) then becomes the file extension after the period. Examples of complete file names then are KRMTSLO.DP4 and KRMTSUP.M3.

It is not necessary to follow our file naming convention, and AGEPROF will accept files whose names are constructed differently.

Data Entry: Program DENTDATA

AGEPROF assumes nine pieces of information for each tooth. Additionally, the nine items must occur in the following order:

1) Provenience unit within a site.
2) Sex of the tooth's owner (male, female, or indeterminate).
3) Side of the tooth (left, right, or indeterminate).
4) Wear State of the tooth (Unworn, Very Early Wear, Early Wear, Middle Wear, Late Wear).
5) Tooth length.
6) Tooth breadth.
7) Crown height of the first (anteriormost) lobe or loph.

8) Crown height of the second lobe or loph.

9) Catalog number of the tooth.

We defined the crown height measurement we make on ungulate teeth in chapter 4. It is illustrated in figure 4.2, which also shows the length and breadth dimensions we think are most useful. Length is the anteroposterior dimension of a tooth at the crown base, just above the junction between the enamel of the crown and the dentine of the roots. Breadth is the mediolateral or buccolingual dimension of the anterior lobe, again at the base of the crown. On teeth that are not composed of lobes or lophs (e.g. carnivore teeth), breadth is simply the maximum mediolateral (buccolingual) dimension, wherever it occurs at the base of the crown.

Measured in this way, length and breadth do not change with age. Thus, variability in length and breadth can be used to test sample homogeneity. Excessive variability, as expressed by the coefficient of variation [= (100 x the standard deviation)/the mean], might indicate confusion between adjacent teeth of a species (e.g. M1 and M2) or even between teeth of two similar species. Plots of length or breath or length versus breadth may then be used to sort specimens between categories in such mixed samples. Assuming sample homogeneity, dental length and breadth may serve as proxies for live individual size, and mean lengths and breadths may be compared among samples to see if they differ in mean individual size. We discuss these matters in more detail in chapter 8 under the program BONESTAT.

To ensure that all nine items are recorded in the right order, we have written the program DENTDATA, which prompts the user for them. DENTDATA includes "error traps" that reduce possible entry error, and it automatically enters an item of information when this has been predetermined by a previous entry.

Figure 7.1 lists DENTDATA, and figure 7.2 shows two sample sessions. Figure 7.3 shows the files created in the sample sessions. Table 7.1 summarizes the DENTDATA prompts, with possible responses and their effects.

DENTDATA asks first "Do you want to enter a catalog number for each tooth (Y/N)." If the answer is Y, DENTDATA will prompt the user for individual catalog numbers in a subsequent session. Otherwise it will record each catalog number as "#". We routinely answer N for reasons discussed in the introduction to Part 2.

DENTDATA next asks "Is Sex Known (Y/N)." For most dental samples, the answer will be N. Exceptions are modern comparative samples and the occasional fossil samples in which whole skulls are common. In many species, sex may then be readily determined from the skull (e.g. by the presence or shape of horns or antlers in bovids and cervids). If the response to the sex prompt is N, DENTDATA will automatically record sex as indeterminate for each tooth in a sample. If the answer is Y, DENTDATA will prompt the user for the sex of each tooth.

DENTDATA next asks "Enter one Crown Height or Two (1/2)." If the

FIGURE 7.1: Listing of the program DENTDATA for recording dental length, breadth, and crown height in a computer file.

```
1000 PRINT "DENTDATA -- Places dental lengths, breadths, and heights in a"
1010 PRINT "file. For use with compiled versions of AGEPROF and BONESTAT."
1020 REM IBM Personal Computer BASIC (R. G. Klein, 6 January 1984)
1030 PRINT
1040 KEY 1, "CHANGE" + CHR$(13)
1050 FILEENTERED=0
1060 '
1070 CNYN$=""
1080 WHILE CNYN$<>"Y" AND CNYN$<>"N"
1090   INPUT "Do you want to enter a catalog number for each tooth (Y/N)";
          ANS$:GOSUB 2360:CNYN$=ANS$
1100   IF CNYN$<>"Y" AND CNYN$<>"N" THEN BEEP
1110 WEND
1120 '
1130 SXYN$=""
1140 WHILE SXYN$<>"Y" AND SXYN$<>"N"
1150   INPUT "Is Sex known (Y/N)"; ANS$:GOSUB 2360:SXYN$=ANS$
1160   IF SXYN$<>"Y" AND SXYN$<>"N" THEN BEEP
1170 WEND
1180 '
1190 SDYN$=""
1200 WHILE SDYN$<>"Y" AND SDYN$<>"N"
1210   INPUT "Is Side known (Y/N)";ANS$:GOSUB 2360:SDYN$=ANS$
1220   IF SDYN$<>"Y" AND SDYN$<>"N" THEN BEEP
1230 WEND
1240 '
1250 CH%=0
1260 WHILE CH%<>1 AND CH%<>2
1270   INPUT "Enter one crown height or two (1/2)";CH%
1280   IF CH%<>1 AND CH%<>2 THEN BEEP
1290 WEND
1300 '
1310 IF FILEENTERED=0 THEN INPUT "File Name";FILE$:FILEENTERED=-1
1320 CLOSE:OPEN FILE$ FOR APPEND AS #1
1330 '
1340 NEWSITE=-1
1350 CONTINUE=-1
1360 WHILE CONTINUE
1365 CHANGE=0:QUIT=0
1370   IF NEWSITE THEN INPUT "Site (carriage return if no site wanted)";ANS$:
          GOSUB 2360:S$=ANS$:NEWSITE=0
1380   IF S$="QUIT" THEN QUIT=-1
1390   IF S$="CHANGE" THEN CHANGE=-1
1400   IF NOT CHANGE AND NOT QUIT THEN
          INPUT "Provenience Unit (carriage return for no unit)";ANS$:
          GOSUB 2360:P$=ANS$
1410   IF P$="QUIT" THEN QUIT=-1
1420   IF P$="CHANGE" THEN CHANGE=-1:NEWSITE=-1
1430   P$=S$+P$
1440   IF P$<>"" THEN CONTINUE=0 ELSE BEEP:
          PRINT "Must have site name or provenience unit!"
1445   IF P$="CHANGE" AND NEWSITE THEN CONTINUE=-1
1450 WEND
1460 IF CHANGE THEN 1070
1470 IF QUIT THEN CLOSE:CLS:END
1480 '
1490 CONTINUE=-1:CHANGE=0:QUIT=0
1500 IF SXYN$="N" THEN SX$="I":CONTINUE=0
1510 WHILE CONTINUE
```

177

```
1520   INPUT "Sex (M/F/I)";ANS$:GOSUB 2360:SX$=ANS$
1530   IF SX$="M" OR SX$="F" OR SX$="I" THEN CONTINUE=0
1540   IF SX$="CHANGE" THEN CHANGE=-1:CONTINUE=0
1550   IF SX$="QUIT" THEN QUIT=-1:CONTINUE=0
1560   IF CONTINUE THEN BEEP
1570 WEND
1580 IF CHANGE THEN 1350
1590 IF QUIT THEN CLOSE:CLS:END
1600 '
1610 CONTINUE=-1:QUIT=0:CHANGE=0
1620 IF SDYN$="N" THEN SD$="I":CONTINUE=0
1630 WHILE CONTINUE
1640   INPUT "Side (L/R/I)";ANS$:GOSUB 2360:SD$=ANS$
1650   IF SD$="L" OR SD$="R" OR SD$="I" THEN CONTINUE=0
1660   IF SD$="QUIT" THEN QUIT=-1:CONTINUE=0
1670   IF SD$="CHANGE" THEN CHANGE=-1:CONTINUE=0
1680   IF CONTINUE THEN BEEP
1690 WEND
1700 IF CHANGE THEN 1350
1710 IF QUIT THEN CLOSE:CLS:END
1720 '
1730 CONTINUE=-1:QUIT=0:CHANGE=0
1740 WHILE CONTINUE
1750   INPUT "Wear State (UW/VEW/EW/MW/LW/I)";ANS$:GOSUB 2360:WS$=ANS$
1760   IF WS$="UW" OR WS$="VEW" OR WS$="EW" OR WS$="MW" OR WS$="LW" OR
          WS$="I" THEN CONTINUE=0
1770   IF WS$="CHANGE" THEN CHANGE=-1:CONTINUE=0
1780   IF WS$="QUIT" THEN QUIT=-1:CONTINUE=0
1790   IF CONTINUE THEN BEEP
1800 WEND
1810 IF CHANGE THEN 1350
1820 IF QUIT THEN CLOSE:CLS:END
1830 '
1840 L!=0
1850 WHILE L!=0
1860   INPUT "Length";ANS$:GOSUB 2360:L$=ANS$
1870   L!=VAL(L$)
1880   IF L$="CHANGE" OR L$="QUIT" THEN L!=-1
1890   IF L!=0 THEN BEEP
1900 WEND
1910 IF L$="CHANGE" THEN 1350
1920 IF L$="QUIT" THEN CLOSE:CLS:END
1930 '
1940 B!=0
1950 WHILE B!=0
1960   INPUT "Breadth";ANS$:GOSUB 2360:B$=ANS$
1970   B!=VAL(B$)
1980   IF B$="CHANGE" OR B$="QUIT" THEN B!=-1
1990   IF B!=0 THEN BEEP
2000 WEND
2010 IF B$="CHANGE" THEN 1350
2020 IF B$="QUIT" THEN CLOSE:CLS:END
2030 '
2040 H1!=0
2050 WHILE H1!=0
2060   INPUT "Crown Height 1";ANS$:GOSUB 2360:H1$=ANS$
2070   H1!=VAL(H1$)
2080   IF H1$="CHANGE" OR H1$="QUIT" THEN H1!=-1
2090   IF H1!=0 THEN BEEP
```

```
2100 WEND
2110 IF H1$="CHANGE" THEN 1350
2120 IF H1$="QUIT" THEN CLOSE:CLS:END
2130 '
2140 IF CH%=1 THEN H2!=-1 ELSE H2!=0
2150 WHILE H2!=0
2160   INPUT "Crown Height 2";ANS$:GOSUB 2360:H2$=ANS$
2170   H2!=VAL(H2$)
2180   IF H2$="QUIT" OR H2$="CHANGE" THEN H2!=-1
2190   IF H2!=0 THEN BEEP
2200 WEND
2210 IF H2$="CHANGE" THEN 1350
2220 IF H2$="QUIT" THEN CLOSE:CLS:END
2230 '
2240 IF CNYN$="N" THEN CN$="#" ELSE CN$=""
2250 WHILE CN$=""
2260   INPUT "Catalog Number";ANS$:GOSUB 2360:CN$=ANS$
2270   IF CN$="" THEN CN$="#"
2280 WEND
2290 IF CN$="CHANGE" THEN 1350
2300 IF CN$="QUIT" THEN CLOSE:CLS:END
2310 '
2320 PRINT #1,P$",","SX$","SD$","WS$","L!","B!","H1!","H2!","CN$
2330 PRINT
2340 GOTO 1490 'start over again from sex
2350 '
2360 REM Capitalization
2370   FOR LTR=1 TO LEN(ANS$)
2380     LTR$ = MID$(ANS$,LTR,1)
2390     IF "a"<=LTR$ AND LTR$<="z" THEN MID$(ANS$,LTR,1)=CHR$(ASC(LTR$)-32)
2400   NEXT LTR
2410 RETURN
```

FIGURE 7.2: DENTDATA sample sessions showing the entry of lower dP4 and M3 crown length, breadth, and height for steenbok (*Raphicerus campestris*) from Equus Cave, South Africa.

DENTDATA -- Places dental lengths, breadths, and heights in a file.
For use with AGEPROF and BONESTAT.

Do you want to enter a catalog number for each tooth (Y/N) ? N
Is Sex known (Y/N) ? N
Is Side known (Y/N) ? Y
Enter one crown height or two (1/2) ? 2
File Name ? EQCRCLO.DP4
Site (carriage return if site name not wanted) ?
Provenience Unit (carriage return for no unit) ? 2A
Side (L/R/I) ? R
Wear State (UW/VEW/EW/MW/LW/I) ? EW
Length ? 101
Breadth ? 35
Crown Height 1 ? 50
Crown Height 2 ? 51

Side (L/R/I) ? CHANGE
Provenience Unit (carriage return for no unit) ? 2B
Side (L/R/I) ? R
Wear State (UW/VEW/EW/MW/LW/I) ? MW
Length ? 98
Breadth ? 30
Crown Height 1 ? 29
Crown Height 2 ? 35

Side (L/R/I) ? R
Wear State (UW/VEW/EW/MW/LW/I) ? MW
Length ? 102
Breadth ? 31
Crown Height 1 ? 24
Crown Height 2 ? 35

Side (L/R/I) ? R
Wear State (UW/VEW/EW/MW/LW/I) ? EW
Length ? 112
Breadth ? 30
Crown Height 1 ? 50
Crown Height 2 ? 61

Side (L/R/I) ? QUIT

DENTDATA -- Places dental lengths, breadths, and heights in a file.
For use with AGEPROF and BONESTAT.

Do you want to enter a catalog number for each tooth (Y/N) ? N
Is Sex known (Y/N) ? N
Is Side known (Y/N) ? Y
Enter one crown height or two (1/2) ? 2
File Name ? EQCRCLO.M3
Site (carriage return if site name not wanted) ?
Provenience Unit (carriage return for no unit) ? 2A
Side (L/R/I) ? R
Wear State (UW/VEW/EW/MW/LW/I) ? VEW
Length ? 162
Breadth ? 62
Crown Height 1 ? 116
Crown Height 2 ? 123

Side (L/R/I) ? R
Wear State (UW/VEW/EW/MW/LW/I) ? EW
Length ? 146
Breadth ? 54
Crown Height 1 ? 113
Crown Height 2 ? 120

Side (L/R/I) ? CHANGE
Provenience Unit (carriage return for no unit) ? 2B
Side (L/R/I) ? R
Wear State (UW/VEW/EW/MW/LW/I) ? EW
Length ? 128
Breadth ? 46
Crown Height 1 ? 110
Crown Height 2 ? 112

Side (L/R/I) ? R
Wear State (UW/VEW/EW/MW/LW/I) ? UW
Length ? 142
Breadth ? 52
Crown Height 1 ? 125
Crown Height 2 ? 135

Side (L/R/I) ? QUIT

2A,I,R,EW,101,35,50,51,#
2B,I,R,MW,98,30,29,35,#
2B,I,R,MW,102,31,24,35,#
2B,I,R,EW,112,30,50,61,#

2A,I,R,VEW,162,62,116,123,#
2A,I,R,EW,146,54,113,120,#
2B,I,R,EW,128,46,110,112,#
2B,I,R,UW,142,52,125,135,#

FIGURE 7.3: The files created by the DENTDATA sample sessions shown in figure 7.2 (dP4s above, M3s below.)

response is "1", DENTDATA will ask the user for only one crown height for each tooth in a sample. It will automatically record the second crown height as "-1", our code for a missing value. If the response is "2", DENTDATA will prompt the user for two crown heights of each tooth. If two crown heights are to be entered, entry should obviously always be in the same order. For example, on a bilobed tooth, the anterior lobe should be entered first and the posterior lobe second, or vice versa.

DENTDATA next asks for "File Name", meaning the name of the file in which dental measurements are to be stored. The next request is for "Site (carriage return if site name not wanted)." If the response is "CHANGE", DENTDATA restarts the prompt series from "Do you want to enter a catalog number for each tooth (Y/N)." This response is only meaningful for samples that contain some teeth with catalog numbers and some without, or some of unknown sex and some of known sex, or some for which only one crown height is available and some for which two are available. In this case, the CHANGE response permits all the teeth in a sample to be entered economically in one DENTDATA session, assuming the user has first grouped the teeth according to whether they have catalog numbers, whether sex is known, and how many crown heights have been measured on each.

If the response to "Site (carriage return if site name not wanted)" is QUIT, DENTDATA closes the file and terminates the session. If a site name is entered, it becomes part of the provenience information on each tooth. In most instances the site name will be superfluous, since a file will contain only teeth from one site, and the site name will already be incorporated in the file name. If this is the case, the user should respond to the site request with a carriage return. A site name should be entered only if the user wants to include teeth from more than one site in the same file. In general, we do not recommend this. It is desirable only if the user intends to construct a single age profile based on teeth from two or more sites. If a site name is entered, it should be kept as brief as possible. Virtually any combination of letters or numbers will do.

The next prompt is for "Provenience Unit (carriage return for no unit)."

TABLE 7.1 DENTDATA Prompts with Accepted Responses and Their Effects.

Prompts	Responses
1) Do you want to enter a catalog number for each tooth (Y/N)	Y -- causes the program to prompt for a catalog number for each tooth. N -- causes the catalog number of each tooth to be recorded as "#".
2) Is Sex Known (Y/N)	Y -- causes the program to prompt for the sex of each tooth. N -- causes the program to record the sex of each tooth as indeterminate without prompting.
3) Is Side Known (Y/N)	Y -- causes the program to prompt for the side of each tooth. N- causes the program to record the side of each tooth as indeterminate without prompting.
4) Enter one crown height or two (1/2)	1 -- causes the program to prompt for only one crown height for each tooth (the second is automatically recorded as "-1", meaning missing.) 2 -- causes the program to prompt for two crown heights for each tooth.
5) File Name	A naming convention is suggested in the text.
6) Site	Site name, including imbedded blanks if desired (best to use a mnemonic abbreviation.) Will be concatenated with "Provenience Unit" to form a single provenience label. Carriage return (= no entry) -- if there is no reason to include the site name in the provenience label. QUIT -- closes file and terminates session. CHANGE -- causes prompt sequence to begin again from "Do you want to enter a catalog number for each tooth (Y/N)"
7) Provenience Unit	A mnemonic abbreviation for a field unit. Will be grafted on to site name to form a

single provenience label.

Carriage return (= no entry), if a site name has already been entered and will suffice as a provenience label.

QUIT -- closes file and terminates session.

CHANGE -- causes prompt sequence to begin again from "Site".

---

8) Sex (M/F/I)

M, F, or I -- causes sex to be recorded, leading to prompt for "Side (L/R/I)".

QUIT -- closes file and terminates session.

CHANGE -- causes prompt sequence to begin again from "Provenience Unit".

---

9) Side (L/R/I)

L, R, or I -- causes side to be recorded, leading to prompt for "Length".

QUIT -- closes file and terminates session.

CHANGE -- causes prompt sequence to begin again from "Provenience Unit".

---

10) Wear State (UW/VEW/EW/ MW/LW/I)

UW (unworn), VEW (very early wear), EW (early wear), MW (medium wear), LW (late wear), or I (indeterminate)

QUIT -- closes file and terminates session.

CHANGE -- causes prompt sequence to begin again from "Provenience Unit".

---

11) Length
12) Breadth
13) Crown Height 1
14) Crown Height 2

-1, if no value for the dimension is available.

CHANGE, in response to request for any dimension causes prompt sequence to begin again from "Provenience Unit".

QUIT -- closes file and terminates session.

A number greater than 0 -- the known value of a dental dimension.

---

15) Catalog Number

CHANGE -- causes prompt sequence to begin again from "Provenience Unit."

QUIT -- closes file and terminates session.

Carriage return -- for no number.

A catalog number comprising any combination of letters and numbers.

Note: Each response must be followed by a carriage return.

The response may be virtually any combination of letters and numbers, but we suggest a mnemonic abbreviation for a field unit (e.g. 1WA for the First White Ash). If the user has entered a site name and now enters a provenience unit, DENTDATA concatenates the two. For example, if the site name was KRM1 (for Klasies River Mouth 1) and the user enters 14 (for level 14) in response to the provenience unit prompt, DENTDATA will concatenate KRM1 and 14 into a single provenience label KRM114. This means that it is not necessary to provide a specific provenience unit if a site name has been entered that is adequate by itself to describe provenience. In this case, the user may respond to the provenience unit request with a simple carriage return. However, DENTDATA must have some provenience information. Therefore, if the user did not enter a site name previously, a provenience unit must be supplied. Otherwise DENTDATA prints an error message and reprompts first for site name and then for provenience unit. A response of CHANGE to the provenience unit request also restarts the prompt series from site name. A response of QUIT closes the file and terminates the session. QUIT has the same effect in response to all subsequent prompts.

If the user has indicated that the sex of each tooth is known, DENTDATA next asks "Sex (M/F/I)." A response of CHANGE restarts the prompt series from provenience unit. CHANGE has the same effect in response to all subsequent prompts. Any response to Sex but M (male), F (female), I (indeterminate), CHANGE, or QUIT leads to an error message and a renewed request for sex. If the user has indicated that the sex of each tooth is unknown, DENTDATA automatically records the sex for each tooth as indeterminate.

The next request is for "Side (L/R/I)." The response must be L (left), R (right), I (indeterminate), CHANGE, or QUIT. Otherwise DENTDATA prints an error message and reprompts.

DENTDATA next asks "Wear State (UW/VEW/EW/MW/LW/I)", meaning the user's qualitative evaluation of the wear on a tooth. The response must be CHANGE, QUIT, UW (unworn), VEW (very early wear), EW (early wear), MW (medium wear), LW (late wear), or I (indeterminate wear). Unworn teeth and teeth in late wear (with the crown largely worn away) are easy to identify. The other wear states are more subjective, and their consistent determination requires experience. With regard to the bovids and cervids that dominate samples we have studied, we ordinarily employ very early wear for teeth on which the first lobe is in wear but the second is not. Early Wear is for a tooth on which the second lobe has only recently come into wear, and Medium Wear is for a tooth between Early Wear and Late Wear.

It is particularly important to designate completely unworn teeth or teeth in very early wear, since their mean height is a vital datum for age profile construction. The program BONESTAT discussed in the next chapter can process DENTDATA files to calculate mean crown height and associated statistics for teeth in any designated wear state or combination of wear states.

185

Site __E QUUS CAVE__   Date __4 / 21 /83__   DENTAL MEASUREMENTS

Species __RAPHICERUS CAMPESTRIS__   Tooth __M3__

S$	P$	SX$	SD$	WS$	L	B	H1	H2	NO$	NOTES
	2B	I	L	UW	139	52	152	155		
	"	I	L	MW	154	59	106	113		
	"	I	L	MW	145	53	131	137		
	"	I	L	MW	138	48	115	121		
	"	I	R	UW	139	52	146	-1		
	2A	I	R	LW	-1	-1	-1	49		
	"	I	L	LW	136	58	60	58		
	"	I	R	LW	-1	-1	-1	59		
	1B	I	L	MW	138	58	118	121		

Department of Anthropology, University of Chicago
1126 East 59th Street, Chicago, IL 60637 USA

DENTAL MEASUREMENTS

FIGURE 7.4: A coding form for dental length, breadth, and crown heights to be entered into a file by the program DENTDATA. The columns are labelled with the names for the variables in the program. S$ stands for site, P$ for provenience unit (within a site), SX$ for sex (male, female, or indeterminate), SD$ for side (left, right, or indeterminate), L for

186

Once wear state has been successfully entered, DENTDATA asks sequentially for "Length," "Breadth," "Crown Height 1," and "Crown Height 2." If a particular measurement is not available, the user should enter a negative number, indicating a missing value. We recommend "-1". For each request, the response must be CHANGE, QUIT, or a number. Otherwise DENTDATA prints an error message and repeats the request. If the user indicated previously that only one crown height was available, DENTDATA does not prompt for "Crown Height 2."

DENTDATA next asks "Catalog Number" (unless the user indicated previously that catalog numbers were not wanted.) Appropriate responses are CHANGE, QUIT, a catalog number (comprising any combination of letters and numbers), or a carriage return (signifying no number). In the last case, the number will be recorded as "#". DENTDATA writes information to file only after the catalog number has been entered (or after the last crown height, if the user is not entering catalog numbers). This is the reason for allowing a return to "Provenience Unit" by responding CHANGE to any prompt --the result is that an erroneous response to a previous prompt can be erased before it is permanently recorded. Once data are permanently recorded in a DENTDATA file, they can be changed only with an external text editor.

After the information on a tooth has been written to a file, DENTDATA asks for information on the next tooth. If the user indicated that sex information is available, DENTDATA begins the new prompt series with a request for "Sex (M/F/I)." Otherwise it begins with a request for "Side (L/R/I)." In either case, it assumes that the provenience unit for the new tooth is the same as the provenience unit for the previous one, unless the user responds CHANGE to "Sex" or "Side." This feature has been incorporated so that grouping teeth by provenience unit saves entry time and also reduces the likelihood of entry error.

We have found that DENTDATA is easiest to use if the analyst records the necessary information for each tooth on a form like the one illustrated in figure 7.4.

Automatic Entry of Age and Crown Height Parameters: Program CRNHGT

To compute a complete age profile, AGEPROF needs the potential ecological longevity of a species, the age at shedding of the deciduous tooth and age at eruption of the permanent tooth on which the profile is based, and the initial (unworn) crown heights of the two teeth. The permanent tooth must be one that erupts before the deciduous tooth is shed. In most cases the

---

crown length, B for crown breadth, H1 and H2 for (two) separate crown heights, and NO$ for catalog number. Note that site does not have to be recorded (or entered) if the file to be created by DENTDATA contains measurements from only one site.

permanent tooth will be M1, M2, or M3. In bovids and cervids the deciduous tooth will usually be dP4, in equids dP2. We explained the reasons for this in chapter 4. Incisors and canines will almost never be chosen, partly because they tend to be rarer than cheek teeth in fossil samples and partly because they are often difficult to identify to species. Also, incisor and canine wear may depart significantly from the pattern assumed by Spinage's model for calculating age from crown height. This is especially true in cervids and bovids.

The various parameters required by AGEPROF must be entered for each age profile, even when the user is calculating age profiles for the same species over and over again. Recurrent calculation may be necessary, for example, when one species is well represented in successive levels of the same site. In this case entering and re entering the background data to run AGEPROF for each level can prove very tiresome, and there is a strong likelihood of entry error. It is with this problem in mind that we have written the program CRNHGT.

CRNHGT creates a file in which the shedding and eruption ages, initial (unworn) crown heights, and potential ecological longevity of important species can be stored. In a subsequent AGEPROF session, the user need only tell AGEPROF the species name, the names of the deciduous and permanent teeth on which the age profile will be based, and the name of the file created by CRNHGT. AGEPROF can then obtain the crucial age and crown height parameters from the file. However, for any species, even one "on file," AGEPROF always allows these parameters to be entered directly from the keyboard. A user who wishes to do this in all cases can safely skip the rest of this section.

CRNHGT is listed in figure 7.5. Figure 7.6 presents a sample session. Figure 7.7 shows the file created by the session. Table 7.2 lists the CRNHGT prompts and appropriate responses.

CRNHGT asks first for "File Name." This is the file in which the shedding/eruption ages and initial crown heights will be stored. We recommend using the file name "CRNHGT.DAT."

If the file already exists, CRNHGT lists the species it contains so the user will not enter the same species twice. CRNHGT allows only the addition of entries (new entries are placed at the end of an existing file). Deletion must be done with an external editor.

If the file does not already exist, CRNHGT prints "New File" and asks "Species". If the user responds QUIT, CRNHGT closes the file and terminates the session. Otherwise the species name should correspond exactly to the one used in AGEPROF sessions. Perhaps the safest convention is to use the scientific (Latin) name for a species. The user need not worry about name length; no scientific name we are aware of exceeds system length limitations.

CRNHGT now prompts sequentially for "Age at Potential Ecological Longevity," "Age of dP2 shedding," "Age of dP3 shedding," "Age of dP4 shedding," "Age of M1 eruption," "Age of M2 eruption," "Age of M3 eruption," "Unworn dP2 crown height," "Unworn dP3 crown height,"

FIGURE 7.5: Listing of the program CRNHGT for placing ages of dental eruption and shedding, potential ecological longevity, and unworn crown heights in a file.

```
100 PRINT "CRNHGT -- creates a file containing species names (in Latin) and"
110 PRINT "age and crown height parameters.  Ages to be entered in months"
120 PRINT "and crown heights in tenths of a millimeter.  To exit, type 'QUIT'"
130 PRINT "in response to 'Species.'"
140 REM IBM Personal Computer BASIC (R. G. Klein, 12 January 1984)
150 PRINT
160 ON ERROR GOTO 1000
165 '
170 INPUT "File Name";FILE$:GOSUB 900
180 CLOSE:OPEN FILE$ FOR INPUT AS #1
185 '
190 PRINT "These species are already on file:"
200     WHILE NOT EOF(1)
210         INPUT#1,SP$,PEL!,DP2S!,DP3S!,DP4S!,M1E!,M2E!,M3E!
220         INPUT#1,DP2H!,DP3H!,DP4H!,P2H!,P3H!,P4H!,M1H!,M2H!,M3H!
230         PRINT SP$
240     WEND
245 '
250 CLOSE:OPEN FILE$ FOR APPEND AS #1
260 INPUT "Species";ANS$:GOSUB 900:SP$=ANS$
270 IF SP$="QUIT" THEN CLOSE:CLS:END
272 '
277     PEL!=0
279     WHILE PEL!<12 OR PEL!>1200
280         INPUT "Age at Potential Ecological Longevity in months (12-1200)";PEL!
290         IF PEL!<12 OR PEL!>1200 THEN BEEP
300     WEND
305 '
307     TOOTH$="DP2":GOSUB 600:DP2S!=AGE!
309     TOOTH$="DP3":GOSUB 600:DP3S!=AGE!
311     TOOTH$="DP4":GOSUB 600:DP4S!=AGE!
315 '
320     TOOTH$="M1":GOSUB 700:M1E!=AGE!
330     TOOTH$="M2":GOSUB 700:M2E!=AGE!
340     TOOTH$="M3":GOSUB 700:M3E!=AGE!
350 '
360     MAXHGT!=1000
365     TOOTH$="DP2":GOSUB 800:DP2H!=HEIGHT!
370     TOOTH$="DP3":GOSUB 800:DP3H!=HEIGHT!
380     TOOTH$="DP4":GOSUB 800:DP4H!=HEIGHT!
390     MAXHGT!=1250
400     TOOTH$="P2":GOSUB 800:P2H!=HEIGHT!
410     TOOTH$="P3":GOSUB 800:P3H!=HEIGHT!
420     TOOTH$="P4":GOSUB 800:P4H!=HEIGHT!
430     TOOTH$="M1":GOSUB 800:M1H!=HEIGHT!
440     TOOTH$="M2":GOSUB 800:M2H!=HEIGHT!
450     TOOTH$="M3":GOSUB 800:M3H!=HEIGHT!
460 '
470     YN$=""
475     WHILE YN$<>"Y" AND YN$<>"N"
480         INPUT "Are all entries satisfactory (Y/N)";ANS$:GOSUB 900:YN$=ANS$
490         IF YN$<>"Y" AND YN$<>"N" THEN BEEP
500     WEND
510 '
520 PRINT #1,SP$","PEL!","DP2S!","DP3S!","DP4S!","M1E!","M2E!","M3E!
530 PRINT #1,DP2H!","DP3H!","DP4H!","P2H!","P3H!","P4H!","M1H!","M2H!","M3H!
540 PRINT
550 '
560 GOTO 260    'start again from species
```

```
590 '
600 REM Entry of shedding ages
605 AGE!=-1
610 WHILE AGE!<0 OR AGE!>PEL!
615    PRINT "Age of "TOOTH$" shedding in months ( 0 - "PEL")";:INPUT AGE!
620    IF AGE!<0 OR AGE!>PEL! THEN BEEP
625 WEND
630 RETURN
700 '
710 REM Entry of eruption ages
715 AGE!=-1
720 WHILE AGE!<0 OR AGE!>PEL!
725    PRINT "Age of "TOOTH$" eruption in months ( 0 - "PEL")";:INPUT AGE!
730    IF AGE!<0 OR AGE!>PEL! THEN BEEP
735 WEND
740 RETURN
745 '
800 REM Entry of unworn crown heights
802 HEIGHT!=-1
805 WHILE HEIGHT!<0 OR HEIGHT!>MAXHGT!
810    PRINT "Unworn "TOOTH$" crown height in tenths of a millimeter ";:
       PRINT "( >0 - "MAXHGT!")";:INPUT HEIGHT!
812    IF HEIGHT!<0 OR HEIGHT!>MAXHGT! THEN BEEP
815 WEND
820 RETURN
825 '
900 REM Capitalization
910 FOR LTR=1 TO LEN(ANS$)
920    LTR$=MID$(ANS$,LTR,1)
930    IF "a"<=LTR$ AND LTR$<="z" THEN MID$(ANS$,LTR,1)=CHR$(ASC(LTR$)-32)
940 NEXT
950 RETURN
960 '
1000 IF ERR=53 THEN BEEP: PRINT "New file!": RESUME 250
```

"Unworn dP4 crown height," "Unworn P2 crown height," "Unworn P3 crown height," "Unworn P4 crown height," "Unworn M1 crown height," "Unworn M2 crown height," and "Unworn M3 crown height." CRNHGT does not request ages of eruption for P2, P3, and P4, because it assumes these are the same as the ages of shedding for dP2, dP3, and dP4 respectively.

All ages should be entered in months and all crown heights in tenths of a millimeter. CRNHGT will not accept an age at potential ecological longevity less than 12 months or greater than 1200, ages of shedding and eruption less than 0 months or greater than the age at potential ecological longevity, unworn deciduous crown heights less than 0 tenths of a millimeter or greater than 1000, or unworn permanent crown heights less than 0 tenths of a millimeter or greater than 1250. For any age or unworn crown height whose value is not known, the user may enter 0 (or simply a carriage return). Of course, 0 values should not be used in a subsequent AGEPROF session.

Once "Unworn M3 crown height" has been successfully entered, CRNHGT asks "Are all the entries satisfactory (Y/N)." If the answer is N, CRNHGT restarts the prompt series from "Species" without recording any of the values entered previously. The user can now enter the correct values. If the answer is Y, CRNHGT first writes all entered values to the file before restarting the prompt series from "Species." (In this case, "Species" means the next species.)

As it is now written, CRNHGT does not allow a user to enter one set of initial crown heights for upper teeth and a second set for lower. In our experience, the initial crown heights of corresponding upper and lower teeth (e.g. lower M1 and upper M1) are similar enough so that the estimate of initial crown height for a lower tooth usually suffices for the corresponding upper, and vice versa. For each tooth in an upper-lower pair, we ordinarily enter the initial crown height estimate based on the larger number of available specimens, whether upper or lower.

CRNHGT also allows only one initial crown height per tooth. We ordinarily enter the initial crown height of the anteriormost lobe or loph of each tooth, since this is the lobe or loph we use most often in age calculation. In any case, on most multilobed or multilophed teeth, the initial crown height of the anterior lobe or loph is an adequate estimate of the initial crown height of posterior ones. The dP4's of cervids and bovids are the most prominent exception to this rule, since the posterior lobes are generally much higher than the anteriormost lobe. Thus, if a CRNHGT file contains the initial crown height of the anterior lobe of a cervid or bovid dP4 and the user wishes to process crown heights of one of the posterior lobes, the initial crown height of the posterior lobe (and all other basic parameters) will have to be entered from the keyboard in an AGEPROF session.

FIGURE 7.6: A sample CRNHGT session. Eruption/shedding ages and unworn crown heights have been entered only for those teeth the authors customarily use to calculate age profiles for the specified species.

CRNHGT -- creates a file containing species names (in Latin) and age and crown height parameters. Ages to be entered in months and crown heights in tenths of a millimeter. To exit, type 'QUIT' in response to 'Species.'

File Name ? CRNHGT.DAT

New File!
Species ? TAUROTRAGUS ORYX
Age at Potential Ecological Longevity in months (12-1200) ? 240
Age of dP2 shedding in months (0-240) ?
Age of dP3 shedding in months (0-240) ?
Age of dP4 shedding in months (0-240) ? 37
Age of M1 eruption in months (0-240) ?
Age of M2 eruption in months (0-240) ?
Age of M3 eruption in months (0-240) ? 24
Unworn dP2 crown height in tenths of a millimeter (0-1000) ?
Unworn dP3 crown height in tenths of a millimeter (0-1000) ?
Unworn dP4 crown height in tenths of a millimeter (0-1000) ? 190
Unworn P2 crown height in tenths of a millimeter (0-1250) ?
Unworn P3 crown height in tenths of a millimeter (0-1250) ?
Unworn P4 crown height in tenths of a millimeter (0-1250) ?
Unworn M1 crown height in tenths of a millimeter (0-1250) ?
Unworn M2 crown height in tenths of a millimeter (0-1250) ?
Unworn M3 crown height in tenths of a millimeter (0-1250) ? 448
Are all entries satisfactory (Y/N) ? Y

Species ? REDUNCA ARUNDINUM
Age at Potential Ecological Longevity in months (12-1200) ? 144
Age of dP2 shedding in months (0-144) ?
Age of dP3 shedding in months (0-144) ?
Age of dP4 shedding in months (0-144) ? 22
Age of M1 eruption in months (0-144) ?
Age of M2 eruption in months (0-144) ?
Age of M3 eruption in months (0-144) ? 16
Unworn dP2 crown height in tenths of a millimeter (0-1000) ?
Unworn dP3 crown height in tenths of a millimeter (0-1000) ?
Unworn dP4 crown height in tenths of a millimeter (0-1000) ? 130
Unworn P2 crown height in tenths of a millimeter (0-1250) ?
Unworn P3 crown height in tenths of a millimeter (0-1250) ?
Unworn P4 crown height in tenths of a millimeter (0-1250) ?
Unworn M1 crown height in tenths of a millimeter (0-1250) ?

Unworn M2 crown height in tenths of a millimeter (0-1250) ?
Unworn M3 crown height in tenths of a millimeter (0-1250) ? 340
Are all entries satisfactory (Y/N) ? Y

Species ? CERVUS ELAPHUS
Age at Potential Ecological Longevity in months (12-1200) ? 192
Age of dP2 shedding in months (0-192) ?
Age of dP3 shedding in months (0-192) ?
Age of dP4 shedding in months (0-192) ? 26
Age of M1 eruption in months (0-192) ? 6
Age of M2 eruption in months (0-192) ? 12
Age of M3 eruption in months (0-192) ?
Unworn dP2 crown height in tenths of a millimeter (0-1000) ?
Unworn dP3 crown height in tenths of a millimeter (0-1000) ?
Unworn dP4 crown height in tenths of a millimeter (0-1000) ? 140
Unworn P2 crown height in tenths of a millimeter (0-1250) ?
Unworn P3 crown height in tenths of a millimeter (0-1250) ?
Unworn P4 crown height in tenths of a millimeter (0-1250) ?
Unworn M1 crown height in tenths of a millimeter (0-1250) ? 270
Unworn M2 crown height in tenths of a millimeter (0-1250) ? 296
Unworn M3 crown height in tenths of a millimeter (0-1250) ?
Are all entries satisfactory (Y/N) ? Y

Species ? EQUUS BURCHELLI
Age at Potential Ecological Longevity in months (12-1200) ? 264
Age of dP2 shedding in months (0-264) ? 36
Age of dP3 shedding in months (0-264) ?
Age of dP4 shedding in months (0-264) ?
Age of M1 eruption in months (0-264) ?
Age of M2 eruption in months (0-264) ?
Age of M3 eruption in months (0-264) ? 36
Unworn dP2 crown height in tenths of a millimeter (0-1000) ? 270
Unworn dP3 crown height in tenths of a millimeter (0-1000) ?
Unworn dP4 crown height in tenths of a millimeter (0-1000) ?
Unworn P2 crown height in tenths of a millimeter (0-1250) ? 600
Unworn P3 crown height in tenths of a millimeter (0-1250) ?
Unworn P4 crown height in tenths of a millimeter (0-1250) ?
Unworn M1 crown height in tenths of a millimeter (0-1250) ?
Unworn M2 crown height in tenths of a millimeter (0-1250) ?
Unworn M3 crown height in tenths of a millimeter (0-1250) ? 750
Are all entries satisfactory (Y/N) ? Y

Species ? QUIT

TAUROTRAGUS ORYX,240,0,0,37,0,0,24
0,0,190,0,0,0,0,0,448
REDUNCA ARUNDINUM,144,0,0,22,0,0,16
0,0,130,0,0,0,0,0,340
CERVUS ELAPHUS,192,0,0,26,6,12,0
0,0,140,0,0,0,270,296,0
EQUUS BURCHELLI,264,36,0,0,0,0,36
270,0,0,600,0,0,0,0,750

FIGURE 7.7: The file created by the CRNHGT session shown in figure 7.6. Note that "0" implies no entry, not a 0 value for a variable.

A Sample Session with AGEPROF

AGEPROF is listed in figure 7.8. Table 7.3 contains AGEPROF prompts and appropriate responses. In this section, we present a sample session.

AGEPROF asks first for "Site." The site name is used only to label the printout, and the answer may be virtually any combination of letters and numbers, including embedded blanks. We recommend restricting site name to fifty characters (or fewer) for legibility in program output.

AGEPROF next requests "Species (Latin name)." In fact, the Latin name is necessary only if the user wants AGEPROF to obtain the species' age at potential ecological longevity, shedding/eruption ages, and initial unworn crown heights from a file created by CRNHGT. Otherwise the species name is used only to label the printout, and virtually any name will suffice.

The next prompt is for "Sex (M/F/B)." This is to determine if the user wants an age profile based only on male teeth, only on female teeth, or on both. In most samples, tooth sex will be indeterminate, and the proper response to "Sex (M/F/B)" is B. (If a sample contains only indeterminate teeth, a response of M or F will produce an age profile in which the number of individuals in each class is 0.)

AGEPROF next asks "Side (L/R/B)." The answer depends on whether the user wants a profile based just on left teeth, just on right teeth, or on both.

Once side has been successfully entered, AGEPROF asks "How many provenience units to enter (ALL or 1-30)." We have arbitrarily limited the maximum number to thirty. There is no fundamental programmatic reason why the number could not be increased, however, if the user wished.

When the number of provenience units has been entered, AGEPROF asks the user to list them, one at a time, in response to the prompt "Provenience Unit." Entries must correspond precisely to the ones that AGEPROF will encounter in the DENTDATA file it is going to process. In its calculations, AGEPROF will treat the teeth from all the provenience units listed as if they came from a single provenience unit. If the user wants AGEPROF to process all teeth in a file regardless of provenience unit, he or she should respond ALL to the "Number of provenience units to enter."

TABLE 7.2 CRNHGT Prompts with Accepted Responses and Their Effects.

Prompts	Responses and effects
1) File Name	Any name acceptable to system. CRNHGT.DAT recommended.
2) Species	Scientific (Latin) name recommended. QUIT -- closes file and terminates session.
3) Age at potential ecological longevity.	The appropriate Figure between 12 and 1200 months.

Age of shedding in months of:

4) dP2	0 (or simply a carriage return) if the value
5) dP3	is unknown.
6) dP4	The appropriate value between 0 months and age at potential ecological longevity.

Age of eruption in months of:

7) M1	0 (or simply a carriage return) if the value
8) M2	is unknown
9) M3	The appropriate value between 0 months and age at potential ecological longevity.

Unworn crown height in tenths of a millimeter of:

10) dP2	0 (or simply a carriage return) if the value
11) dP3	is unknown.
12) dP4	The appropriate value between 0 and 1000 tenths of a millimeter.

Unworn crown height in tenths of a millimeter of:

13) P2	0 (or simply a carriage return) if the value
14) P3	is unknown.
15) P4	The appropriate value between 0 and 1250
16) M1	tenths of a millimeter.
17) M2	
18) M3	

19) Are all entries satisfactory (Y/N)	Y -- program writes all entered values to file and prompts for next "Species". N -- program reprompts from "Species"; nothing written to file.

Note: Each response must be followed by a carriage return.

Once the last provenience unit has been entered, AGEPROF asks "Kind of deciduous tooth (dP#/None)." The response must begin with D or N or AGEPROF will repeat the question. If the answer is None (or simply N), AGEPROF immediately asks "Kind of Permanent Tooth (P#/M#/None)." If the answer is dP1, dP2, dP3, or dP4, AGEPROF next asks "Deciduous lobe to consider (1 or 2)."

Once the deciduous lobe has been successfully entered, AGEPROF asks "Kind of permanent tooth (P#/M#/None)." If the answer is None (or simply N), the next prompt is "Background data from File or Keyboard (F/K)." If the answer is a permanent premolar (P1, P2, P3, or P4) or molar (M1, M2, or M3), the next prompt is "Permanent lobe to consider (1 or 2)."

When the permanent lobe has been entered, AGEPROF asks "Background data from File or Keyboard (F/K)." F is the proper answer if the user wants AGEPROF to obtain potential ecological longevity, shedding/eruption ages, and initial (unworn) crown heights from a file created by CRNHGT. K is the correct answer if the user wishes to enter these parameters from the keyboard.

If the answer is F, AGEPROF asks "Name of file with background data." If AGEPROF cannot locate the file in the system, it repeats "Background data from File or Keyboard (F/K)". If it locates the file but the file does not contain the species name as specified at the beginning of the session, AGEPROF tells the user to enter background data from the keyboard.

If the species name is found in the CRNHGT file, AGEPROF will use the associated potential ecological longevity, shedding/eruption ages, and initial crown heights to calculate an age profile. It also lists the parameters on the screen so the user can check their accuracy. It then asks "Name of file with deciduous crown heights," followed by "Name of file to write ages to." This second request permits the user to create a file in which calculated ages will be stored sequentially, along with the provenience, sex, and side of each tooth providing an age. The user can then scan the file visually or process it with other programs, such as BONESTAT. For example, BONESTAT could be used to determine if calculated ages are discontinuously distributed in a way that suggests seasonally limited bone accumulation.

If the user does not want a file of calculated ages, the proper response to "Name of file to write ages to" is NONE. If the user wants a file, we recommend a name with the extension "AGE", preceded by a composite abbreviation incorporating site name, species name, and the name of the tooth from which ages were calculated. For example, BCTOUDP4.AGE could be used to store ages of Border Cave *Taurotragus oryx* (eland) calculated from upper dP4s.

When either NONE or a file name has been entered, AGEPROF proceeds to calculate ages from deciduous crown heights. It then asks "Name of file with permanent crown heights," followed by "Name of file to write ages to." Again the user has the option of responding NONE to the second question. Whatever the response, AGEPROF calculates ages from

FIGURE 7.8: Listing of the program AGEPROF for calculating ungulate age (mortality) profiles from dental crown heights.

```
1000 PRINT "AGEPROF--Program to construct an age profile based on 10% of"
1010 PRINT "lifespan segments; age estimated from dental crown heights."
1020 PRINT
1030 REM IBM Personal Computer BASIC (R. G. Klein, 4 January 1983)
1040 REM For a deciduous tooth, age is calculated from crown height using:
1050 REM    AGE = (AGEs((CH|2)/CHo|2)) - (2*(AGEs)*(CH/CHo)) + AGEs
1060 REM For a permanent tooth, age is calculated from crown height using:
1070 REM    AGE = (((AGEpel - AGEe)/(CHo|2))*(CH|2))
1080 REM                - ((2*(AGEpel - AGEe)/CHo)*CH) + AGEpel
1090 REM              CHo = Initial (Unworn) Crown Height
1100 REM              AGEs = Age at which a deciduous tooth is shed
1110 REM              AGEe = Age at which a permanent tooth erupts
1120 REM              AGEpel = Age at Potential Ecological Longevity
1130 DEFINT A-Z
1140 DIM D(10), P(10), PU$(30)
1150 ON ERROR GOTO 4040
1160 INPUT "Site";ST$
1170 INPUT "Species (Latin name)";ANS$:GOSUB 3970:SP$=ANS$
1180 '
1190 MF$=""
1200 WHILE MF$<>"M" AND MF$<>"F" AND MF$<>"B"
1210    INPUT "Sex (M/F/B)";ANS$:GOSUB 3970:MF$=ANS$
1220    IF MF$<>"M" AND MF$<>"F" AND MF$<>"B" THEN BEEP
1230 WEND
1240 '
1250 LR$=""
1260 WHILE LR$<>"L" AND LR$<>"R" AND LR$<>"B"
1270    INPUT "Side (L/R/B)";ANS$:GOSUB 3970:LR$=ANS$
1280    IF LR$<>"L" AND LR$<>"R" AND LR$<>"B" THEN BEEP
1290 WEND
1300 '
1310 NPU=0
1320 WHILE NPU<1 OR NPU>30
1330    INPUT "How many provenience units to enter (ALL or 1-30)";ANS$:
           GOSUB 3970:NPU$=ANS$
1340    NPU=VAL(NPU$)
1350    IF NPU$="ALL" THEN PU$(1)="ALL":NPU=1
1360    IF NPU<1 OR NPU>30 THEN BEEP
1370 WEND
1380 '
1390 IF NPU$="ALL" THEN I=1 ELSE I=0
1400 WHILE I<NPU
1410    I=I+1
1420    INPUT "Provenience unit";ANS$:GOSUB 3970:PU$(I)=ANS$
1430 WEND
1440 '
1450 D$=""
1460 WHILE LEFT$(D$,1)<>"N" AND LEFT$(D$,1)<>"D"
1470    INPUT "Kind of deciduous tooth (dP#/None)";ANS$:GOSUB 3970:D$=ANS$
1480    IF LEFT$(D$,1)<>"N" AND LEFT$(D$,1)<>"D" THEN BEEP
1490 WEND
1500 '
1510 DLB=0
1520 WHILE LEFT$(D$,1)="D" AND DLB<>1 AND DLB<>2
1530    INPUT "Deciduous lobe to consider (1 or 2)";DLB
1540    IF DLB<>1 AND DLB<>2 THEN BEEP
1550 WEND
1560 '
1570 P$=""
```

```
1580 WHILE LEFT$(P$,1)<>"N" AND LEFT$(P$,1)<>"P" AND LEFT$(P$,1)<>"M"
1590   NPUT "Kind of permanent tooth (P#/M#/None)";ANS$:GOSUB 3970:P$=ANS$
1600   IF LEFT$(P$,1)<>"N" AND LEFT$(P$,1)<>"P" AND LEFT$(P$,1)<>"M" THEN BEEP
1610 WEND
1620 '
1630 PLB=0
1640 WHILE LEFT$(P$,1)<>"N" AND PLB<>1 AND PLB<>2
1650   INPUT "Permanent lobe to consider (1 or 2)";PLB
1660   IF PLB<>1 AND PLB<>2 THEN BEEP
1670 WEND
1680 '
1690 FK$=""
1700 WHILE FK$<>"F" AND FK$<>"K"
1710   INPUT "Background data from File or Keyboard (F/K)";ANS$:GOSUB 3970:
         FK$=ANS$
1720   IF FK$<>"F" AND FK$<>"K" THEN BEEP
1730 WEND
1740 '
1750 IF FK$="F" THEN GOSUB 3580 'obtain background info from file
1760 IF FK$="K" THEN GOSUB 1910 'obtain background info on deciduous tooth
1770 IF FK$="K" AND LEFT$(P$,1)<>"N" THEN GOSUB 2120
         'obtain background info on permanent tooth
1780 '
1790 IF LEFT$(D$,1)<>"N" THEN GOSUB 2260 'open file and calculate decid ages
1800 IF LEFT$(P$,1)<>"N" THEN GOSUB 2620 'open file and calculate perm ages
1810 GOSUB 3040     'calculate and print age profile
1820 '
1830 YN$=""
1840 WHILE YN$<>"N" AND YN$<>"Y"
1850   INPUT "Want to run program again (Y/N)";ANS$:GOSUB 3970:YN$=ANS$
1860   IF YN$<>"Y" AND YN$<>"N" THEN BEEP
1870 WEND
1880 IF YN$="Y" THEN CLOSE:RUN 1000
1890 IF YN$="N" THEN CLOSE:CLS:END
1900 '
1910 PEL!=0
1920 WHILE PEL!<12 OR PEL!>1200
1930   INPUT "Age at potential ecological longevity in months (12-1200)";PEL!
1940   IF PEL!<12 OR PEL!>1200 THEN BEEP
1950 WEND
1960 IF LEFT$(D$,1)="N" THEN RETURN
1970 '
1980 REM Deciduous background information from keyboard
1990 AGES!=0
2000 WHILE AGES!<=0 OR AGES!>PEL!
2010   PRINT "Age at which "D$" is shed in months ( >0 - ";PEL!;")";:
         INPUT AGES!
2020   IF AGES!<=0 OR AGES!>PEL! THEN BEEP
2030 WEND
2040 '
2050 DCH0!=0
2060 WHILE DCH0!<=0 OR DCH0!>1000
2070   PRINT "Initial (Unworn) "D$" crown height in tenths of a mm ";:
         PRINT"(>0 - 1000)";:INPUT DCH0!
2080   IF DCH0!<=0 OR DCH0!>1000 THEN BEEP
2090 WEND
2100 RETURN
2110 '
2120 REM Permanent background information from keyboard
```

```
2130 AGEE!=0
2140 WHILE AGEE!<=0 OR AGEE!>PEL!
2150  PRINT "Eruption age of "P$" in months ( >0 - ";PEL!;")";:INPUT AGEE!
2160  IF AGEE!<=0 OR AGEE!>PEL! THEN BEEP
2170 WEND
2180 '
2190 PCH0!=0
2200 WHILE PCH0!<=0 OR PCH0!>1250
2210  PRINT "Initial (Unworn) "P$" crown height in tenths of a mm ";:
         PRINT "(>0-1250)";:INPUT PCH0!
2220  IF PCH0!<=0 OR PCH0!>1250 THEN BEEP
2230 WEND
2240 RETURN
2250 '
2260 REM Read deciduous crown heights from file
2270  INPUT "Name of File with deciduous crown heights";DINFILE$:
         FILE$=DINFILE$
2280  CLOSE:OPEN DINFILE$ FOR INPUT AS #1
2290  INPUT "Name of File to write Ages to";ANS$:GOSUB 3970:DOUTFILE$=ANS$
2300  IF DOUTFILE$<>"NONE" THEN OPEN DOUTFILE$ FOR OUTPUT AS #2
2310  WHILE NOT EOF(1)
2320    SEX=0:SIDE=0:PROVUNIT=0
2330    INPUT #1,LV$,SX$,SD$,WS$,L!,B!,CH1!,CH2!,CN$
2340    IF LEFT$(LV$,1) = "#" THEN LV$ = MID$(LV$,2)
2350    SX$ = LEFT$(SX$,1):SD$ = LEFT$(SD$,1)
2360    IF MF$ = "B" OR SX$ = MF$ THEN SEX=-1
2370    IF LR$ = "B" OR SD$ = LR$ THEN SIDE=-1
2380    IF PU$(1)="ALL" THEN PROVUNIT=-1
2390    IF SEX AND SIDE AND NOT PROVUNIT THEN GOSUB 2980 'check provunit
2400    IF DLB=1 THEN CH!=CH1!
2410    IF DLB=2 THEN CH!=CH2!
2420    IF SEX AND SIDE AND PROVUNIT AND CH!<0 THEN GOSUB 2470
           'count unmeasurable teeth by wear state
2430    IF SEX AND SIDE AND PROVUNIT AND CH!>=0 THEN GOSUB 2550
           'calculate age
2440  WEND
2450 RETURN
2460 '
2470 REM Count unmeasurable deciduous teeth by wear state
2480  IF WS$ = "UW" THEN NUWD = NUWD + 1
2490  IF WS$ = "VEW" THEN NVEWD = NVEWD + 1
2500  IF WS$ = "EW" THEN NEWD = NEWD + 1
2510  IF WS$ = "MW" THEN NMWD = NMWD + 1
2520  IF WS$ = "LW" THEN NLWD = NLWD + 1
2530 RETURN
2540 '
2550 REM Calculate deciduous ages and tally
2560  AGE!=(AGES!*(CH!|2))/(DCH0!|2) - ((2*AGES!/DCH0!)*CH!) + AGES!
2570  IF DOUTFILE$<>"NONE" THEN PRINT#2,LV$,"SX$","SD$","AGE!
2580  G=INT(AGE!*(10/PEL!))
2590  D(G)=D(G)+1
2600 RETURN
2610 '
2620 REM Read permanent crown heights from file
2630  INPUT "Name of File with permanent crown heights";PINFILE$:
         FILE$=PINFILE$
2640  CLOSE:OPEN PINFILE$ FOR INPUT AS #1
2650  INPUT "Name of File to write Ages to";ANS$:GOSUB 3970:POUTFILE$=ANS$
2660  IF POUTFILE$<>"NONE" THEN OPEN POUTFILE$ FOR OUTPUT AS #2
```

```
2670   WHILE NOT EOF(1)
2680     SEX = 0:SIDE = 0:PROVUNIT = 0
2690     INPUT #1,LV$,SX$,SD$,WS$,L!,B!,CH1!,CH2!,CN$
2700     IF LEFT$(LV$,1) = "#" THEN LV$ = MID$(LV$,2)
2710     SX$ = LEFT$(SX$,1):SD$ = LEFT$(SD$,1)
2720     IF MF$ = "B" OR SX$ = MF$ THEN SEX=-1
2730     IF LR$ = "B" OR SD$ = LR$ THEN SIDE=-1
2740     IF PU$(1)="ALL" THEN PROVUNIT=-1
2750     IF SEX AND SIDE AND NOT PROVUNIT THEN GOSUB 2980 'check provunit
2760     IF PLB=1 THEN CH!=CH1!
2770     IF PLB=2 THEN CH!=CH2!
2780     IF SEX AND SIDE AND PROVUNIT AND CH!<0 THEN GOSUB 2830
           'count unmeasurable teeth by wear state
2790     IF SEX AND SIDE AND PROVUNIT AND CH!>=0 THEN GOSUB 2910
           'calculate age
2800   WEND
2810 RETURN
2820 '
2830 REM Count unmeasurable permanent teeth by wear state
2840   IF WS$ = "UW" THEN NUWP = NUWP + 1
2850   IF WS$ = "VEW" THEN NVEWP = NVEWP + 1
2860   IF WS$ = "EW" THEN NEWP = NEWP + 1
2870   IF WS$ = "MW" THEN NMWP = NMWP + 1
2880   IF WS$ = "LW" THEN NLWP = NLWP + 1
2890 RETURN
2900 '
2910 REM Calculate permanent ages and tally
2920   AGE!=(((PEL!-AGEE!)/(PCH0!|2))*(CH!|2))-(2*((PEL!-AGEE!)/PCH0!)*(CH!))
           +PEL!
2930   IF POUTFILE$<>"NONE" THEN PRINT#2,LV$","SX$","SD$","AGE!
2940   G=INT(AGE!*(10/PEL!))
2950   P(G)=P(G)+1
2960 RETURN
2970 '
2980 REM check provenience unit
2990   FOR I=1 TO NPU
3000     IF LV$=PU$(I) THEN PROVUNIT=-1:I=NPU
3010   NEXT
3020 RETURN
3030 '
3040 REM Combine deciduous and permanent counts
3050   FOR G=0 TO 9
3060     IF P(G)<D(G) THEN P(G)=D(G)
3070   NEXT G
3080 REM Calculate total number of individuals)
3090   FOR G=0 TO 9
3100     T=T+P(G)
3110   NEXT G
3120 '
3130 REM Print the age profile
3140   HC$="":SOFTCOPY=-1
3150   WHILE HC$<>"N" AND SOFTCOPY=-1
3160     IF HC$="" THEN CLOSE:OPEN "SCRN:" FOR OUTPUT AS #1
3170     IF HC$="Y" THEN SOFTCOPY=0:CLOSE:OPEN "LPT1:" FOR OUTPUT AS #1
3180 PRINT#1, "                              "; DATE$;" "TIME$
3190 PRINT#1, ST$                            "
3200 PRINT#1, "AGE PROFILE OF " SP$ " (SEX = "MF$ " and SIDE = "LR$")"
3210 PRINT#1, "assuming that the unworn crown heights of " D$ " lobe" DLB "and"
3220 PRINT#1, P$ " lobe"PLB"are" DCH0!"and" PCH0!"tenths of a mm and that the"
```

```
3230 PRINT#1, "age at which " D$" is shed is"AGES!"months, the age at which "P$
3240 PRINT#1, "erupts is" AGEE!"months and the age at potential ecological"
3250 PRINT#1, "longevity is" PEL!"months.  Provenience units: ";
3260 PPU$=""
3270 FOR I=1 TO NPU
3280    PPU$=PPU$+PU$(I)+" "
3290 NEXT I
3300 PRINT#1,PPU$
3310 PRINT#1, "  "
3320 PRINT#1, "  "
3330 PRINT#1, "   AGE INTERVALS (in months)"
3340 PRINT#1, "At least", "But below", "Number"
3350 PRINT#1, "-----------------------------"
3360    FOR G = 0 TO 9
3370       PRINT#1, (PEL!*G)/10, (PEL!*(G+1)/10), P(G)
3380    NEXT G
3390 PRINT#1, "-----------------------------"
3400 PRINT#1, "TOTAL NUMBER OF INDIVIDUALS=" T
3410 IF HC$<>"Y" THEN PRINT "Press <ENTER> to continue...";:YY$=INKEY$:
       WHILE YY$="":YY$=INKEY$:WEND
3420 PRINT#1, "    "
3430 PRINT#1, "Number of unmeasurable teeth:"
3440 PRINT#1, TAB(5) "Deciduous  Permanent"
3450 PRINT#1, "UW   " NUWD; TAB(17) NUWP
3460 PRINT#1, "VEW  " NVEWD; TAB(17) NVEWP
3470 PRINT#1, "EW   " NEWD; TAB(17) NEWP
3480 PRINT#1, "MW   " NMWD; TAB(17) NMWP
3490 PRINT#1, "LW   " NLWD; TAB(17) NLWP
3500 CLOSE: PRINT
3510    WHILE HC$<>"N" AND HC$<>"Y"
3520       INPUT "Want hard copy (Y/N)";ANS$:GOSUB 3970:HC$=ANS$
3530       IF HC$<>"Y" AND HC$<>"N" THEN BEEP
3540    WEND
3550 WEND
3560 RETURN
3570 '
3580 REM To obtain species parameters from CRNHGT file
3590    INPUT "Name of file with background data";BACKFILE$:FILE$=BACKFILE$
3600    CLOSE:OPEN BACKFILE$ FOR INPUT AS #1
3610    WHILE S$<>SP$ AND NOT EOF(1)
3620       INPUT #1,S$,PEL!,DP2S!,DP3S!,DP4S!,M1E!,M2E!,M3E!
3630       INPUT #1,DP2CH0!,DP3CH0!,DP4CH0!,P2CH0!,P3CH0!,P4CH0!,M1CH0!,M2CH0!,
          M3CH0!
3640    WEND
3650    IF S$<>SP$ THEN FK$="K":BEEP:PRINT "Species not on file! ";:
          PRINT "Must enter background data from keyboard.":RETURN
3660    PRINT: PRINT S$
3670    PRINT "dP2 shed (and P2 erupts) at" DP2S!"months"
3680    PRINT "dP3 shed (and P3 erupts) at" DP3S!"months"
3690    PRINT "dP4 shed (and P4 erupts) at" DP4S!"months"
3700    PRINT "M1 erupts at" M1E!"months"
3710    PRINT "M2 erupts at" M2E!"months"
3720    PRINT "M3 erupts at" M3E!"months"
3730    PRINT "Age at potential ecological longevity is" PEL!"months"
3740    PRINT "Unworn dP2 crown height is" DP2CH0!"tenths of a mm"
3750    PRINT "Unworn dP3 crown height is" DP3CH0!"tenths of a mm"
3760    PRINT "Unworn dP4 crown height is" DP4CH0!"tenths of a mm"
3770    PRINT "Unworn P2 crown height is" P2CH0!"tenths of a mm"
3780    PRINT "Unworn P3 crown height is" P3CH0!"tenths of a mm"
```

```
3790   PRINT "Unworn P4 crown height is" P4CH0!"tenths of a mm"
3800   PRINT "Unworn M1 crown height is" M1CH0!"tenths of a mm"
3810   PRINT "Unworn M2 crown height is" M2CH0!"tenths of a mm"
3820   PRINT "Unworn M3 crown height is" M3CH0!"tenths of a mm"
3830   PRINT
3840 '
3850   IF LEFT$(D$,3)="DP2" THEN DCH0!=DP2CH0!:AGES!=DP2S!
3860   IF LEFT$(D$,3)="DP3" THEN DCH0!=DP3CH0!:AGES!=DP3S!
3870   IF LEFT$(D$,3)="DP4" THEN DCH0!=DP4CH0!:AGES!=DP4S!
3880 '
3890   IF LEFT$(P$,2)="P2" THEN PCH0!=P2CH0!:AGEE!=DP2S!
3900   IF LEFT$(P$,2)="P3" THEN PCH0!=P3CH0!:AGEE!=DP3S!
3910   IF LEFT$(P$,2)="P4" THEN PCH0!=P4CH0!:AGEE!=DP4S!
3920   IF LEFT$(P$,2)="M1" THEN PCH0!=M1CH0!:AGEE!=M1E!
3930   IF LEFT$(P$,2)="M2" THEN PCH0!=M2CH0!:AGEE!=M2E!
3940   IF LEFT$(P$,2)="M3" THEN PCH0!=M3CH0!:AGEE!=M3E!
3950 RETURN
3960 '
3970 REM Capitalization
3980   FOR N=1 TO LEN(ANS$)
3990     LTR$=MID$(ANS$,N,1)
4000     IF "a"<=LTR$ AND LTR$<="z" THEN MID$(ANS$,N,1)=CHR$(ASC(LTR$)-32)
4010   NEXT N
4020 RETURN
4030 '
4040 REM Error traps
4050   IF ERR=53 AND FILE$=DINFILE$ THEN BEEP:PRINT "No such file":RESUME 2270
4060   IF ERR=53 AND FILE$=PINFILE$ THEN BEEP:PRINT "No such file":RESUME 2630
4070   IF ERR=53 AND FILE$=BACKFILE$ THEN BEEP:PRINT "No such file":RESUME 1690
4080   IF ERR=27 THEN BEEP:PRINT "Turn on printer!":HC$="":RESUME 3510
```

TABLE 7.3 AGEPROF Prompts and Acceptable Responses.

Prompts	Responses
1) Site	Site name, including embedded blanks, if desired.
2) Species (Latin name)	Latin name or name recorded in a CRNHGT file if AGEPROF is to obtain shedding/eruption ages, potential ecological longevity, and initial (unworn) crown heights from such a file; otherwise any name.
3) Sex (M/F/B)	M (male), F (female), or B (both) -- leads to prompt for "Side (L/R/B)"
4) Side (L/R/B)	L (left), R (right), B (both) -- leads to prompt for "How many provenience units to enter."
5) How many pro- venience units to enter	ALL -- if AGEPROF is to process all teeth in a file. A number between 1 and 30.
6) Provenience Unit	Any combination of letters and numbers -- combinations must match combinations used to designate provenience units in data files.
7) Kind of deciduous tooth (dP#/None)	dP1, dP2, dP3, or dP4. N(one) -- causes program to request "Kind of permanent tooth (P#/M#/None)"
n.b. This prompt does not appear if answer to 7 was None.	
8) Deciduous lobe to consider (1 or 2)	1 -- causes age to be calculated from the first crown height of each deciduous tooth. 2 -- causes age to be calculated from the second crown height of each deciduous tooth.
9) Kind of permanent tooth (P#/M#/None)	P1, P2, P3, P4, M1, M2, or M3 N(one) -- causes program to request "Background data from File or Keyboard."

n.b. This prompt does not appear if the answer to 9 was None.

| 10) Permanent lobe to consider (1 or 2) | 1 -- causes age to be calculated from the first crown height of each permanent tooth. 2 -- causes age to be calculated from the second crown height of each permanent tooth. |

| 11) Background data from file or keyboard (F/K) | F -- if potential ecological longevity, shedding/eruption ages, and initial crown heights are stored in a CRNHGT file. K -- if potential ecological longevity and other parameters are to be entered from the keyboard. |

---

n.b. This prompt only appears if the answer to 11 was F.

| 12) Name of file with back-ground data. | File in which potential ecological longevity, shedding/eruption ages, and initial crown heights are stored. |

---

n.b. These prompts only appear if the answer to 11 was K.

| 13) Age at potential ecological longevity. | An appropriate age between 12 and 1200 months. |

| 14) Age at shedding | The age between 0 months and potential ecological longevity when the deciduous tooth of prompt 7 is shed. |

| 15) Initial (unworn) deciduous crown height | The appropriate height between 0 and 1000 tenths of a millimeter. |

| 16) Eruption age of permanent tooth. | The age between 0 months and potential ecological longevity when the permanent tooth of prompt 9 erupts. |

| 17) Initial (unworn) permanent tooth crown height | The appropriate height between 0 and 1250 tenths of a millimeter. |

| 18) Name of file with deciduous | The name of the file in which deciduous crown heights are stored. |

crown heights

19) Name of file to write ages to	Name of file into which estimated deciduous ages are to be placed. None -- if no such file is wanted.
20) Name of file with permanent crown heights	Name of the file in which permanent crown heights are stored.
21) Name of file to write ages to	Name of file into which estimated permanent ages are to be placed. None -- if no such file is wanted.
22) Want hard copy (Y/N)	Y -- forces results to attached printer, N -- leads immediately to prompt 23.
23) Run Program Again (Y/N)	Y -- starts program from scratch, with prompt for "Site". N -- terminates session.

Note: Each response must be followed by a carriage return.

permanent crown heights. It then displays the age profile on the screen.

The final questions are "Want hard copy (Y/N)" and "Run program again (Y/N)." Y in response to the second question initiates a completely fresh session in which all variables are initially set to zero. N terminates the session.

If the answer to "Background data from File or Keyboard" is K, the prompt sequence is identical to the one we have just described, except the user will be asked first to enter the age at potential longevity, shedding and eruption ages, and unworn crown heights. Acceptable responses are the same as those discussed in the section on CRNHGT.

Results of an AGEPROF Session

Figure 7.9 presents the output from the sample session of AGEPROF "photoed" in the same Figure. The first part of the output is a caption listing the site and species for which the age profile was calculated, the deciduous and permanent teeth on which it was based, and the age at potential ecological longevity, the shedding/eruption ages, and the initial (unworn) crown heights used to calculate the profile. The second part is the age profile itself, presented in tabular form. The first two columns of the table define ten successive life-span segments, each of which represents exactly 10% of the potential ecological longevity of the species. The third column is the number of individuals in each life-span segment.

To produce the third column, AGEPROF compared the number of individuals placed in a particular life-span segment by deciduous crown

FIGURE 7.9: Left: A sample AGEPROF session. Right: Output from the sample session. The files processed in the sample session were created by DENTDATA in figure 7.2 and are illustrated in figure 7.3. Except for illustrative purposes, the authors would not ordinarily compute an age profile from so few teeth.

AGEPROF--Program to construct an age profile based on 10% of life-span segments; age estimated from dental crown heights.

Site ? EQUUS CAVE
Species (Latin name) ? RAPHICERUS CAMPESTRIS
Sex (M/F/B) ? B
Side (L/R/B) ? B
How many provenience units to enter (ALL or 1-30) ? ALL
Kind of deciduous tooth (dP#/None) ? DP4
Deciduous lobe to consider (1 or 2) ? 1
Kind of permanent tooth (P#/M#/None) ? M3
Permanent lobe to consider (1 or 2) ? 1
Background data from File or Keyboard (F/K) ? K
Age at potential ecological longevity in months (12-1200) ? 72
Age at which dP4 is shed in months (>0- 72) ? 12
Initial (Unworn) dP4 crown height in tenths of a millimeter (>0-1000) ? 60
Eruption age of M3 in months (>0- 72) ? 9.6
Initial (Unworn) M3 crown height in tenths of a millimeter (>0-1250) ? 156
Name of File with deciduous crown heights ? EQCRCLO.DP4
Name of File to write Ages to ? NONE
Name of File with permanent crown heights ? EQCRCLO.M3
Name of File to write Ages to ? NONE

4-16-83 10:53:32

EQUUS CAVE

AGE PROFILE OF RAPHICERUS CAMPESTRIS (SEX = B and SIDE = B)
assuming that the unworn crown heights of DP4 lobe 1 and
M3 lobe 1 are 60 and 156 tenths of a mm and that the
age at which DP4 is shed is 12 months, the age at which M3
erupts is 9.6 months and the age at potential ecological
longevity is 72 months. Provenience units: ALL

AGE INTERVALS (in months)

At least	But below	Number
0	7.2	5
7.2	14.4	4
14.4	21.6	1
21.6	28.8	0
28.8	36	0
36	43.2	0
43.2	50.4	0
50.4	57.6	0
57.6	64.8	0
64.8	72	0

TOTAL NUMBER OF INDIVIDUALS= 10
Press <ENTER> to continue ...

Number of unmeasurable teeth:

	Deciduous	Permanent
UW	0	0
VEW	0	0
EW	0	0
MW	0	0
LW	0	0

Want hard copy (Y/N) ? N
Want to run the program again (Y/N) ? N

height measurements with the number placed in the same segment by permanent ones. The final tabulation includes only the larger of the two numbers. In most species, the deciduous teeth are shed before the end of the second life-span segment or early in the third, while the permanent teeth begin to erupt only during the first segment. This means that most of the individuals represented by both the deciduous tooth and the permanent tooth used to construct the age profile will fall in the second life-span segment. They will rarely fall in any life-span segment after the third.

If a user wished, AGEPROF could report the numbers of individuals placed in the same life-span segment by deciduous and permanent teeth separately, without (or before) choosing the larger number. Another potential modification that might interest some users would be to present the age profile as a histogram instead of (or as well as) a table. This could be accomplished with minimal reprogramming but would mean more prompts and greater processing time.

In most samples we have studied, crown height is measurable on the overwhelming majority of teeth. It is therefore unlikely that unmeasurable teeth have seriously distorted the age profile. However, there are samples in which unmeasurable teeth are common. As the final item, AGEPROF thus displays the number of unmeasurable teeth in each subjective wear category (UW, VEW, EW, MW, and LW) so that the possibility of age profile distortion may be assessed.

Comparing Age Profiles: Program SMIRNOV
In chapter 4, we stressed the value of the Kolmogorov-Smirnov test for determining the probability that two age profiles differ simply by chance. The test is seldom included in standard statistical packages, particularly in a form that is convenient for comparing age profiles, patterns of skeletal part representation, or other data that are pertinent to faunal analysts. We have thus written the program SMIRNOV and describe its use briefly here.

Figure 7.10 lists SMIRNOV, and figure 7.11 shows a sample session based on the two age profiles used to illustrate the test in the previous chapter. Table 7.4 lists the SMIRNOV prompts and appropriate responses.

SMIRNOV asks first for "Title of Run." This is solely to label the printout and may consist of virtually any combination of letters and numbers, including embedded blanks. The next prompt is for "Number of categories in each sample." In the case of an age profile created by AGEPROF, the answer is obviously 10 (for the ten successive life-span segments into which AGEPROF groups ages.)

SMIRNOV next asks "Number of items in category 1 of SAMPLE 1." In the case of an age profile created by AGEPROF, the appropriate answer is the number of individuals in the first (youngest) life-span segment in whichever sample is to be entered first. SMIRNOV then requests the number of items in each of the remaining categories. In the case of an AGEPROF age profile, the last prompt in the series is for "Number of items in category 10 of SAMPLE 1."

FIGURE 7.10.: Listing of the program SMIRNOV for comparing two samples using the Kolmogorov-Smirnov test.

```
1000 PRINT "Kolmogorov-Smirnov two-sample test"
1010 REM IBM Personal Computer BASIC (R. G. Klein, 11 January 1984)
1020 DEFINT A-Z
1030 ON ERROR GOTO 1910
1040 DIM S1(100),S2(100),TS1(100),TS2(100),QS1!(100),QS2!(100),D!(100)
1050 PRINT
1060 INPUT "Title of Run"; TR$
1070 '
1080 WHILE B2$<>"2"
1090 NC=0
1100   WHILE NC<=1 OR NC>100
1110     INPUT "Number of categories in each sample (2-100)";NC
1120     IF NC<=1 OR NC>100 THEN BEEP
1130   WEND
1140 '
1150   FOR I = 1 TO NC
1160     PRINT "Number of items in category" I "of SAMPLE 1";:INPUT S1(I)
1170   NEXT I
1180   B2$="2"
1190 WEND
1200 PRINT
1210 '
1220 FOR I = 1 TO NC
1230   PRINT "Number of items in category" I "of SAMPLE 2";:INPUT S2(I)
1240 NEXT I
1250 '
1260 REM Cumulative Frequency Distributions
1270   TS1(1) = S1(1): TS2(1) = S2(1)
1280   FOR I = 2 TO NC
1290     TS1(I) = TS1(I-1) + S1(I)
1300     TS2(I) = TS2(I-1) + S2(I)
1310   NEXT I
1320 REM Cumulative Percentage Distributions and Maximum Difference
1330   MAX!=0
1340   FOR I = 1 TO NC
1350     QS1!(I) = TS1(I)/TS1(NC)
1360     QS2!(I) = TS2(I)/TS2(NC)
1370     D!(I) = ABS(QS1!(I) - QS2!(I))
1380     IF D!(I) >= MAX! THEN MAX! = D!(I)
1390   NEXT I
1400 REM Compute Kolmogorov-Smirnov Z
1410   KSZ! = MAX!/((((TS1(NC)+TS2(NC))/(TS1(NC)*TS2(NC)))|(1/2))
1420 REM Results
1430 HC$="":SOFTCOPY=-1
1440 WHILE HC$<>"N" AND SOFTCOPY=-1
1450   IF HC$="" THEN CLOSE:OPEN "SCRN:" FOR OUTPUT AS #1
1460   IF HC$="Y" THEN SOFTCOPY=0:CLOSE:OPEN "LPT1:" FOR OUTPUT AS #1
1470 PRINT
1480 PRINT#1, "                    "DATE$" "TIME$
1490 PRINT#1, TR$
1500 PRINT#1, " "
1510 PRINT#1, "Total number of items in SAMPLE 1 ="TS1(NC)
1520   IF TS1(NC)<40 THEN PRINT#1,"Caution: SAMPLE 1 contains <40 items!"
1530 PRINT#1, "Number of items in SAMPLE 2 ="TS2(NC)
1540   IF TS2(NC)<40 THEN PRINT#1,"Caution: SAMPLE 2 contains <40 items!"
1550 PRINT#1, "Maximum absolute difference =" MAX!
1560 PRINT#1, "Kolmogorov-Smirnov Z =" KSZ!
1570 PRINT#1, " "
1580 PRINT#1, "A Z value of >= 1.22 is significant at the 0.10 level or below"
```

```
1590 PRINT#1, "A Z value of > = 1.36 is significant at the 0.05 level or below"
1600 PRINT#1, "A Z value of > = 1.63 is significant at the 0.01 level or below"
1610 PRINT#1, "A Z value of > = 1.95 is significant at the 0.001 level or below"
1620 PRINT
1630   WHILE HC$<>"Y" AND HC$<>"N"
1640     INPUT "Want hard copy (Y/N)";ANS$:GOSUB 1840:HC$=ANS$
1650     IF HC$<>"N" AND HC$<>"Y" THEN BEEP
1660   WEND
1670 WEND
1680 '
1690 YN$=""
1700 WHILE YN$<>"Y" AND YN$<>"N"
1710   INPUT "Run Program Again (Y/N)";ANS$:GOSUB 1840:YN$=ANS$
1720   IF YN$<>"Y" AND YN$<>"N" THEN BEEP
1730 WEND
1740 IF YN$="N" THEN CLS:CLOSE:END
1750 '
1760 B2$=""
1770 WHILE B2$<>"B" AND B2$<>"2"
1780 INPUT "Change entries for both samples or just second (B/2)";ANS$:
       GOSUB 1840:B2$=ANS$
1790   IF B2$<>"B" AND B2$<>"2" THEN BEEP
1800 WEND
1810 PRINT
1820 GOTO 1060   'run again
1830 '
1840 REM Capitalization
1850 FOR LTR=1 TO LEN(ANS$)
1860   LTR$=MID$(ANS$,LTR,1)
1870   IF "a"<=LTR$ AND LTR$<="z" THEN MID$(ANS$,LTR,1)=CHR$(ASC(LTR$)-32)
1880 NEXT
1890 RETURN
1900 '
1910 REM error trap
1920   IF ERR=27 THEN BEEP:PRINT "Turn on printer!":
       PRINT "Press any key to continue ...":Y$=INKEY$:WHILE Y$="":Y$=INKEY$:
       WEND:RESUME 1460
```

Kolmogorov-Smirnov two-sample test

Title of Run ? KRM ELAND AND GIANT BUFFALO AGE PROFILES
Number of categories in each sample ? 10
Number of items in category 1 of SAMPLE 1 ? 20
Number of items in category 2 of SAMPLE 1 ? 17
Number of items in category 3 of SAMPLE 1 ? 13
Number of items in category 4 of SAMPLE 1 ? 23
Number of items in category 5 of SAMPLE 1 ? 23
Number of items in category 6 of SAMPLE 1 ? 16
Number of items in category 7 of SAMPLE 1 ? 3
Number of items in category 8 of SAMPLE 1 ? 4
Number of items in category 9 of SAMPLE 1 ? 2
Number of items in category 10 of SAMPLE 1 ? 0

Number of items in category 1 of SAMPLE 2 ? 44
Number of items in category 2 of SAMPLE 2 ? 2
Number of items in category 3 of SAMPLE 2 ? 3
Number of items in category 4 of SAMPLE 2 ? 0
Number of items in category 5 of SAMPLE 2 ? 2
Number of items in category 6 of SAMPLE 2 ? 9
Number of items in category 7 of SAMPLE 2 ? 5
Number of items in category 8 of SAMPLE 2 ? 5
Number of items in category 9 of SAMPLE 2 ? 0
Number of items in category 10 of SAMPLE 2 ? 0

4-20-83 08:21:17

KRM ELAND AND GIANT BUFFALO AGE PROFILES

Total number of items in SAMPLE 1 = 121
Number of items in SAMPLE 2 = 70
Maximum absolute difference = 0.4632822
Kolmogorov-Smirnov Z = 3.08511

A Z value of $>=$ 1.22 is significant at the 0.10 level or below
A Z value of $>=$ 1.36 is significant at the 0.05 level or below
A Z value of $>=$ 1.63 is significant at the 0.01 level or below
A Z value of $>=$ 1.95 is significant at the 0.001 level or below

Want hard copy (Y/N) ? N
Run Program Again (Y/N) ? N

FIGURE 7.11: A SMIRNOV sample session comparing two hypothetical
age profiles. The difference between the profiles is highly significant in
conventional statistical terms.

TABLE 7.4 SMIRNOV Prompts and Acceptable Responses.

Prompt	Response
1) Title of run	Any combination of letters and numbers, including embedded blanks. Used solely to label printout.
2) Number of categories in each sample.	The number of categories into which each sample has been subdivided (cannot exceed 100.)
3) Number of items in category 1 of SAMPLE 1.	The number of items in the first category of sample 1. The prompt is repeated for each category in the sample, up to the number of categories specified in prompt 2.
4) Number of items in category 1 of SAMPLE 2.	The number of items in the first category of sample 2. The prompt is repeated for each category in the sample, up to the number of categories specified in prompt 2.
5) Want hard copy (Y/N)	Y -- forces results to attached printer, followed by prompt 6. N -- leads immediately to prompt 6.
6) Run Program Again (Y/N)	Y -- leads to prompt 7. N -- terminates session.
7) Change entries for both samples or just second (B/2).	B -- initiates a completely new run, with all previous entries erased. 2 -- initiates a new run , but with previous entries for sample 1 preserved. Only the numbers of items in each category of sample 2 are requested.

Note: Each response must be followed by a carriage return.

When the number of items in the last category of the first sample has been entered, SMIRNOV repeats the same set of prompts for the second sample. In the case of an AGEPROF age profile (with ten categories), the first prompt in the new series is "Number of items in category 1 of SAMPLE 2," and the last prompt is "Number of items in category 10 of SAMPLE 2."

After the number of items in the last category of sample 2 has been entered, SMIRNOV displays the total number of items in each sample, the maximum absolute difference between their cumulative distributions, and the Kolmogorov-Smirnov value, called "Z." It warns the user if the total number of items in either sample is less than forty, in which case the test may provide misleading results. It may then be advisable to use some other procedure such as the Mann-Whitney test. Finally, SMIRNOV shows the Z values associated with the .10, .05, .01, and .001 levels of statistical significance.

SMIRNOV next asks "Want hard copy (Y/N)." Whatever the response, the next question is "Run Program Again" (Y/N)." If the answer is N, SMIRNOV terminates the session. If the answer is Y, SMIRNOV asks "Change entries for both samples or just second (B/2)." This is to permit a user to compare one sample with two or more in a row, without having to reenter the values for the first sample each time. If the answer is 2, SMIRNOV first requests "Title of Run" and then "Number of items in category 1 of Sample 2." This is followed by requests for the number of items in each of the remaining categories in Sample 2 and a display of the results. If the answer is B, SMIRNOV initiates a completely new run, with the full series of prompts that have already been discussed. All entries from the previous run are erased.

As we indicated in chapter 4, the Kolmogorov-Smirnov test can be used to compare any two samples that comprise the same number of categories, as long as the categories are arranged in the same logical order within each sample. Thus, we often use the test to compare patterns of skeletal part representation. In this instance, the categories involved are skeletal parts listed in anatomical order or in any other order that makes good faunal analytic sense. The number of items to be entered for each skeletal part category can be either the number of bones assigned to it or the minimum number of individuals from which the bones derive. We provided concrete illustrations in chapter 5.

As it is now written, SMIRNOV allows the user to enter up to one hundred categories in each of two samples. The number could be increased, but we believe one hundred will suffice for virtually all faunal analytic applications.

MEASUREMENTS OF BONES AND TEETH: PROGRAMS

BONESTAT AND **BONEDATA**

In Part 1, we illustrated the use of measurements for estimating the sex ratio and age structure of a fossil species sample, for differentiating morphologically similar elements within a species, and for describing individual size. These are but a few of the ways faunal analysts can use measurements. In this chapter, we present the program BONESTAT, which calculates the mean, the standard deviation, the median, the observed range, other useful statistics, and histograms from bone and tooth measurements.

File Names
In the last chapter, we described the program DENTDATA which creates a file containing the provenience, side, sex, wear state, length, breadth, two separate crown heights, and a catalog number for each tooth in a fossil species sample. We suggested a convention for naming DENTDATA files. The program AGEPROF uses the crown heights they contain to construct an age profile. BONESTAT can also process DENTDATA files and provides summary statistics and histograms for tooth length, breadth, or crown height, at the user's choice.

In the previous chapter we also noted that AGEPROF can create a file containing the provenience, side, sex, and age estimated from crown height for each tooth in a sample. We suggested that such a file be named to indicate the site, species, and kind of tooth from which estimated ages were obtained. BONESTAT can also process this kind of file and will provide summary statistics and histograms for the estimated ages. A histogram is particularly useful for detecting age discontinuities that indicate seasonal death or seasonal bone accumulation.

Finally, BONESTAT processes files that contain measurements on bones. For the moment, the only measurements it expects are total bone length (assuming a complete bone) and the mediolateral and anteroposterior diameters of one epiphysis (proximal or distal). The last two measurements are the ones that are most practical in the faunal samples we have studied, which tend to be highly fragmented. We have included total bone length mainly to indicate the potential of BONESTAT. With minimal rewriting, it could be made to accept and process a much wider range of measurements on each bone, including (for example) the minimum diameter of the shaft and the diameters of both epiphyses. Alternatively, it could be made to accept a variable number of measurements at the user's choice. However, this would make the program somewhat harder to use while increasing the chances of data entry error.

We have developed a convention for naming files that contain those bone measurements BONESTAT currently expects. We assume that a single file will contain measurements and associated data (provenience, side, sex, catalog number) for only one skeletal part of one species. We further assume that the file will contain bones from only one site. We then use the first 2 to 3 letters in the file name for the site (e.g. KRM for Klasies River Mouth) and the next 2 to 3 letters for the species. Ordinarily, we designate the species by the first letters of its Latin binomial (e.g. TS for *Tragelaphus scriptus*), but if such a combination of letters could represent more than one species, we add letters to make this designation unique (e.g. TSC for *Tragelaphus scriptus* in a site that also contains *Tragelaphus strepsiceros* .)

The final letters before the period in the file name are PR for proximal and DI for distal, denoting the position of the epiphysis whose diameters are in the file. The file extension after the period is then a three-letter abbreviation for the skeletal part of the epiphysis (e.g. HUM for humerus or RAD for radius). Examples of complete file names then are KRMTSDI.HUM or KRMTSPR.RAD.

If BONESTAT is rewritten to accept a wider range of measurements, including proximal and distal ones in the same file, the file-naming convention must obviously be changed. BONESTAT will in fact accept any file name that is acceptable to the system on which it is running.

Entry of Bone Measurements: Program BONEDATA

The dental measurements and estimated ages that BONESTAT processes are entered into files via DENTDATA and AGEPROF, as discussed previously. For the entry of bone measurements, we have written the program BONEDATA, which asks the user for seven items of information on each bone, in the following order:

1) Provenience.
2) Sex.
3) Side.
4) Mediolateral diameter of the epiphysis being measured.
5) Anteroposterior diameter of the epiphysis being measured.
6) Total length of the bone (assuming it is complete).
7) Catalog number of bone.

Figure 8.1 lists BONEDATA, and Figure 8.2 shows a sample session. Figure 8.3 shows the file created by the sample session. Table 8.1 summarizes the BONEDATA prompts, with possible responses and their effects.

BONEDATA asks first "Do you want to enter a catalog number for each bone (Y/N)." If the answer is Y, BONEDATA will routinely prompt for such a number in the subsequent session. If the answer is N it will not, and the catalog number of each bone will be recorded as "#". For reasons we presented in the introduction to Part 2, we routinely answer N.

BONEDATA next asks "Is Sex Known (Y/N)." For most bone samples the answer will be N. The principal exceptions will be modern comparative samples. If the response is N, BONEDATA will automatically record sex

FIGURE 8.1: Listing of the program BONEDATA for placing the mediolateral and anteroposterior diameters of an epiphysis and total bone length in a data file.

```
1000 PRINT "BONEDATA. For limbbone epiphyses. Places the medio-lateral"
1010 PRINT "and antero-posterior diameters and the total bone length in a"
1020 PRINT "file. For missing measurements, enter -1. To change Site, enter"
1030 PRINT "'CHANGE' in response to 'Provenience Unit.' To change"
1040 PRINT "'Provenience Unit' enter 'CHANGE' in response to any prompt."
1050 PRINT "To end, enter 'QUIT' in response to any prompt."
1060 PRINT
1070 REM IBM Personal Computer BASIC (R. G. Klein, 11 January 1984)
1080 DEFINT A-Z
1090 KEY 1, "CHANGE" + CHR$(13)
1100 FILEENTERED=0
1110 '
1120 CNYN$=""
1130 WHILE CNYN$<>"N" AND CNYN$<>"Y"
1140   INPUT "Do you want to enter a catalog number for each bone (Y/N)";
          ANS$:GOSUB 2250:CNYN$=ANS$
1150   IF CNYN$<>"N" AND CNYN$<>"Y" THEN BEEP
1160 WEND
1170 '
1180 SXYN$=""
1190 WHILE SXYN$<>"N" AND SXYN$<>"Y"
1200   INPUT "Is sex known (Y/N)";ANS$:GOSUB 2250:SXYN$=ANS$
1210   IF SXYN$<>"Y" AND SXYN$<>"N" THEN BEEP
1220 WEND
1230 '
1240 SDYN$=""
1250 WHILE SDYN$<>"N" AND SDYN$<>"Y"
1260   INPUT "Is side known (Y/N)";ANS$:GOSUB 2250:SDYN$=ANS$
1270   IF SDYN$<>"N" AND SDYN$<>"Y" THEN BEEP
1280 WEND
1290 '
1300 TLYN$=""
1310 WHILE TLYN$<>"N" AND TLYN$<>"Y"
1320   INPUT "Total Length to be entered (Y/N)";ANS$:GOSUB 2250:TLYN$=ANS$
1330   IF TLYN$<>"N" AND TLYN$<>"Y" THEN BEEP
1340 WEND
1350 '
1360 IF FILEENTERED=0 THEN INPUT "File Name";FILE$:FILEENTERED=-1
1370 CLOSE:OPEN FILE$ FOR APPEND AS #1
1380 '
1390 NEWSITE=-1
1400 CONTINUE=-1:CHANGE=0:QUIT=0
1410 WHILE CONTINUE
1420   IF NEWSITE THEN INPUT "Site (carriage return if no site name wanted)";
          ANS$:GOSUB 2250:S$=ANS$:NEWSITE=0
1430   IF S$ = "QUIT" THEN QUIT=-1
1440   IF S$ = "CHANGE" THEN CHANGE=-1
1450   IF NOT QUIT AND NOT CHANGE THEN
          INPUT "Provenience Unit (carriage return for no unit)";ANS$:
          GOSUB 2250:P$=ANS$
1460   IF P$ = "QUIT" THEN QUIT=-1
1470   IF P$ = "CHANGE" THEN CHANGE=-1:NEWSITE=-1
1480   P$=S$+P$
1490   IF P$<>"" THEN CONTINUE=0 ELSE BEEP:
          PRINT "Must have Site Name or Provenience   Unit!":
1495   IF P$="CHANGE" AND NEWSITE THEN CONTINUE=-1
1500 WEND
1510 IF CHANGE THEN 1120
1520 IF QUIT THEN CLOSE:CLS:END
```

216

```
1530 '
1540 CONTINUE=-1:CHANGE=0:QUIT=0
1550 IF SXYN$="N" THEN SX$="I":CONTINUE=0
1560 WHILE CONTINUE
1570   INPUT "Sex (M/F/I)";ANS$:GOSUB 2250:SX$=ANS$
1580     IF SX$="M" OR SX$="F" OR SX$="I" THEN CONTINUE=0
1590     IF SX$="QUIT" THEN QUIT=-1:CONTINUE=0
1600     IF SX$="CHANGE" THEN CHANGE=-1:CONTINUE=0
1610     IF CONTINUE THEN BEEP
1620 WEND
1630 IF QUIT THEN CLOSE:CLS:END
1640 IF CHANGE THEN 1400
1650 '
1660 CONTINUE=-1:CHANGE=0:QUIT=0
1670 IF SDYN$="N" THEN SD$="I":CONTINUE=0
1680 WHILE CONTINUE
1690   INPUT "Side (L/R/I)";ANS$:GOSUB 2250:SD$=ANS$
1700     IF SD$="L" OR SD$="R" OR SD$="I" THEN CONTINUE=0
1710     IF SD$="QUIT" THEN QUIT=-1:CONTINUE=0
1720     IF SD$="CHANGE" THEN CHANGE=-1:CONTINUE=0
1730     IF CONTINUE THEN BEEP
1740 WEND
1750 IF CHANGE THEN 1400
1760 IF QUIT THEN CLOSE:CLS:END
1770 '
1780 ML!=0:CHANGE=0:QUIT=0
1790 WHILE ML!=0
1800   INPUT "Medio-lateral diameter";ANS$:GOSUB 2250:ML$=ANS$
1810   ML!=VAL(ML$)
1820   IF ML$="QUIT" THEN QUIT=-1:ML!=-1
1830   IF ML$="CHANGE" THEN CHANGE=-1:ML!=-1
1840     IF ML!=0 THEN BEEP
1850 WEND
1860 IF CHANGE THEN 1400
1870 IF QUIT THEN CLOSE:CLS:END
1880 '
1890 AP!=0:CHANGE=0:QUIT=0
1900 WHILE AP!=0
1910   INPUT "Antero-posterior diameter";ANS$:GOSUB 2250:AP$=ANS$
1920   AP!=VAL(AP$)
1930   IF AP$="QUIT" THEN QUIT=-1:AP!=-1
1940   IF AP$="CHANGE" THEN CHANGE=-1:AP!=-1
1950   IF AP!=0 THEN BEEP
1960 WEND
1970 IF CHANGE THEN 1400
1980 IF QUIT THEN CLS:CLOSE:END
1990 '
2000 TL!=0:CHANGE=0:QUIT=0
2010 IF TLYN$="N" THEN TL!=-1
2020 WHILE TL!=0
2030   INPUT "Total length";ANS$:GOSUB 2250:TL$=ANS$
2040   TL!=VAL(TL$)
2050   IF TL$="CHANGE" THEN CHANGE=-1:TL!=-1
2060   IF TL$="QUIT" THEN QUIT=-1:TL!=-1
2070   IF TL!=0 THEN BEEP
2080 WEND
2090 IF CHANGE THEN 1400
2100 IF QUIT THEN CLS:CLOSE:END
2110 '
```

```
2120 CN$=""
2130 IF CNYN$="N" THEN CN$="#"
2140 WHILE CN$=""
2150   INPUT "Catalog Number";ANS$:GOSUB 2250:CN$=ANS$
2160   IF CN$="" THEN CN$="#"
2170 WEND
2180 IF CN$="CHANGE" THEN 1400
2190 IF CN$="QUIT" THEN CLS:CLOSE:END
2200 '
2210 PRINT #1, P$","SX$","SD$","ML!","AP!","TL!","CN$
2220 PRINT
2230 GOTO 1540   'start again from sex
2240 '
2250 REM Capitalization
2260 FOR LTR=1 TO LEN(ANS$)
2270   LTR$ = MID$(ANS$,LTR,1)
2280   IF "a"<=LTR$ AND LTR$<="z" THEN MID$(ANS$,LTR,1)=CHR$(ASC(LTR$)-32)
2290 NEXT LTR
2300 RETURN
```

as indeterminate for each bone in a sample. If the answer is Y, BONEDATA will prompt the user for the sex of each bone.

BONEDATA next asks "Is Side Known (Y/N)." For most bone samples, the answer will be Y. However, there may be times when side has not been recorded or is irrelevant. In this case, N is the appropriate response. BONEDATA will then automatically record the side of each bone as indeterminate. If the answer is Y, it will prompt the user for the side of each bone.

BONEDATA next asks "Total Length to be entered (Y/N)." If the answer is Y, BONEDATA will prompt the user for the total length of each bone. If the answer is N, BONEDATA automatically records total length for each bone as "-1", our code for a missing value.

BONEDATA next requests "File Name," meaning the name of the file in which the bone measurements are to be stored. This is followed by a request for "Site (carriage return if no site name wanted)." If the response is CHANGE, BONEDATA restarts the prompt series from "Do you want to enter a catalog number for the bone (Y/N)." CHANGE is meaningful only for samples that contain some bones with catalog numbers and some without, some of unknown sex and some of known sex, some of unknown side and some of known side, or some on which total length is measurable and some on which it is not. In this case the CHANGE response permits all bones in a sample to be entered economically in one BONEDATA session, assuming the user has previously grouped the bones according to whether they have catalog numbers and whether sex, side, and total length are known.

If the response to "Site (carriage return if site name not wanted)" is QUIT, BONEDATA closes the file and terminates the session. If a site name is entered, it becomes part of the provenience information on each bone. In most instances the site name will be superfluous, since a file will contain bones from only one site, and the site name will already be incorporated in the file name. If this is the case, the user should respond to the site request with a carriage return. A site name should be entered only if the user wants to include bones from more than one site in the same file. In general, we do not recommend this. It is desirable only if there is some reason to calculate descriptive statistics based on bones from more than one site. If a site name is entered, it should be kept as brief as possible. Virtually any combination of letters and numbers will do.

The next prompt is for "Provenience Unit (carriage return for no unit)." The response may be virtually any combination of letters and numbers, but we suggest a mnemonic abbreviation for a field unit (e.g. 1WA for First White Ash.) If the user has entered a site name and now enters a provenience unit, BONEDATA concatenates the two. For example, if the site name was KRM1 (for Klasies River Mouth 1) and the user enters 14 (for level 14) in response to the provenience unit prompt, BONEDATA will concatenate KRM1 and 14 into the single provenience label KRM114. This means that it is not necessary to provide a specific provenience unit if a site name has been entered that is adequate by itself to describe provenience. In this case, the user may respond to the provenience unit request with a simple carriage return. However, BONEDATA must have some provenience information. Therefore, if the user did not enter a site name previously, a provenience unit must be supplied. Otherwise BONEDATA prints an error message and reprompts first for site name and then for provenience unit. A response of CHANGE to the provenience unit request also restarts the prompt series from site name. A response of QUIT closes the file and terminates the session. QUIT has the same effect in response to all subsequent requests.

If the user has indicated that the sex of each bone is known, BONEDATA next asks "Sex (M/F/I)." A response of CHANGE restarts the prompt series from provenience unit. CHANGE has the same effect in response to all subsequent prompts. With regard to the request for sex, any response but M (for male), F (for female), I (for indeterminate), CHANGE, or QUIT leads to an error message and a renewed request. If the user has indicated that the sex of each bone is unknown, BONEDATA automatically records the sex for each bone as indeterminate.

FIGURE 8.2: A BONEDATA sample session, involving distal humeri of the extinct monachine seal *Homiphoca capensis* from Langebaanweg, South Africa.

BONEDATA. For limbbone epiphyses. Places the medio-lateral and antero-posterior diameters and the total bone length in a file. For missing measurements, enter -1. To change Site, enter 'CHANGE' in response to 'Provenience Unit.' To change 'Provenience Unit' enter 'CHANGE' in response to any prompt. To end, enter 'QUIT' in response to any prompt.

Do you want to enter a catalog number for each bone ? N
Is sex known (Y/N) ? N
Is side known (Y/N) ? Y
Total Length to be entered (Y/N) ? Y
File Name ? LBWHCDI.HUM
Site (carriage return if no site name wanted) ?
Provenience Unit (carriage return for no unit) ? 3AN
Side (L/R/I) ? R
Medio-lateral diameter ? 482
Antero-posterior diameter ? 289
Total length ? -1

Side (L/R/I) ? R
Medio-lateral diameter ? 494
Antero-posterior diameter ? 269
Total length ? 1301

Side (L/R/I) ? R
Medio-lateral diameter ? 451
Antero-posterior diameter ? -1
Total length ? 1181

Side (L/R/I) ? L
Medio-lateral diameter ? 478
Antero-posterior diameter ? 457
Total length ? -1

Side (L/R/I) ? CHANGE
Provenience Unit (carriage return for no unit) ? 3AS
Side (L/R/I) ? L
Medio-lateral diameter ? 469
Antero-posterior diameter ? 269
Total length ? -1

Side (L/R/I) ? R
Medio-lateral diameter ? 488

Antero-posterior diameter ? 267
Total length ? -1

Side (L/R/I) ? R
Medio-lateral diameter ? 474
Antero-posterior diameter ? 299
Total length ? 1321

Side (L/R/I) ? QUIT

          3AN,I,R,482,289,-1,#
          3AN,I,R,494,269,1301,#
          3AN,I,R,451,-1,1181,#
          3AN,I,L,478,457,-1,#
          3AS,I,L,469,269,-1,#
          3AS,I,R,488,267,-1,#
          3AS,I,R,474,299,1321,#

FIGURE 8.3: The file created by the BONEDATA sample session in Figure
8.2.

If the user has indicated that the side of each bone is known,
BONEDATA next asks "Side (L/R/I)." The response must be L (for left), R
(for right), I (for indeterminate), CHANGE, or QUIT, or BONEDATA
repeats the prompt. If the user has indicated previously that the side of
each bone is unknown, BONEDATA automatically records the side for each
bone as indeterminate.

Once side has been successfully entered, BONEDATA asks sequentially
for "mediolateral diameter," "anteroposterior diameter," and "total length."
If a particular measurement is not available, the user should enter a
negative number, indicating a missing value. We recommend "-1". In
response to each request, the answer must be CHANGE, QUIT or a
number. If the user indicated previously that total length was not available,
BONEDATA does not prompt for it. Instead, it automatically records -1 for
the total length of each bone in the sample.

Following the successful entry of "Total Length," BONEDATA requests
"Catalog Number". (It omits this request, however, if the user previously
declined to enter individual catalog numbers.) Appropriate responses are
CHANGE, QUIT, a carriage return (for no number), or a catalog number
consisting of any combination of letters and numbers.

BONEDATA writes information to a file only after "Catalog Number"
has been entered. This is the reason for allowing a return to "Provenience
Unit" following any prompt -- the result is that an erroneous response to a
previous prompt can be erased before it is permanently recorded. Once
data are permanently recorded in a BONEDATA file, they can be changed
only with an external text editor.

TABLE 8.1 BONEDATA Prompts with Accepted Responses and Their
            Effects.

Prompts	Responses and effects
1) Do you want to enter a catalog number for each bone (Y/N)	Y -- causes the program to prompt for a catalog number for each bone. N -- causes the program to record the catalog number of each bone as #.
2) Is Sex Known (Y/N)	Y -- if sex is known for any specimens. Will cause BONEDATA to prompt for the sex of each bone as it is entered. N -- if sex is not known. Will cause BONEDATA to record sex as indeterminate for each bone.
3) Is Side Known (Y/N)	Y -- if side is known for any specimens. Will cause BONEDATA to prompt for the side of each bone as it is entered. N -- if side is not known or is irrelevant. Will cause BONEDATA to record side as indeterminate for each bone.
4) Total Length to be Entered (Y/N)	Y -- if total length is known for any specimens. Will cause BONEDATA to prompt for total length of each bone as it is entered. N -- if total length is not known. Will cause BONEDATA to record total length as "-1" (missing) for each bone.
5) File Name	The name of the file to contain the bone measurements. Any name that is acceptable to the system.
6) Site	CHANGE -- restarts the prompt series from "Do you want to enter a catalog number for each bone." QUIT -- closes file and terminates session. CARRIAGE RETURN -- if no site name wanted Name of a site, as brief as possible. Will be concatenated with "Provenience Unit" supplied in response to prompt 7.
7) Provenience Unit	CHANGE -- restarts prompt series from

"Site".
QUIT -- closes file and terminates session.
Carriage return -- if no provenience
unit wanted.
Provenience Unit -- any combination of
letters and numbers, as brief as
possible.

n.b. BONEDATA must have a site name or a provenience unit. Thus, if the user enters a carriage return in response to both prompts 6 and 7, BONEDATA will reprompt for "Site" (prompt 6).

| 8) Sex (M/F/I) | M (for male), F (for female), or I (for indeterminate). CHANGE -- restarts prompt series from "Provenience Unit." QUIT -- closes file and terminates session. |

| 9) Side (L/R/I) | L (for left), R (for right), or I (for indeterminate). CHANGE -- restarts prompt series from "Provenience Unit." QUIT -- closes file and terminates session. |

---

10) Medio-lateral diameter	Any number (a negative number indicates a missing value)(-1 recommended).
11) Antero-posterior diameter	CHANGE -- restarts prompt series from "Provenience Unit".
12) Total length	QUIT -- closes file and terminates session.

| 13) Catalog Number | CHANGE -- restarts prompt series from "Provenience Unit". QUIT -- closes file and terminates session. Carriage return -- for no number. A Catalog Number, consisting of any combination of letters and numbers. |

---

n.b. Prompts 7, 8, and 11 appear only if the user has indicated that sex, side, and total length are available for each bone. Prompt 13 appears only if the user previously indicated a desire to enter a catalog number for each bone.

Note: Each response must be followed by a carriage return.

Site __L ANGEBAANWEG__   Date __4__ /__21__ /__83__   BONE MEASUREMENTS

Species __HOMIPHOCA CAPENSIS__   Bone __DISTAL FEMUR__

S$	P$	SX$	SD$	ML	AP	TL	NO$	COMMENTS
	QSM	I	R	634	336	-1	33108	
	"	I	L	566	313	-1	34102	
	"	I	L	616	337	-1	2902	
	3AN	I	R	601	333	997	40106	
	"	I	R	-1	284	861	2803	
	"	I	L	620	333	-1	40107	
	"	I	R	604	339	915	40109	
	3AS	I	R	595	319	924	35106	

Department of Anthropology, University of Chicago
1126 East 59th Street, Chicago, IL 60637 USA   BONE MEASUREMENTS

FIGURE 8.4: A coding form for the medio-lateral and anteroposterior diameters of an epiphysis and for total bone length to be entered into a file by the program BONEDATA. The columns are labelled with the names for the variables in the program. S$ stands for site, P$ for provenience unit (within a site), SX$ for sex (male, female, or

After the information on a bone has been written to a file, BONEDATA requests information on the next bone. If the user indicated that sex information is available, the new prompt series begins with a request for "Sex (M/F/I)." If the user indicated that sex was not available but side was, the prompt series begins with "Side (L/R/I)." Otherwise the first request is for "Medio-Lateral Diameter." In any case, BONEDATA assumes that the provenience unit for the new bone is the same as the provenience unit for the previous one unless the user responds CHANGE to "Sex" or "Side." This feature has been incorporated so that grouping teeth by provenience unit saves entry time and also reduces the likelihood of entry error.

We have found that BONEDATA is easiest to use if the analyst records the necessary information for each tooth on a form like the one illustrated in figure 8.4.

A Sample Session With Bonestat

In this section, we present a sample session with BONESTAT. Figure 8.5 lists BONESTAT. Figure 8.6 is a "photo" of the sample session with output. Table 8.2 lists the BONESTAT prompts and appropriate responses.

BONESTAT asks first for "Name of Dataset." This is used solely to label the printout and may consist of any combination of letters and numbers, including embedded blanks. BONESTAT next asks "Analyze Bones, Teeth, or Ages (B/T/A)." The answer must be B, T, or A. Otherwise BONESTAT prints an error message and repeats the question.

If the answer is B, BONESTAT next asks "Variable to analyze (ML, AP, or TL)," where ML is the mediolateral diameter (of an epiphysis), AP is the anteroposterior diameter (of the same epiphysis), and TL is the total length. If the answer is T, BONESTAT next asks "Variable to analyze (L, B, CH1, or CH2)," where L is tooth length, B is breadth, and CH1 and CH2 are two possible, separate crown heights. In the case of either bones or teeth, the appropriate response to variable to analyze is the variable for which the user wants descriptive statistics. If the response in either case is not one of the variables in the list (ML, AP, or TL for bones; L, B, CH1, or CH2 for teeth), BONESTAT asks again for variable to analyze.

If the variable to analyze is a tooth dimension, BONESTAT next asks "How many wear states to analyze (ALL or 1-5)." Acceptable answers are ALL for all wear states (= all teeth) or a number between 1 and 5. If the

---

indeterminate); SD$ for Side (left, right, or indeterminate), ML for mediolateral diameter, AP for anteroposterior diameter, TL for total length, and NO$ for catalog number. Note that site does not have to be recorded if the file to be created by BONEDATA contains measurements from only one site. Note also that provenience unit does not have to be reentered until provenience unit changes.

FIGURE 8.5: Listing of the program BONESTAT for calculating descriptive statistics from bone or tooth measurements.

```
1000 PRINT "BONESTAT -- Summary statistics and histogram for bone and tooth"
1010 PRINT "measurements.  Requires files.  ML = medio-lateral diameter;"
1020 PRINT "AP = antero-posterior diameter; TL = total length.  L = crown"
1030 PRINT "length; B = crown breadth; CH1 = height of lobe 1; CH2 = height"
1040 PRINT "of lobe 2."
1050 PRINT
1060 REM IBM Personal Computer BASIC (R. G. Klein, 5 January 1984)
1070 ON ERROR GOTO 4750
1080 DEFINT A-Z
1090 DIM WSA$(5),PU$(30),X!(5000),P(50),MID!(50),Y!(20),Z!(20)
1100 '
1110 INPUT "Name of Dataset";ND$
1120 '
1130 BTA$=""
1140 WHILE BTA$<>"B" AND BTA$<>"T" AND BTA$<>"A"
1150   INPUT "Analyze Bones, Teeth, or Ages (B/T/A)";ANS$:GOSUB 4680:BTA$=ANS$
1160   IF BTA$<>"B" AND BTA$<>"T" AND BTA$<>"A" THEN BEEP
1170 WEND
1180 '
1190 CONTINUE=-1
1200 WHILE BTA$="B" AND CONTINUE
1210   INPUT "Variable to analyze (ML,AP,or TL)";ANS$:GOSUB 4680:VAR$=ANS$
1220   IF VAR$="ML" OR VAR$="AP" OR VAR$="TL" THEN CONTINUE=0 ELSE BEEP
1230 WEND
1240 '
1250 WHILE BTA$="T" AND CONTINUE
1260   INPUT "Variable to analyze (L,B,CH1,or CH2)";ANS$:GOSUB 4680:VAR$=ANS$
1270   IF VAR$="L" OR VAR$="B" OR VAR$="CH1" OR VAR$="CH2" THEN CONTINUE=0
         ELSE BEEP
1280 WEND
1290 '
1300 NWS=0:EWS=0
1310 WHILE BTA$="T" AND NWS<1
1320   INPUT "How many wear states to analyze (ALL or 1-5)";ANS$:GOSUB 4680:
         NWS$=ANS$
1330   NWS=VAL(NWS$)
1340   IF NWS$="ALL" THEN WSA$(1)="ALL":NWS=1:EWS=-1
1350   IF NWS<1 OR NWS>5 THEN BEEP
1360 WEND
1370 '
1380 WHILE BTA$="T" AND EWS<>-1
1390   FOR J=1 TO NWS
1400     WHILE WSA$(J)<>"ALL" AND WSA$(J)<>"UW" AND WSA$(J)<>"EW" AND
           WSA$(J)<>"VEW" AND WSA$(J)<>"MW" AND WSA$(J)<>"LW"
1410       INPUT "Wear State (UW,VEW,EW,MW, or LW)";ANS$:
             GOSUB 4680:WSA$(J)=ANS$
1420       IF WSA$(J)<>"ALL" AND WSA$(J)<>"UW" AND WSA$(J)<>"EW" AND
             WSA$(J)<>"VEW" AND WSA$(J)<>"MW" AND WSA$(J)<>"LW" THEN BEEP
1430     WEND
1440   NEXT J
1450   EWS=-1
1460 WEND
1470 '
1480 NPU=0:EPU=0
1490 WHILE NPU<1 OR NPU>30
1500   INPUT "How many provenience units to analyze (ALL or 1-30)";ANS$:
         GOSUB 4680:NPU$=ANS$
1510   NPU=VAL(NPU$)
1520   IF NPU$="ALL" THEN PU$(1)="ALL":NPU=1:EPU=-1
```

```
1530   IF NPU<1 OR NPU>30 THEN BEEP
1540 WEND
1550 '
1560 CHANGE=0
1570 WHILE EPU<>-1
1580   FOR J=1 TO NPU
1590     INPUT "Provenience Unit";ANS$:GOSUB 4680:PU$(J)=ANS$
1600     IF PU$(J)="CHANGE" THEN J=NPU:CHANGE=-1
1610   NEXT
1620   EPU=-1
1630 WEND
1640 IF CHANGE THEN 1480
1650 '
1660 MF$=""
1670 WHILE MF$<>"M" AND MF$<>"F" AND MF$<>"B"
1680   INPUT "Sex to analyze (M/F/B)";ANS$:GOSUB 4680:MF$=ANS$
1690   IF MF$<>"M" AND MF$<>"F" AND MF$<>"B" THEN BEEP
1700 WEND
1710 '
1720 LR$=""
1730 WHILE LR$<>"L" AND LR$<>"R" AND LR$<>"B"
1740   INPUT "Side to analyze (L/R/B)"; ANS$:GOSUB 4680:LR$=ANS$
1750   IF LR$<>"L" AND LR$<>"R" AND LR$<>"B" THEN BEEP
1760 WEND
1770 '
1780 INPUT "File name";FILE$
1790 OPEN FILE$ FOR INPUT AS #1
1800 WHILE NOT EOF(1)
1810   WEARSTATE=0:SEX=0:SIDE=0:PROVUNIT=0
1820   IF BTA$="B" THEN INPUT#1,LV$,SX$,SD$,ML!,AP!,TL!,CN$
1830   IF BTA$="T" THEN INPUT#1,LV$,SX$,SD$,WS$,L!,B!,CH1!,CH2!,CN$
1840   IF BTA$="A" THEN INPUT#1,LV$,SX$,SD$,AGE!
1850   IF LEFT$(LV$,1)="#" THEN LV$=MID$(LV$,2)
1860   SX$=LEFT$(SX$,1):SD$=LEFT$(SD$,1)
1870   IF BTA$<>"T" THEN WEARSTATE=-1
1880   IF BTA$="T" AND WSA$(1)="ALL" THEN WEARSTATE=-1 ELSE GOSUB 1990
          'check wearstate
1890   IF MF$="B" OR SX$=MF$ THEN SEX=-1
1900   IF LR$="B" OR SD$=LR$ THEN SIDE=-1
1910   IF PU$(1)="ALL" THEN PROVUNIT=-1 ELSE GOSUB 2060 'check provunit
1920   IF WEARSTATE AND SEX AND SIDE AND PROVUNIT THEN GOSUB 2110 'establish
          sample size
1930 WEND
1940 GOSUB 2220  'calculate statistics
1950 IF N<=1 THEN GOSUB 4580 'run program again?
1960 IF N>1 THEN GOSUB 3450:GOSUB 4580 'calculate histogram & run again?
1970 CLOSE:CLS:END
1980 '
1990 REM Check wear state
2000   FOR J=1 TO NWS
2010     IF WS$=WSA$(J) THEN WEARSTATE=-1:J=NWS
2020   NEXT J
2030 RETURN
2040 '
2050 REM Check provenience unit
2060   FOR J=1 TO NPU
2070     IF LV$=PU$(J) THEN PROVUNIT=-1:J=NPU
2080   NEXT
2090 RETURN
```

```
2100 '
2110 REM Establish Sample Size
2120   IF VAR$="ML" AND ML!>0 THEN N=N+1:X!(N)=ML!
2130   IF VAR$="AP" AND AP!>0 THEN N=N+1:X!(N)=AP!
2140   IF VAR$="TL" AND TL!>0 THEN N=N+1:X!(N)=TL!
2150   IF VAR$="L" AND L!>0 THEN N=N+1:X!(N)=L!
2160   IF VAR$="B" AND B!>0 THEN N=N+1:X!(N)=B!
2170   IF VAR$="CH1" AND CH1!>0 THEN N=N+1:X!(N)=CH1!
2180   IF VAR$="CH2" AND CH2!>0 THEN N=N+1:X!(N)=CH2!
2190   IF BTA$="A" THEN N=N+1:X!(N)=AGE!
2200 RETURN
2210 '
2220 REM Messages for samples with 0 and 1 specimen.
2230   IF N=0 THEN PRINT "No specimens in this sample!":RETURN
2240   IF N=1 THEN PRINT "Only one specimen in this sample!  Specimen size=";
           X!(1):RETURN
2250 REM Mean and standard deviation
2260   FOR I=1 TO N
2270     T!= T!+X!(I)
2280     TSQ!= TSQ!+(X!(I)|2)
2290   NEXT I
2300   M!=T!/N
2310   S!=SQR((TSQ!-(T!|2)/N)/(N-1))
2320 REM Coefficient of variation
2330   CV!=(100*S!)/M!
2340 REM Standard error of the mean
2350   SE!=S!/(N|(1/2))
2360 REM 95% confidence limits for the mean
2370   IF N-1=1 THEN ST!=12.706
2380   IF N-1=2 THEN ST!=4.303
2390   IF N-1=3 THEN ST!=3.182
2400   IF N-1=4 THEN ST!=2.776
2410   IF N-1=5 THEN ST!=2.571
2420   IF N-1=6 THEN ST!=2.447
2430   IF N-1=7 THEN ST!=2.365
2440   IF N-1=8 THEN ST!=2.306
2450   IF N-1=9 THEN ST!=2.262
2460   IF N-1=10 THEN ST!=2.228
2470   IF N-1=11 THEN ST!=2.201
2480   IF N-1=12 THEN ST!=2.179
2490   IF N-1=13 THEN ST!=2.16
2500   IF N-1=14 THEN ST!=2.145
2510   IF N-1=15 THEN ST!=2.131
2520   IF N-1=16 THEN ST!=2.12
2530   IF N-1=17 THEN ST!=2.11
2540   IF N-1=18 THEN ST!=2.101
2550   IF N-1=19 THEN ST!=2.093
2560   IF N-1=20 THEN ST!=2.086
2570   IF N-1=21 THEN ST!=2.08
2580   IF N-1=22 THEN ST!=2.074
2590   IF N-1=23 THEN ST!=2.069
2600   IF N-1=24 THEN ST!=2.064
2610   IF N-1=25 THEN ST!=2.06
2620   IF N-1=26 THEN ST!=2.056
2630   IF N-1=27 THEN ST!=2.052
2640   IF N-1=28 THEN ST!=2.048
2650   IF N-1=29 THEN ST!=2.045
2660   IF N-1>=30 AND N-1<40 THEN ST!=2.042
2670   IF N-1>=40 AND N-1<60 THEN ST!=2.021
```

```
2680   IF N-1>=60 AND N-1<120 THEN ST!=2
2690   IF N-1=120 THEN ST!=1.98
2700   IF N-1>120 THEN ST!=1.96
2710      LCL!= M!-(ST!*SE!)
2720      UCL!= M!+(ST!*SE!)
2730 REM Arrange data in ascending order
2740   D=4
2750   IF D<N THEN D=D+D:GOTO 2750
2760   D=INT(D/2)
2770   IF D<1 THEN 2880
2780   FOR J=1 TO (N-D)
2790      FOR I=J TO 1 STEP -D
2800         IF X!(I+D)>X!(I) THEN 2850
2810            Y!=X!(I)
2820            X!(I)=X!(I+D)
2830            X!(I+D)=Y!
2840      NEXT I
2850   NEXT J
2860   GOTO 2760
2870 REM Calculate Median for even number of cases
2880   IF N/2=INT(N/2) THEN MD!=(X!(N/2)+X!((N/2)+1))/2
2890 REM Calculate Median for odd number of cases
2900   IF N/2<>INT(N/2) THEN MD!=X!((N+1)/2)
2910 REM Observed Range
2920   MIN!=X!(1)
2930   MAX!=X!(N)
2940 REM Print Results
2950   IF VAR$ = "ML" THEN VAR$ = "Medio-lateral diameter"
2960   IF VAR$ = "AP" THEN VAR$ = "Antero-posterior diameter"
2970   IF VAR$ = "TL" THEN VAR$ = "Total length"
2980   IF VAR$ = "L" THEN VAR$ = "Basal Length"
2990   IF VAR$ = "B" THEN VAR$ = "Basal Breadth"
3000   IF VAR$ = "CH1" THEN VAR$ = "Crown Height - First Lobe"
3010   IF VAR$ = "CH2" THEN VAR$ = "Crown Height - Second Lobe"
3020   IF MF$ = "M" THEN MF$ = "Male"
3030   IF MF$ = "F" THEN MF$ = "Female"
3040   IF MF$ = "B" THEN MF$ = "Both"
3050   IF LR$ = "L" THEN LR$ = "Left"
3060   IF LR$ = "R" THEN LR$ = "Right"
3070   IF LR$ = "B" THEN LR$ = "Both"
3080 '
3090 HC$="":SOFTCOPY=-1
3100 WHILE HC$<>"N" AND SOFTCOPY=-1
3110   IF HC$="" THEN CLOSE:OPEN "SCRN:" FOR OUTPUT AS #1
3120   IF HC$="Y" THEN SOFTCOPY=0:CLOSE:OPEN "LPT1:" FOR OUTPUT AS #1
3130 PRINT#1, "                    " DATE$" "TIME$
3140 PRINT#1, " "
3150 PRINT#1, ND$
3160 PRINT#1, "From provenience units: ";
3170 PPU$=""
3180 FOR J = 1 TO NPU
3190   PPU$=PPU$+PU$(J)+" "
3200 NEXT J
3210 PRINT#1,TAB(25) PPU$
3220 PRINT#1, "Variable = " VAR$
3230 PRINT#1, "Sex = " MF$, "Side = " LR$
3240 IF BTA$="T" THEN PRINT#1,"Wear States: ";:
        FOR J=1 TO NWS:PRINT #1,TAB(15+(4*J)) WSA$(J);:NEXT J
3250 PRINT#1, " "
```

```
3260 PRINT#1, " "
3270 PRINT#1, "Mean = "; TAB(40) M!
3280 PRINT#1, "Standard deviation = "; TAB(40) S!
3290 PRINT#1, "Sample size = "; TAB(40) N
3300 PRINT#1, "Coefficient of variation = "; TAB(40) CV!
3310 PRINT#1, "Observed Range = "; TAB(40) MIN!"-"MAX!
3320 PRINT#1, "Standard error of the mean = "; TAB(40) SE!
3330 PRINT#1, "95% confidence limits of the mean = "; TAB(40) LCL!"-"UCL!
3340 PRINT#1, "Mean + or - one standard deviation = "; TAB(40) M!-S!"-"M!+S!
3350 PRINT#1, "Median ="; TAB(40) MD!
3360 CLOSE: PRINT
3370 '
3380    WHILE HC$<>"Y" AND HC$<>"N"
3390       INPUT "Want hard copy (Y/N)";ANS$:GOSUB 4680:HC$=ANS$
3400       IF HC$<>"Y" AND HC$<>"N" THEN BEEP
3410    WEND
3420 WEND
3430 RETURN
3440 '
3450 REM Histogram background
3460 YN$=""
3470 WHILE YN$<>"Y" AND YN$<>"N"
3480    INPUT "Do you want a histogram (Y/N)";ANS$:GOSUB 4680:YN$=ANS$
3490    IF YN$<>"Y" AND YN$<>"N" THEN BEEP
3500 WEND
3510 IF YN$="N" THEN RETURN
3520 '
3530 HISTOGRAM=-1
3540    WHILE HISTOGRAM
3550    SP$=""
3560    WHILE SP$<>"Y" AND SP$<>"N"
3570       INPUT "Is the minimum a satisfactory starting point (Y/N)";ANS$:
              GOSUB 4680:SP$=ANS$
3580       IF SP$<>"Y" AND SP$<>"N" THEN BEEP
3590    WEND
3600    IF SP$="Y" THEN SP!=MIN!
3610    IF SP$="N" THEN INPUT "Starting point";SP!
3620 '
3630    EP$=""
3640    WHILE EP$<>"Y" AND EP$<>"N"
3650       INPUT "Is the maximum a satisfactory end point (Y/N)";ANS$:
              GOSUB 4680:EP$=ANS$
3660       IF EP$<>"Y" AND EP$<>"N" THEN BEEP
3670    WEND
3680    IF EP$="Y" THEN EP!=MAX!
3690    IF EP$="N" THEN INPUT "End point";EP!
3700 '
3710    CI$=""
3720    WHILE CI$<>"N"
3730       INPUT "Width of class interval";WID!
3740       NC=CINT(((EP!-SP!)/WID!)+.5)
3750       IF NC>50 THEN BEEP:PRINT ">50 classes.  Choose a smaller interval!"
3760       IF NC<=50 THEN PRINT "That means";NC; "classes.  ";
3770       CLASSINT=0
3780       WHILE NC<=50 AND CLASSINT=0
3790          INPUT "Want to choose another class interval (Y/N)";ANS$:
                 GOSUB 4680:CI$=ANS$
3800          IF CI$="Y" OR CI$="N" THEN CLASSINT=-1 ELSE BEEP
3810       WEND
```

```
3820   WEND
3830 REM Initialize with 0 in each class
3840   K=0:L=0 'initialize arrays for outliers
3850   FOR G=1 TO NC
3860      P(G)=0
3870   NEXT G
3880 REM Place observation in class and tally
3890   FOR I=1 TO N
3900      IF X!(I)<SP! THEN K=K+1:Y!(K)=X!(I) 'low outliers
3910      IF X!(I)>EP! THEN L=L+1:Z!(L)=X!(I) 'high outliers
3920      IF X!(I)>=SP! AND X!(I)<=EP! THEN G=INT((X!(I)-SP!)/WID!)+1:
             P(G)=P(G)+1
3930   NEXT I
3940 REM Establish number of items in largest class
3950   MAXG=P(1)
3960   FOR G=2 TO NC
3970      IF P(G)>MAXG THEN MAXG=P(G)
3980   NEXT G
3990 REM Calculate class midpoints
4000   FOR G=1 TO NC
4010      MID!(G)=SP!+(WID!/2)+(WID!*(G-1))
4020   NEXT G
4030 REM Print histogram
4040   HC$="":SOFTCOPY=-1
4050   WHILE HC$<>"N" AND SOFTCOPY=-1
4060      IF HC$="" THEN CLOSE:OPEN "SCRN:" FOR OUTPUT AS #1
4070      IF HC$="Y" THEN SOFTCOPY=0:CLOSE:OPEN "LPT1:" FOR OUTPUT AS #1
4080 PRINT
4090 PRINT#1, "                    " DATE$" "TIME$
4100 PRINT#1, " "
4110 REM Print Frequency Scale
4120   TOOMUCH=0
4130   IF MAXG>60 THEN TOOMUCH=-1:
             PRINT#1,">60 items in the largest class, cannot print bars!"
4140   IF NOT TOOMUCH THEN FOR J=1 TO 12:PRINT#1,TAB((J*5)-1);(J*5);:NEXT
4150      PRINT#1, TAB(65); "Midpoint"; TAB(75); "n"
4160      PRINT#1, " "
4170 REM Print bars
4180   IF NOT TOOMUCH THEN FOR G=1 TO NC:FOR J=1 TO P(G):PRINT#1,"¦ ";:NEXT J:
             PRINT#1,TAB(65);MID!(G);TAB(75);P(G):NEXT G
4190   IF TOOMUCH THEN FOR G=1 TO NC:PRINT#1,TAB(65);MID!(G);TAB(75);P(G):NEXT
4200 PRINT#1, " "
4210 PRINT#1, "Off histogram at low end are: "
4220   FOR I=1 TO K
4230      PRINT#1, Y!(I);
4240   NEXT I
4250 PRINT#1, " "
4260 PRINT#1, "Off histogram at high end are: "
4270   FOR I=1 TO L
4280      PRINT#1, Z!(I);
4290   NEXT I
4300 PRINT#1, " ": PRINT#1, " "
4310 PRINT#1, ND$
4320 PRINT#1, "From provenience units: ";
4330   PPU$=""
4340   FOR J=1 TO NPU
4350      PPU$=PPU$+PU$(J)+" "
4360   NEXT J
4370 PRINT#1, TAB(25) PPU$
```

```
4380 PRINT#1, " "
4390 PRINT#1, "Variable = " VAR$
4400 PRINT#1, "Sex = " MF$, "Side = " LR$
4410 IF BTA$="T" THEN PRINT#1,"Wear States: ";:
        FOR J=1 TO NWS:PRINT #1,TAB(15+(4*J)) WSA$(J);:NEXT J
4420 PRINT#1," ": CLOSE: PRINT
4430    WHILE HC$<>"Y" AND HC$<>"N"
4440       INPUT "Want hard copy (Y/N)";ANS$:GOSUB 4680:HC$=ANS$
4450       IF HC$<>"Y" AND HC$<>"N" THEN BEEP
4460    WEND
4470  WEND
4480 '
4490  YN$=""
4500  WHILE YN$<>"Y" AND YN$<>"N"
4510     INPUT "Want another histogram (Y/N)";ANS$:GOSUB 4680:YN$=ANS$
4520     IF YN$<>"Y" AND YN$<>"N" THEN BEEP
4530  WEND
4540  IF YN$="N" THEN HISTOGRAM=0
4550 WEND
4560 RETURN
4570 '
4580 REM Run program again
4590  YN$=""
4600  WHILE YN$<>"Y" AND YN$<>"N"
4610     INPUT "Run program again (Y/N)";ANS$:GOSUB 4680:YN$=ANS$
4620     IF YN$<>"Y" AND YN$<>"N" THEN BEEP
4630  WEND
4640  IF YN$="N" THEN RETURN
4650  IF YN$="Y" THEN CLS:CLOSE:RUN 1000
4660 RETURN
4670 '
4680 REM Capitalization
4690  FOR LTR=1 TO LEN(ANS$)
4700     LTR$=MID$(ANS$,LTR,1)
4710     IF "a"<=LTR$ AND LTR$<="z" THEN MID$(ANS$,LTR,1)=CHR$(ASC(LTR$)-32)
4720  NEXT LTR
4730 RETURN
4740 '
4750 REM Error messages
4760 IF ERR=53 THEN BEEP: PRINT "File not found": RESUME 1780
4770 IF ERR=27 THEN BEEP: CLOSE: PRINT "Turn on printer.":
        PRINT "Press any key to continue ...";:YY$=INKEY$:WHILE YY$="":
        YY$=INKEY$:WEND:RESUME 3120
4780 IF ERL=3900 THEN BEEP:PRINT "> 20 data points excluded. ";:
        PRINT "Choose new starting point":RESUME 3550
4790 IF ERL=3910 THEN BEEP:PRINT "> 20 data points excluded. ";:
        PRINT "Choose new end point":RESUME 3630
```

response is a number, BONESTAT then asks the user to list the wear states in response to the prompt "Wear State (UW,VEW,EW,MW, or LW)". The answer to each prompt must be UW (Unworn), VEW (Very Early Wear), EW (Early Wear), MW (Medium Wear), or LW (Late Wear). We discussed criteria for defining these wear states in the section on DENTDATA in the previous chapter. We anticipate that the most frequent response to "How many wear states to analyze" will be "1", followed by the wear state UW. This permits a user to obtain mean unworn crown heights for age profile construction via the program AGEPROF.

BONESTAT next asks "How many provenience units to analyze (ALL or 1-30)." It asks this question immediately after "Variable to analyze (ML, AP, or TL)" if bones are to be processed or after "Analyze Bones, Teeth, or Ages (B/T/A)" if ages are to be processed. The number of provenience units to enter is the number of units that the user wants to lump for computational purposes. We have arbitrarily limited this number to thirty units maximum, but there is no basic programmatic reason why it cannot be more. If the user wants BONESTAT to process all items in a file regardless of provenience unit, the proper answer to "How many provenience units to analyze" is ALL.

When the number of provenience units has been entered, BONESTAT asks the user to list them one at a time, in response to the prompt "Provenience Unit." Entries must correspond precisely to the ones that BONESTAT will encounter in the files it is going to process. In its calculations, BONESTAT will treat objects from all the provenience units listed as if they came from a single provenience unit.

Once the last provenience unit has been entered, BONESTAT asks "Sex to Analyze (M/F/B)." This is to determine if the user wants statistics and histograms only for male bones, only for female bones, or for both. In most samples, bone sex will be indeterminate, and the proper response to "Sex (M/F/B)" is B. (If a sample contains only indeterminate bones, a response of M or F will cause BONESTAT to print "No specimens in this sample" after scanning the file.) If the response is not M, F, or B, BONESTAT reprompts for sex.

BONESTAT next asks "Side to Analyze (L/R/B)." The answer depends on whether the user wants statistics based just on left bones, just on right bones, or on both. BONESTAT will not accept any answer but L, R, or B.

Once side has been successfully entered, BONESTAT asks "File Name." This is the name of the file that contains the bone measurements, tooth measurements, or ages to be processed. If BONESTAT cannot locate the file in the system, it prints an error message and requests "File Name" again. Otherwise it opens the file and begins calculations on the subsample defined by the provenience unit(s), wear states (for teeth), sex, and side specified by the user. If this subsample contains no specimens or only one, it prints "No specimens in sample" or "Only one specimen in sample" and computes no statistics. If the subsample contains two specimens or more, it displays statistics on the screen in the format shown in figure 8.6.

The next prompt is "Want hard copy (Y/N)". If the answer is Y,

FIGURE 8.6: A BONESTAT sample session with sample output.

BONESTAT -- Summary statistics and histogram for bone and tooth
measurements. Requires files. ML = medio-lateral diameter;
AP = antero-posterior diameter; TL = total length. L = crown
length; B = crown breadth; CH1 = height of lobe 1; CH2 = height
of lobe 2.

Name of Dataset ? MELLIVORA CAPENSIS Lower M1 Length (South Africa)
Analyze Bones, Teeth, or Ages (B/T/A) ? T
Variable to analyze (L, B, CH1, or CH2) ? L
How many wear states to analyze (ALL or 1-5) ? ALL
How many provenience units to analyze (ALL or 1-30) ? 2
Provenience Unit ? TVL
Provenience Unit ? SCP
Sex to analyze (M/F/B) ? B
Side to analyze (L/R/B) ? B
File Name ? MELCAPLO.M1

4-23-83 10:36:27

MELLIVORA CAPENSIS Lower M1 Length (South Africa)
From provenience units: TVL SCP
Variable = Basal Length
Sex = Both   Side = Both
Wear States: ALL

Mean =	139.4286
Standard deviation =	5.813973
Sample size =	14
Coefficient of variation =	4.169858
Observed Range =	130 - 152
Standard error of the mean =	1.55385
95% confidence limits of the mean =	136.0723 - 142.7849
Mean + or - one standard deviation =	133.6146 - 145.2425
Median =	139.5

Want hard copy (Y/N) ? N

Do you want a histogram (Y/N) ? Y
Is the minimum a satisfactory starting point (Y/N) ? Y
Is the maximum a satisfactory end point (Y/N) ? Y
Width of class interval ? 3

That means 7 classes. Want to choose another class interval (Y/N) ? N

23-Apr-83 10:39

5	10	15	20	25	30	35	40	45	50	55	Midpoint	n
I											131.5	1
I											134.5	1
IIII											137.5	4
IIII											140.5	4
II											143.5	2
											146.5	0
I											149.5	1
I											152.5	1

Off histogram at low end are:

Off histogram at high end are:

MELLIVORA CAPENSIS Lower M1 Length (South Africa)
From provenience units: TVL SCP

Variable = Basal Length
Sex = Both   Side = Both
Wear States: ALL

Want hard copy (Y/N) ? N
Want another histogram (Y/N) ? N
Run program again (Y/N) ? N

BONECODE forces the results on the screen to an attached printer. Whether or not the user requests printed copy, BONESTAT next asks "Do you want a histogram (Y/N)." If the answer is N, it terminates the run and asks "Run Program Again (Y/N)." If the answer to the histogram request is Y, it asks "Is the minimum a satisfactory starting point (Y/N)." This is to determine if the user wishes the minimum value in histogram calculation to be the smallest measurement in the sample (the left hand figure in the Observed Range printed out previously.) If the answer is N, BONESTAT asks "Starting point," meaning a user-defined minimum value for histogram construction. It then asks "Is the maximum a satisfactory end point (Y/N)." If the answer is N, BONESTAT requests a user-defined "End point."

Ordinarily we expect the minimum and maximum values in a sample will be the best starting and end points for histogram construction. We have allowed different, user-defined starting and end points for two reasons. First, there will be occasions when the user wants to examine the detailed distribution of data points over a range that is smaller than the

TABLE 8.2 BONESTAT Prompts with Responses and Their Effects:

Prompts	Responses
1) Name of Dataset	Any combination of letters and numbers, including embedded blanks. Used solely to label output.
2) Analyze Bones, Teeth, or Ages (B/T/A)	B (for Bones), T (for Teeth), or A (for Ages)
3a) (If answer to 2 was bones) Variable to Analyze (ML, AP, or TL)	ML -- mediolateral diameter AP -- anteroposterior diameter TL -- total length
3b) (If answer to 2 was teeth) Variable to Analyze (L, B, CH1, or CH2)	L -- tooth length B -- tooth breadth CH1 -- first crown height CH2 -- second crown height
4) (If the answer to 2 was teeth) How many wear states to analyze	ALL -- if BONESTAT is to process all teeth regardless of wear. An integer between 1 and 5 if BONESTAT is to process only teeth in selected wear states.
5) (If the answer to 2 was teeth) Wear State (UW, VEW,EW,MW, or LW)	UW (for Unworn), VEW (for Very Early Wear), EW (for Early Wear), MW (for Medium Wear), or LW (for Late Wear).
6) How many provenience units to analyze	ALL -- if BONESTAT is to process all items in a file regardless of provenience unit. An integer between 1 and 30.
7) Provenience Unit	Any combination of letters and numbers -- combinations must match those used to designate provenience units in the file to be processed.
8) Sex to Analyze (M/F/B)	M (for male), F (for female), or B (for both). If bone sex is indeterminate, then B.

9) Side to Analyze (L/R/B)	L (for left), R (for right), B (for both). If bone side is indeterminate, then B.
10) File name	Name of file that contains the data to be analyzed.
11) Want hard copy (Y/N)	Y -- forces results to attached printer, followed by prompt 12. N -- leads directly to prompt 12.
12) Do you want a histogram (Y/N)	Y -- if a histogram is desired (leads to prompts 13-18) N -- if no histogram is desired (leads to prompt 19)
13) Is the minimum a satisfactory starting point (Y/N)	Y -- if minimum is satisfactory. N -- if user wants to supply a different starting point. Leads to prompt 14.
14) Starting point	Any suitable figure.
15) Is the maximum a satisfactory end point (Y/N)	Y -- if maximum is satisfactory. N -- if user wants to supply a different end point. Leads to prompt 16.
16) End polnt	Any suitable figure.
15) Width of Class Interval	Any number (if this interval results in more than fifty classes, BONESTAT will request a broader interval).
16) That means XX Classes. Want to choose another interval (Y/N).	Y -- if number of classes is not satisfactory. Leads to renewed prompt 15. N -- if number of classes is satisfactory.
17) Want hard copy (Y/N)	Y -- forces histogram to attached printer, followed by prompt 18. N -- leads directly to prompt 18.
18) Want another histogram (Y/N)	Y -- if user wants to construct another histogram with the same data. N -- if no more histograms are wanted.

---

19) Run Program Again (Y/N)	Y -- erases all previous entries, restarts prompt series from prompt 1.	
	N -- closes file and terminates session.	

Note: Each response must be followed by a carriage return.

total observed range. Second, there will be times when the user wants to produce completely comparable histograms for several samples, each with its own minimum and maximum. For example, the user may want to compare histograms for the same measurement in successive layers of a site. In this case, the appropriate starting and end points for each histogram are the minimum and maximum measurements for the site as a whole. To obtain these values, the user should first run BONESTAT for the entire site. This means responding ALL to the "Number of Provenience Units to Enter". The result will be summary statistics for all specimens in the site, regardless of their provenience. The resultant Observed Range provides the appropriate starting and end points for the histogram of each layer.

After the starting point and end point have been determined, BONESTAT asks "Width of class interval." This is the interval on which the histogram will be based. In general, the choice of an interval depends on the problem the user is investigating and on sample size. Too narrow an interval may result in a histogram that consists of widely spaced bars one or two units high. Too broad an interval may result in a histogram with too few classes to define the shape of a distribution. In most cases, a good interval is one that results in 8 to 16 classes, the number that is usually necessary and sufficient for defining distribution shape. In the case of measurements on basal tooth breadth, the diameters of a fused epiphysis, or other skeletal dimensions that do not change with age, a class interval equal to one half the standard deviation usually results in 8 to 16 classes.

Once the class interval has been entered, BONESTAT calculates the number of classes that will result. If the number exceeds fifty, it requests a broader class interval. This is because a histogram based on more than fifty classes will not fit on most computer terminal screens and, with its caption, will also exceed paper length on many printers. If the number of classes is fifty or fewer, BONESTAT prints the number and asks "Want to choose another class interval (Y/N)." If the answer is Y, it prompts for a new "Width of class interval." If the answer is N, it proceeds to calculate the histogram.

If histogram calculation shows that there are more than twenty data points below the starting point or above the end point for the histogram specified by the user, BONESTAT will print an appropriate message to the screen and request a new starting or end point, whichever is the problem. Otherwise it will display the histogram on the screen, along with a list of those data points excluded by the user-specified starting and end points.

If there are more than sixty items in the largest class, BONESTAT displays only the midpoints of the classes and the number of items in each class. This is to accommodate the space limitations of most screens and printers. If there are fewer than sixty items in the largest class, BONESTAT prints histogram bars in addition to the class midpoints and the number of items in each class.

BONESTAT then asks "Want hard copy (Y/N)." If the answer is Y, it forces the histogram to an attached printer. The next request is "Want another histogram (Y/N)." If the answer is N, it asks "Run program again (Y/N)", meaning a completely new run, with fresh data. If the answer to "Want another histogram (Y/N)" is Y, it re-initiates the prompt series from "Is the minimum a satisfactory starting point (Y/N)."

If the user responds N to both "Want another histogram (Y/N)" and "Run program again (Y/N)," BONESTAT terminates the session. If the user responds Y to "Run program again (Y/N)," it initiates a new run in which all previous entries will be erased.

The Results of a BONESTAT Session

Figure 8.6 presents the printout from a sample BONESTAT session. In descending order, BONESTAT prints the mean, standard deviation, sample size, coefficient of variation, observed range, standard error of the mean, 95% confidence limits of the mean, the mean plus or minus one standard deviation, and the median for a sample of measurements. Our purpose here is to outline some features of these statistics that are particularly pertinent to faunal analysts. For in-depth discussions of the statistics, there are many excellent texts. For faunal analysts we particularly recommend *Quantitative Zoology* by Simpson, Roe, and Lewontin (1960) or *Biometry* by Sokal and Rohlf (1969).

In general, it can be assumed that measurements on skeletal dimensions that do not change with age or growth are normally distributed in the statistical sense. For such skeletal dimensions (e.g. basal tooth breadth or the diameters of fused epiphyses), the arithmetic mean is usually the best index of central tendency and the standard deviation is the best index of sample dispersion.

For dimensions that change with age or growth, statistical normality cannot be assumed and is in fact unlikely. For such dimensions (e.g. crown height), the median may be best index of central tendency, while a histogram depicting the sample distribution may be most useful for judging sample dispersion. We particularly recommend the median and histograms for describing and comparing age distributions such as those produced by the program AGEPROF.

The coefficient of variation [= (100 x the standard deviation)/(the mean), often abbreviated CV or V] is a measure of absolute dispersion that is useful for determining whether a sample is homogeneous or not (Simpson, Roe, and Lewontin 1960). For bone measurements that do not reflect age or continuing growth (i.e. ones from normally distributed populations), a CV greater than 10 suggests sample mixture. In the case

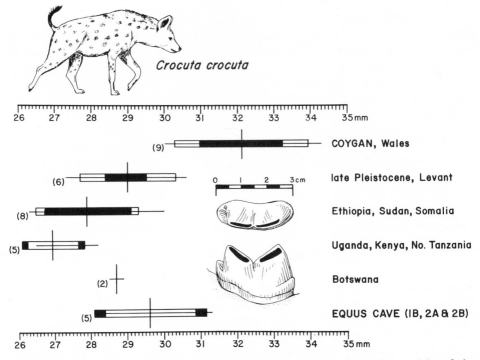

FIGURE 8.7: A Dice-Leraas diagram for the length of the lower M1 of the spotted hyena (*Crocuta crocuta*) from Pleistocene fossil sites in Wales (Coygan), the Levant, and South Africa (Equus Cave) and in recent samples from eastern and southern Africa. The vertical line is the mean for each sample, the horizontal line is the observed range, the open bar is the standard deviation, the closed bar is the 95% confidence interval for the mean, and the number in parentheses is the number of specimens in each sample. The figure indicates that spotted hyenas tend to be larger in colder climates (see figure 5.7 for a similar diagram making the same point from black-backed jackal lower M1 lengths). The Levant data are from Kurtén (1965); the remaining data are from measurements made by the authors.

of the basal breadth of a tooth, for example, a CV greater than 10 might mean that a sample comprises teeth of two very similar species or perhaps similar adjacent teeth (e.g. the M1 and M2) of one species. A CV less than 4 suggests unusual homogeneity. This might occur if a sample were made up overwhelmingly of bones from siblings.

The 95% confidence limits of the mean and the mean plus or minus one standard deviation are useful for constructing Dice-Leraas diagrams (Simpson, Roe, and Lewontin 1960). These diagrams facilitiate comparisons between samples derived from normally distributed populations. We offer an example here in figure 8.7. Commonly, in such a diagram, the mean of each sample is represented by a vertical line, the observed range by a horizontal line, the mean plus or minus one standard deviation by a solid bar, and the 95% confidence limits by an open (blank) bar. Sample means whose 95% confidence limits do not overlap may be considered different at the .05 level of probability or below. Conventionally, sample means that differ from one another at the .05 level or below are said to be "significantly different," meaning that the numerical difference between them is not likely to be due to chance. Thus, the 95% confidence limits may be used as a partial replacement for "Student's t-test" to determine if two means are significantly different at the .05 level. However, the means of two samples may differ at the .05 level (or below), even if the 95% confidence limits do overlap. Thus, in cases of overlap, it is still necessary to apply Student's t.

The 95% confidence interval and the mean plus or minus one standard deviation are not particularly useful for comparing samples on variables like age that are not normally distributed. As we indicated previously, in the case of a variable like age, the Kolmogorov-Smirnov test is often an appropriate and useful procedure for determining whether two samples are likely to have been drawn from the same population--that is, for determining the likelihood that two samples differ for some reason other than chance.

APPENDIX. Principal Variables in the Program MNI

Set-up Variables:

S$	Site name
SP$	Species name
FAM$, FM$	Zoological family
FILE$	File with bones, dentitions, or skeletal part divisors (used to trap error if named file does not exist in system)
FK$	Read skeletal part divisors from file or keyboard
DIVFILE$	Name of file with skeletal part divisors
BONEFILE$	Name of file with bones
DENTFILE$	Name of file with dentitions
NCR$, NCR	Number of bone states to include
CR$(6)	Bone state
NPU$, NPU	Number of provenience units
PU$(30)	Provenience unit
IR$	Ignore/Recognize left/right distinction
RI$	Ignore/Recognize fused/unfused distinction
SKPT$(46)	To hold skeletal part lookup table
TOOTH$(24)	To hold tooth lookup table
FUST(5)	To hold fusion state lookup table
GOODREC	True if the provenience unit, state of a bone or dentition indicate it should be included in NISP and MNI counts; false otherwise.

Variables read from bone (BONECODE) file

LV$	Level (or provenience unit)
SK$	Skeletal part
LR$	Side (left/right)
PD$	Part of bone (proximal/distal)
PES$	State of fusion-proximal
FP!	Fraction-proximal
DES$	State of fusion-distal
FD!	Fraction-distal
CT$	Comment
CN$	Catalog Number

Variables read from dental (DENTCODE) file

LV$	Level (or provenience unit)
UL$	Jaw (upper/lower)
LRB$	Side of dentition (left/right/both)

LR$	Side of dentition to enter (left/right)
NT	Number of teeth (or sockets) in dentition
TH$	Tooth (name)
CN$	Catalog number
CT$	Comment

Variables that format output

CCR$(6)	To print bone states
PPU$(10)	To print provenience units
SOFTCOPY,HC	To provide a screen listing first, followed optionally by printed copy

Variables That Count Skeletal Parts Other Than Dentitions

To count NISPs:

TB(50)	Total bones (specimens) for each skeletal part
TP(22)	Total specimens for each proximal end
TD(22)	Total specimens for each distal end

To sum fractions for each proximal/distal element:

L!(22,10)	Left bones
R!(22,10)	Right bones
I!(22,10)	Bones of indeterminate side
TL(22,10)	Total lefts (lefts + 1/2 indeterminates)
TR(22,10)	Total rights (rights + 1/2 indeterminates)
T(22,10)	Final total (larger of lefts or rights)

To sum fractions by state of fusion:

TPFE(22)	Proximal, fused epiphysis
TDFE(22)	Distal, fused epiphysis
TPUE(22)	Proximal, unfused epiphysis
TDUE(22)	Distal, unfused epiphysis
TPU(22)	Proximal, unfused (larger of shaft or epiphysis)
TDU(22)	Distal, unfused (larger of shaft or epiphysis)

To sum fractions for non-proximal/distal elements:

LB!(50)	Left bones
RB!(50)	right bones
IB!(50)	Indeterminate bones

MNIs for limb bones, ribs, vertebrae, and scapula:

| MNIP(22) | Proximal |
| MNID(22) | Distal |

MNIs for non-proximal/distal elements, fusion irrelevant

| TLB(50) | Left bones |
| TRB(50) | Right bones |

Summary MNIs:
MNI(50)

To allocate fusion states for bones of indeterminate fusion:
DEI   Distal
PEI   Proximal

To allocate indeterminate metapodials:
MP

To count total NISP and MNI:
SK   Total number of bones entered
MNIB   Total MNI for bones
NISP   Grand total of all "bones" (including dentitions)

Divisors for skeletal parts:
NDS   Number of distal sesamoids per individual
NLM   Number of lateral metapodials per side per
                      individual
NLU   Number of lumbar vertebrae per individual
NMC   Number of metacarpals per side per individual
NMT   Number of metatarsals per side per individual
NP1   Number of first phalanges per side per individual
NP2   Number of second phalanges per side per individual
NP3   Number of third phalanges per side per individual
NPS   Number of proximal sesamoids per individual
NRI   Number of ribs per individual
NSA   Number of sacral vertebrae per individual
NTH   Number of thoracic vertebrae per individual

To allocate frontlets of indeterminate sex:
SEX

To sum fractions for frontlets:
IS!(2)   Indeterminate side
LS!(2)   Left side
RS!(2)   Right side

MNIs for frontlets:
TLS(2)   Lefts
TRS(2)   Rights
TS(2)   MNI (larger of lefts or rights)

Variables That Count Dentitions

MNIs for individual teeth:

LMAX(19,3)	Left maxilla
RMAX(19,3)	Right maxilla
IMAX(19,3)	Maxilla of indeterminate side
LMAND(19,3)	Left mandible
RMAND(19,3)	Right mandible
IMAND(19,3)	Mandible of indeterminate side

To combine isolated teeth and teeth in sockets:

LMNT!(19)	Left mandible, teeth
RMNT!(19)	Right mandible, teeth
LMXT!(19)	Left maxilla, teeth
RMXT!(19)	Right maxilla, teeth

To combine teeth in sockets and empty sockets:

LMNS!(19)	Left mandible, sockets
RMNS!(19)	Right mandible, sockets
LMXS!(19)	Left maxilla, sockets
RMXS!(19)	Right maxilla, sockets

To pick largest number (teeth or sockets):

RMX!(19)	Right maxilla
LMX!(19)	Left maxilla
RMN!(19)	Right mandible
LMN!(19)	Left mandible

To hold final MNIs for each dental position (deciduous and permanent)

MAND(27)	For mandibular teeth
MAX(27)	For maxillary teeth

To count number of dentitions entered:

UT	Upper dentitions (left not joined to right)
BUT	Upper dentitions (left and right joined)
LT	Lower dentitions (left not joined to right)
BLT	Lower dentitions (left and right joined)

To count totals for dentitions:

MNIT	"Total" MNI for teeth
TT	Total number of dentitions

To input indeterminate teeth:

DI$(4)	Deciduous incisors
DP$(4)	Deciduous premolars
I$(4)	Incisors
M$(7)	Molars

Appendix

P\$(4)	Premolars
T\$	General "tooth"

To allocate indeterminate teeth:

XDI, IDI	Deciduous incisors
XDP, IDP	Deciduous premolars
XI, II	Incisors
XM, IM	Molars
XP, IP	Premolars

To allocate dentitions of indeterminate jaw (upper or lower)
UL

To input number of indistinguishable teeth of each type:

NDI	Number of deciduous incisors
NDP	Number of deciduous premolars
NI	Number of incisors
NM	Number of molars
NP	Number of premolars

REFERENCES

Altuna, J. 1976. Los mamiferos del yacimiento prehistorico de Tito Bustillo (Asturias). In *Excavaciones en la Cueva de "Tito Bustillo" (Asturias): Trabajos de 1975*, ed. J. A. Moure Romanillo and H. Cano Herrera, 151-94. Oviedo: Instituto de Estudios Asturianos.

Attwell, C. A. M. 1980. Age determination of the blue wildebeest *Connochaetes taurinus* in Zululand. *South African Journal of Zoology* 15:121-30.

Attwell, C. A. M. and Jeffrey, R. C. V. 1980. Aspects of molariform tooth attrition in eland and wildebeest. *South African Journal of Wildlife Research* 11:31-34.

Avery, D. M. 1982. Micromammals as palaeoenvironmental indicators and an interpretation of the late Quaternary in the southern Cape Province, South Africa. *Annals of the South African Museum* 85:183-374.

Bailey, G. 1983. Economic change in Late Pleistocene Cantabria. In *Hunter-gatherer economy in prehistory: A European perspective*, ed. G. Bailey, 149-65. Cambridge: Cambridge University Press.

Barandiaran, I., Freeman, L. G., Gonzalez Echegaray, J. & Klein, R. G. 1984. *Excavaciones en el Yacimiento de "El Juyo,"* vol. 1. Santillana: Museo y Centro de Investigaciones de Altamira.

Bearder, S. K. 1977. Feeding habits of spotted hyenas in a woodland habitat. *East African Wildlife Journal* 15:263-80.

Bedord, J. N. 1978. A new technique of sex determination in mature bison metapodials. *Plains Anthropologist Memoir* 14:40-43.

Behrensmeyer, A. K. 1975. The taphonomy and paleoecology of the Plio-Pleistocene vertebrate assemblages east of Lake Rudolf, Kenya. *Bulletin of the Museum of Comparative Zoology* 146:473-578.

⸺. 1978. Taphonomic and ecologic information from bone weathering. *Paleobiology* 4:150-62.

Behrensmeyer, A. K. and Hill, A., eds. 1980. *Fossils in the making*. Chicago: University of Chicago Press.

Benn, D. W. 1974. Annuli in the dental cementum of white-tailed deer from archeological contexts. *Wisconsin Archeologist* 55:90-98.

Binford, L. R. 1978. *Nunamiut ethnoarchaeology*. New York: Academic Press.

⸺. 1981. *Bones: Ancient men and modern myths*. New York: Academic Press.

Blalock, H. M. 1972. *Social statistics*. New York: McGraw-Hill.

Boessneck, J. 1969. Osteological differences between sheep (*Ovis aries* Linne) and goats (*Capra hircus* Linne). In *Science in archaeology*, ed. E. Brothwell and E. Higgs, 331-58. London: Thames and Hudson.

Boessneck, J., and von den Driesch, A. 1978. The significance of measuring animal bones from archaeological sites. *Peabody Museum of Archaeology Bulletin* (Harvard University) 2:25-39.

Bökönyi, S. 1970. A new method for the determination of the number of individuals in animal bone material. *American Journal of Archaeology* 74:291-92.

Bonnichsen, R. 1979. Pleistocene bone technology in the Beringian Refugium. *Archaeological Survey of Canada Paper* 89:1-280.

Bonnichsen, R., and Sanger, D. 1977. Integrating faunal analysis. *Canadian Journal of Archaeology* 1:109-33.

Bordes, F. & Prat, F. 1965. Observations sur les faunes du Riss et du Würm I en Dordogne. *L'Anthropologie* 69:31-45.

Bourque, B. J., Morris, K. & Spiess, A. 1978. Determining season of death of mammal teeth from archeological sites: A new sectioning technique. *Science* 149:530-31.

Boyer-Klein, A. 1982. Cadre climatique du Magdalenien Cantabrique. Essai de reconstitution par la palynologie. *Cahiers du Centre de Recherches Préhistoriques* (Université de Paris I) 8:91-97.

Brain, C. K. 1975. An introduction to the South African australopithecine bone accumulations. In *Archaeozoological studies*, ed. A. T. Clason, 109-19. New York: American Elsevier.

_____. 1976. Some principles in the interpretation of bone accumulations associated with man. In *Human origins*, ed. G. Ll. Isaac and E. McCown, 121-38. Menlo Park, Calif.: W. A. Benjamin.

_____. 1981. *The hunters or the hunted: An introduction to African cave taphonomy.* Chicago: University of Chicago Press.

Bunn, H. T. 1981. Archaeological evidence for meat-eating by Plio-Pleistocene hominids from Koobi Fora and Olduvai Gorge. *Nature* 291:574-77.

_____. 1982. *Meat-eating and human evolution: Studies on the diet and subsistence patterns of Plio-Pleistocene hominids in East Africa.* Ph.D. dissertation, University of California at Berkeley.

Butzer, K. W. 1978a. Sediment stratigraphy of the Middle Stone Age sequence at Klasies River Mouth. *South African Archaeological Bulletin* 33:141-51.

_____. 1978b. Climate patterns in an unglaciated continent. *Geographic Magazine* 51:201-8.

_____. n.d. Second preliminary report (1982) on the Beniali Research Project, Sierra de Espadan, Spain. Unpublished manuscript, University of Chicago.

Casteel, R. W. 1977a. Characterization of faunal assemblages and the minimum number of individuals determined from paired elements: Continuing problems in archaeology. *Journal of Archaeological Science* 4:125-34.

_____. 1977b. A consideration of the behaviour of the minimum number of individuals index: A problem in faunal characterization. *Ossa* 3/4:141-51.

_____. 1978. Faunal assemblages and the "Weigemethode" or weight method. *Journal of Field Archaeology* 5:71-77.

Chaplin, R. E. 1971. *The study of animal bones from archaeological sites*. New York: Seminar Press.

Clark, G. A., and Straus, L. G. 1983. Late Pleistocene huntergatherer adaptations in Cantabrian Spain. In *Hunter-gatherer economy in prehistory: A European perspective*, ed. G. Bailey, 149-65. Cambridge: Cambridge University Press.

Clark, J., and Kietzke, K. K. 1967. Paleoecology of the Lower Nodular Zone, Brule Formation, in the Big Badlands of South Dakota. *Fieldiana: Geology Memoirs* 5:111-37.

Clason, A. T. 1972. Some remarks on the use and presentation of archaeozoological data. *Helinium* 12:139-53.

Clason, A. T., and Prummel, W. 1977. Collecting, sieving and archaeozoological research. *Journal of Archaeological Science* 4:171-75.

Cornwall, I. W. 1974. *Bones for the archaeologist*. London: Phoenix House.

Cutress, T. W., and Healy, W. B. 1965. Wear of sheep's teeth. II. Effects of pasture juices on dentine. *New Zealand Journal of Agricultural Research* 8:753-62.

Davis, S. J. M. 1977. The ungulate remains from Kebara Cave. *Eretz-Israel (Archaeological, Historical, and Geographical Studies)* 13:150-63.

_____. 1981. The effects of temperature change and domestication on the body size of late Pleistocene to Holocene mammals of Israel. *Paleobiology* 7:101-14.

Deacon, H. J. 1979. Excavations at Boomplaas Cave--a sequence through the Upper Pleistocene and Holocene in South Africa. *World Archaeology* 10:241-57.

Deacon, J. 1978. Changing patterns in the late Pleistocene/early Holocene prehistory of southern Africa, as seen from the Nelson Bay Cave stone artifact sequence. *Quaternary Research* 10:84-111.

_____. 1984. Later Stone Age people and their descendants in southern Africa. In *Southern African prehistory and palaeoenvironments*, ed. R. G. Klein. Rotterdam, A. A. Balkema, forthcoming.

Delpech, F. 1975. *Les faunes du Paléolithique Supérieur dans le Sud-Ouest de la France*. Thèse de Doctorat d'Etat es Sciènces Naturelles, Université de Bordeaux.

Ducos, P. 1968. *L'origine des animaux domestiques en Palestine*. Bordeaux: Delmas.

_____. 1975. Analyse statistique des collections d'ossements d'animaux. In *Archaeozoological studies*, ed. A. T. Clason, 35-44. New York: American Elsevier.

Eberhardt, L. L. 1971. Population analysis. In *Wildlife management techniques*, 3d ed. rev., ed. R. H. Giles, Jr., 457- 495. Washington: The Wildlife Society.

Edwards, J. K., Marchinton, R. L., and Smith, G. F. 1982. Pelvic girdle criteria for sex determination of white-tailed deer. *Journal of Wildlife Management* 46:544-47.

Fieller, N. R. J., and Turner, A. 1982. Number estimation in vertebrate samples. *Journal of Archaeological Science* 9:49- 62.

Freeman, L. G., Klein, R. G., and Gonzalez Echegaray, J. 1983. A stone age sanctuary. *Natural History* 92(8):46-53.

Frison, G. C. 1978a. Animal population studies and cultural inference. *Plains Anthropologist Memoir* 14:44-52.

_____. 1978b. *Prehistoric hunters of the High Plains*. New York: Academic Press.

Gejvall, N.-G. 1969. *Lerna, a pre-classical site in the Argolid. Vol. 1. The fauna.* Princeton: American School of Classical Studies at Athens.

Gifford, D. P. 1981. Taphonomy and paleoecology: A critical review of archaeology's sister disciplines. *Advances in Archaeological Method and Theory* 4:365-438.

Gifford, D. P. and Crader, D. C. 1977. A computer coding system for archaeological faunal remains. *American Antiquity* 42:225- 238.

Gilbert, B. M. 1980. *Mammalian osteo-archaeology*. Laramie, Wyo.: B. Miles Gilbert.

Gordon, B. C. 1980. Seasonality of French Magdalenian sites using microscopic analysis of annuli of reindeer teeth. Unpublished Progress Report no. 3 (1 May 1980), Archaeological Survey of Canada.

Grasse, P. 1955, 1967. *Traite de zoologie.* Vols. 16 and 17. Paris: Masson et Cie.

Grayson, D. K. 1973. On the methodology of faunal analysis. *American Antiquity* 38:432-39.

_____. 1979. On the quantification of vertebrate archaeofaunas. *Advances in Archaeological Method and Theory* 2:199-237.

_____. 1981. A critical view of the use of archaeological vertebrates in paleoenvironmental reconstruction. *Journal of Ethnobiology* 1:28-38.

Grigson, C. 1983. Review of *Bones: Ancient men and modern myths* (by L. R. Binford). *Journal of Archaeological Science* 10:296- 97.

Grimsdell, J. J. R. 1973. Age determination of the African buffalo, *Syncerus caffer* Sparrman. *East African Wildlife Journal* 11:31-53.

Grue, H., and Jensen, B. 1979. Review of the formation of incremental lines in tooth cementum of terrestrial mammals. *Danish Review of Game Biology* 11(3):1-48.

Guilday, J. E. 1971. The Pleistocene history of the Appalachian mammal fauna. In *The distributional history of the biota of the southern Appalachians*, ed. P. C. Holt, 233-62. Blacksburg: Virginia Polytechnic Institute and State University.

Hanson, C. B. 1980. Fluvial taphonomic processes: Models and experiments. In *Fossils in the making*, ed. A. K. Behrensmeyer and A. P. Hill, 156-81. Chicago: University of Chicago Press.

Healy, W. B. 1965. Ingestion of soil by sheep in New Zealand in relation to wear of teeth. *Nature* 208:806-7.

Healy, W. B., and Ludwig, T. G. 1965. Wear of sheep's teeth. I. The role of ingested soil. *New Zealand Journal of Agricultural Research* 8:737-52.

Hendey, Q. B. 1981. Palaeoecology of the late Tertiary fossil occurrences in "E" Quarry, Langebaanweg, South Africa, and a reinterpretation of their geological context. *Annals of the South African Museum* 84:1-104.

———. 1982. *Langebaanweg: A record of past life.* Cape Town, South African Museum.

Henschel, J. R., Tilson, R., and von Blottnitz, F. 1979. Implications of a spotted hyaena bone assemblage in the Namib Desert. *South African Archaeological Bulletin* 34:127-31.

Holtzman, R. C. 1979. Maximum likelihood estimation of fossil assemblage composition. *Paleobiology* 5:77-89.

Hulbert, R. C. 1982. Population dynamics of the three-toed horse *Neohipparion* from the late Miocene of Florida. *Paleobiology* 8:159-67.

Irby, L. R. 1979. Reproduction in mountain reedbuck (*Redunca fulvorufula*). *Mammalia* 43:191-213.

Jarman, P. J. 1974. The social organization of antelope in relation to their ecology. *Behaviour* 48:215-67.

Kay, M. 1974. Dental annuli age determination on white-tailed deer from archaeological sites. *Plains Anthropologist* 19:224- 27.

Kerr, M. A., and Roth, H. H. 1970. Studies on the agricultural utilisation of semi-domesticated eland (*Taurotragus oryx*) in Rhodesia. Horn development and tooth eruption as indicators of age. *Rhodesian Journal of Agricultural Research* 8:149-55.

Klein, R. G. 1972. The late Quaternary mammalian fauna of Nelson Bay Cave (Cape Province, South Africa): Its implications for megafaunal extinctions and environmental and cultural change. *Quaternary Research* 2:135-42.

———. 1973. *Ice-Age hunters of the Ukraine.* Chicago: University of Chicago Press.

———. 1975. Paleoanthropological implications of the nonarcheological bone assemblage from Swartklip 1, South-Western Cape Province, South Africa. *Quaternary Research* 5:275-88.

———. 1976. The mammalian fauna of the Klasies River Mouth sites, southern Cape Province, South Africa. *South African Archaeological Bulletin* 31:75-98.

———. 1978. Stone age predation on large African bovids. *Journal of Archaeological Science* 5:195-217.

———. 1979. Stone age exploitation of animals in southern Africa. *American Scientist* 67:151-60.

———. 1980a. The interpretation of mammalian faunas from Stone Age archaeological sites, with special reference to sites in the southern Cape Province, South Africa. In *Fossils in the making*, ed. A. K. Behrensmeyer and A. Hill, 223-246. Chicago: University of Chicago Press.

———. 1980b. Environmental and ecological implications of large mammals from Upper Pleistocene and Holocene sites in southern Africa. *Annals of the South African Museum* 81:223-83.

———. 1981. Stone Age predation on small African bovids. *South African Archaeological Bulletin* 36:55-65.

_____. 1982a. Age (mortality) profiles as a means of distinguishing hunted species from scavenged ones in Stone Age archaeological sites. *Paleobiology* 8:151-58.

_____. 1982b. Patterns of ungulate mortality and ungulate mortality profiles from Langebaanweg (early Pliocene) and Elandsfontein (Middle Pleistocene), south-western Cape Province, South Africa. *Annals of the South African Museum* 90:49-94.

Klein, R. G., Allwarden, K., and Wolf, C. 1983. The calculation and interpretation of ungulate age profiles from dental crown heights. In *Hunter-gatherer economy in prehistory: A European perspective*, ed. G. Bailey, 47-57. Cambridge: University of Cambridge Press.

Klein, R. G. and Cruz-Uribe, K. 1983a. The computation of ungulate age (mortality) profiles from dental crown heights. *Paleobiology* 9:70-78.

_____. 1983b. Stone Age population numbers and average tortoise size at Byneskranskop Cave 1 and Die Kelders Cave 1, southern Cape Province, South Africa. *South African Archaeological Bulletin* 38:26-30.

_____. 1984. An overview of the Torralba fauna. In *Torralba: An Acheulean butchering site on the Spanish Meseta*, ed. L. G. Freeman and F. C. Howell. New York: Academic Press, forthcoming.

Klingel, H. 1965. Notes on tooth development and ageing criteria in the plains zebra *Equus quagga boehmi* Matschie. *East African Wildlife Journal* 3:127-29.

Krantz, G. S. 1968. A new method of counting mammal bones. *American Journal of Archaeology* 72:285-88.

Kruuk, H. 1972. *The spotted hyena.* Chicago: University of Chicago Press.

Kurtén, B. 1953. On the variation and population dynamics of fossil and recent mammal populations. *Acta Zoologica Fennica* 76:1-122.

_____. 1959. Rates of evolution in fossil mammals. *Cold Spring Harbor Symposia on Quantitative Biology* 24:205-15.

_____. 1965. The Carnivora of the Palestine caves. *Acta Zoologica Fennica* 107:1-74.

Lie, R. W. 1980. Minimum number of individuals from osteological samples. *Norwegian Archaeological Review* 13:24-30.

Lowe, V. P. W. 1967. Teeth as indicators of age with special reference to Red deer (*Cervus elaphus*) of known age from Rhum. *Journal of Zoology* (London) 152:137-53.

Ludwig, T. G., Healy, W. B., and Cutress, T. W. 1966. Wear on sheep's teeth. III. Seasonal variation in wear and ingested soil. *New Zealand Journal of Agricultural Research* 9:157-164.

Lyman, R. L. 1979. Faunal analysis: an outline of method and theory with some suggestions. *Northwest Anthropological Research Notes* 13:22-35.

_____. 1982. Archaeofaunas and subsistence studies. *Advances in Archaeological Method and Theory* 5:331-93.

McArdle, J. 1975-77. A numerical (computerized) method for quantifying zooarcheological comparisons. *Paleorient* 3:181- 90.

Manson, J. 1974. Aspects of the biology and behavior of the Cape grysbok *Raphicerus melanotis* Thunberg. M. A. Thesis, University of

Stellenbosch.

Meadow, R. H. 1978. "BONECODE"--a system of numerical coding for faunal data from Middle Eastern sites. *Bulletin of the Peabody Museum of Archaeology and Ethnology* (Harvard University) 2:169-86.

_____. 1980. Animal bones: Problems for the archaeologist together with some possible solutions. *Paleorient* 6:65-77.

Mentis, M T. 1972. A review of some life history features of the large herbivores of Africa. *Lammergeyer* 16:1-89.

Mills, M. G. L. 1973. The brown hyaena. *African Wildlife* 27:150-53.

_____. 1978a. The comparative socio-ecology of the Hyaenidae. *Carnivore* 1:1-6.

_____. 1978b. Foraging behaviour of the brown hyaena (*Hyaena brunnea*, Thunberg, 1820) in the southern Kalahari. *Zeitschrift fur Tierpsychologie* 48:113-41.

Mills, M. G. L., and Mills, M. E. J. 1977. An analysis of bones collected at hyaena breeding dens in the Gemsbok National Parks (Mammalia: Carnivora). *Annals of the Transvaal Museum* 30:145-55.

Mitchell, B. 1965. Breeding, growth and ageing criteria of Lichtenstein's Hartebeest. *Puku* 3:97-104.

_____. 1967. Growth layers in dental cement for determining the age of red deer (*Cervus elaphus* L.). *The Journal of Animal Ecology* 36:279-93.

Morris, P. 1972. A review of mammalian age determination methods. *Mammal Review* 2:69-104.

_____. 1978. The use of teeth for estimating the age of wild mammals. In *Development, function and evolution of teeth*, ed. P. M. Butler and K. A. Joysey, 483-94. New York: Academic Press.

Nichol, R. K., and Creak, G. A. 1979. Matching paired elements among archaeological bone remains: A computer procedure and some practical limitations. *Newsletter of Computer Archaeology* 14:6-16.

Nimmo, B. W. 1971. Population dynamics of a Wyoming pronghorn cohort from the Eden-Farson site, 48SW304. *Plains Anthropologist* 16:285-88.

Noe-Nygaard, N. 1977. Butchering and marrow fracturing as a taphonomic factor in archaeological deposits. *Paleobiology* 2:218-37.

Olsen, S. J. 1971. *Zooarchaeology: Animal bones in archaeology and their interpretation.* Reading, Mass.: Addison-Wesley.

Owens, D., and Owens, M. 1979. Notes on social organization and behavior of brown hyenas (*Hyaena brunnea*). *Journal of Mammalogy* 60:405-8.

Owens, M., and Owens, D. 1978. Feeding ecology and its influence on social organization in brown hyenas (*Hyaena brunnea*, Thunberg) of the central Kalahari Desert. *East African Wildlife Journal* 16:113-35.

1979. The secret society of the brown hyenas. *African Wildlife* 33(3):113-35.

Pales, L., and Garcia, M. A. 1981. *Atlas ostéologique des mammifères*, Vol. 2. Paris: Central National de la Recherche Scientifique.

Pales, L., and Lambert, Ch. 1971. *Atlas ostéologique des mammifères*, Vol 1. Paris: Centre National de la Recherche Scientifique.

Payne, S. 1972a. Partial recovery and sample bias: the results of some sieving experiments. In *Papers in economic prehistory*, ed. E. S. Higgs, 49-64. Cambridge: Cambridge University Press.

_____. 1972b. On the interpretation of bone samples from archaeological sites. In *Papers in economic prehistory*, ed. E. S. Higgs, 65-81. Cambridge: Cambridge University Press.

_____. 1973. Kill-off patterns in sheep and goats: The mandibles from Asvan Kale. *Anatolian Studies* 23:281-303.

_____. 1975. Partial recovery and sample bias. In *Archaeozoological studies*, ed. A. T. Clason, 7-17. New York: American Elsevier.

Perkins, D. 1973. A critique on the methods of quantifying faunal remains from archaeological sites. In *Domestikationsforschung und Geschichte der Haustiere*, ed. J. Matolsci, 367-70. Budapest: Akademiai Kiado.

Perkins, D., and Daly, P. 1968. A hunters' village in Neolithic Turkey. *Scientific American* 219(11): 97-106.

Poplin, F. 1976. Rémarques théoriques et pratiques sur les unites utilisées dans les études d'ostéologie quantitative, particulièrement en archéologie préhistorique. *Union Internationale des Sciènces Préhistoriques, IXe Congrès, Nice, Themes Specialisées*, 124-41.

Potts, R., and Shipman, P. 1981. Cutmarks made by stone tools on bones from Olduvai Gorge, Tanzania. *Nature* 291:577-80.

Quimby, D. C., and Gaab, J. E. 1957. Mandibular dentition as an age indicator in Rocky Mountain elk. *Journal of Wildlife Management* 21:435-51.

Rautenbach, I. L. 1971. Ageing criteria in the springbok, *Antidorcas marsupialis* (Zimmermann, 1780)(Artiodactyla: Bovidae). *Annals of the Transvaal Museum* 27:83-133.

Redding, R. W., Pires-Ferreira, J. W., and Zeder, M. A. 1975-77. A proposed system for computer analysis of identifiable faunal material from archaeological sites. *Paleorient* 3:190-203.

Redding, R. W., Zeder, M. A., and McCardle, J. 1978. "BONESORT II"--a system for the computer processing of identifiable faunal material. *Bulletin of the Peabody Museum of Archaeology and Ethnology* (Harvard University) 2:135-47.

Reher, C. A. 1978. Buffalo population and other deterministic factors in a model of adaptive process on the shortgrass plains. *Plains Anthropologist Memoir* 14:23-39.

Robinette, W. L., and Child, G. F. T. 1964. Notes on the biology of the lechwe (*Kobus leche*). *Puku* 2:85-117.

Ryder, M. L. 1969. *Animal bones in archaeology*. Mammal Society Handbooks. Oxford, Blackwell Scientific Publications.

Schmid, E. 1972. *Atlas of animal bones*. Amsterdam, Elsevier.

Schweitzer, F. R. 1974. Archaeological evidence for sheep at the Cape. *South African Archaeological Bulletin* 29:75-82.

_____. 1979. Excavations at Die Kelders, Cape Province, South Africa: The Holocene deposits. *Annals of the South African Museum* 78:101-233.

References

Shipman, P. 1981. *Life history of a fossil.* Cambridge: Harvard University Press.

Shipman, P., and Rose, J. 1983. Early hominid hunting, butchering, and carcass-processing behaviors: approaches to the fossil record. *Journal of Anthropological Archaeology* 2:57-98.

Shotwell, A. J. 1955. An approach to the paleoecology of mammals. *Ecology* 36:327-37.

_____. 1958. Inter-community relationships in Hemphillian (midPliocene) mammals. *Ecology* 39:271-73.

Siegel, S. 1956. *Non-parametric statistics for the behavioral sciences.* New York: McGraw-Hill.

Silver, I. A. 1969. The ageing of domestic animals. In *Science in archaeology,* ed. D. Brothwell and E. S. Higgs, 283-302. London: Thames and Hudson.

Simpson, C. D. 1966. Tooth eruption, growth and ageing criteria in the greater kudu--*Tragelaphus strepsiceros* Pallas. *Arnoldia* 2(21):1-12.

_____. 1973. Tooth replacement, growth and ageing criteria for the Zambesi bushbuck--*Tragelaphus scriptus ornatus* Pocock. *Arnoldia* 6(6):1-25.

Simpson, G. G., Roe, A., and Lewontwin, R. C. 1960. *Quantitative zoology.* New York: Brace and World.

Sinclair, A. R. E. 1977. *The African buffalo.* Chicago: University of Chicago Press.

Singer, R., and Wymer, J. 1982. *The Middle Stone Age at Klasies River Mouth in South Africa.* Chicago: University of Chicago Press.

Smith, B. D. 1975. Toward a more accurate estimation of the meat yield of animal species at archaeological sites. In *Archaeozoological studies,* ed. A. T. Clason, 99-106. New York: American Elsevier.

_____. 1976. "Twitching": a minor ailment affecting human paleoecological research. In *Cultural change and continuity,* ed. C. Cleland, 275-292. New York: Academic Press.

Smuts, G. L. 1974. Age determination in Burchell's zebra (*Equus burchelli antiquorum*) from the Kruger National Park. *Journal of the Southern African Wildlife Management Association* 4:103- 15.

Sokal, R. R., and Rohlf, F. J. 1969. *Biometry.* San Francisco: W. H. Freeman.

Speth, J. D. 1983. *Bison kills and bone counts: Decision making by ancient hunters.* Chicago: University of Chicago Press.

Spiess, A. E. 1979. *Reindeer and caribou hunters: An archaeological study.* New York: Academic Press.

Spinage, C. A. 1971. Geratodontology and horn growth of the impala (*Aepyceros melampus*). *Journal of Zoology* (London) 164:209-25.

_____. 1972. Age estimation of zebra. *East African Wildlife Journal* 10:273-77.

_____. 1973. A review of the age determination of mammals by means of teeth, with especial reference to Africa. *East African Wildlife Journal* 11:165-87.

_____. 1976. Age determination of the female Grant's gazelle. *East African Wildlife Journal* 14:121-34.

Stewart, F. L., and Stahl, F. W. 1977. Cautionary note on edible meat poundage figures. *American Antiquity* 42:267-70.

Straus, L. G., Altuna, J., Clark, G. A., Gonzalez Morales, M., Laville, H., Leroi-Gourhan, Arl., Menendez de la Hoz, M., and Ortea, J. A. 1981. Paleoecology at La Riera (Asturias, Spain). *Current Anthropology* 22:655-82.

Sutcliffe, A. J. 1970. Spotted hyaena: Crusher, gnawer, digester, and collector of bones. *Nature* 227:1110-13.

Taber, R. D. 1956. Characteristics of the pelvic girdle in relation to sex in black-tailed and white-tailed deer. *California Department of Fish and Game* 42:15-21.

_____. 1971. Criteria of sex and age. In *Wildlife management techniques*, ed. R. H. Giles, 325-401. Washington, D. C.: The Wildlife Society.

Thomas, D. H. 1971. On distinguishing natural from cultural bone in archaeological sites. *American Antiquity* 36:366-71.

Turner, A. T. 1983. The quantification of relative abundances in fossil and sub-fossil bone assemblages. *Annals of the Transvaal Museum* 33:311-21.

Uerpmann, H.-P. 1973. Animal bone finds and economic archaeology: A critical study of "osteoarchaeological" method. *World Archaeology* 4:307-22.

_____. 1978. The "Knocod" system for processing data on animal bones from archaeological sites. *Bulletin of the Peabody Museum of Archaeology and Ethnology* (Harvard University) 2:149-67.

Van Valen, L. 1964. Age in two fossil horse populations. *Acta Zoologica* 45:93-106.

Volman, T. P. 1984. Early prehistory of Southern Africa. In *Southern African prehistory and palaeoenvironments*, ed. R. G. Klein. Rotterdam, A. A. Balkema, forthcoming.

Von den Driesch, A. 1976. A guide to the measurement of animal bones from archaeological sites. *Bulletin of the Peabody Museum of Archaeology and Ethnology* (Harvard University) 1:1- 136.

Von Richter, W. 1971. Observations on the biology and ecology of the black wildebeest (*Connochaetes gnou*). *Journal of the Southern African Wildlife Management Association* 1:3-16.

_____. 1974. *Connochaetes gnou*. *Mammalian Species* 50:1-6.

Voorhies, M. R. 1969. Taphonomy and population dynamics of an early Pliocene vertebrate fauna, Knox County, Nebraska. *University of Wyoming Special Contributions to Geology Special Paper* 1:1-69.

Vrba, E. S. 1975. Some evidence of chronology and palaeoecology of Sterkfontein, Swartkrans and Kromdraai from the fossil Bovidae. *Nature* 254:301-4.

_____. 1976. The fossil Bovidae of Sterkfontein, Swartkrans and Kromdraai. *Transvaal Museum Memoir* 21:1-166.

_____. 1980. The significance of bovid remains as indicators of environment and predation patterns. In *Fossils in the making*, ed. A. K. Behrensmeyer and A. Hill, 247-71. Chicago: University of Chicago Press.

Watson, J. P. N. 1979. The estimation of the relative frequencies of mammalian species: Khirokitia 1972. *Journal of Archaeological Science* 6:127-37.

White, T. E. 1953. A method of calculating the dietary percentage of various food animals utilized by aboriginal peoples. *American Antiquity* 18:396-98.

Wilson, M. 1980. Population dynamics of the Garnsey Site Bison. In *Late prehistoric bison procurement in southeastern New Mexico: The 1978 season at the Garnsey Site (LA-18399)*, by J. D. Speth and W. J. Parry, 88-129. Technical Report 12. Ann Arbor: University of Michigan Museum of Anthropology.

Wilson, V. J., and Roth, H. H. 1967. The effects of tsetse control operations on common duiker in Eastern Zambia. *East African Wildlife Journal* 5:53-64.

Ziegler, A. C. 1973. *Inference from prehistoric faunal remains. Addison-Wesley Module in Anthropology* 43. Reading, Mass.: Addison-Wesley.

INDEX

Acheulean, 7, 67, 76, 77
Aepyceros melampus, 18
Alcelaphine, 79
Alcelaphus buselaphus, 49, 50, 66
Alcelaphus lichtensteini, 51
Allwarden, K., 48, 62, 70
Altamira Cave, Spain, 99
Altuna, J., 40, 41
Ambrona, Spain, 7, 8
Antidorcas australis, 49, 50
Antidorcas bondi, 49, 50
Antidorcas marsupialis, 49, 50
Attritional age profile, definition of, 56-57
Attwell, C. A. M., 50, 51
Aurochs, 19, 49, 50, 70, 76. *See also Bos primigenius*
Australopithecine, 69, 85
Avery, D. M., 95

Bailey, G., 97
Barandiaran, I., 70
Bearder, S. K., 82
Bedord, J. N., 41
Behrensmeyer, A. K., 7, 8, 67
Beniali, Spain, 166, 167
Benn, D. W., 45, 62
Bergmann's rule, 94-95
Binford, L. R., 6, 65, 73
Bison, 19, 34, 61, 65, 70, 76
Black-backed jackal. *See* Jackal, black-backed
Blalock, H. M., 57
Blesbok, 49, 50, 66. *See also Damaliscus dorcas*
Blue antelope, 49, 50, 66 *See also Hippotragus leucophaeus*
Boessneck, J., 39, 40, 41
Bökönyi, S., 24, 26
"Bone Circle." *See* Elandsfontein
Bonnichsen, R., 6, 103

Bontebok, 54. *See also Damaliscus dorcas*
Boomplaas Cave A, South Africa, 31, 64-65, 66, 67, 68, 69-70, 72-73, 74, 84
Border Cave, South Africa, 84
Bordes, F., 76
Bos primigenius, 49, 50
Bourque, B. J., 45
Bovid, 64-67, 73, 74, 85
Boyer-Klein, A., 70
Brain, C. K., 7, 8, 14, 64, 65, 69, 85
Breadth (of tooth), definition of, 176
Buccal, definition of, 16
Buffalo: Cape, 12, 19, 49, 50, 51, 76, 78, 79, 80, 81, 87-89; giant, 49, 50, 211. *See also Pelorovis antiquus, Syncerus caffer*
Bunn, H. T., 6, 8, 82
Burning, of bones, 6
Bushbuck, 49, 50, 51, 76 78, 79. *See also Tragelaphus scriptus*
Bushpig, 76, 78, 79
Butzer, K. W., 7, 94, 95
Byneskranskop Cave 1, South Africa, 89, 93

Calcaneum, recording of, 121, 123
Canis mesomelas, 42, 82
Capra hircus, 109, 166, 167
Caracal, 12. *See also Felis caracal*
Carpals, recording of, 127
Casteel, R. W., 24, 26, 29-30, 31, 35
Catastrophic age profile, definition of, 56-57
Cattle, 64
Cementum, 44-45, 62
Cervid, 85
Cervus elaphus, 49, 50, 72, 193,

194; *C. e. canadensis*, 48

Chaplin, R. E., 24, 35, 41, 43

Chersina angulata, 94

Child, G. F. T., 51

Clark, G. A., 97

Clark, J., 3

Clason, A. T., 3, 24

Clavicle, recording of, 121

Climatic change, Africa, 94-95

Coefficient of variation, 176, 239-40

Connochaetes, 66; *C. gnou*, 20; *C. taurinus*, 49, 50

Cornwall, I. W., x, 11

Coygan, Wales, 240

Crader, D. C., 103

Cranial/postcranial ratio, 67-69, 83

Creak, G. A., 27

Crocuta crocuta, 82, 240

Crown height, definition of, 46

Cruz-Uribe, K., 8, 67, 97, 102

Cutress, T. W., 52

Daly, P., 64

Damaliscus dorcas, 49, 50, 54, 66

Davis, S. J. M., 46, 92

Deacon, H. J., 66

Deacon, J., 77

Deer, red, 33, 40, 47, 49, 50, 51, 55, 70-74, 76; roe, 34, 70; white-tailed, 62. *See also Cervus elaphus*

Delpeche, F., 76

Dentine, 44

Diaphysis, definition of, 13

Dice-Leraas diagrams, 240

Die Kelders Cave 1, South Africa, 84, 86-87, 89, 91, 93, 97

Distal, definition of, 15

Dog, Cape hunting, 19. *See also Lycaon pictus*

Ducos, P., 24, 46

Duiker, gray, 49, 50, 51. *See also Sylvicapra grimmia*

Dwarfing, 92

Early Stone Age, 77. *See also* Acheulean

Eberhardt, L. L., 56

Edwards, J. K., 39

Efremov, I. A., 8

El Juyo Cave, Spain, 5, 55, 70-75, 99

Eland, 17, 49, 50, 78, 79, 81, 196, 211; age profiles, 80, 87-89. *See also Taurotragus oryx*

Elands Bay Cave, South Africa, 89, 93

Elandsfontein, South Africa, 7, 90, 93; "Bone Circle," 84

Elk, Rocky Mountain, 48, 51, 62. *See also Cervus elaphus canadensis*

Epiphysis, definition of, 13

Equus Cave, South Africa, 31, 67, 68, 69-70, 73, 74, 75, 84, 85, 93, 180, 206, 207, 240

Equus burchelli, 49, 50, 193, 194

Equus capensis, 49, 50

Equus przewalskii, 49, 50

Extinction, 89

Felis caracal, 12

Femur, recording of, 121

Fibula, recording of, 121, 128

Fieller, N. R., 35-36, 37

Fish, 79

France, southwestern, 76, 77

Freeman, L. G., 70

Frison, G. C., 55, 56, 61

Frontlet, recording of, 127-28, 129, 141, 143-44

Fynbos, 76, 77, 91, 95, 96

Gaab, J. E., 51

Garcia, M. A., 11

Garnsey Site, New Mexico, 65

Gejvall, N.-G., 32, 33

Giant Cape horse, 49, 50. *See also Equus capensis*

Gifford, D. P., 8, 103

Gilbert, B. M., 11

Goat, 64, 109, 166. *See also Capra hircus*

Gonzalez Echegaray, J., 70

Gordon, B. C., 62
Grayson, D. K., 4, 6, 24
Grigson, C., 7
Grimsdell, J. J. R., 51
Grue, H., 44
Grysbok, 66, 76, 78, 79; Cape, 49,
50, 51, 90-91, 92, 93, 122, 136.
See also Raphicerus melanotis
Guilday, J. E., 94

Hanson, C. B., 67
Hartebeest, 66; Cape, 49, 50, 51;
giant, 49, 50; Lichtenstein's, 51.
*See also Alcelaphus buselaphus,
A. lichtensteini, Megalotragus
priscus*
Healy, W. B., 52
Hendey, Q. B., 7, 90
Henschel, J. R., 82
Hill, A., 8
Hippotragus equinus, 49, 50
Hippotragus leucophaeus, 49, 50, 66
Histogram, construction of, 235,
238, 239
Hoedjies Punt, South Africa, 84
Holtzman, R. C., 34
Homiphoca capensis, 220
Horse, 49, 50, 70, 76. *See also
Equus przewalskii*
Hottentot, 64
Hulbert, R. C., 61
Humerus, recording of, 121
Hunting: of buffalo, 88; of eland, 89
Hyaena brunnea, 15, 16, 82
Hyena, 67, 68, 69, 70, 73, 81-85,
89-90; brown, 9, 15, 16, 82, 85;
spotted, 82, 85, 240. *See also
Crocuta crocuta, Hyaena brunnea*
Hyoid, recording of, 127
Hystrix africaeaustralis, 6

Ibex, 70
Impala, 18. *See also Aepyceros
melampus*
Innominate, recording of, 108, 127
Irby, L. R., 51

Jackal, black-backed, 42, 47, 82,
85, 94, 240; size change, 95-96.
See also Canis mesomelas
Jarman, P. J., 91
Jeffrey, R. C. V., 50, 51
Jensen, B., 44
Juyo Cave, Spain. *See* El Juyo Cave

Kalahari Desert, 85
Kay, M., 62
Kerr, M. A., 50
Kietzke, K. K., 3
Klasies River Mouth Cave 1, South
Africa, 5, 31, 67, 68, 69-70,
78-81, 84, 87-89, 90, 93, 113,
114, 122, 136, 175, 185, 215,
219
Klein, R. G., 7, 8, 24, 48, 56, 57,
62, 67, 70, 76, 78, 82, 88, 89,
90, 92, 95, 97, 102
Klingel, H., 51
Klipspringer, 66. *See also Oreotra-
gus oreotragus*
Kobus leche, 49, 50
Koobi Fora, Kenya, 8
Krantz, G. S., 35
Kruuk, H., 82
Kudu, 49, 50, 51, 66. *See also
Tragelaphus strepsiceros*
Kuiseb River, 64
Kurtén, B., 55, 61, 62, 94, 240

Lambert, Ch., 11
Langebaanweg, South Africa, 6, 90,
92, 220
Later Stone Age, 5, 76, 77, 79, 81,
84, 86, 89, 91, 93, 97, 98
Lateral, definition of, 16
Lateral malleolus, recording of, 128
Lechwe, 49, 50, 51. *See also Kobus
leche*
Length (of tooth), definition of, 176
Lewontin, R. C., 239, 240
Lie, R. W., 24, 30, 35
Limpet, 81, 94, 98, 99. *See also
Patella vulgata*
Lingual, definition of, 16

Lion, 88
Lowe, V. P. W., 51
Ludwig, T. G., 52
Lycaon pictus, 19
Lyman, R. L., 4, 5, 24
Lynx, African. *See* Caracal

Macchia. *See* Fynbos
Magdalenian, 5, 55, 70, 76, 97, 99
Mandibular condyle, recording of, 127, 129
Mann-Whitney test, 213
Manson, J., 51
Marchinton, R. L., 39
Meadow, R. H., 3, 103
Medial, definition of, 16
Megalotragus priscus, 49, 50
Mellivora capensis, 234, 235
Mentis, M. T., 50, 91
Mesolithic, 71
Metapodials, recording of, 111, 121, 141, 143-44, 146, 149
Microlith, 79
Middle Stone Age, 5, 76, 77, 78, 79, 81, 84, 89, 93, 97, 98
Mills, M. E. J., 82, 85
Mills, M. G. L., 82, 85
Mitchell, B., 51
Mollusk, 78, 79, 96-98, 99. *See also* Limpet
Morris, K., 45
Morris, P., 44
Mousterian, 76

McArdle, J., 103

Namib Desert, 64
Nelson Bay Cave, South Africa, 5, 77, 78-81, 84, 87-89, 90, 93
Neolithic, 64
Nichol, R. K., 27
Nimmo, B. W., 56
Noe-Nygaard, N., 71
Nyala, 13, 14. *See also Tragelaphus angasi*
Nyanzachoerus, 92

Occipital condyle, recording of, 127, 128
Olduvai Gorge, Tanzania, 8
Olsen, S. J., 11
Oreotragus oreotragus, 66
Owens, D., 82
Owens, M., 82
Oxygen-isotope analysis, 78

Pales, L., 11
Pascal, 101
Patella, recording of, 127
Patella vulgata, 94
Payne, S., 2, 24, 87
Pelea capreolus, 49, 50, 113
Pelorovis antiquus, 49, 50
Penguin, 79
Perkins, D., 24, 30, 33, 34, 37, 64
Phalanges, recording of, 109, 111, 121, 123, 146, 149
Pig, 35
Pires-Ferreira, J. W., 103
Poplin, F., 24
Porcupine, 6, 8, 67, 90. *See also Hystrix africaeaustralis*
Potts, R., 8
Prat, F., 76
Predator-prey relationship, 89
Procavia capensis, 113, 114
Proximal, definition of, 15
Prummel, W., 3

Quimby, D. C., 51

Radius, recording of, 121
Raphicerus, 66, 92; *R. campestris*, 49, 50, 91, 180, 206, 207; *R. melanotis*, 49, 50, 91, 122, 136
Rautenbach, I. L., 51
Red deer. *See* Deer, red
Redding, R. W., 103
Redunca arundinum, 49, 50, 192, 194
Redunca fulvorufula, 49, 50
Reedbuck, 82; mountain, 49, 50, 51; southern, 49, 50. *See also Redunca arundinum, R.*

fulvorufula
Reher, C. A., 56
Reindeer, 62, 76
Ribs, recording of, 109, 123, 127
Roan antelope, 49, 50. *See also*
  Hippotragus equinus
Robinette, W. L., 51
Roe, A., 239, 240
Roe deer. *See* Deer, roe
Rohlf, F. J., 239
Rose, J., 6, 7
Roth, H. H., 50, 51
Ryder, M. L., 11

Saldanha Man site, South Africa, 7.
  See also Elandsfontein
Sanger, D., 103
Scapula, recording of, 108, 121
Scavenging, 88
Schlepp effect, 64-65
Schmid, E., 11
Schweitzer, F. R., 86
Sea Harvest, South Africa, 84, 93
Seabird, 79
Seal, 41, 78, 79, 220
Seasonal mortality, 45, 60-61
Sesamoids, recording of, 111, 128,
  146, 149
Sheep, 33, 43, 52, 64; age/sex pro-
  files, 86-87
Shipman, P., 6, 7, 8
Shotwell, A. J., 34
Siegel, S., 57
Silver, I. A., 43, 86
Simpson, C. D., 51
Simpson, G. G., 239, 240
Sinclair, A. R. E., 88
Skull, recording of, 108, 128-29
Smith, B. D., 24, 34
Smith, G. F., 39
Smuts, G. L., 51
Sokal, R. R., 239
Solutrean, 76, 97
Speth, J. D., 65
Spiess, A., 45, 62
Spinage, C. A., 44, 45, 48, 53, 62,
  175, 188

Springbok, 49, 50, 51, 76, 82;
  Bond's, 49, 50; southern, 49, 50.
  *See also Antidorcas australis, A.
  bondi, A. marsupialis*
Stahl, F. W., 34
Steenbok, 49, 50, 66, 76, 180; age
  profiles, 92, 93; sex ratio, 91.
  See also Raphicerus campestris
Stewart, F. L., 34
Straus, L. G., 97
Student's t-test, 241
Suberde, Turkey, 64
Sutcliffe, A. J., 7, 82
Swartklip 1, South Africa, 31, 67,
  68, 69-70, 73, 84, 85, 93, 95
Sylvicapra grimmia, 49, 50
Syncerus caffer, 12, 49, 50, 80

Taber, R. D., 39
Tarsals, recording of, 127, 128
Taurotragus oryx, 17, 49, 50, 80,
  192, 194, 196
Thomas, D. H., 6
Tibia, recording of, 121
Tilson, R., 82
Torralba, Spain, 8, 67
Tortoise, 81, 94, 96-98. *See also*
  Chersina angulata
Tragelaphus angasi, 13, 14
Tragelaphus scriptus, 49, 50, 175,
  215
Tragelaphus strepsiceros, 66, 175,
  215
Transportation, of bones, 64-67
Turner, A., 35-36, 37

Uerpmann, H.-P., 24, 103
Ukrainian Upper Paleolithic, 82
Ulna, recording of, 121, 128
Utility index, 65

Vaalribbok, 49, 50. *See also Pelea
  capreolus*
Van Valen, L., 55
Vertebrae, recording of, 108, 109,
  127, 128, 146, 149
Volman, T. P., 77

Von Blottnitz, F., 82
Von den Driesch, A., 22, 40, 41
Von Richter, W., 51
Voorhies, M. R., 45, 67
Vrba, E. S., 69

Watson, J. P. N., 24, 30
Wear states, definition of, 185
White, T. E., 26, 34
Wildebeest, 66, 76, 82; black, 20, 49, 50, 51; blue, 49, 50, 51; *See also Connochaetes gnou, C. taurinus*

Wilson, M., 56
Wilson, V. J., 51
Wolf, C., 48, 62, 70

X rays, used to measure crown height, 54-55

Zebra, 76, 78, 82; Burchell's, 49, 50, 51. *See also Equus burchelli*
Zeder, M. A., 103
Ziegler, A. C., 24